FOAMSMITH 2

How to Forge Foam Weapons

Bill Doran

Foamsmith 2: How to Forge Foam Weapons
by Bill Doran
Find Bill on the web at PunishedProps.com

Photography by Bill Doran
Editor and Layout Ninja: Brittany Doran

Printed in Canada

ACKNOWLEDGMENTS

This book is filled, from cover to cover, with a plethora of amazing techniques. I would be fibbing if I said I came up with all of them myself. The prop and cosplay community has been a tremendous support to me both personally and professionally.

When it comes to sussing out the techniques that produce jaw dropping prop pieces, I turn to an incredible pool of creative friends. Thank you Will Morgan, Harrison Krix, Svetlana & Benni, Evil Ted Smith, Eric Jarman, Nic & Tabitha, and David Carpenter. You guys are knowledge monsters and I couldn't have figured this out without you.

Most importantly, thank you to my amazing wife Brittany. Your love, insight, brilliance, and patience have made this all possible. None of this happens, nor is it worth doing, without you.

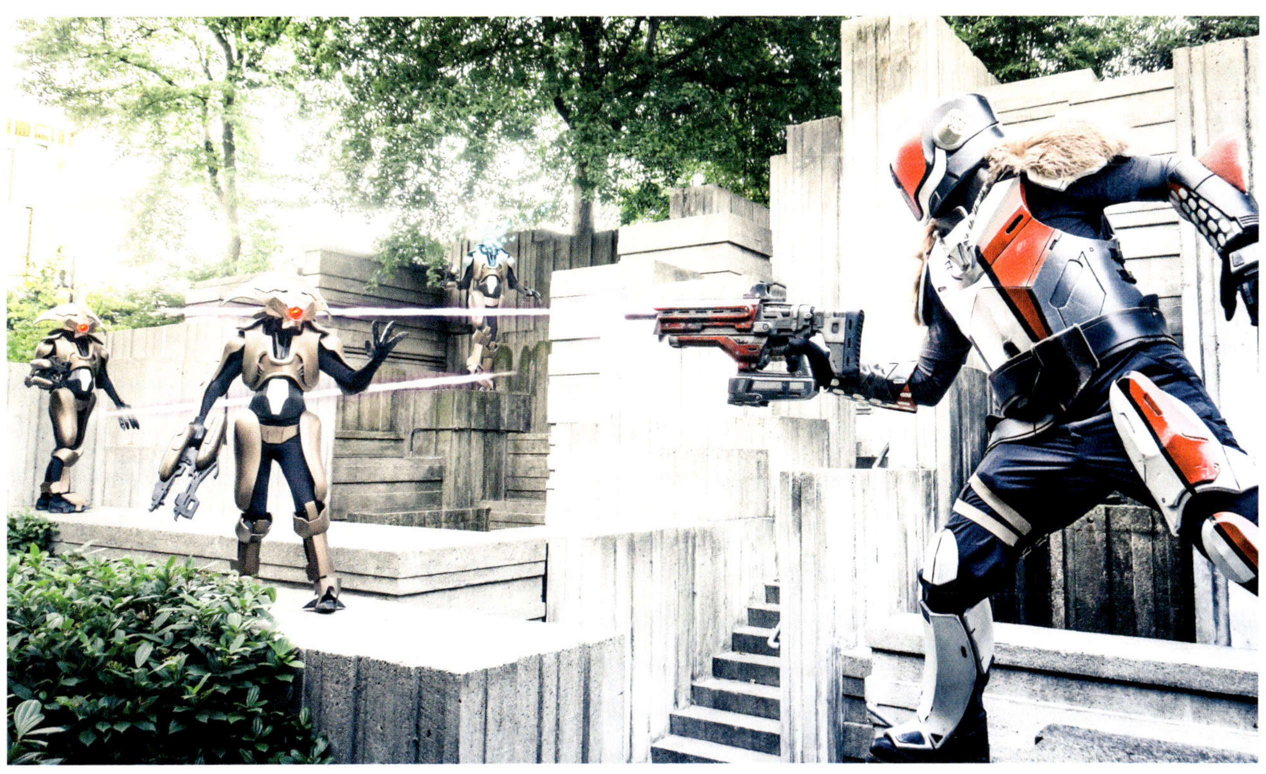

About the Author

Bill Doran is a prop and costume maker, owner of Punished Props, and the author of Foamsmith: How to Create Foam Armor Costumes. He's been building replica props and costumes since his friends convinced him to cosplay with them back in 2009. This opened up an entirely new world of creativity and soon Bill carved out a tidy little career as a prop maker.

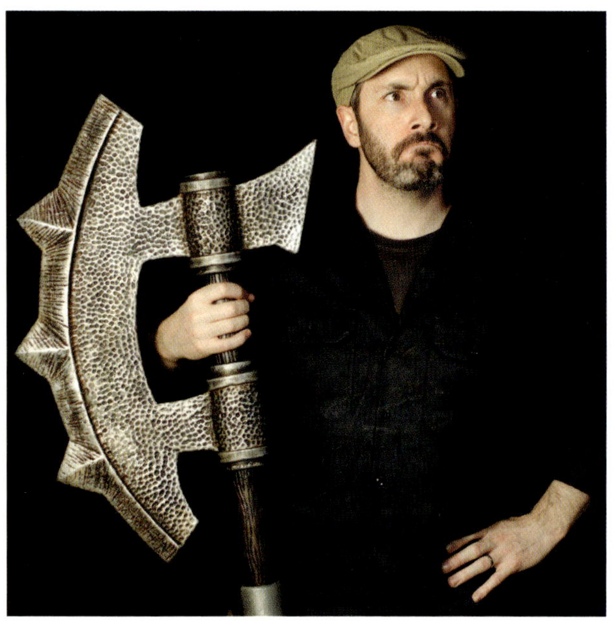

Bill founded Punished Props in 2012 and took his passion for prop making full time, quitting his job in corporate America. Since then, he's built amazing prop replicas for clients all around the world! Along with building incredible things, he also shares his knowledge in detailed blog write-ups and full video tutorials. That passion for instruction led him to write several books on the subject including *A Beginner's Guide to Making Mind Blowing Props* and this *Foamsmith* series!

Nowadays, you can see Bill all around the world at costume and pop culture conventions, spreading his knowledge to those who wish to expand their skills.

Look for *Foamsmith: How to Create Foam Armor Costumes*. The armor book has everything you need to create amazing costume armor from lightweight, low cost EVA foam.

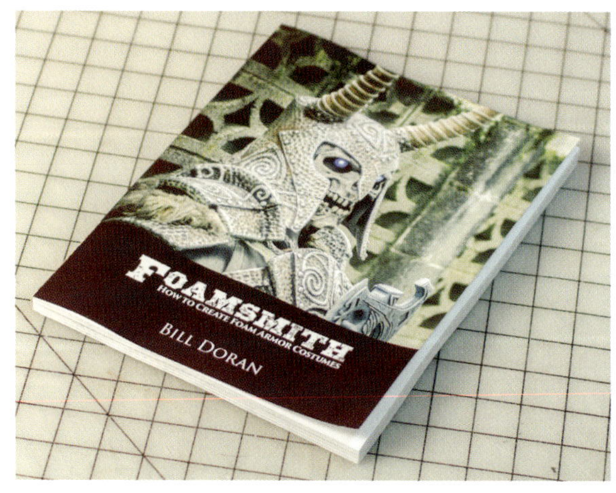

THE FOAMSMITH SERIES

Welcome to *Foamsmith 2:
How to Forge Foam Weapons*

Ever since the first Foamsmith book came out, I've been blown away by seeing the incredible creations my readers have churned out using the techniques they learned. I have never seen a group of people who are so hungry to expand their creative talents and I am humbled by their skill. I knew this second book needed to be just as full of useful knowledge and challenge my readers to do even more. I heard your call dear reader: "Bill, we want to make weapons! Tell us how." Very well. Buckle up kids, we're going on a ride to talent town and the freeway has no speed limit.

This book is designed to empower you. Everybody wants that amazing prop accessory for their incredible costume project, but they don't know where to start. I'm here to tell you that it's much easier and cheaper than you think! The knowledge in this tome will give you the ability to create jaw dropping props quickly and on a budget. Empower yourself; become the Foamsmith!

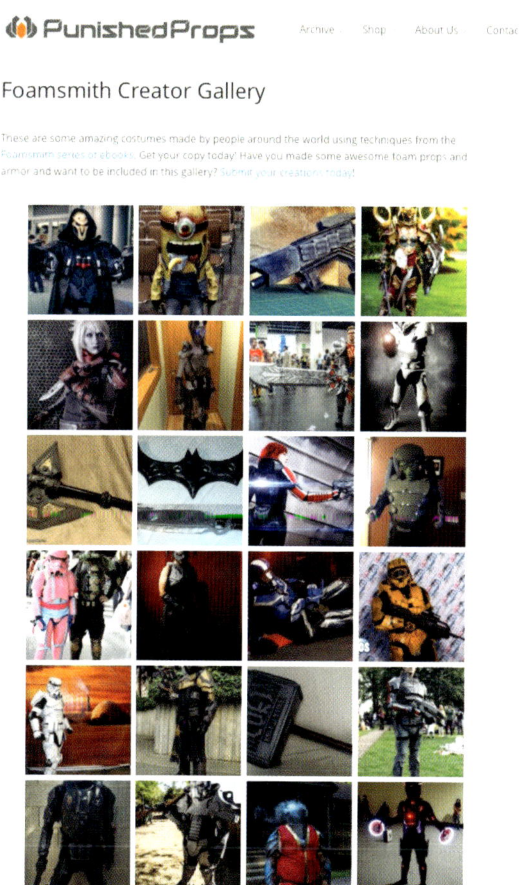

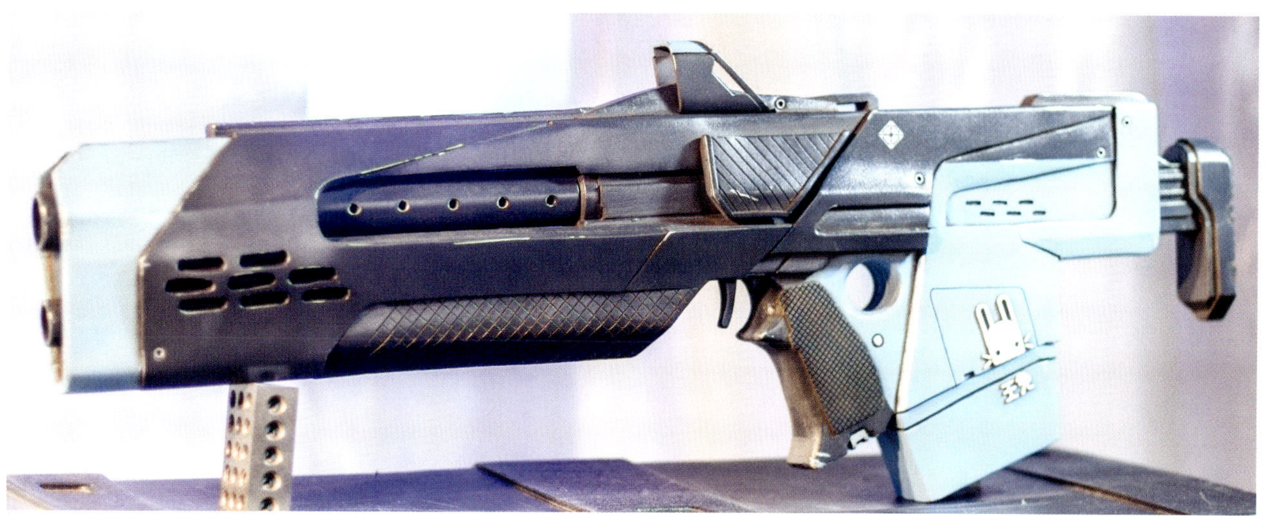

Contents

Axe and Space Gun Templates

A major portion of this book will follow two specific prop builds. These are designed to be examples of how I problem solve the foam prop making process in my shop. I try to be as flexible as possible in the variety of tools that I use (I know not everyone has access to the array of tools I have in my shop), but I also didn't want to hamstring myself. I feel that a genuine look into how I do what I do could be extremely valuable to those of you who are trying to push yourselves to make more ambitious prop projects.

In Part 2 and Part 3 of this book, you can build along with me by printing out the digital files for the axe and space gun!

Download your digital files here:
http://punishedprops.com/foamsmith2

Printing Instructions

The files are already split up into pages to print on a home printer with "Letter" paper size selected. I recommend using thicker, card stock paper.

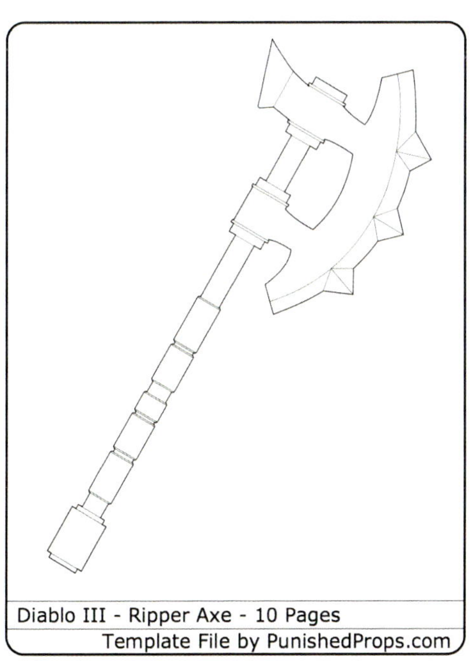

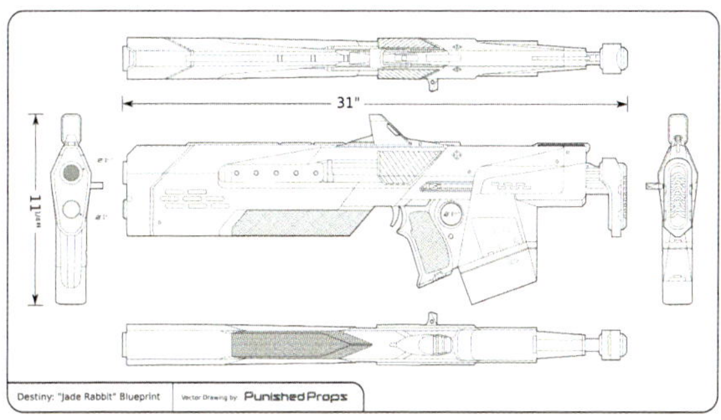

Part 1
Creating Prop Weapons

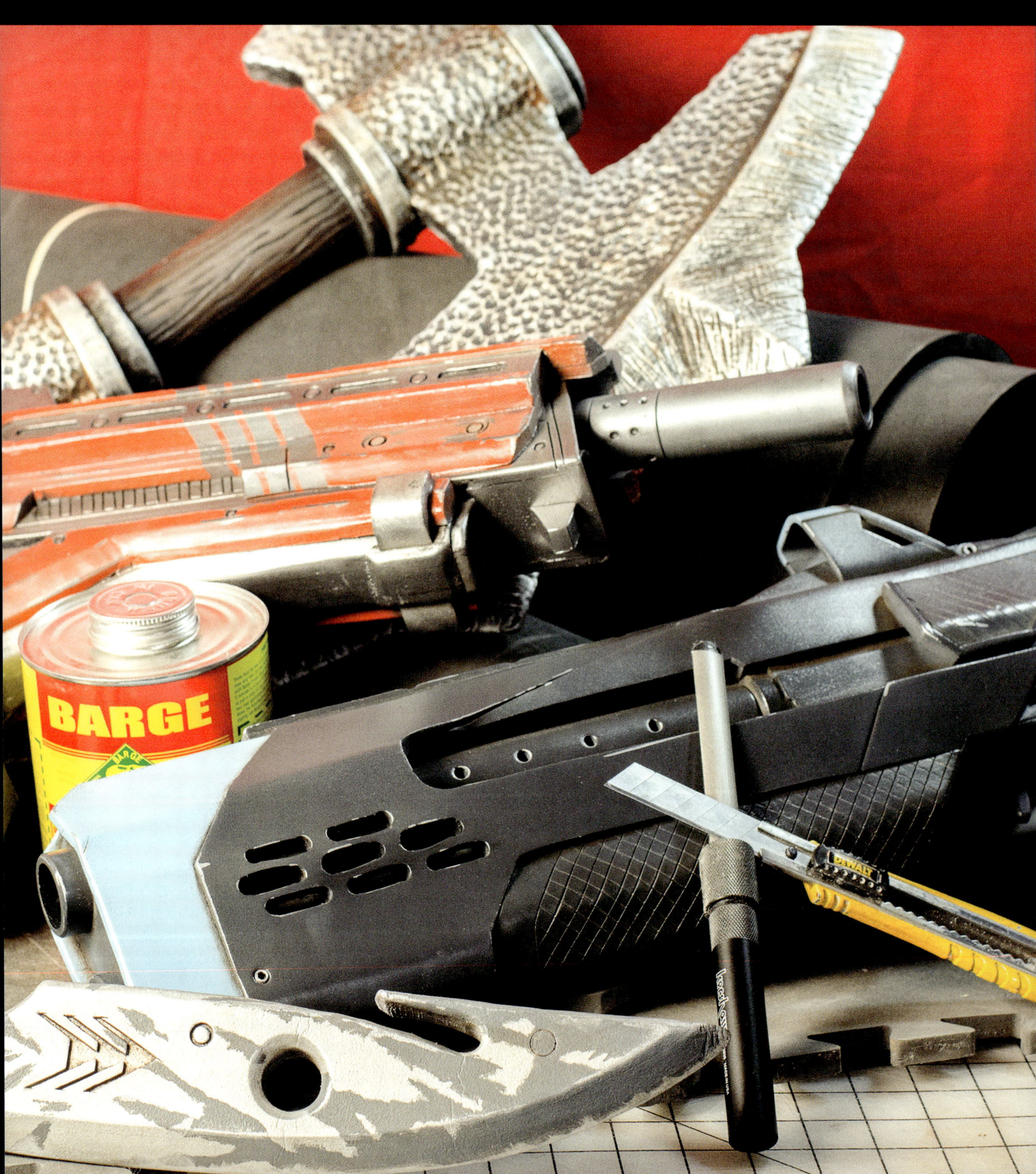

SAFETY FIRST!

It's all fun and games until someone accidentally inhales a bunch of foam dust. When foamsmithing, safety should always come first. For the most part, working with EVA foam is pretty safe. That's one of the many reasons why I enjoy working with it as a material. There are, however, a couple of things we should keep in mind.

Most of the hand tools you will be using are pretty safe, but a good measure of caution must be maintained when wielding sharp things like knives. Believe it or not, a dull knife is much more dangerous than a sharp one, so keep your blades well maintained. You might also take this chance to try some power tools. Always make sure to read the user's manual and take every caution when operating them. A drill press may seem safe enough, but using it in an unsafe manner can cause some serious hurt to your hands. Don't rush, heed the warnings, and be safe!

Protect your lungs. If you end up sanding a lot of foam, especially with power tools, it's going create a lot of dust. You definitely do not want to inhale any of that dust, so keep a healthy supply of dust masks on hand. Safety goggles are a pretty good idea too.

A lot of the glues and spray paints that you may end up using can be pretty hazardous too. For those, you'll want to always work in a well ventilated area (outside if possible) and wear a well maintained respirator.

For good measure, always be sure to read the instructions or material safety data sheets that come with any of the chemical products you use.

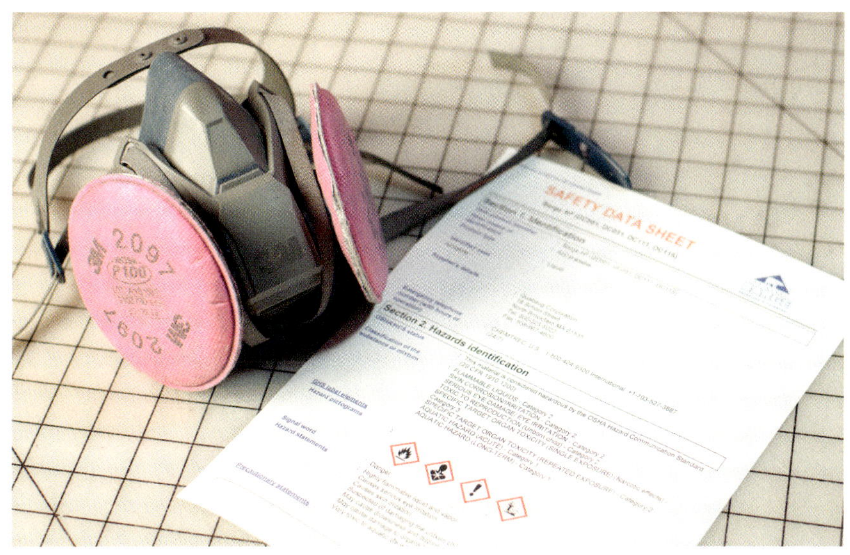

Why Foam Weapons?

I know I've convinced a lot of people to make their armor from EVA foam, but you may not be so convinced when it comes to hand-held props. You may have the impulse to go with wood or rigid plastic materials for your next space gun. Those are wonderful materials, to be sure, but hear me out! EVA foam is a wonder material for props too!

It's cheap & readily available.

At least in the United States, EVA foam can be purchased from a wide range of retailers. I usually pick mine up from the local hardware and craft stores. It's usually cheaper than most woods and plastics too! Since it's so cheap, you can afford to practice with the material a lot to refine your skill.

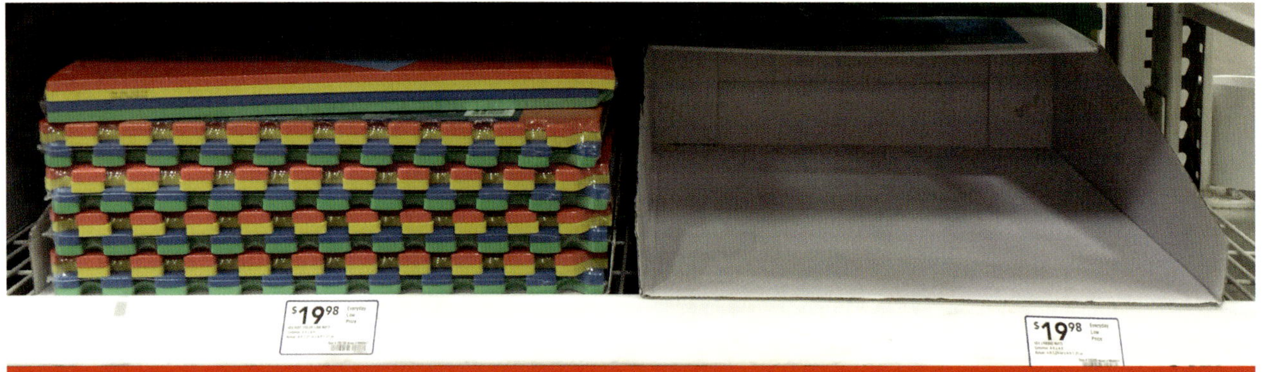

A COSPLAYER WAS HERE

It's lightweight.

Since it's foam, it's made up of a lot of air. That cuts down on the weight considerably. If you have to carry your prop around a comic convention for twelve straight hours, you're going to want a prop that's as light as possible. You'll be surprised how heavy a five pound prop can feel by the end of the day.

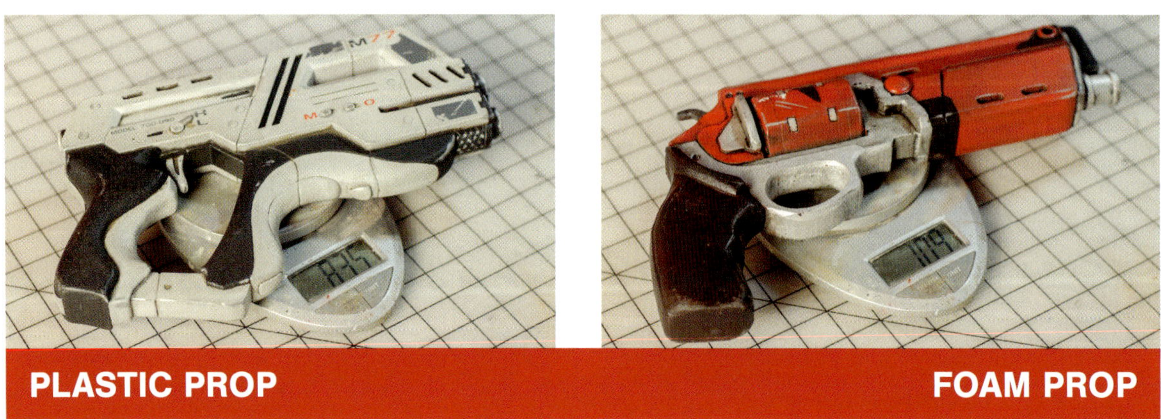

PLASTIC PROP

FOAM PROP

It's fast to work with.

Since EVA foam can be manipulated with just a sharp knife, there's no need to saw away at it endlessly by hand. Cuts can be made quickly, significantly cutting down on your build time. This is especially handy if you find yourself prop-less the day before a convention and need to whip up something fast!

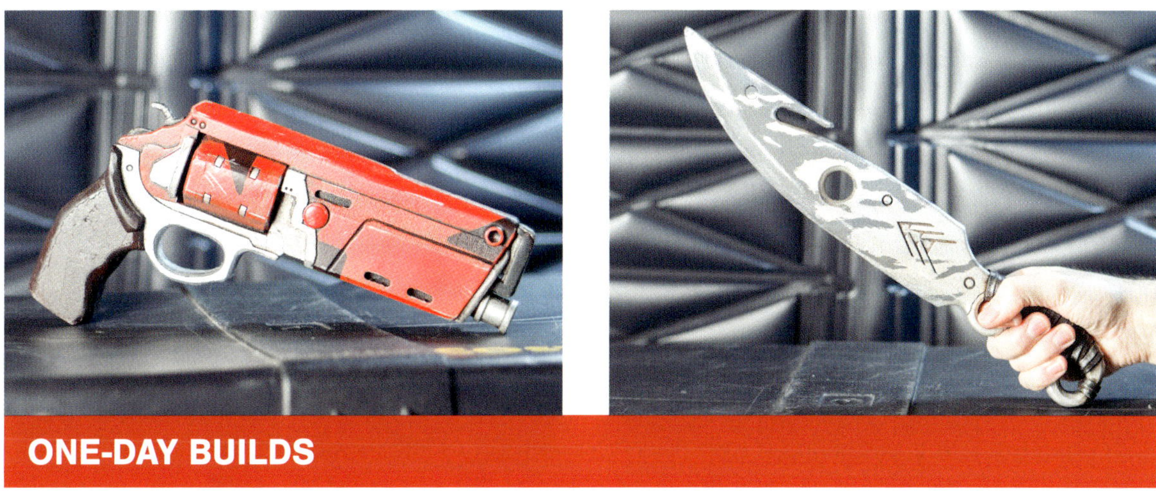

ONE-DAY BUILDS

It's convention safe.

Comic and costume conventions have policies about what type of prop weapons are considered safe for attendees to bring with them. Foam weapons are almost always given the green light when checked by convention security. They're also safe to use as stunt props for your low budget films. It is very unlikely that you'll hurt your friends by bonking them in the head with your foam weapons.

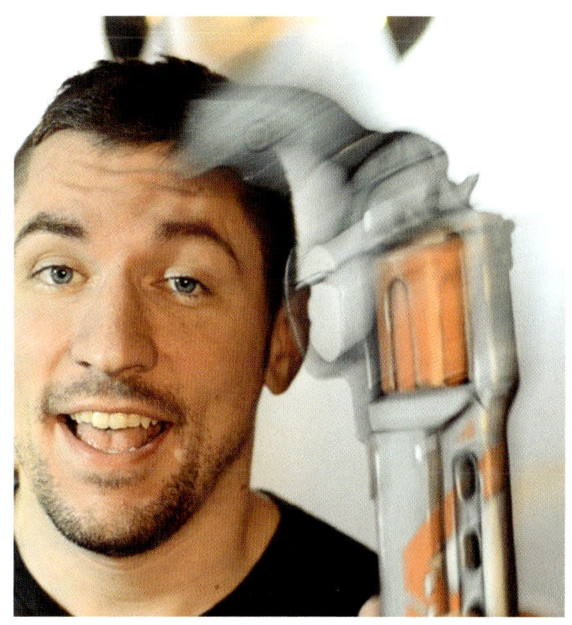

Convention Weapon Policies

Speaking of weapon policies, let's dive into the subject a little bit. Nowadays, cosplay conventions are popping up like weeds. It's become more apparent to convention staff that they need to come up with policies that keep both costumed and non costumed attendees safe at their events. This is especially important when it comes to folks brandishing realistic looking weapons.

Many of these conventions have taken to writing specific rules and guidelines about what's allowed as a costume weapon. If your local convention hasn't done so, I highly recommend you ask them to write guidelines and post them on their website and in their programming material. Getting the rules down on paper can save everyone a lot of confusion and heartache come opening day. Here are some common ground rules for safe convention weapon etiquette. (I played bass for Convention Weapon Etiquette)

The Weapon Check Booth and Peace Bonding

Just about every costume convention has a weapon check booth near the entrance of the event. It's a place where trained staff members can give your weapons a once over to check that they're safe. They will usually mark it with a zip tie or piece of ribbon. This is to let convention staff inside the event space know that you've been checked out and aren't carrying a dangerous weapon.

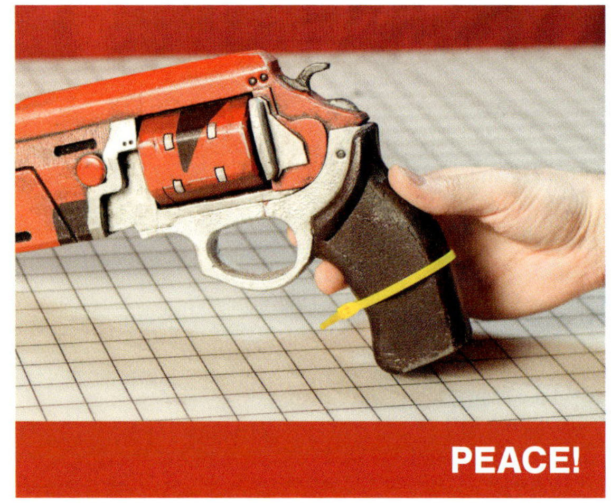
PEACE!

I like to ask that the weapon checking personnel put the zip tie on the handle of my weapon so that I can cover it with my hand when posing for photos. This request is usually honored, which makes me a happy cosplayer!

If your weapon is deemed unsafe for the convention, I would recommend you take it back to your car or hotel room. Leaving it at the front desk to pick up later is probably a bad idea, mostly because you're very likely to forget to recover it at the end of the day.

Seriously, don't bring a real weapon.

No joke, I have seen more than one person try to take an actual, functional crossbow into a convention. They are always, thankfully, turned away at the door. This goes for the same with sharp metal blades. For the convention, real weapons are an extreme liability and an accident just waiting to happen. For you, a real weapon is just a chance to get in trouble, or worse, hurt yourself or others. Keep the real stuff at home.

I would strongly advise against bringing anything that can fire a projectile too. Yes, even Nerf guns and especially Airsoft guns. Permanently disabling the firing mechanisms on those types of "toy" guns might appease the weapon check employees at a convention, but I would ask ahead of time before trying to bring one onto the floor. Leave the functional stuff at home.

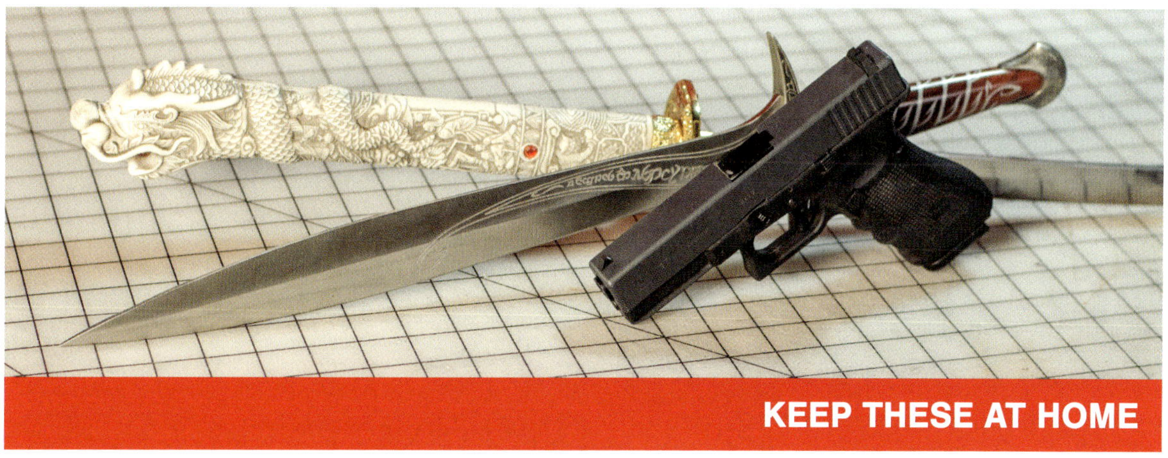

KEEP THESE AT HOME

Be sure to check local laws about weapon carrying policies. Also double check any sort of weapon policies in countries you might be traveling to. I know that Canada is just a short hike from my town in the United States and they have different laws about guns up north. It's best to do your research before you travel to avoid any sort of altercation at the border.

Do not aim guns at people.

Yes, even fake foam guns. Guns make people nervous. Some people get more nervous than others. Some of those people are off duty police officers. If your prop gun is super convincing and you're pointing it at people willy-nilly, it can be misconstrued as a dangerous situation by law enforcement personnel who prefer to carry the real deal.

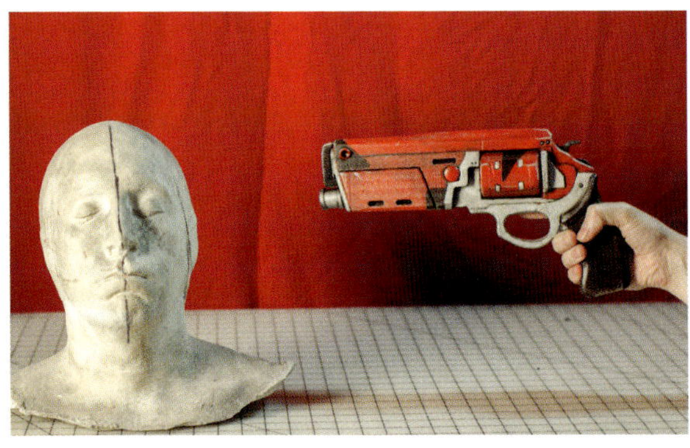

You also don't want to act like a firearm brandishing psycho and scare the bajeezus out of an unsuspecting attendee. If you'd like to arrange a cool photo with another cosplayer, let them know ahead of time how you'll be posing and that you'll be pointing your prop gun near them.

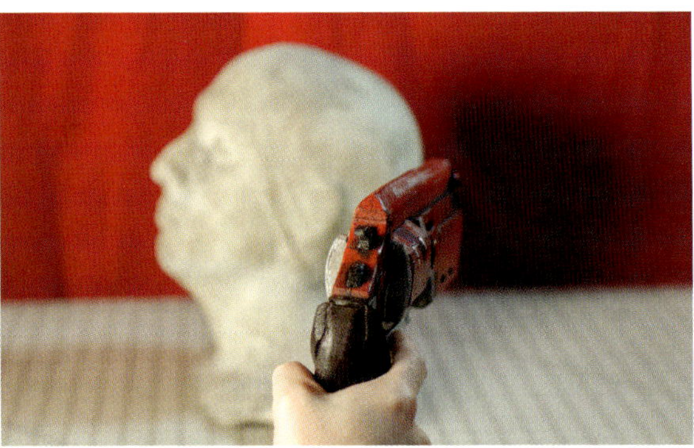

What if you're posing for a super rad photo and absolutely need to point the gun at someone? It's usually a good policy to point it just slightly away from them. It can usually be done in a manner that still looks convincing.

Also, think about posing using correct trigger discipline (finger off the trigger unless you intend to be firing your gun). Not only is it the correct way to handle a firearm, it'll make you look more like you know what you're doing in your photos!

On a similar note, don't pull prop knives on unsuspecting attendees. I've heard of cosplayers thinking it would be funny or cool to pose with their prop knife up to someone else's body. While that might make for a convincing photo, it's not a great surprise to get from a stranger. For any type of interaction in your photos with another cosplayer, talk it out beforehand. No need to make anyone wet their britches mid convention.

NOW I HAVE TRIGGER DISCIPLINE, TRIGGER DISCIPLINE EVERY DAY

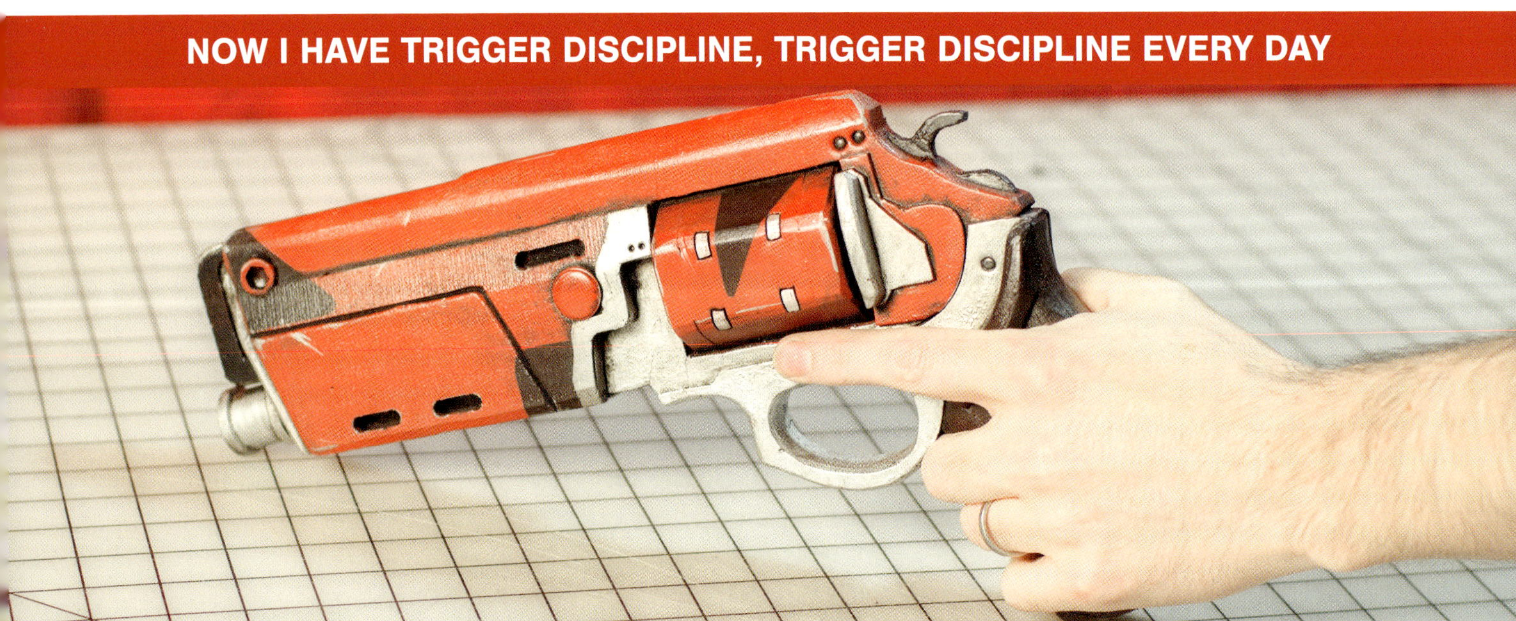

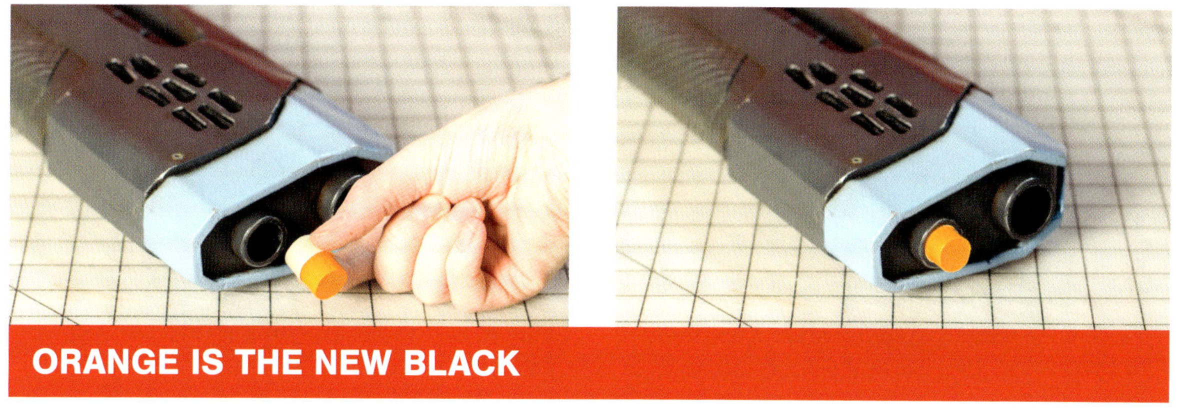

ORANGE IS THE NEW BLACK

Another fantastic policy for your guns is to make one of those obnoxious orange barrel tips. Those tell the rest of the world "Hey, this isn't real, everybody calm yourselves." You can make them removable for photos, so you'll always look legit!

Don't wave your weapons around in public.

You know your sword is made of foam. I know your sword is made of foam. The barista at Starbucks does NOT know your sword is made of foam. For everyone else's personal sanity, keep your weapons sheathed and tucked away until you get inside your costuming event.

Keep that prop wrangled!

Everybody loves a gigantic prop, especially those amazing anime swords. What they don't love is getting bonked in the face, Three Stooges style, when you turn a sharp corner with your Buster Sword strapped to your back.

If you've got a large prop weapon, it falls on you to be extremely aware of your surroundings when moving about a crowded space. Even if your huge sword is squishy foam, you can still cause some damage if you tag a kid in the noggin with it.

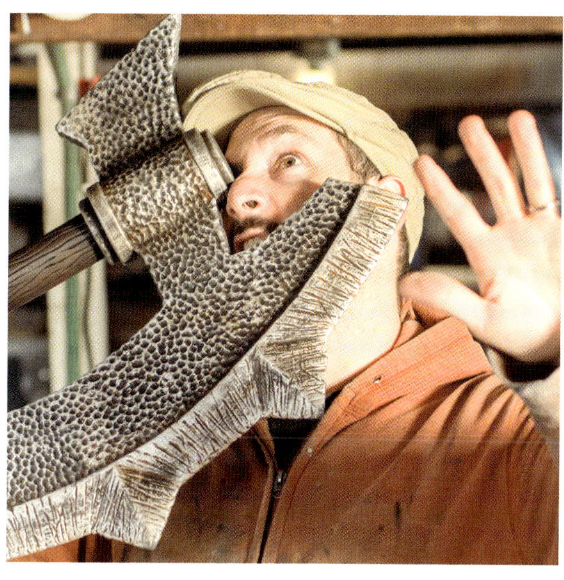

Just follow the rules.

Conventions have rules for a reason; usually because some wacko with a broadsword ruined it for everyone years earlier. If a rule seems unreasonable, then talk to the staff about having it changed for the next years event, but don't break that rule to spite them. Don't be that wacko. You can have your fun and be safe too.

Alright you guys, enough of the safety rundown. It's time to build some sweet prop weapons! Where do we start?

Armor vs. Weapons: Tools, Materials, & Techniques

If you haven't read the first Foamsmith book, this book is going to be a big jump forward, so you may want to study up before moving on. For those of you who are already familiar with basic foamsmithing techniques, you may start to recognize a lot of the material in the following chapters. Rest assured there is all new information here, especially more advanced tools and techniques that are necessary for making incredibly stunning props.

In the last couple of years, I've taken every chance I could get to experiment with a vast array of foams for use in my prop and costume crafting. Most everything can be done with floor mats and craft foam, but there are other options out there. Here's a breakdown of several options as well as some pros and cons.

EVA Foam Floor Mats

Where to get it: Hardware stores as floor mats, Amazon, and craft/hobby stores.

Pros:

- Inexpensive
- Available locally in most places
- Durable

Cons:

- Inconsistent quality
- Textured side may not be desirable
- Limited sizes and thicknesses

L200 (or L300/L400 etc.)

Where to get it: Online stores or local distributors

Pros:

- More consistent quality
- Available without any texture
- Available in large sheets and an array of thicknesses

Cons:

- More expensive than EVA
- Not always available locally

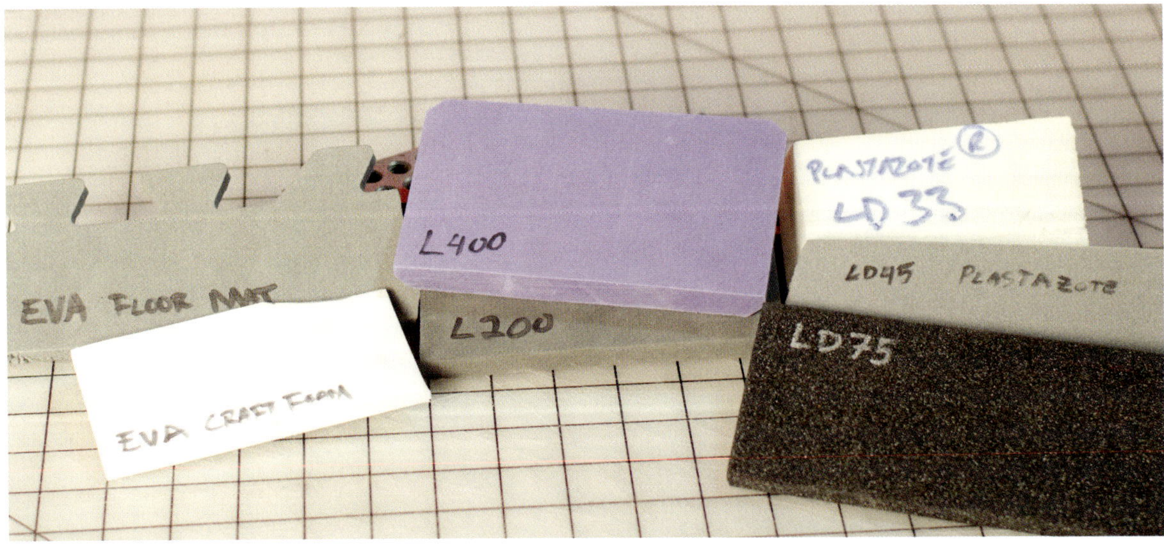

Foam in Other Countries

I fully admit that my foam resource knowledge is mostly limited to the United States. Other countries will have their own foam options. Cosplayers in the Philippines use a similar material called "rubber sheet". Likewise, I have friends in the UK who use foam called Plastazote. I've found the same stuff here in the US, but it's hard to get in small quantities. Most of this foam is usually sold in large lots for use in packaging. Does this mean it's outside your reach? No, but you may need to go in with a handful of friends to place a large order and share it.

No matter what types of foams you have available to you, it's possible to make nearly anything work for your project. You may just need to do a lot of experimenting to get the techniques to work for your props. Your patience and ingenuity will be rewarded.

If you have a local store that sells industrial foam, become their friend! Suppliers end up with small offcuts that you can scoop up for a discount.

Glues

All of your armor foamsmithing adhesives apply to weapons. For most of my projects I stick with a variety of contact cements like DAP or Barge, but if all you can get your hands on is super glue or hot glue, you'll be able to get by!

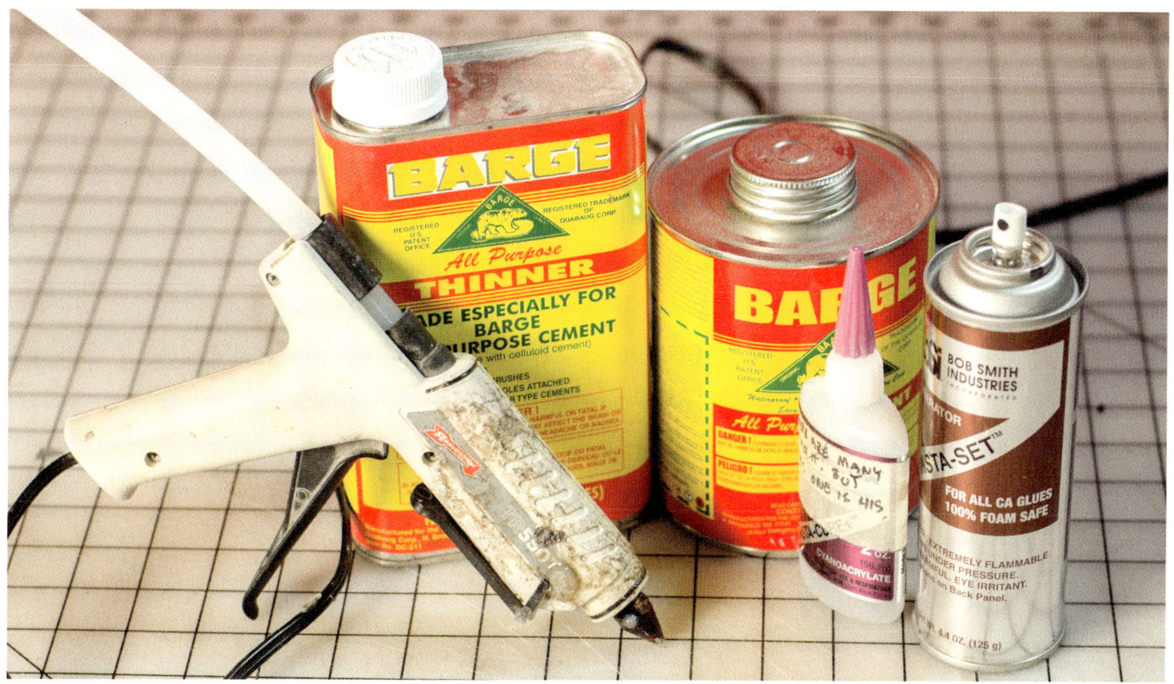

It's Tool Time!

For your foam prop fabrication, all of your standard tools apply. Knives, sharpeners, a heat gun and your trusty rotary tool are going to be absolutely necessary for building that spot-on space gun. Now that you've made the jump to props, however, you should really consider upgrading to some powered tool options. Here are some really fantastic tools that I use every day in my prop making adventures.

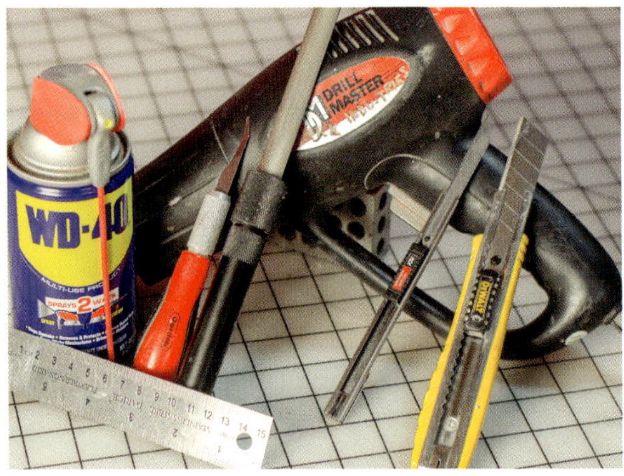

Band saw

I bought my first band saw about a year ago and I can't believe it took me that long to make the investment. Since then I've bought a second one, because they are amazing and I have no self control. The best part is you don't even need a huge, expensive one to get started with your foam weapon fabrication. Mine cost $120 brand new and you can find them for even cheaper, used on Craigslist.

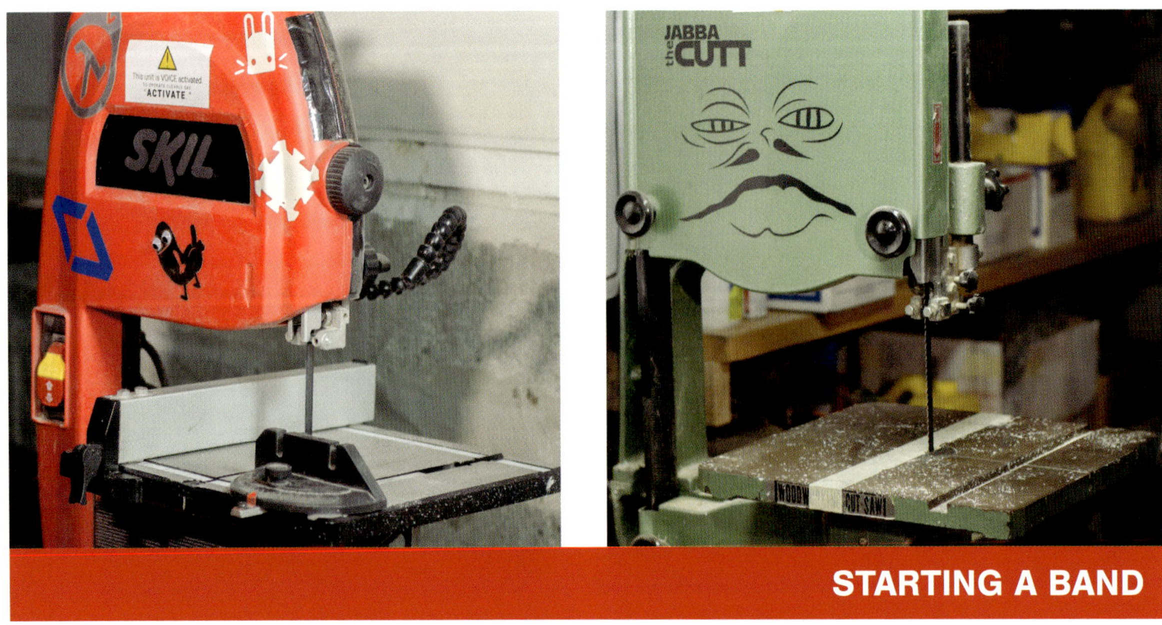

STARTING A BAND

What makes them so incredible, you ask? Bevels. Oh yes, you can create perfect bevels in foam with a band saw. The combination of a tilting bed and a fence means you can run a piece of foam straight along the blade at a precise angle and totally nail a machined looking edge.

The fence and miter gauge means you can also cut multiple pieces in the same thickness, and bevel angle, in a jiffy!

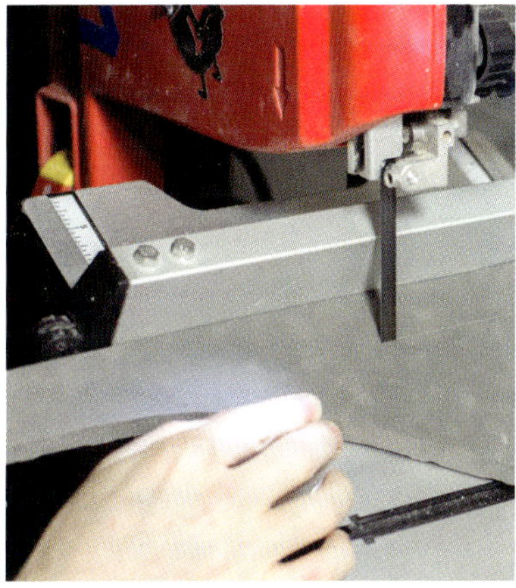

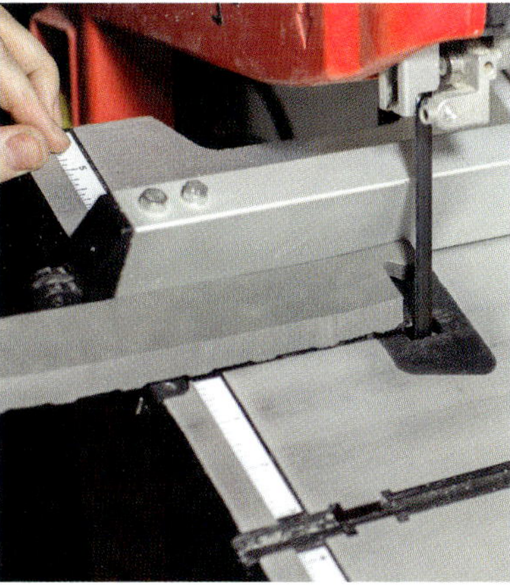

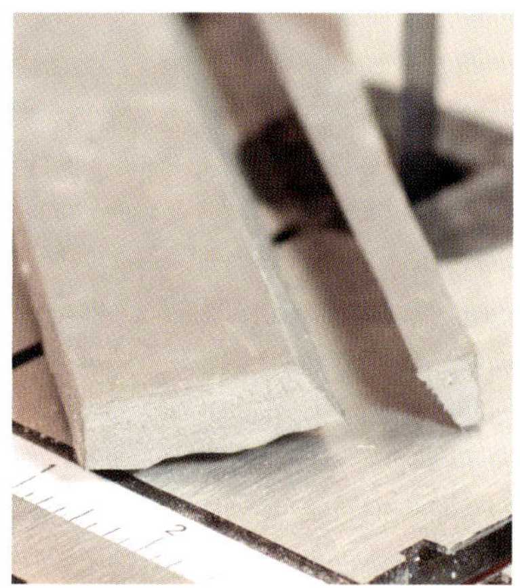

There are a wide assortment of blades available for band saws. New ones usually come with a standard wood cutting blade. These are usually too rough for foamsmithing as they rip right through the material. I recommend picking up a metal cutting blade. It has many more teeth and leaves a less rough texture on the cut edge. You can also get blades specifically for cutting soft materials. These look a lot like knives designed for cutting bread.

Personally, I have a half a dozen different blades and replacements on hand at all times. This way I am always ready to swap out blades for the specific jobs. This is also why I bought a second band saw; less time spent swapping blades.

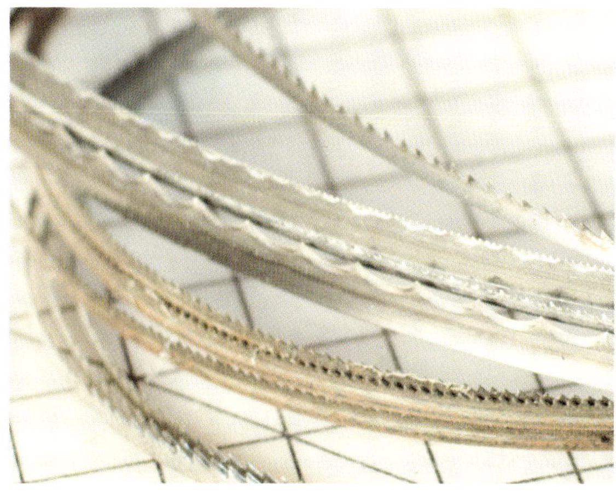

I also keep a fresh pair of shorts nearby in case a blade breaks. It isn't too dangerous when it happens, but it is startling and you may pee a little.

Scroll Saw

While the band saw is my number one foamsmithing power tool, there is one major thing it absolutely cannot do: interior cuts. For that, I need my scroll saw. Every once in awhile a prop demands a weird shaped hole be cut in the interior of the piece and a band saw blade, being a continuous loop, can't make the cut. For that I need to drill a hole and then snake the scroll saw blade in to make the cut.

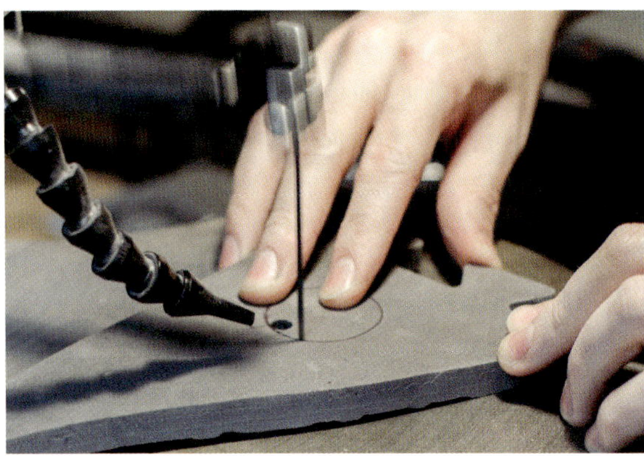

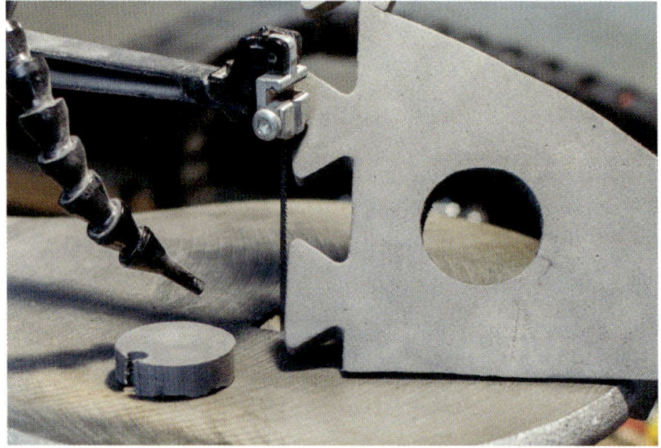

Another thing to consider is the choke of your saw. This is the distance from the blade to the part of the tool that supports the blade. The band saw choke is parallel to the blade and the scroll saw is perpendicular. This means that cutting a particularly wide piece might be impossible on the band saw, but perfectly fine on the scroll saw, and vise versa. So it's worth having both saws for when the situation demands them.

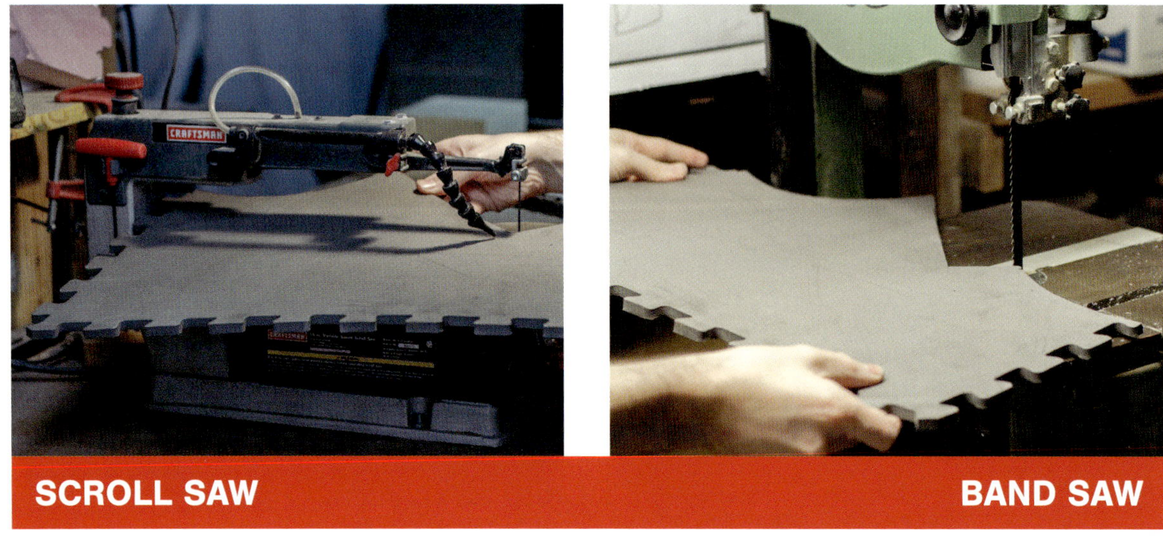

Jig Saw

Looking for the cheapest option? Get your hands on a jig saw. You can pick one up for about 20 bucks new and it does just about everything you need. It can cut interior holes and it doesn't have a choke, so you can cut for miles without concern.

So why waste your money on a band saw and a scroll saw? Accuracy. The jigsaw does everything you need it to, but it only does an OK job. Especially if you need cuts to look perfectly machined, you're going to have a hard time at it without the fence on a band saw.

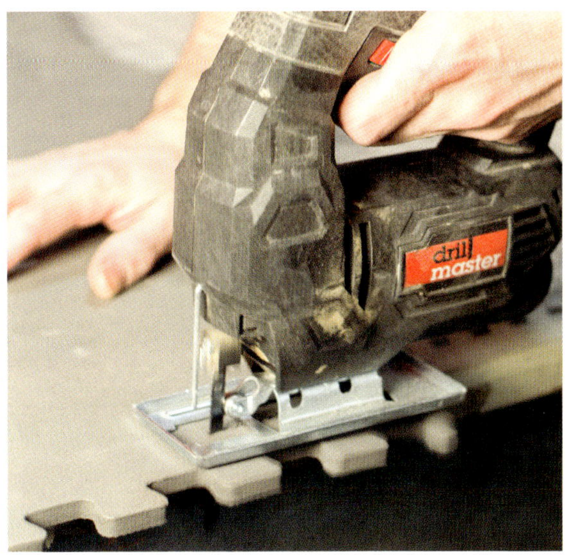

I've also found that a jigsaw can get away from you really fast, ruining a piece you're cutting. A blade with a high tooth per inch count is going to be a must if you plan on running this hand-held monster through foam. Still, it's hard to beat the price and versatility of the jigsaw, especially if working space and budget are a concern.

"The jigsaw does everything you need it to, but it only does an OK job."

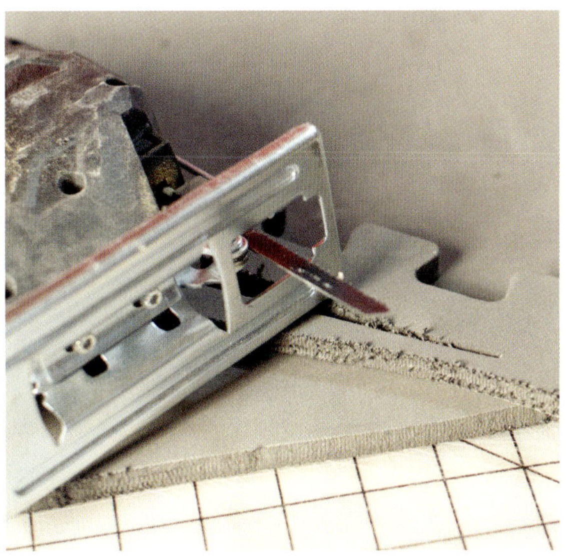

Belt/Disc Sander

"Bill, how do you get clean foam pieces?!" I get this question a lot and the answer is simple: I sold my soul to the devil for elite foam crafting skills. HA! No, I wouldn't sell my soul for anything less than an actual, flying Iron Man suit. The real answer is sanding. The best looking props look so good because a great deal of sanding went into their creation and you can do a lot of sanding with a belt and disc sander.

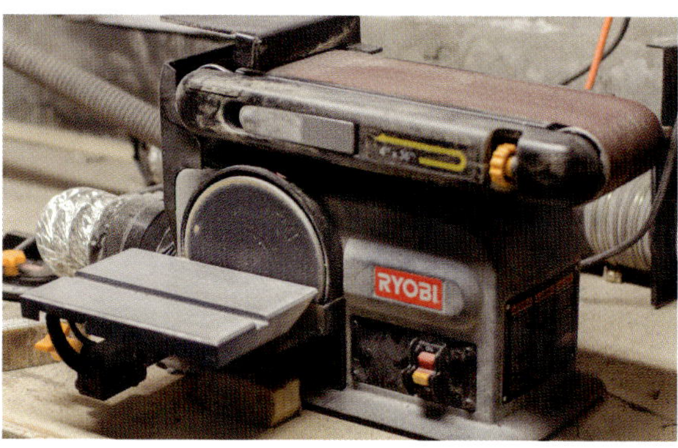

There are many options out there, but it's hard to beat the disc/belt combo. You can nab one of these for just over a hundred bucks new or cheaper used. I recommend getting plenty of replacement sanding belts and discs in 120 grit or higher. Replace them frequently if you use it with other materials, but they should last a long time if you only use them on foam.

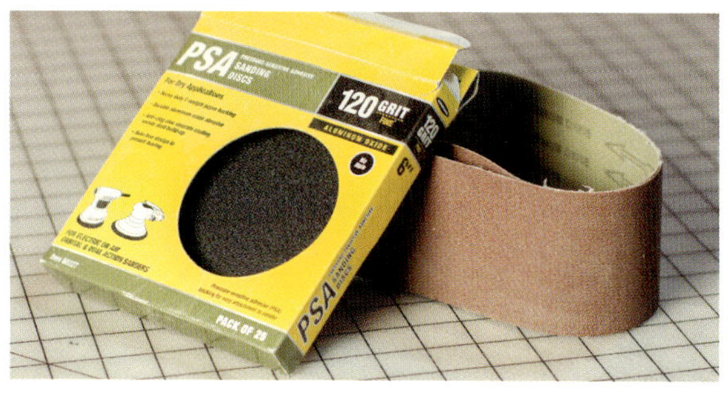

What's so amazing about this mechanical monstrosity? Imagine sanding a piece of foam a thousand times a minute. Yeah, that sounds pretty tiresome. Your sanding machine can do it faster than that without blinking. This results in super clean sanded edges that are impossible to replicate by hand. Most sanders like this also have adjustable beds, so sanding bevels are a snap!

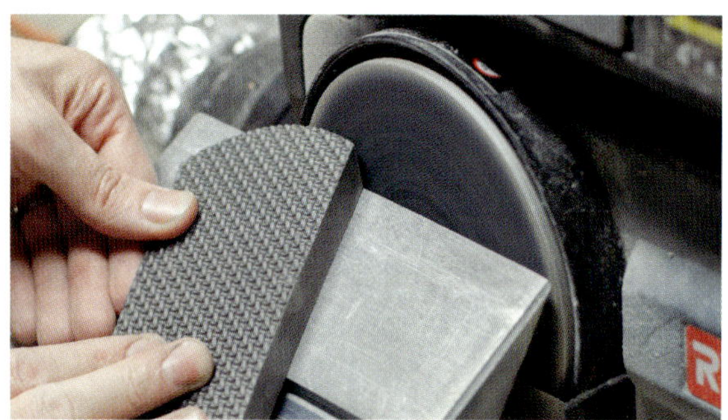

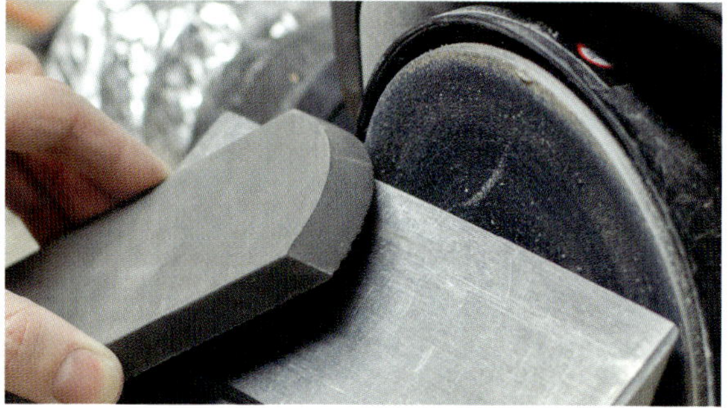

Need to cut out perfect circular shapes? Rough cut it with a knife or band saw then clean it up with your disc or belt sander! Viola! The same can be accomplished with circular, beveled edges.

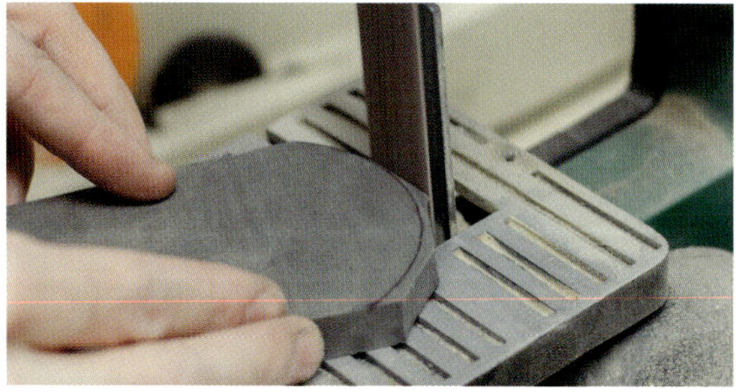

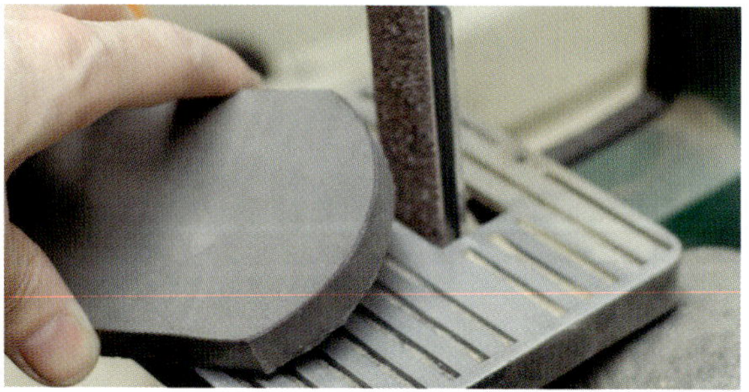

Drill Press

You can get away with using a hand-held power drill for most of your foamsmithing needs, but there comes a time where the drill press is absolutely necessary. Like the other power tools, you can get your hands on one for fairly cheap. What you end up paying for in a more expensive one is size and features, but for most foam work, a small cheap drill press will do most of what you need.

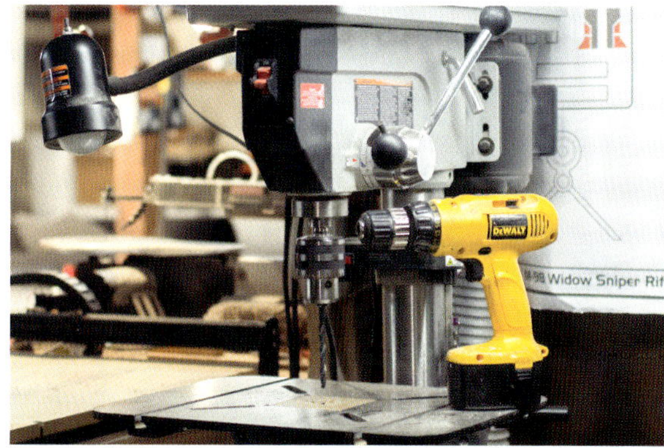

I highly recommend spending the coin on a good set of forstner bits. Unlike normal drill bits, they have a cutting edge on them that will help make very clean holes through foam.

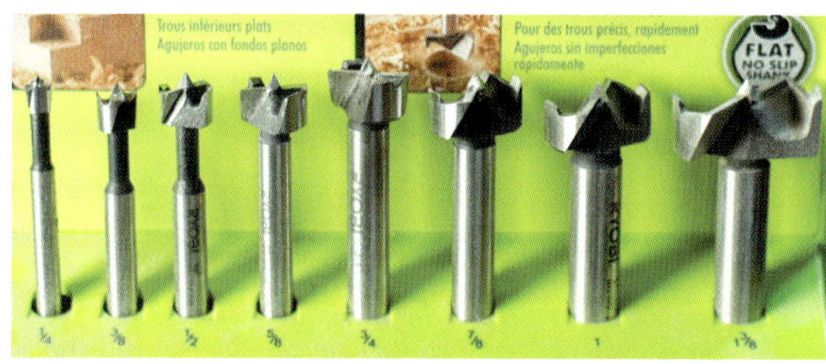

"A drill is a fantastic multitasker."

Believe it or not, drilling holes isn't the main reason why I recommend a drill press for foam smithing. The real reason is because it is a fantastic multitasker. If you pick up a cheap set of sanding drums, you can turn it into a passable spindle sander! Much like the disc sander for exterior rounded edges, the spindle sander is king for getting clean interior, circular shapes.

If you can, get drums with 220 grit; 80 grit drums tend to rip up foam pretty fast. Also make a new bed with a hole drilled in it to accommodate the drum. This bed can be made from some scrap wood and be clamped to the existing drill press bed. This way you can lower the drum below the surface of the bed and be sure to sand the entire edge of the foam.

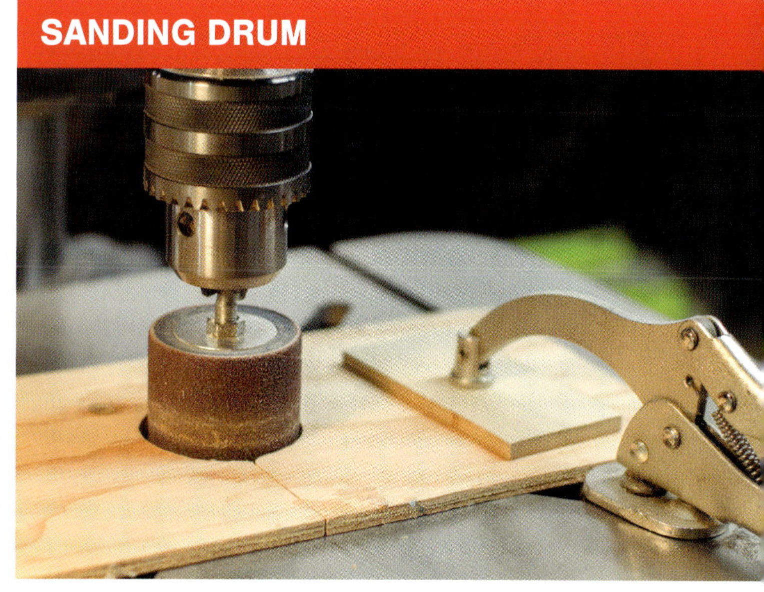

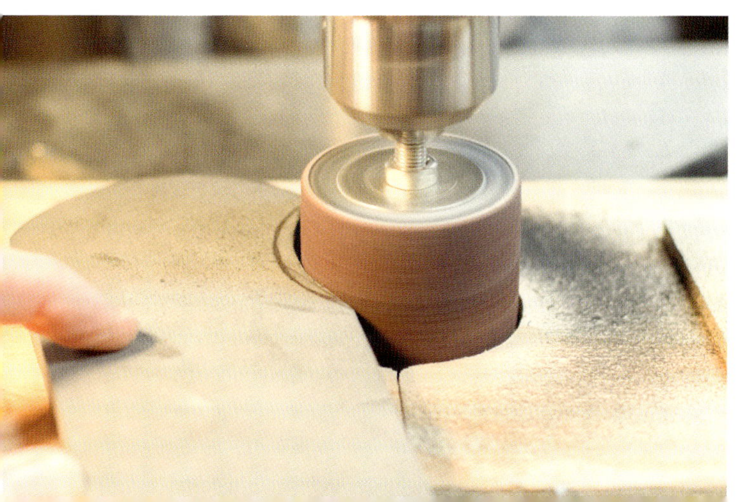

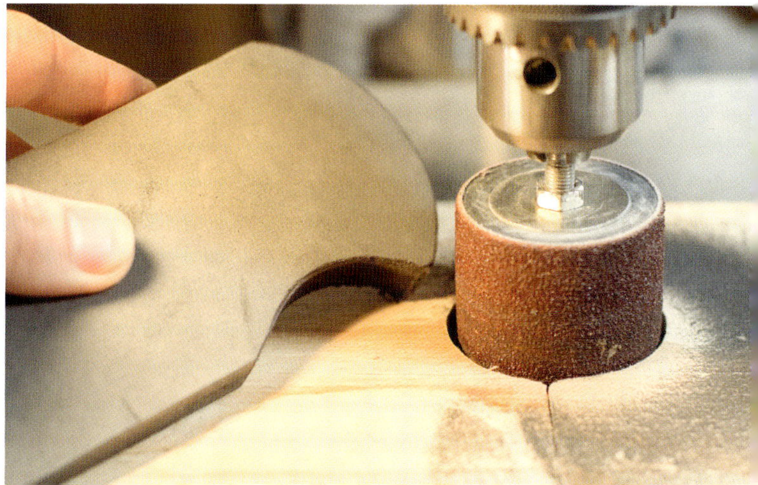

Are these tools necessary?

All of these powered options are not totally necessary. You can still get by with knives and a rotary tool. What you get from these options, however, are speed and accuracy. Especially when you're trying to create prop weapons that have that "machined" look, a combination of power tools will help you meet that look much closer and in much less time. If you're looking to expand your foam prop making portfolio, the investment is well worth it.

Dat Dust Though

The other thing you gain when using crazy awesome power tools is a massive amount of dust. These tools, especially the belt sander, have a knack for kicking up a sandstorm of foam dust that can quickly bury your shop in a desert of debris. If you don't want your workspace to fall prey to this clutter, you really ought to make a dust collection system.

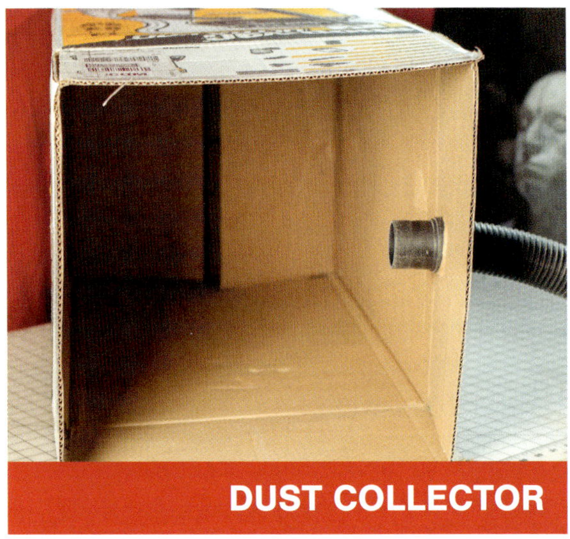
DUST COLLECTOR

Especially if you're working in your home or apartment, some kind of dust collection is going to be a godsend. All you need is a large plastic container or cardboard box, some duct tape and a vacuum. I recommend some kind of beefy shop vac.

Cut off one face of your box so that you can access the area inside when working. Then cut a hole for your vacuum hose to run through and tape it in place. Tah dah! Now you can do all of your powered sanding inside an enclosed space that gobbles up the dust as you work. No more mess! This is particularly handy for use with your rotary tool.

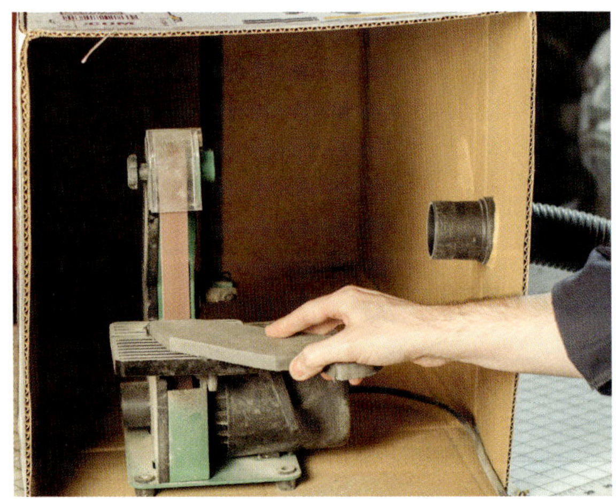

I made my dust box big enough to fit over my belt/disc sander and included a hole to install a cheap light in the top. This way I can see what I'm doing as I work.

References and Scale

Now that you've upgraded your foamsmithing tool arsenal, it's time to start building your super rad prop weapons! Grab your contact cement and start gluing foam together willy nilly! WOOO! Ahhhhh, hold on. Maybe we should do some planning first.

Good planning starts with good reference images. This is one of my favorite steps in prop making because it gives me an excuse to spend three straight hours scouring Google for fun pictures of neat things.

Yes, Google image search is always my first step when approaching a new prop project. It's possible that someone else has already found perfect shots or even drawn up a great set of templates to use. Here are some things to look for when scouring the internet for reference images:

- Highest resolution images possible
- Multiple angles of the item
- Any reference that helps scale the prop

If you can, try to get images that are "orthographic". This means the images have no perspective, like a blueprint. This may not always be possible, especially if you're taking shots from TV or movie footage. For video games, getting your paws on a 3D file that can be viewed directly from the sides will give you the most accurate representation of your prop and all its proportions.

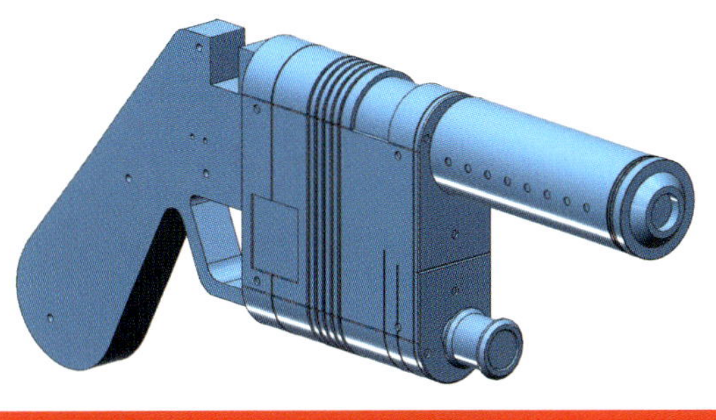

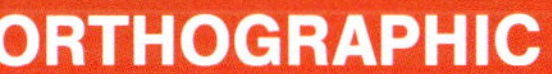

ORTHOGRAPHIC

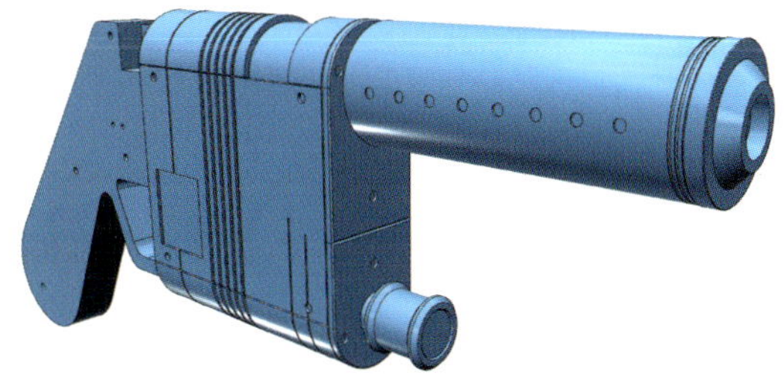

PERSPECTIVE

What if Google comes up empty? How could this be?! I thought they had dominated the world by now. Well, just because the big G couldn't find your prop reference images, doesn't mean you're totally out of luck. You just need to take matters into your own hands. Whether the prop you're trying to replicate is from TV, comics, film, or video games, there is always a way to get decent reference images.

The crucial first step is to get the highest resolution source possible. This might be a blu-ray played on your computer or Playstation, or it might be a real life reference from a museum. Either way, get access to the source and either copy a screen grab on your computer or go all old school and take a photograph. That's right, you can just use your camera to take a photo of your television screen. You laugh, but I've done this more than once and it works like a charm.

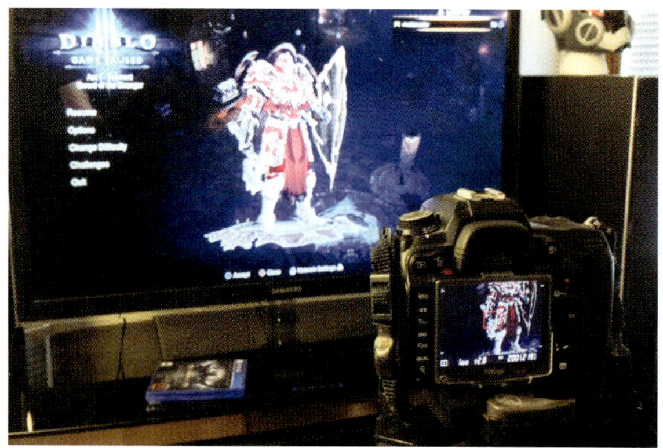

How big should the prop be?

The next big hurdle in prop making is figuring out the scale. It's possible to make your prop way too big or way too small and not even realize it until it's completely finished. For this, getting reference images of the prop in frame alongside the character who holds it can be extremely valuable. Consider Conan's sword in Arnold's mighty paw. Building your sword so that it's scaled to look the same size in your hand will make it look correct for your costume.

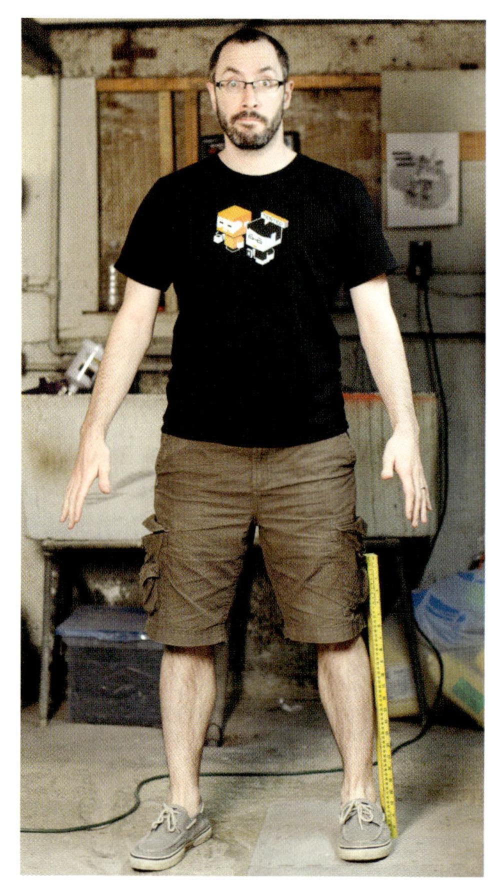

I like to throw a side view of the prop next to a photo of me in Photoshop so that I can look at it in different scales and figure out what is appropriate.

For hand-held items, like a pistol, I utilize a reference photo of my own hand holding a real-sized gun next to a ruler. In Photoshop I can then throw a side view of the prop on top of it and scale it so that it looks right in my hand. Then I can use the ruler in the image to determine how long the prop should be!

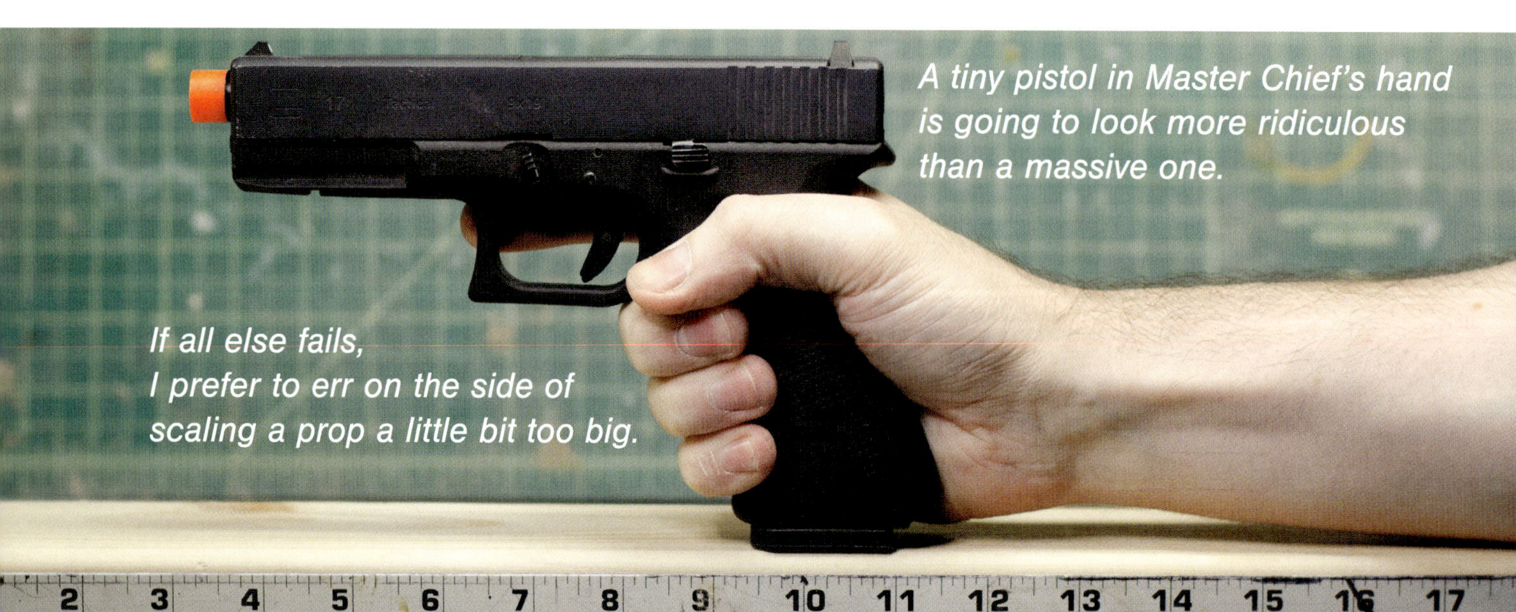

A tiny pistol in Master Chief's hand is going to look more ridiculous than a massive one.

If all else fails, I prefer to err on the side of scaling a prop a little bit too big.

How thick should the weapon be?

It isn't always clear how thick you should build your weapons. Many times, a flat side view is the only decent reference you can get your hands on, so you're stuck scratching your head on certain dimensions. Fortunately there are a couple of things you can do to sleuth your way through this design debacle.

Most props, especially guns, swords, and axes, will have a cylindrical piece somewhere in their design. It could be a handle part or a gun barrel. The great thing about cylinders is that they are the same diameter all the way around. This way, if you can measure their width in your side view, you'll know how thick that part of the prop needs to be in the other views! You can use this measurement as your baseline for judging the thickness for other parts of the prop.

For example, on an axe, if the handle is 1.5" thick, you know the blade needs to be at least that thick and the collar around it needs to be thicker. Even if you don't get the measurements totally "accurate", at least they will look correctly proportional to the handle you build.

You also don't need to go into your design process totally blind. Most of the prop weapons that you'll be building will have real world counterparts that already exist! Don't know how thick your gun handle should be? Measure a real gun handle! Don't have a real gun? Neither do I, but I do have an Airsoft gun that is an almost perfect copy of the genuine article, so I use it as a reference for many of my prop gun builds.

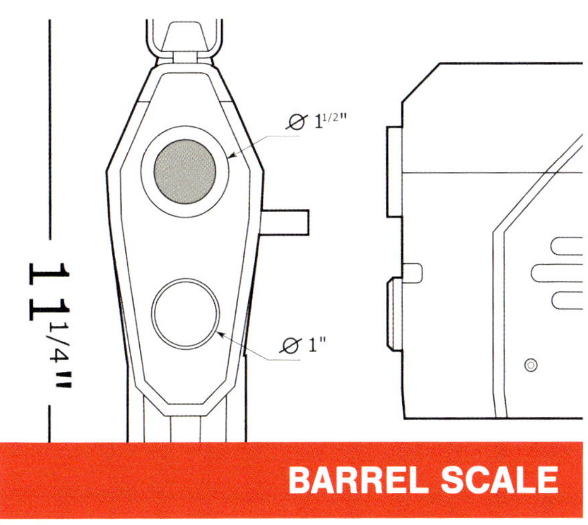

BARREL SCALE

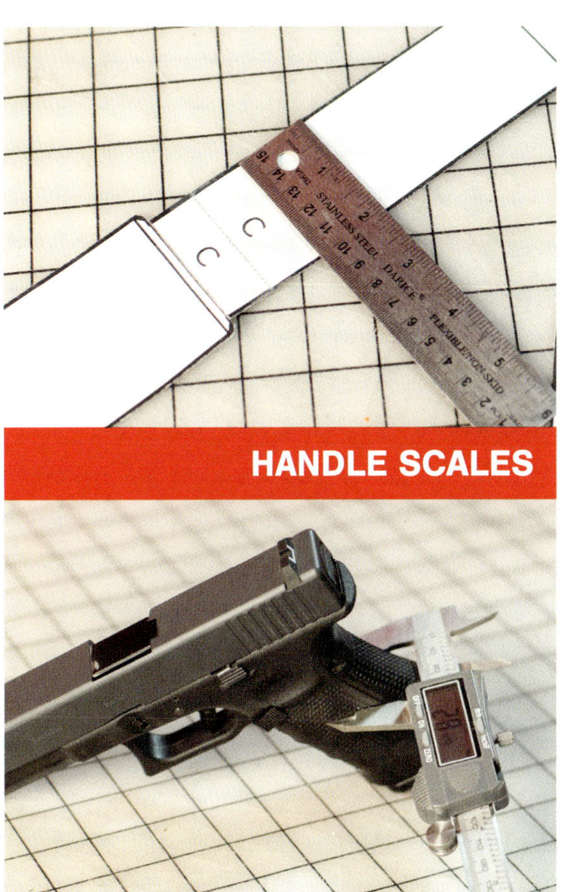

HANDLE SCALES

Practice, and Guess

When push comes to shove, you simply may not be able to get appropriate references for a piece you're trying to replicate and you're going to have to guess on parts of it. That's totally OK and the more you do it, the better you'll get at designing prop weapons that look the way you think they should just by estimating the dimensions.

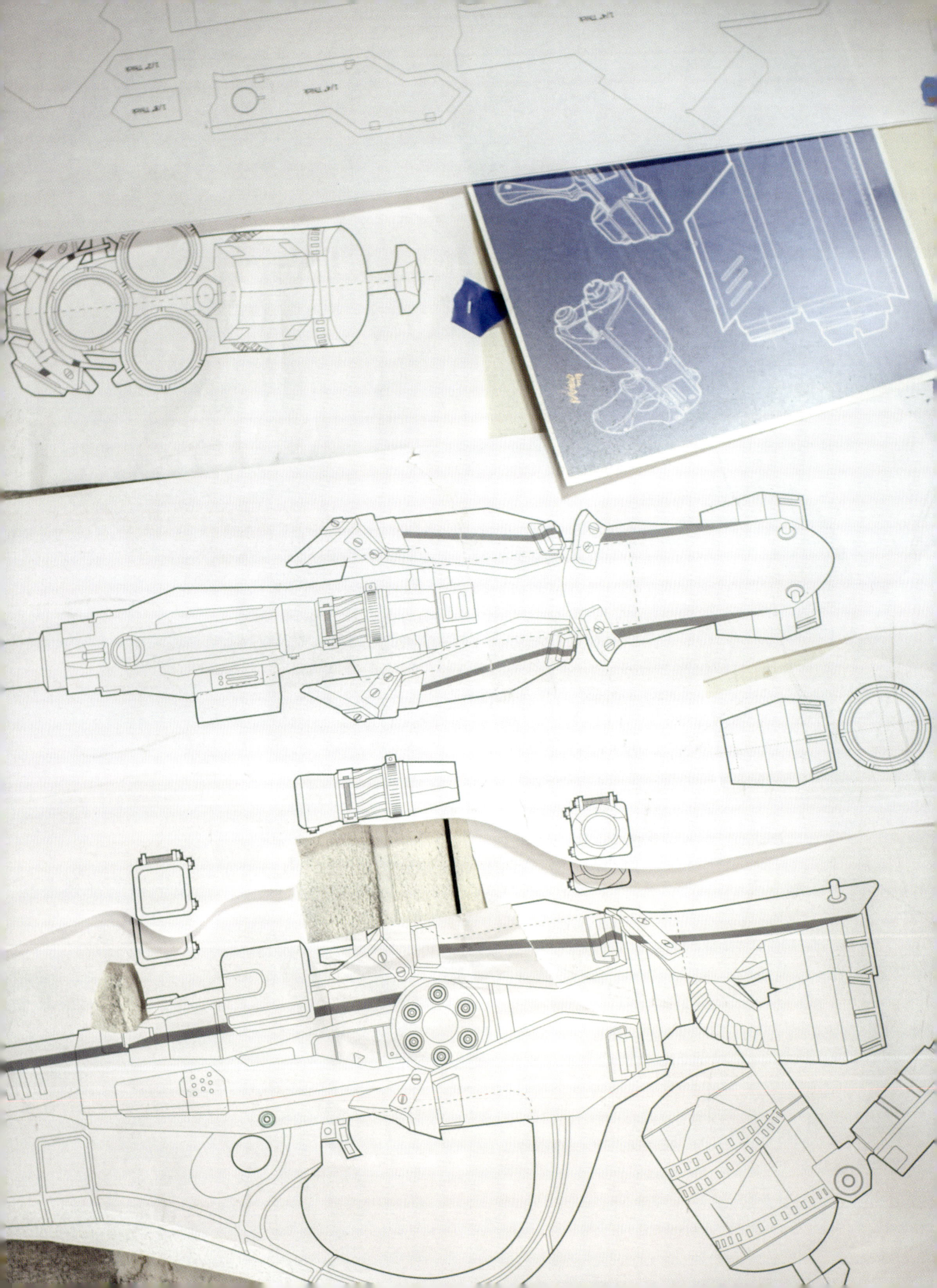

TEMPLATES

To blu or not to blu.

Once you know how big your prop should be, you can start drawing up accurate blueprints of the build. Is this step totally needed? Not necessarily. You could just print out the reference image of your prop at the proper scale and get to work, but I prefer not to skip templating. I consider the blueprinting process the "first build" of a prop. As I draw, I problem solve the entire construction process in my head and make notes on any spots that will require special attention.

Blueprinting can be done in any number of mediums. You could go all old school and draw it on paper (crazy, right?!). I prefer to do all of my drawing digitally and there are many software options:

- SketchUp (Free Version)
- Adobe Illustrator (Paid Subscription)
- Inkscape (Free)

No matter which software package you use, the process is nearly the same. For the purposes of this book, I'll use Inkscape, since it is completely free and, in my opinion, the easiest to use.

For the sake of brevity I'm going to be pretty vague on specific techniques for using Inkscape. YouTube is awash with tutorials on using all of your favorite drawing programs, so I recommend indulging in a few hours of instruction there. That's what I did when I started learning Inkscape!

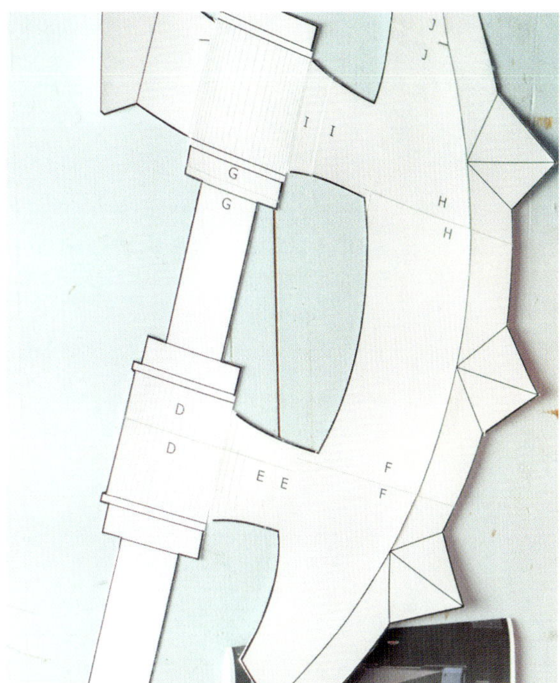

Next, you'll need to choose which views you want to draw. Depending on the size, shape, and complexity of the piece, you may have only one view or you may have several views to draw. You may also be limited by how many angles you were able to get references of. I usually try to draw at least the side, top, and front view of a prop, when necessary.

Once you have all of your reference images laid out in Inkscape, make sure they are all scaled to the same size. This way, the templates are all the same height, thickness, and width. You can use guidelines to make sure everything lines up.

Lock the reference image layer so that you don't move it by accident, create a new layer on top of that and start tracing. That's right, blueprinting is just tracing. Hours and hours of painstaking, digital tracing. Once you get going you'll realize it's not that simple. There's a lot going on when you start translating a 3D object to a 2D orthographic drawing. This is where you begin to learn how much this step is the "first build". As you go, you'll start considering which parts make up different layers of the build and how you'll eventually assemble them.

Even if you can't get a particular view, say a top view of a pistol, you may want to get a top view of of a similar item and draw your "best guess" of that view. This will help you figure out an appropriate thickness for the piece.

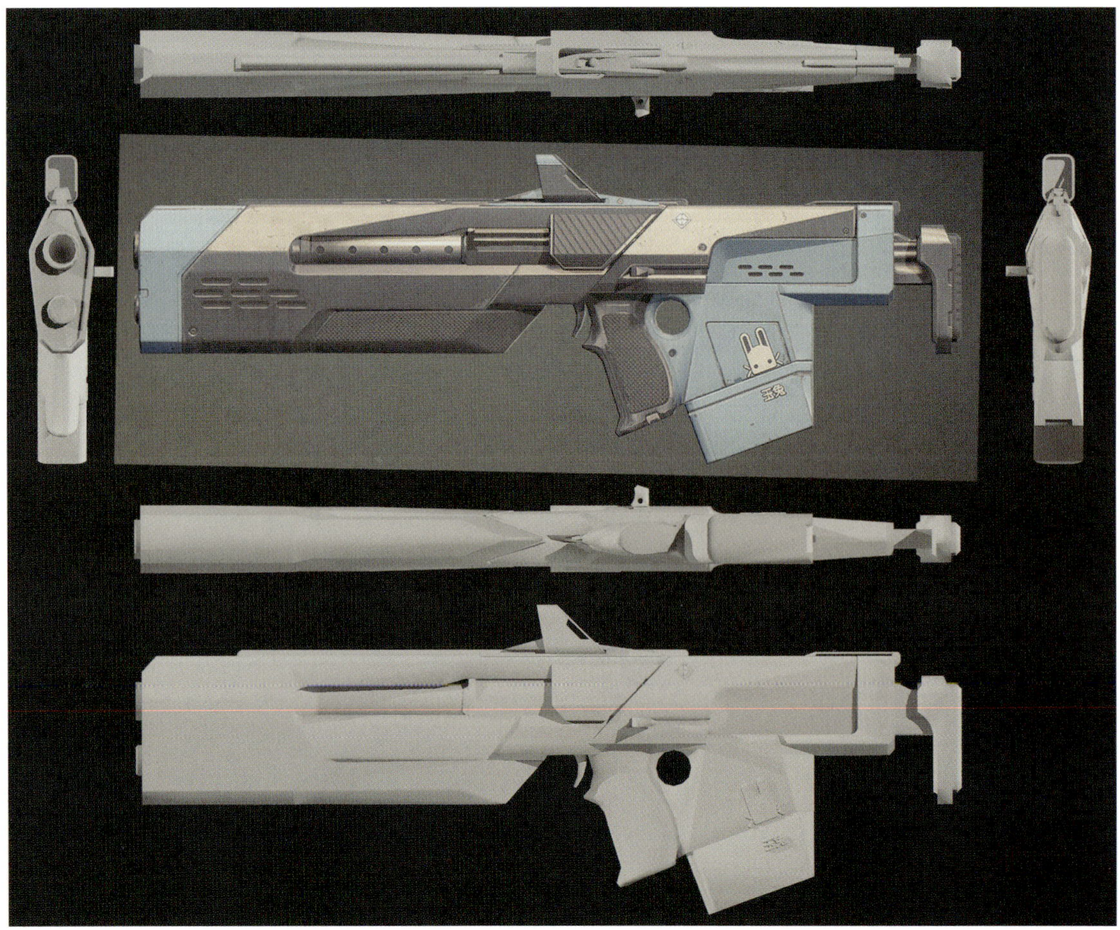

Speaking of layers, consider what foam you'll be working with and the different thicknesses you'll have at your disposal. For most builds, I have foam in ½", 6mm, and 2mm thicknesses. So when I'm drawing my blueprint, especially the top view, I try to design it to accommodate those thicknesses. This may mean you'll end up modifying the original source to match the material you're working with, but so long as you don't go too far, it will look just fine.

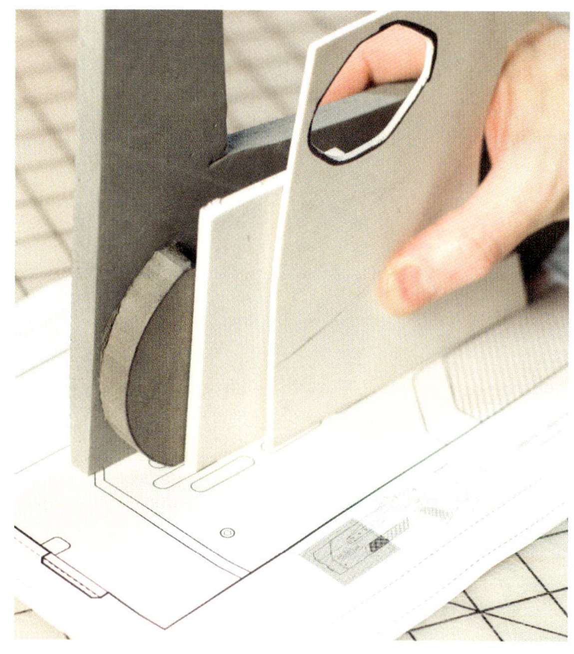

I'll even go so far as to print out half finished blueprints, full scale, and compare them to scraps of foam that I have on hand. This will give me a real world feel for the thickness of the piece. It's too easy to build something far too thick or skinny by accident. With scraps in hand, you can get an actual feel for the piece before you've started building.

If you have a band saw and the pieces aren't too wide, you can rip a piece of foam to whatever thickness you like!

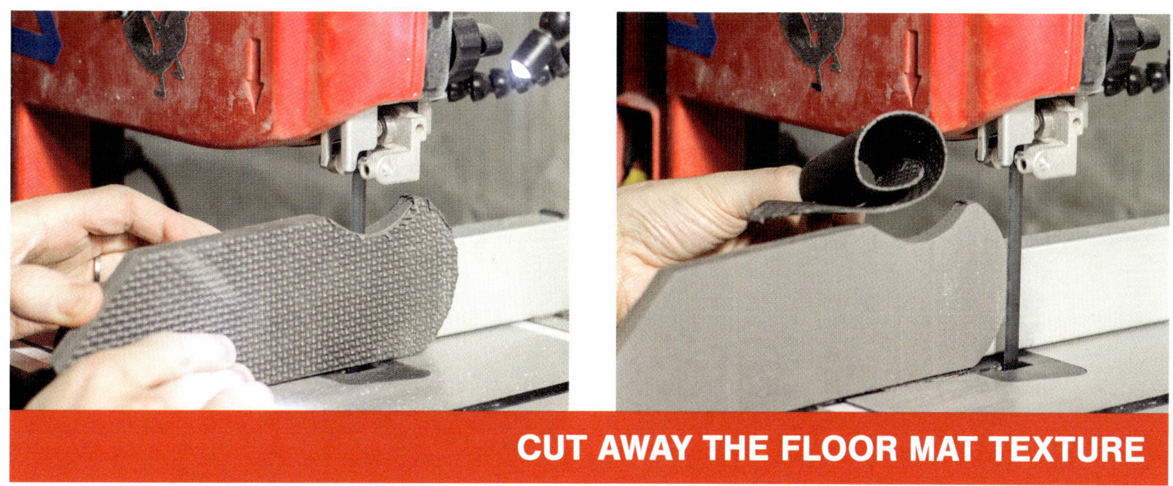

CUT AWAY THE FLOOR MAT TEXTURE

How much should I draw?

Remember that you're essentially drawing a list of instructions for your future self to use during the fabrication. Don't skimp out on details or views that you'll need later on. Even consider exploding out some pieces that should be built separately. I will frequently draw both an exploded and assembled version of a prop if it's particularly complex.

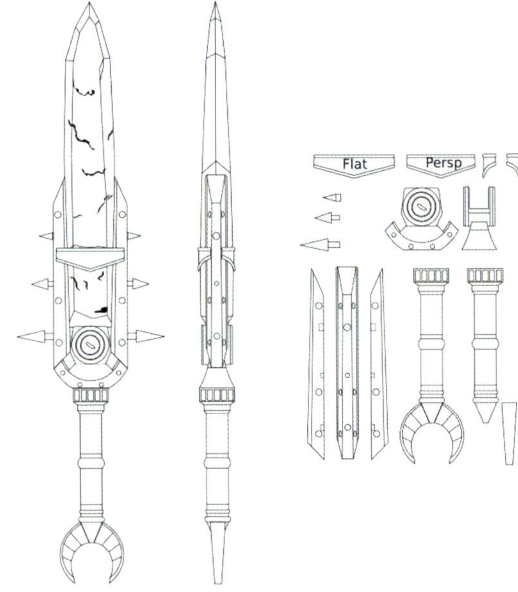

Once you've finished drawing your blueprints it's time to print them out full scale. If it's small enough, you can print it on a normal letter sized printer. You might even be able to get away with printing each view on a different page. If the prop is larger than that, you can split it up on multiple pages and tape them together.

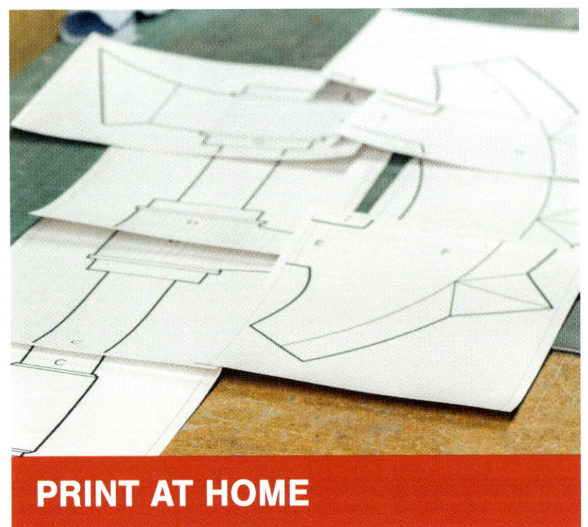
PRINT AT HOME

Another option, my favorite one, is to have the drawing printed on a large format printer. I don't own one, so I save my files as a PDF and bring them to a printer like Office Depot or Staples and have them print it. If you get the cheapest paper and it's all black and white it shouldn't cost more than a few dollars. While you're at it, get two copies printed. It doesn't hurt to have an extra blueprint lying around in case the first one gets ruined.

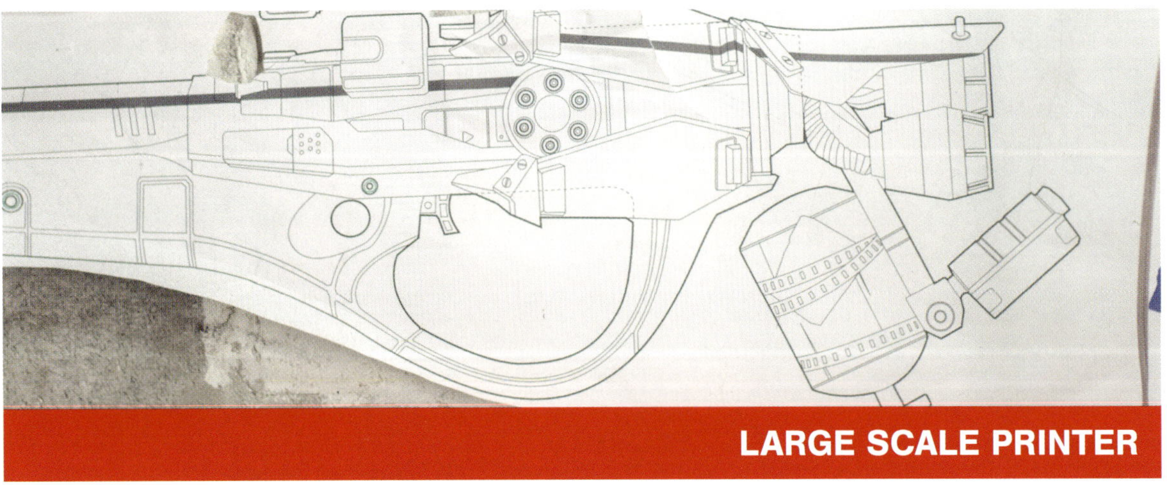
LARGE SCALE PRINTER

Order of Operations

As build time approaches, it will become apparent to you that you can't throw everything together at once. As you design the prop you'll have to decide which parts to build at various stages of the fabrication process. For example, if part of your prop that has both a hole through it and a bevel, you'll want to drill the hole first and then cut the bevel. It can be tricky to drill holes in an angled surface.

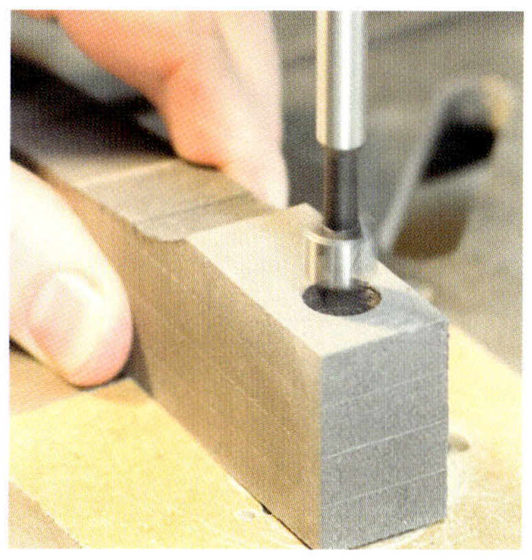

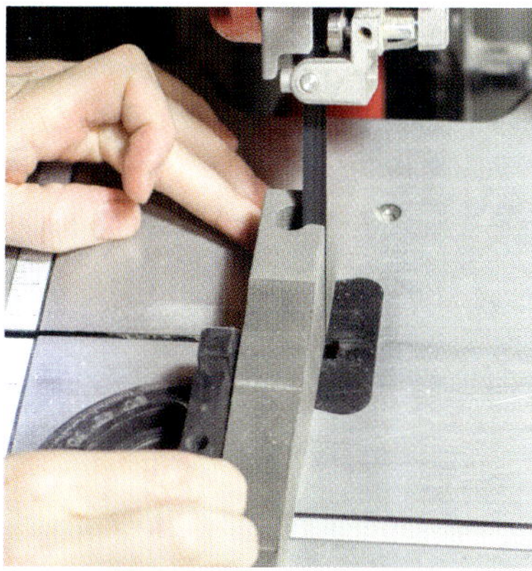

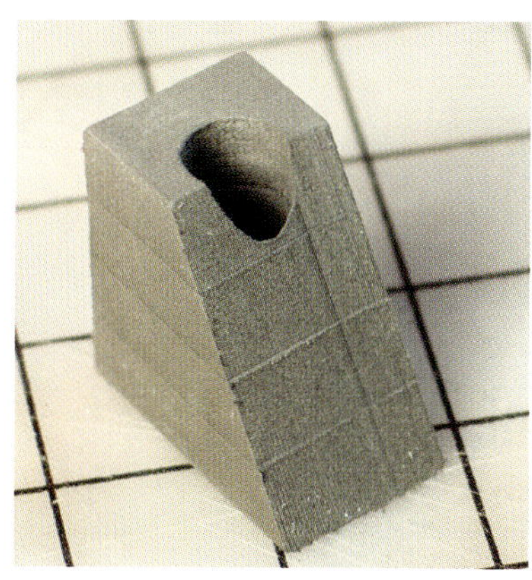

Also consider that your prop may need to be built in several pieces, especially if it's some kind of complex, mechanical weapon. Plan which parts can be built to completion before being attached to the main body part. Making those decisions during the design phase should eliminate confusion later on.

Finally, your prop may need to be taken apart for travel. Decide where on the prop it would be appropriate to add seams for disassembly. Some props may have seams in convenient places by default, but that won't always be the case.

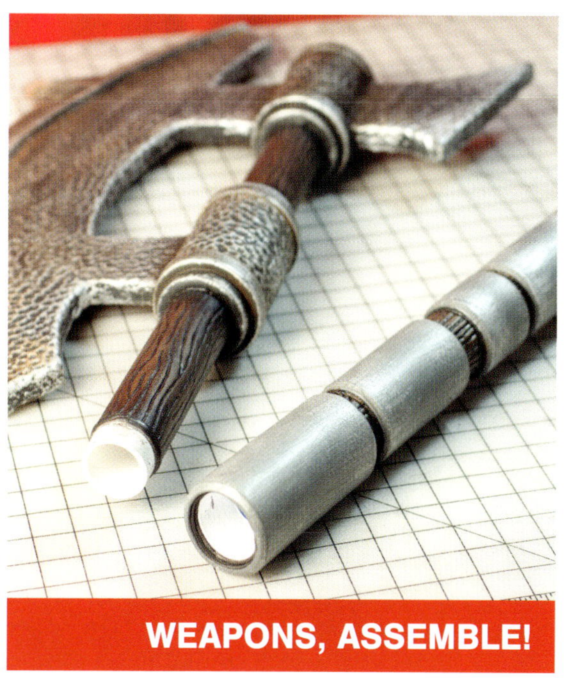

WEAPONS, ASSEMBLE!

"Now is it time to build, Bill?"
Yes, it is time to build! The best part about this step is that you can, in fact, start cutting and gluing pieces together all willy nilly. Since foam is so cheap and quick to work with, it's OK to experiment with your technique as you go. Your blueprint is only a loose instruction manual that you wrote for yourself, so don't feel constricted as you build.

For the most part, the build consists of cutting out a portion of your blueprint, tracing it onto your foam, cutting that foam out, and gluing it to other foam parts. Yes, I know that's a vague set of instructions, but I did that on purpose. You're going to need to get your hands dirty to really learn what you can accomplish with foam. Also, I'll provide a couple of specific, full builds later on in the book that will hand-hold you all the way through the process, so don't fret!

Perfect Cuts

If I've said it once, I've said it a hundred times; keep your knives sharp. Foam dulls a sharp knife with incredible efficiency, so you owe it to your work to invest in a good sharpener and spruce up that edge as soon as it shows signs of dulling.

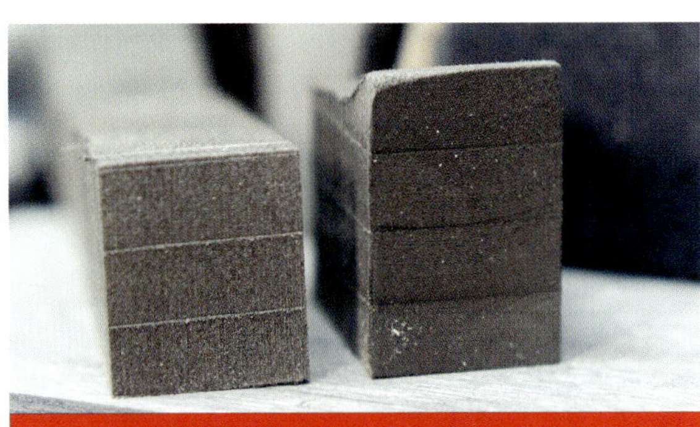

If you use a power saw to make some of your cuts, it's going to be difficult to achieve the same smooth edges that you get with a sharp knife. So, when possible, cut your pieces a little outside the lines and then use a sanding tool to do the final clean up. This is where the disc, belt, and drum sander pays off in spades.

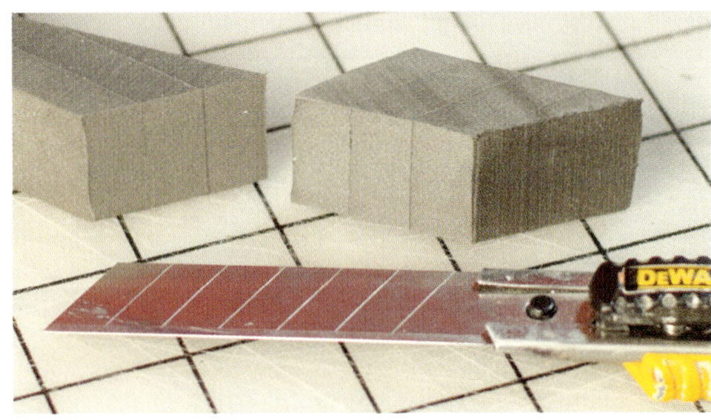

Again, depending on the piece, it won't always be possible to use the power tools on a part depending on the shape of the piece. This is another reason why I try and build out pieces separate from the main prop body before gluing them all together at the end.

If you have multiple layers glued together and want them to look like one solid, homogeneous piece, you'll want to glue the layers together first and then cut and sand them. You can glue the layers together after you've cut them and it's possible to get them close, but if you want that "machined look", glue first.

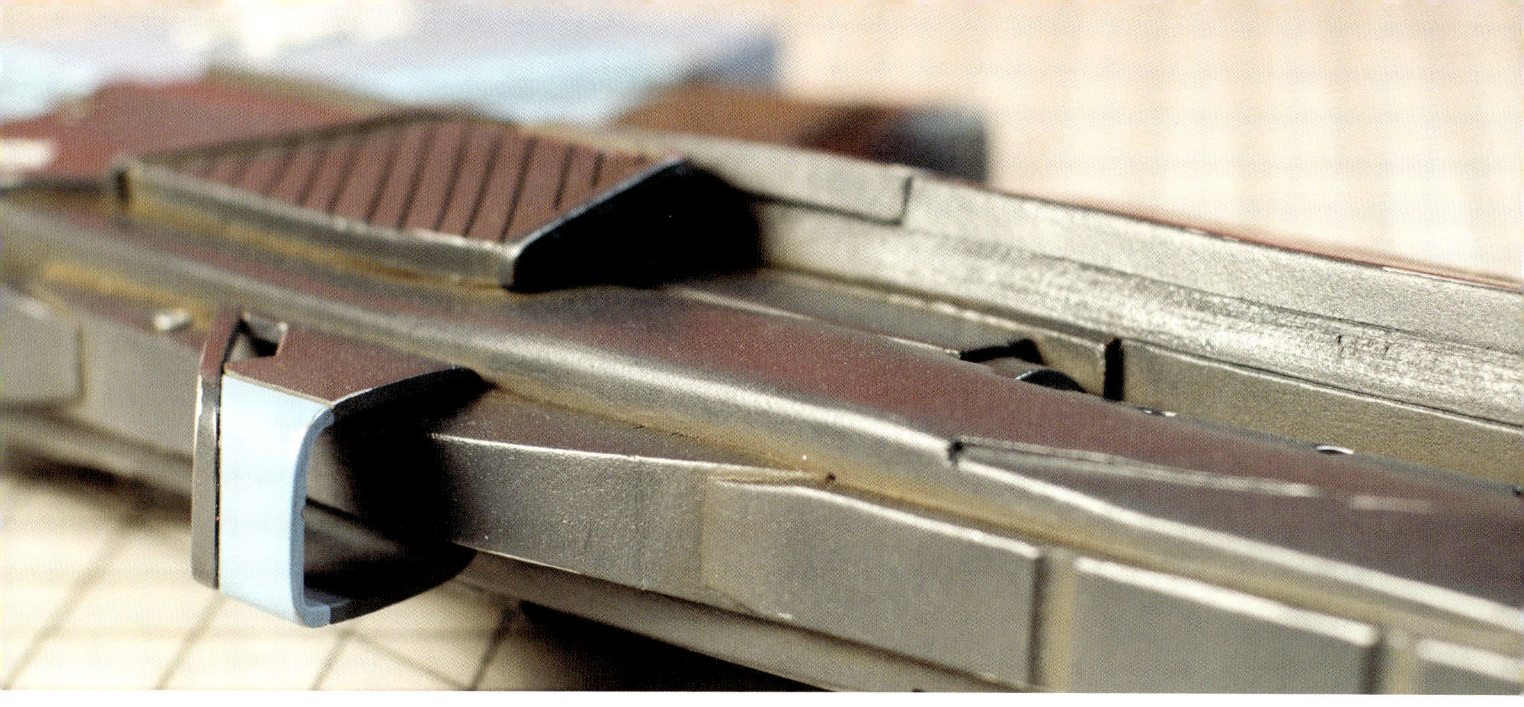

Building in Layers

Nearly every prop I've ever built has been an exercise in cake building. That is to say, they're made of layers, just with less frosting. Most weapons have a geometric look to them and foam comes in flat sheets, so assembling them as individual layers makes a lot of sense. The real art comes from blending layers into one solid looking piece that matches the look you're going for.

Some props will lend themselves very well to this type of building, especially things like space guns and swords. Other pieces with more organic designs will be more difficult to assemble this way, but that doesn't mean you're out of luck. You're just going to have to be more clever about how you bend the material to your will.

I will sometimes leave some layers or parts of a build separate from the main body of the build until they are fully painted. This will save time when painting later on.

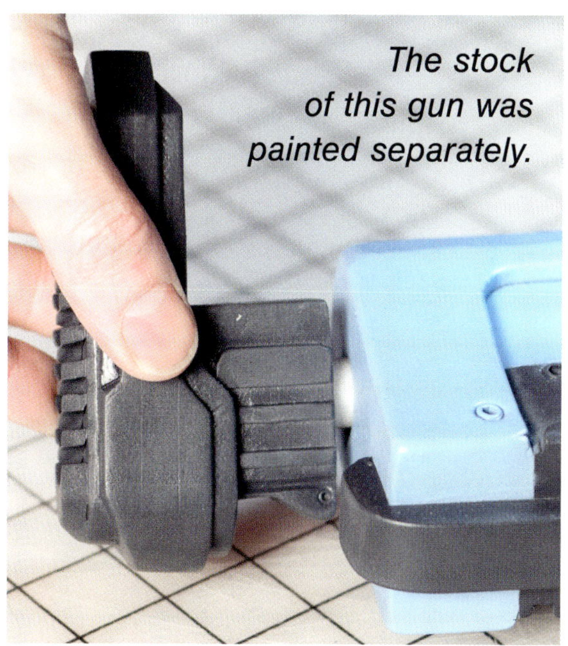

The stock of this gun was painted separately.

Just because you're building your prop from foam, doesn't mean you need to only use foam. You may find that certain pieces will be quicker and easier to make from a material like Worbla or other sculpting mediums. Play to your own strengths and the strengths of different mediums to get the best looking prop you can accomplish!

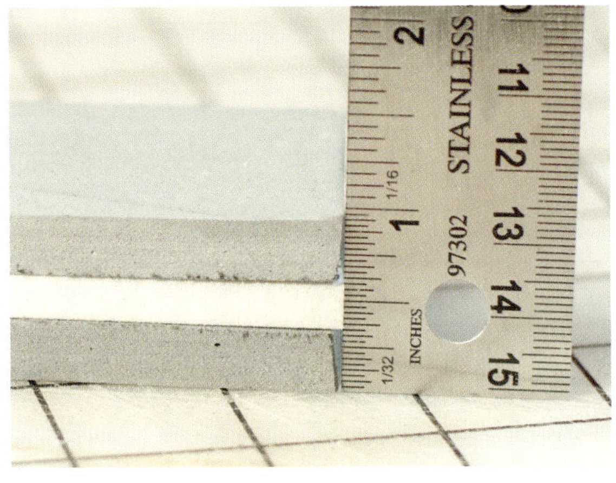

Laminating

Speaking of layers, some of your props might be thick enough to warrant gluing a bunch of foam sheets together to create a thicker part. This is known as laminating. For example, if part of your prop needs to be 2" thick, you need to glue four ½" thick sheets together to achieve that thickness.

Start by cutting out several pieces, each a little larger than the final piece will need to be. It's easier to laminate the foam first and then cut it down to shape. Cut out as many pieces as you'll need to reach the necessary thickness. Also remember that if you're using floor mats, when you remove the texture you'll be making the sheets a little thinner. This will impact the final thickness, so be sure to take that into account. You can always add sheets of different thicknesses to get to the final dimensions.

If you're using some type of foam that doesn't have a textured side, you can skip straight to gluing. If you're using floor mats, like I do, you'll need to remove the textured side. This can be accomplished in a variety of ways. The simplest way is to just sand it off. A belt sander will make short work of that texture, just be careful to keep the piece a uniform thickness. It's surprising how fast that sander will chew through foam.

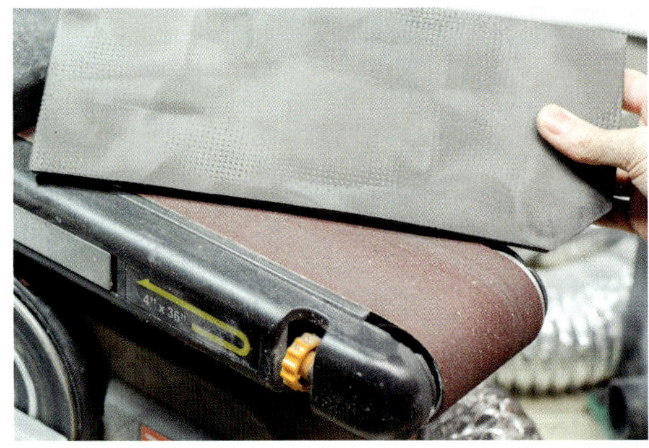

Once your foam pieces are prepared, it's time to glue them all together. A variety of glues will work, but for your money it's hard to beat a good contact cement. I prefer Barge, but there are other options depending on where you live. As always, remember to work in a well ventilated area when using noxious glues.

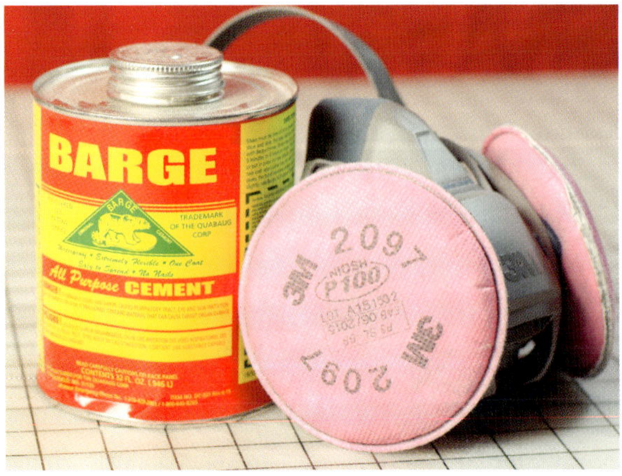

Spread an even coating of cement on all of the faces that need to be glued together and let it dry for 5-10 minutes. It doesn't hurt to wear rubber gloves for this process since some of the pieces will need glue on both sides and you'll have your fingers all over them. For pieces with glue on both sides, you can stand them up on their edges while they dry, so long as the foam is thick enough to do so. I call this technique Foamhenge.

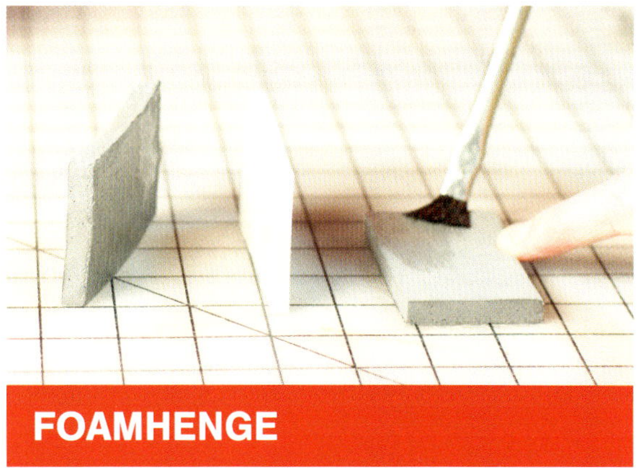

FOAMHENGE

When the glue is ready, you can start stacking your foam pieces to make one large foam block. I recommend just plopping them right down on one another instead of trying to squeegee them onto one another. This can actually cause the pieces to warp a bit. Just stack them up and squish them together.

You can achieve a similar effect with super glue, if necessary. Be sure to cover the entire surface of the foam with glue and work quickly. Glue and stack one piece at a time until you're block is complete.

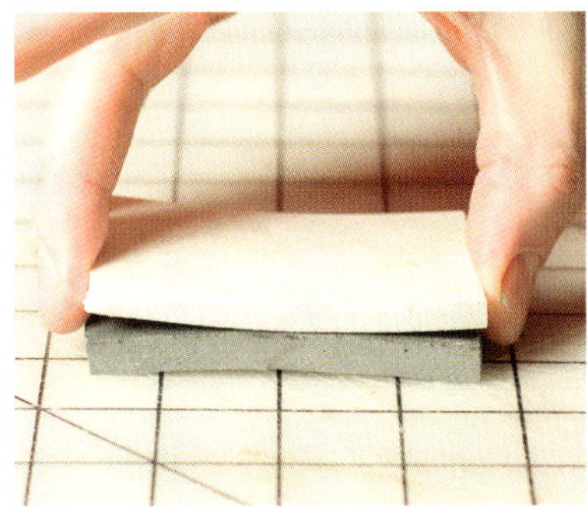

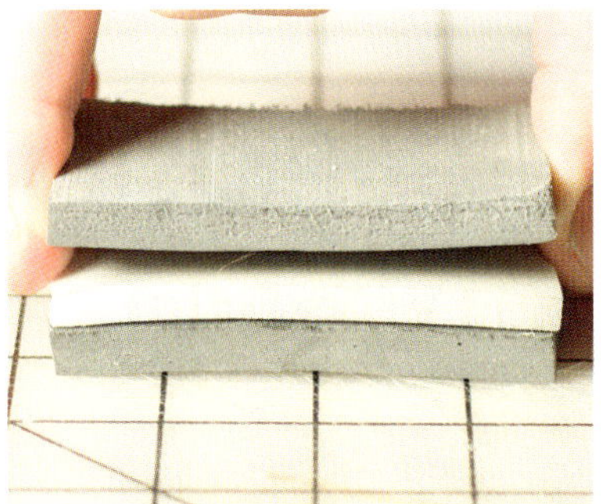

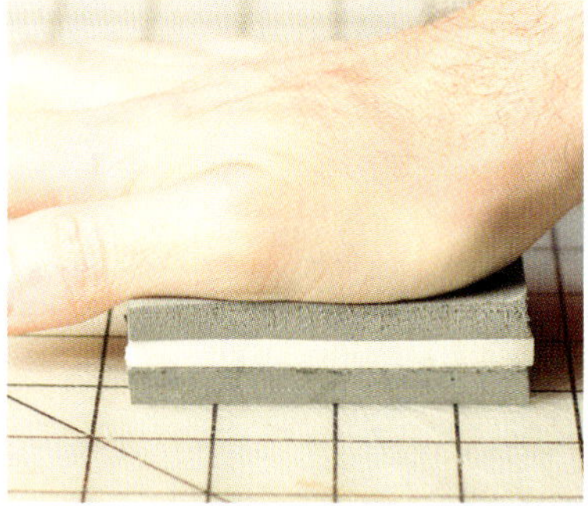

Now that you have your gigantic foam block, you can trace your blueprint onto it and get to cutting! This is where a band saw comes in really handy. If your piece is particularly thick, it's super difficult to get a good 90 degree cut with a knife.

This laminating process can be extremely useful when building the base shape for a large prop. Consider these pieces as platforms that you build the rest of the prop details onto.

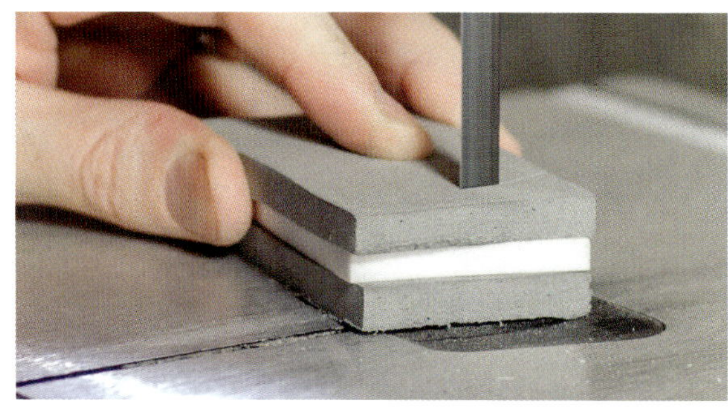

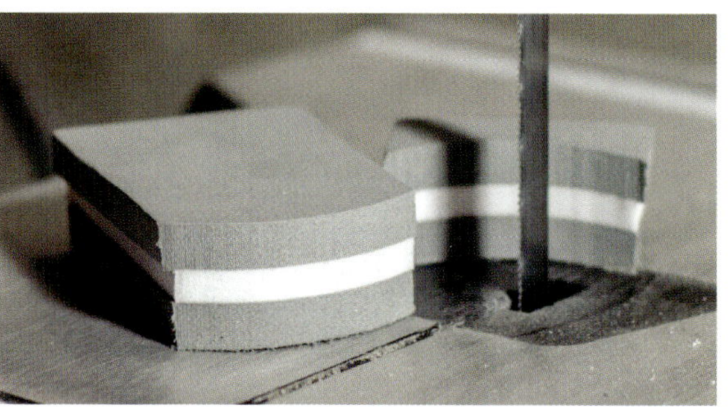

"If the foam is particularly thick, it's super difficult to get a good 90 degree cut with a knife."

Hiding Layer Seams

One shortcoming of using large, laminated blocks of foam are the seam lines between the layers. If you do a really good job and are able to sand those areas with a disc or belt sander you can make them nearly invisible, but that isn't always the case. If need be, you can cover those areas by laminating another thin sheet of craft foam over them. This is another technique that you should keep in mind when designing your build.

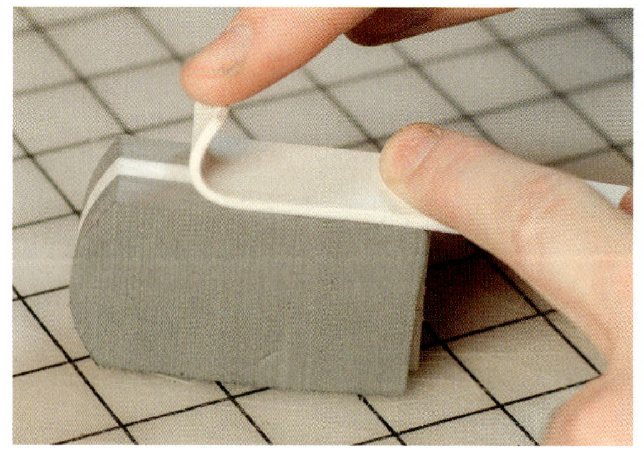

Foam Supports

Getting a Handle on Things

Many weapons have long handles. Foam is a wonder material, but sometimes it can't support its own weight. Props like swords and axes usually have long, thin parts that will need a little extra support. Here are some options for foam support:

- PVC Pipe
- Wooden Dowel
- Fiberglass Rod
- Carbon Fiber Tube

I usually default to using PVC pipe, because it's cheap and readily available in the plumbing section at hardware stores. Also, it can be heat shaped to accommodate any weirdly shaped handles. It's also fairly light and you can use a variety of pipe fixtures to attach parts together, if need be.

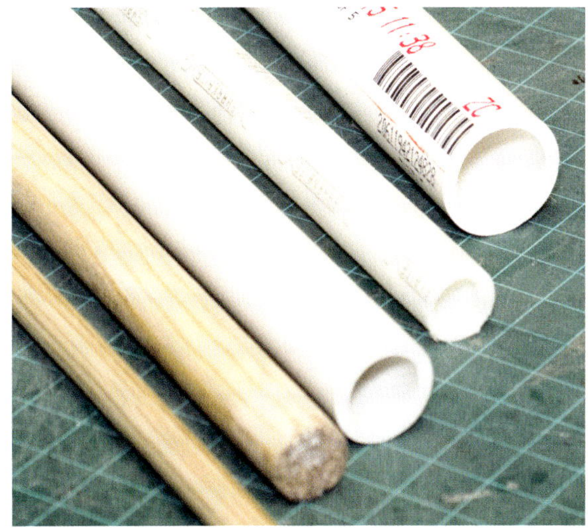

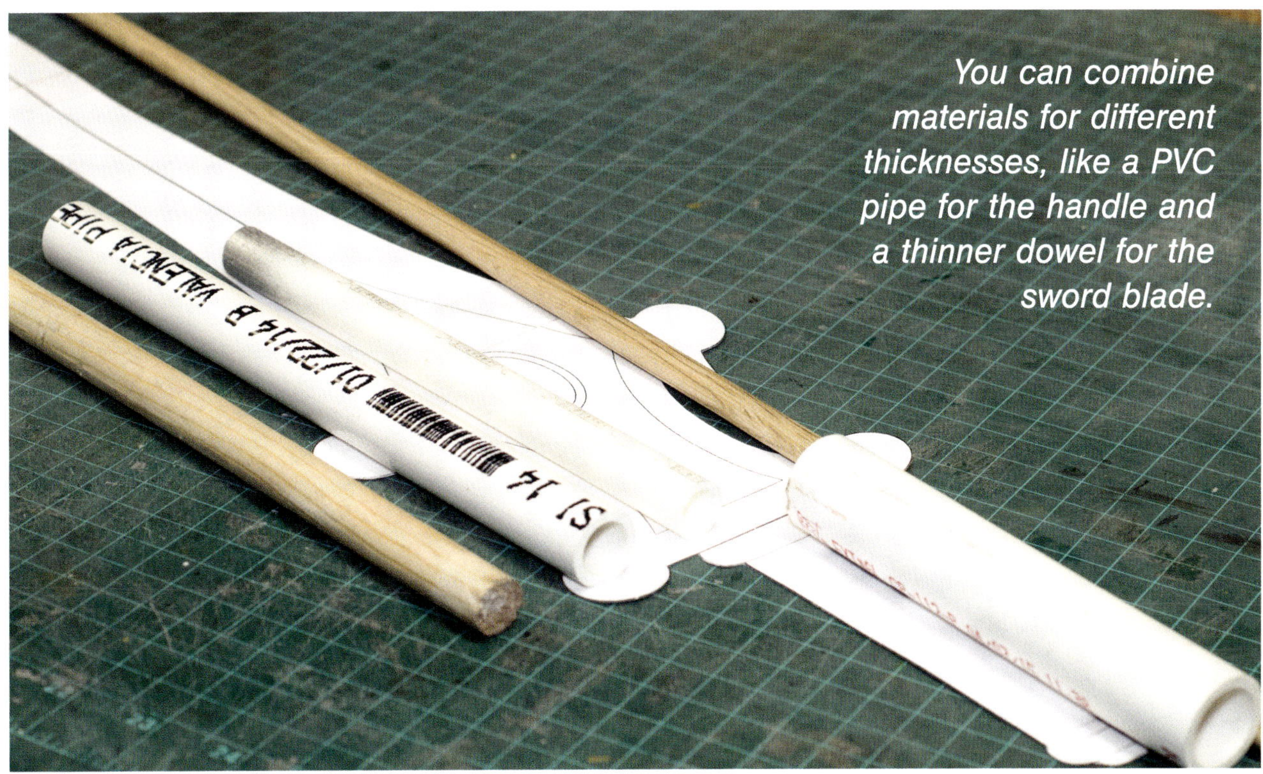

You can combine materials for different thicknesses, like a PVC pipe for the handle and a thinner dowel for the sword blade.

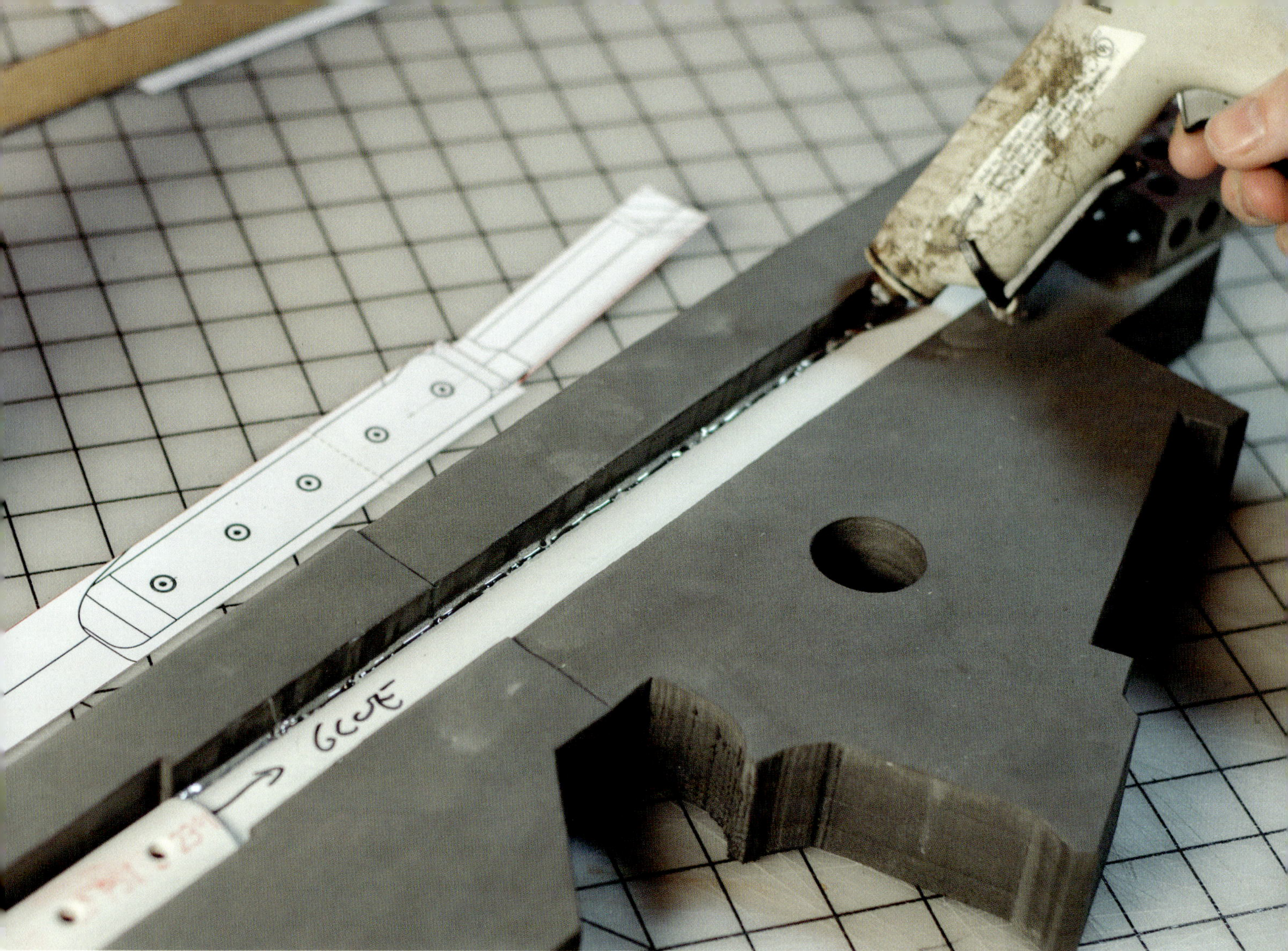

More Support

Long, thin axe handles aren't the only things that might need a little bit of support. If you're building some kind of space rifle, you may find that it gets a little bendy in the middle. Just like the handles, some kind of hidden, rigid material can help keep that piece from being too wobbly.

As with most design decisions, try and consider whether support will be necessary before you start gluing foam parts together. It's much easier to add a PVC pipe support to a prop gun early on. You don't want to have it all assembled only to realize you need to cut it open to glue in some structure pieces.

You might also need to heat bend your pipes for this type of support, especially if your gun is some weird, alien shape. These pipes can be glued into the innermost layer of foam and then covered by the outer layers. Since you won't see it, feel free to secure it with copious amounts of hot glue.

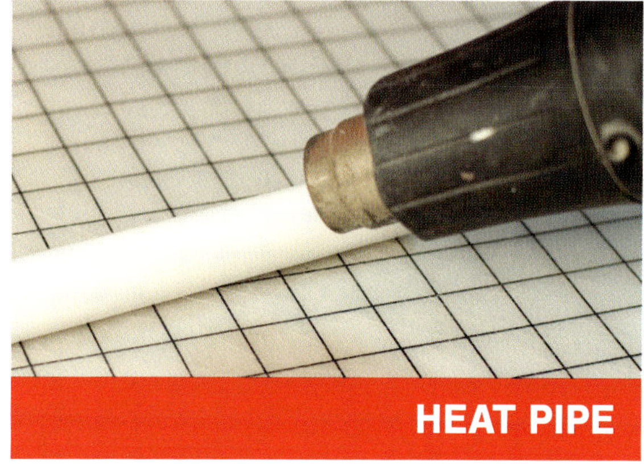

HEAT PIPE

Use a heat gun to make part of a PVC pipe malleable. Don't burn it though. If it starts turning brown you've gone too far and the fumes are toxic. Also note that if you bend it too far it will collapse on itself.

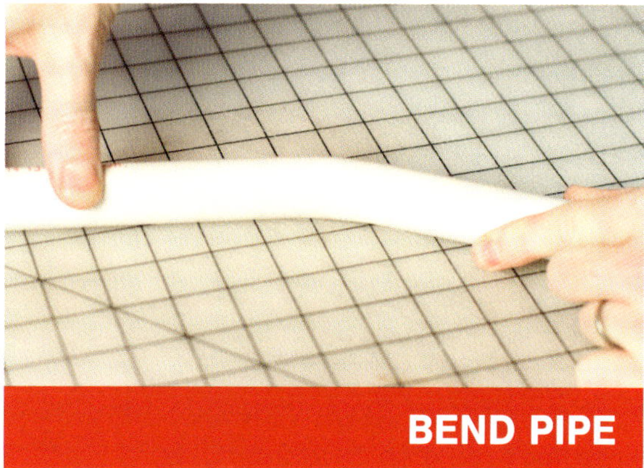

BEND PIPE

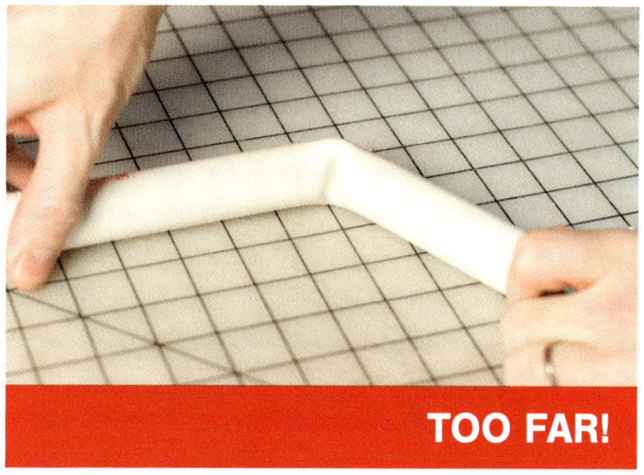

TOO FAR!

Pipes and rods of any material come in a variety of diameters. You can chose to use a pipe that is the same diameter of your handle or get one that's a little thinner and wrap it in foam. I prefer to add foam so that I can texture the piece to match the source art. This is especially useful for wooden handles or anything with a specific texture or pattern.

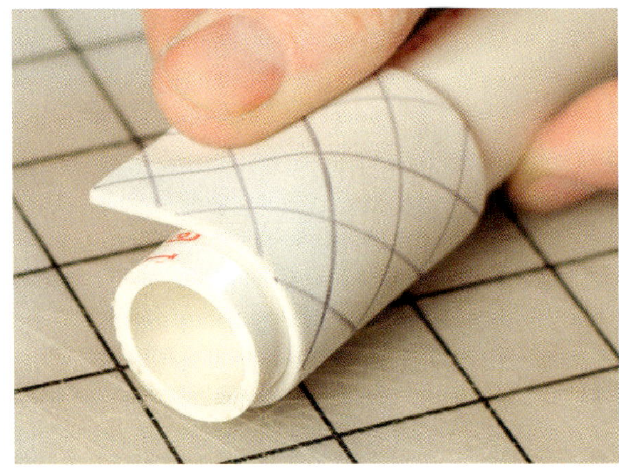

When gluing foam to PVC, be sure to sand the plastic with a low grit sandpaper to give the glue something stick to. Then, you can apply contact cement to both the foam and the plastic, wait a few minutes, and then stick them together.

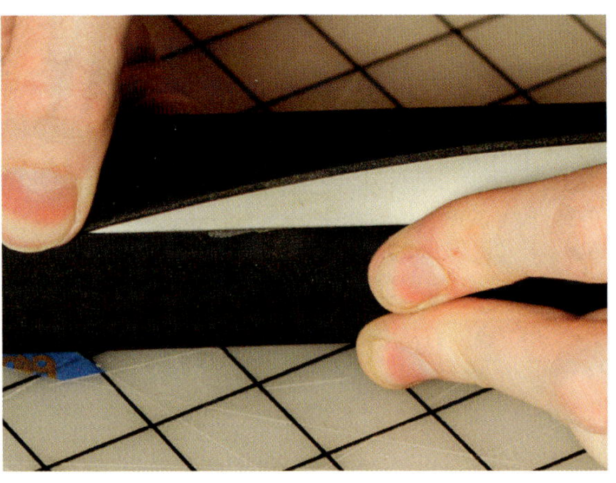

You can cut your designs or patterns into the foam either before or after gluing it to the pipe. It all depends on the look you're going for. For something like wood grain, it's probably easier to carve it into the foam after it's been attached. If you have something more precise, like a diamond pattern, you will probably want to figure that all out on the flat piece of foam before wrapping it around the pipe.

"When gluing foam to PVC, be sure to sand the plastic with a low grit sandpaper to give the glue something stick to."

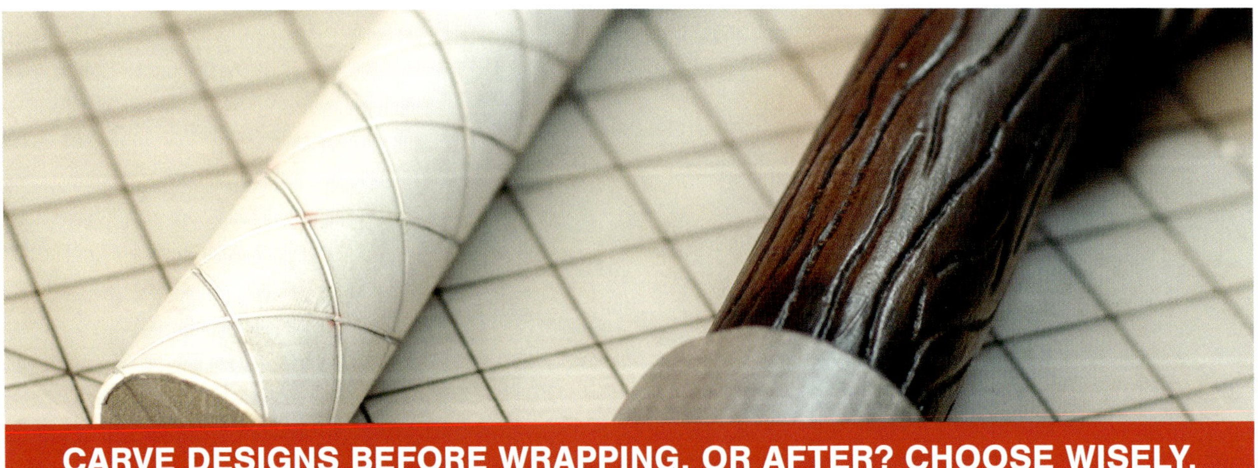

CARVE DESIGNS BEFORE WRAPPING, OR AFTER? CHOOSE WISELY.

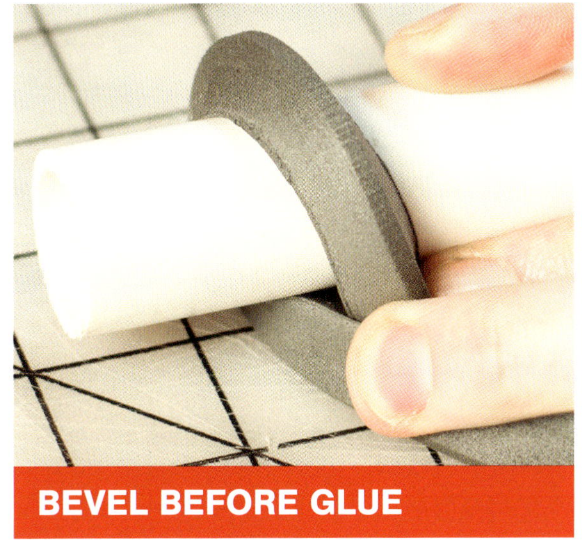

BEVEL BEFORE GLUE

Other parts, like beveled edges, could be difficult to do once they've been glued down, so keep that in mind when trying to map your order of operations.

There are countless designs that can be achieved by wrapping foam pieces around a pipe handle. Thin foam strips act a lot like leather strips, so try duplicating those types of handle wraps! Or use real leather, I'm not the boss of you.

Wrap handles in foam, fabric, leather, and more!

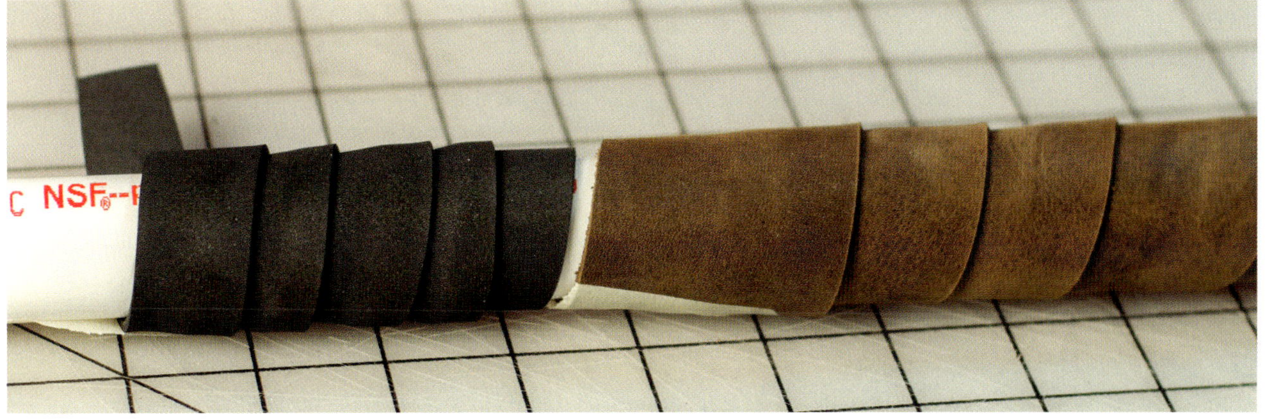

Too Big to Travel?

It is very common for prop weapons to be far too big to fit into your luggage. That's OK, it happens to lots of prop makers! For this very reason, it is a huge benefit to be able to take apart your prop into smaller component parts!

This is another reason why I like using PVC pipe as the interior structure for my props. Many of the fixtures available will fit snugly enough around a pipe that they will stay together with friction and come apart with a small amount of effort.

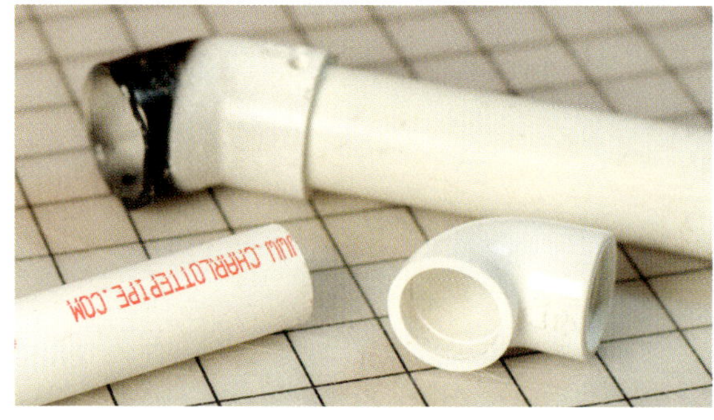

Be prepared for confused hardware store employees as you assemble fixtures in the store aisle.

So long as you design your weapon with these fixture pieces in seam areas, you can simply pop your prop pieces apart at those seams! I will design these pieces so that they each fit into my luggage. I've even redesigned props for the very purpose of fitting them into a specific piece of luggage. These are decisions the traveling cosplayer must make.

I've also seen long stave type weapons built on top of pool cues that can unscrew in the middle. A little more pricey than PVC pipe, but incredibly handy.

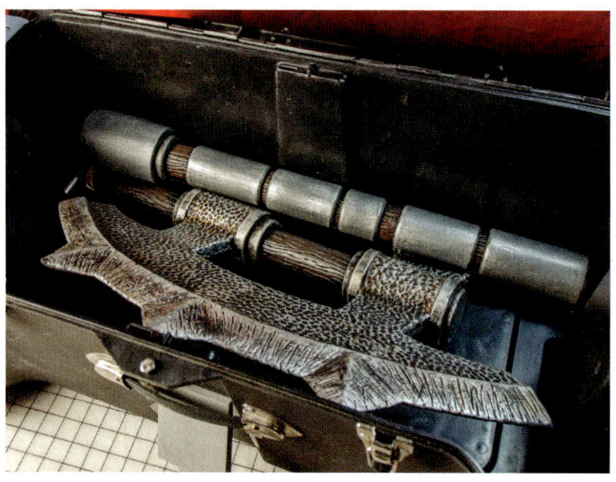

Depending on how much weight they will have to support, props can also be assembled using magnets! While they won't work well for supporting longer pieces, like handles, magnets can be extremely useful for things like battery panels.

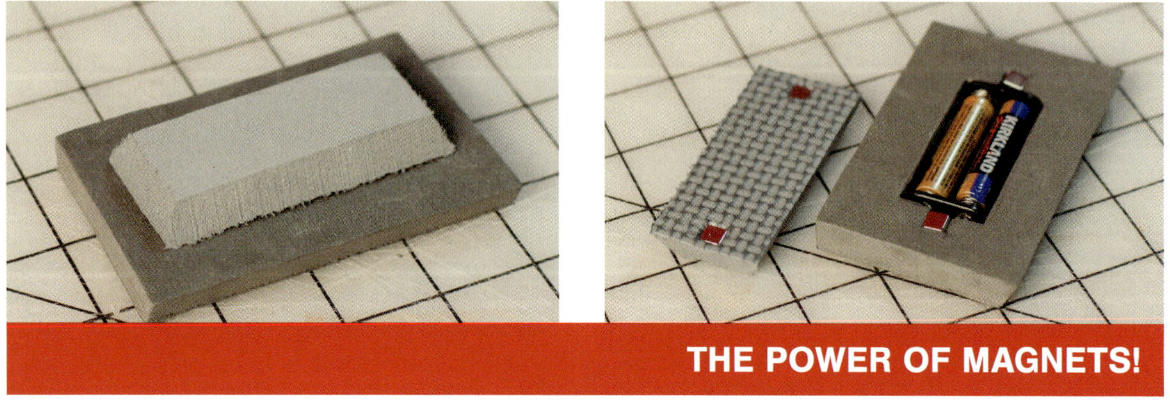

THE POWER OF MAGNETS!

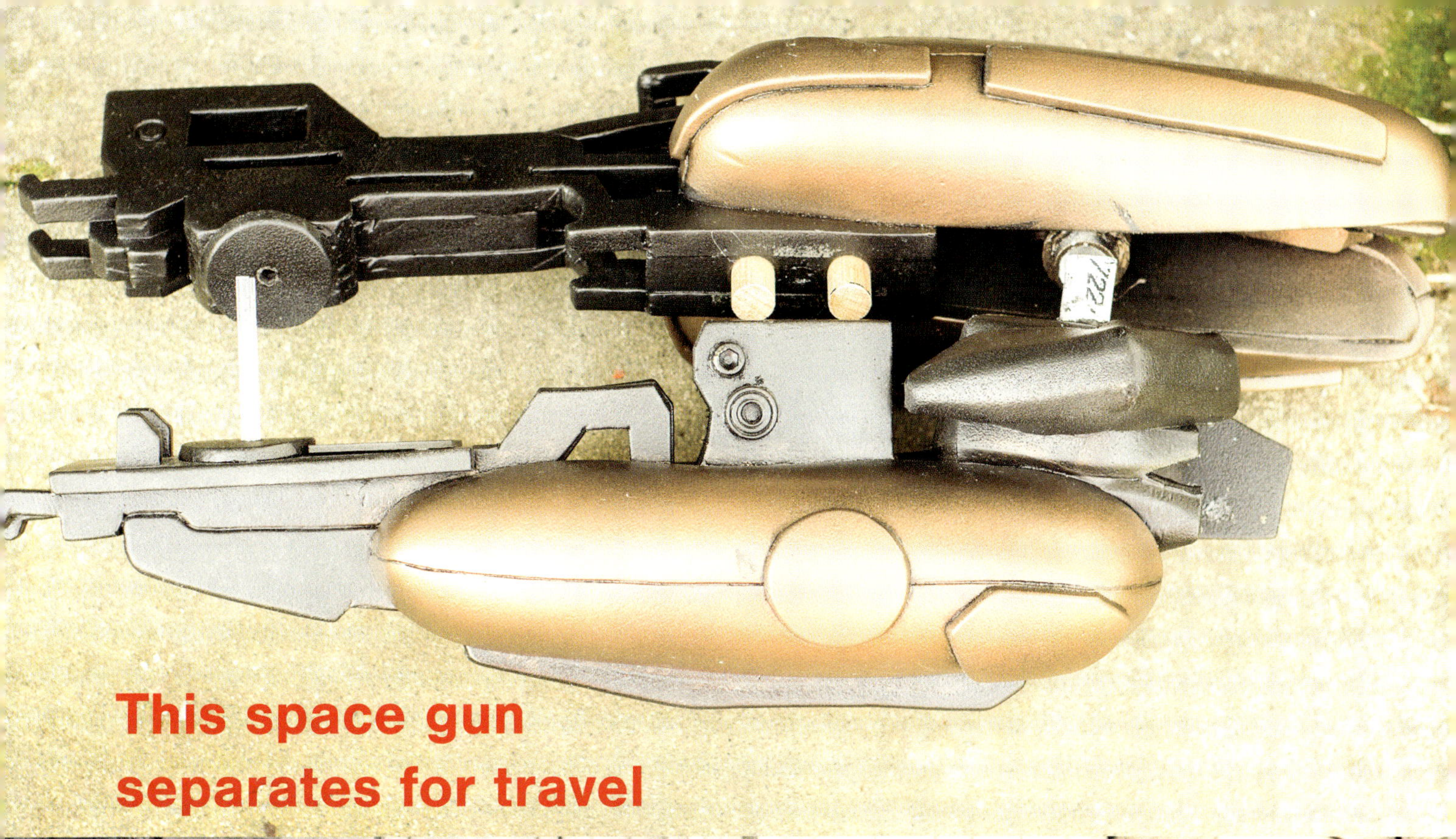

This space gun separates for travel

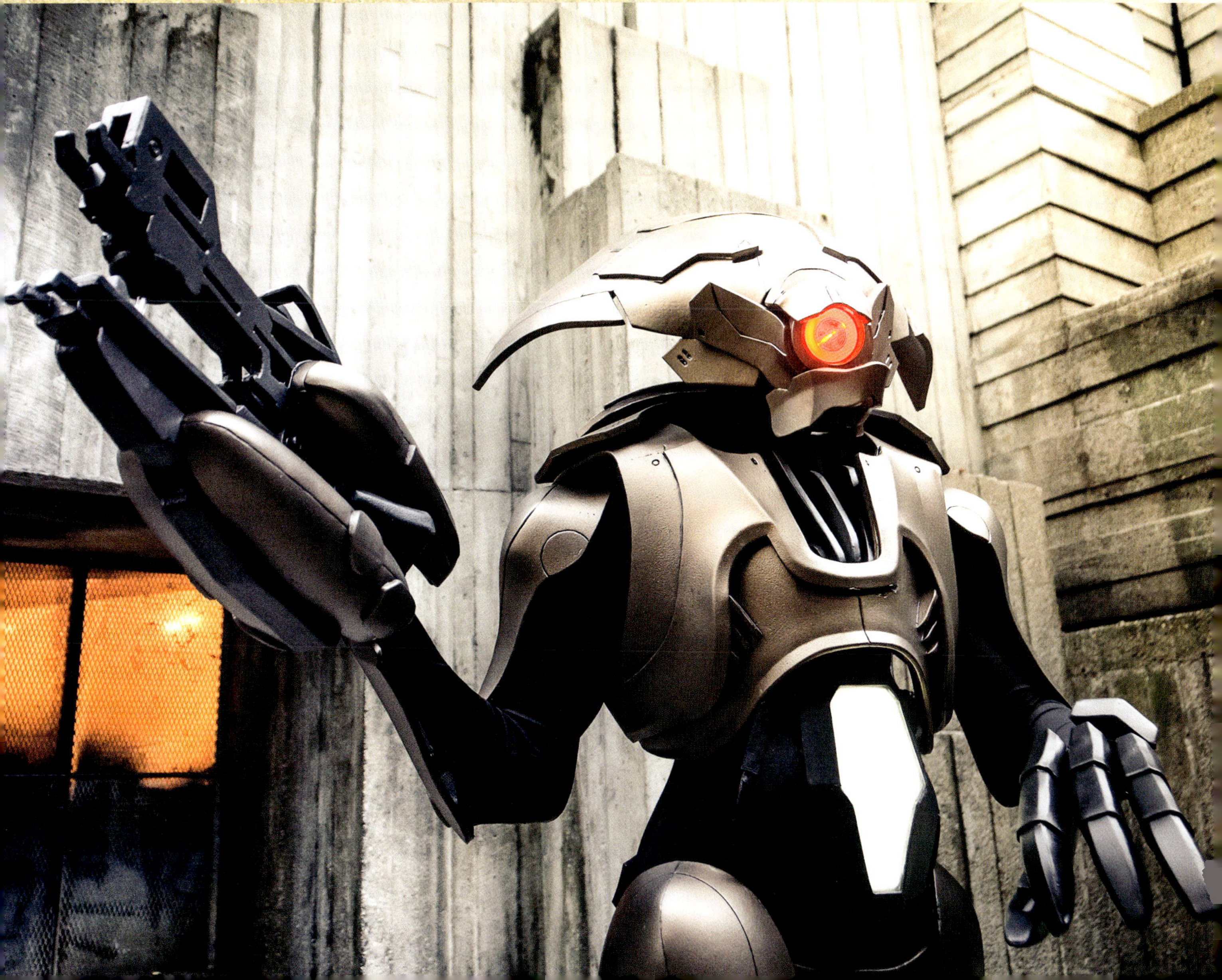

Edged Weapons

I've got an axe to grind!

If you're making any type of edged weapon, you're definitely going to want to sharpen that edge so that it looks properly menacing! This means putting a mean bevel all along the edge of your weapon. This is another place where having power tools will help speed up the process a whole lot, but it isn't totally necessary.

No matter what your tool, I recommend removing as much of the beveled edge with a knife or saw first, before refining it with sanding tools. This means cutting off excess material, but leaving a bit on the prop to finish later when you have more control. This way you can quickly remove a majority of the material without turning it into dust.

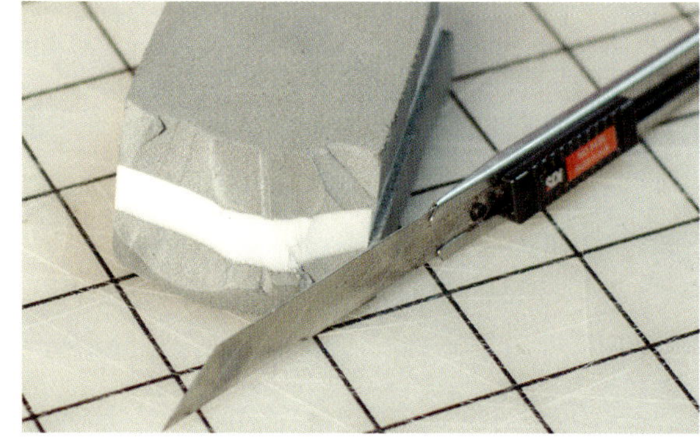

Once you're most of the way there, you can refine that bevel with any number of powered sanding tools. For most jobs, the rotary tool can get you there, just be warned that the smaller diameter drums are prone to digging into the soft foam material. There is a subtle art to creating smooth looking bevels with a Dremel and practice is your friend!

Also be aware that the rotation direction of your tool can make a difference in how much it digs into the foam. Moving the bit with or against the spin direction will yield different results, so try both with each edge you're working on to ensure you're getting the finish you desire.

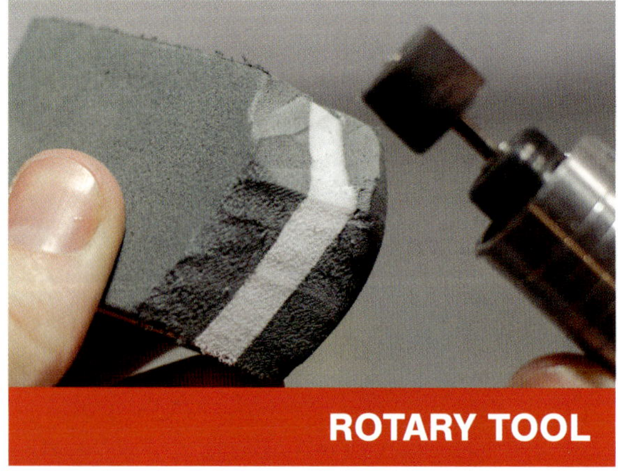

ROTARY TOOL

You can get some clean looking bevels with a belt sander in no time flat! While this is a quicker method, be warned that belt sanders find foam delicious and will gobble it up if you don't pay attention! A practiced hand will ensure a keen sword edge.

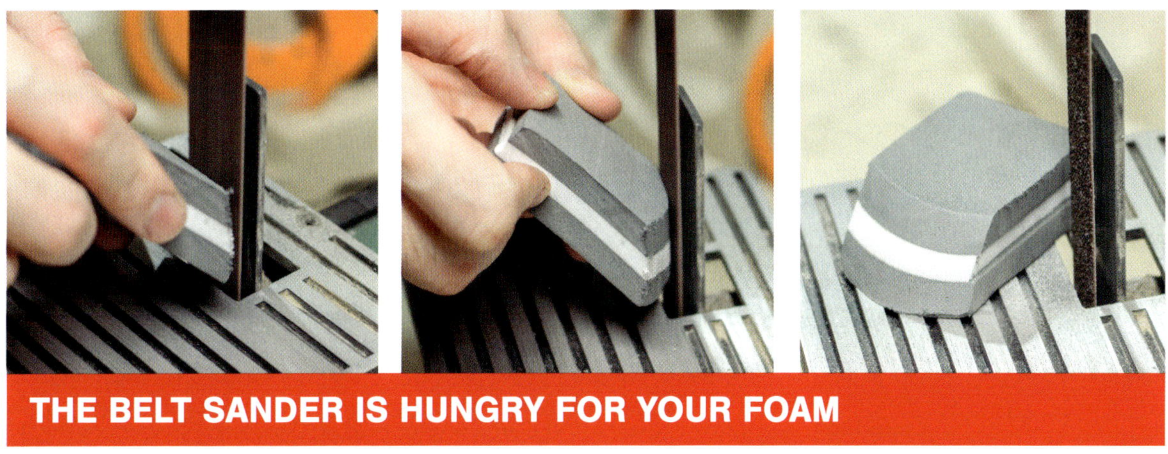

THE BELT SANDER IS HUNGRY FOR YOUR FOAM

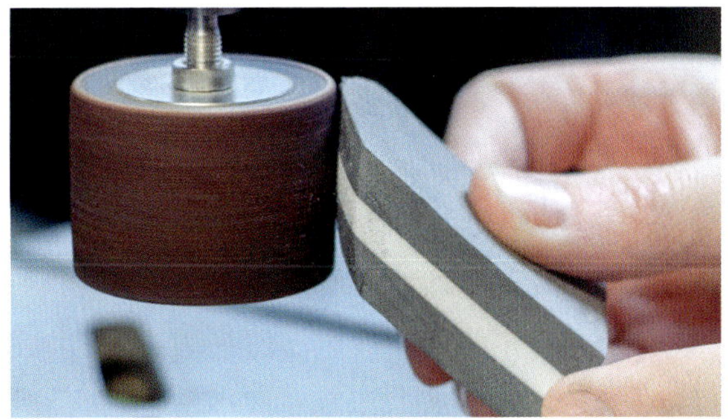

If you've picked up some drum sanding bits for your drill press, this is another great way to utilize them. It's like having a giant rotary tool!

While I do love my large sanding tools, there are some times where the weird shape of your piece can only be refined with a tool as small as your rotary bits. For most foam prop pieces, I'll end up using nearly every sanding tool at my disposal, so it pays to get good at using all of them.

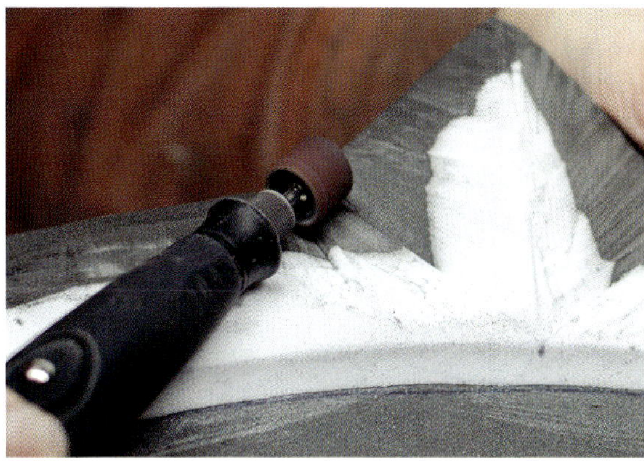

Sealing Foam

Seal of approval

In the first Foamsmith book, we covered a variety of ways to seal your foam armor costumes (Mod Podge, Plasti Dip, Epoxy) and all of those methods apply to your weapons.

Since the release of the first book, I've had a chance to experiment with a couple more advanced methods of sealing and I've settled on my very favorite method: latex rubber.

When sealing your prop, think "will this prop flex?" A thick space gun probably won't bend, but a large, thin blade probably will. Brittle sealants, like wood glue and epoxy, have a great, sandable surface, but aren't flexible. Plasti Dip and Latex are flexible, but can't be sanded. Test out different sealants on scrap foam to see which finish is best for your prop.

Keep in mind that it's totally OK to *not* seal your weapon. It all depends on the finish that you're trying to achieve. In fact, in the example gun build later in this book I'll show you how I seal my props using only spray paint, so stay tuned!

Latex Rubber

If you're looking for a really smooth, flexible finish that's also extremely durable, look no further than latex rubber. Just like with the power tools I mentioned earlier, this is a more advanced method, but it is totally worth the investment.

My preferred latex product is Poly Latex 60. It comes as a thick paste that is ready to be brushed onto any surface. I prefer to thin it 50/50 with distilled water before applying it. This is mostly so that I can spray the liquid rubber from my Critter sprayer to apply it. Feel free to play with the ratio. The more latex you use the thicker your layers will be, but the longer they will take to dry.

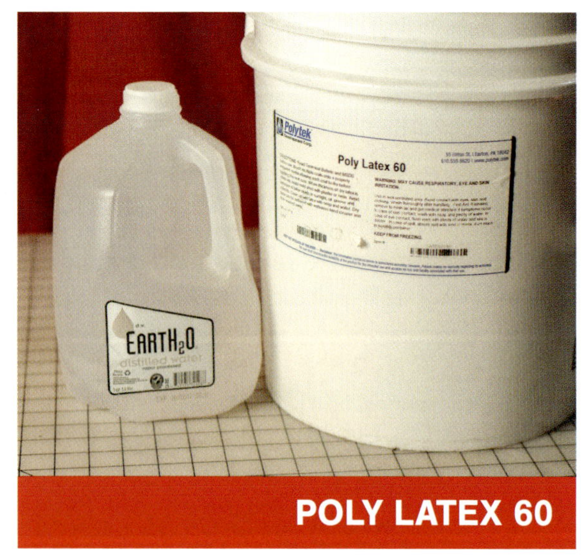

POLY LATEX 60

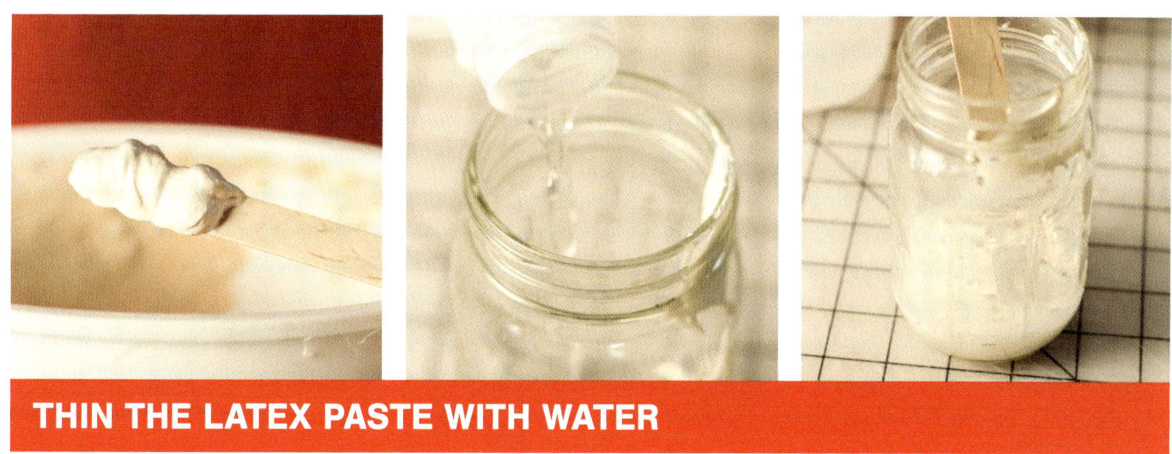

THIN THE LATEX PASTE WITH WATER

Speaking of the sprayer, if you're looking for a chance to spend more money on tools, I've got you covered! To start spraying you'll need the Critter siphon sprayer as well as a good air compressor. This isn't totally necessary. You can definitely just brush on all your layers of latex, but spraying it on is much faster and it allows you to lay down good, even layers of the material without getting any brush strokes.

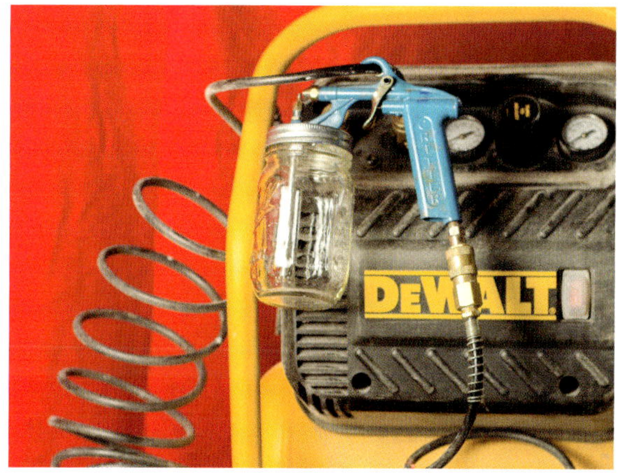

Wear a respirator when spraying Latex!

Something to consider is that as soon as you start laying down rubber it will be extremely difficult to glue down any more foam, so make sure the prop fabrication is completely finished before committing to sealing. You also can't sand the rubber, so get your foam surface close to your desired texture before sealing it with rubber.

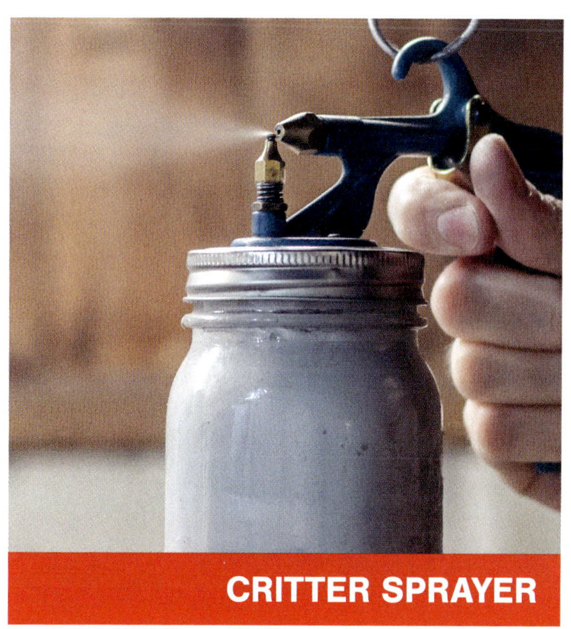

CRITTER SPRAYER

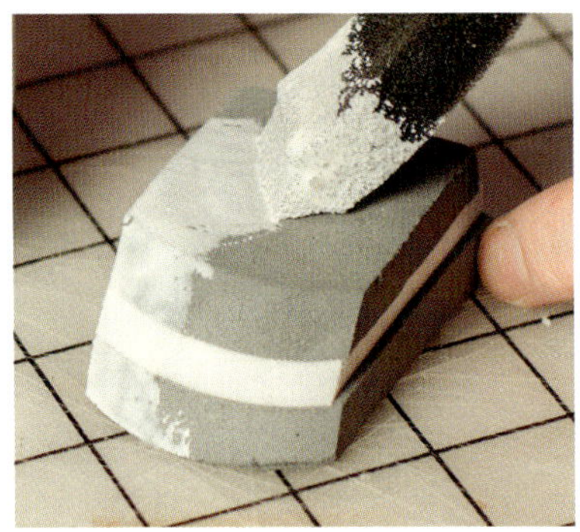
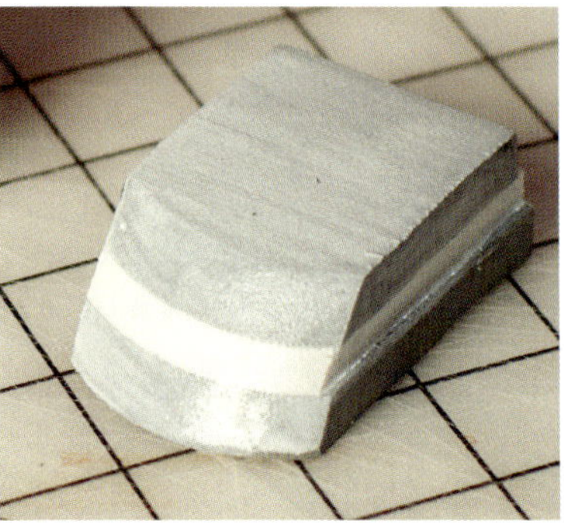
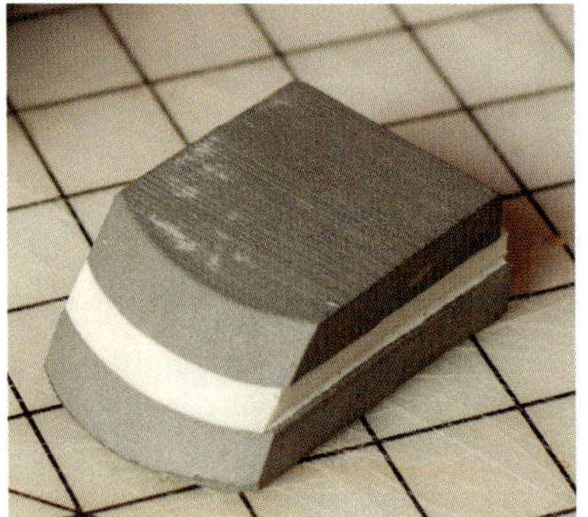

Even if you're going to end up spraying most of your layers, you should still brush on the first couple of passes of latex. This is to ensure you get a little rubber into all of the nooks and crannies of your prop. You can use a simple chip or sponge brush for this application. Brush on a layer and let it almost completely dry before adding the next one. Since this latex is white when wet and transparent when dry, it's very obvious when it's ready for the next layer.

If your piece is small enough you can dunk it into your liquid latex. This will provide quick, total coverage. Just be sure to look out for drips.

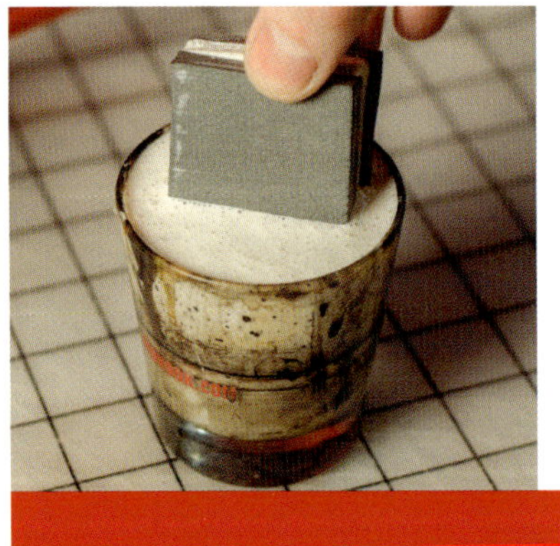
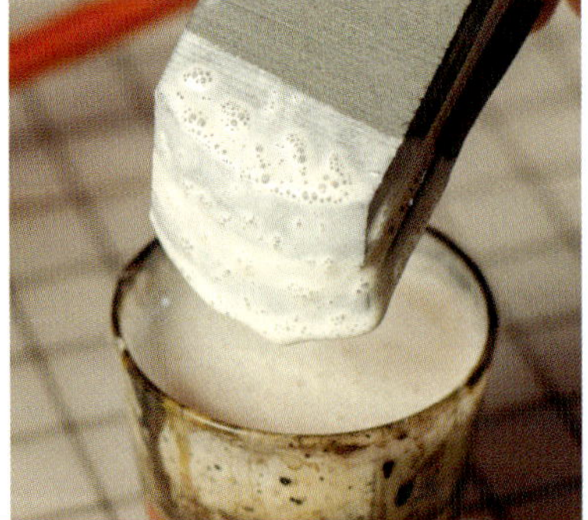
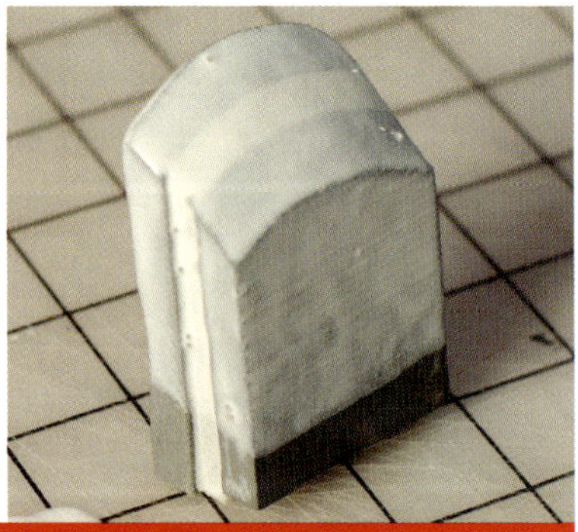

DUNK IT LIKE A COOKIE...BUT DON'T EAT IT.

Color The Latex

You can also tint your rubber before applying it to your prop. If you have a base color for the prop, like a brown for the wood, or a gray/silver for metal parts, you can get a leg up on the painting process by tinting the rubber that you seal it with. There are many types of pigments that can be used for coloring your rubber, but just about any acrylic paints should do the trick. I recommend mixing up a small batch and testing it on some scrap foam before committing a new mixture to your final prop.

Your mixture will be significant lighter than the final, dried color. This is because the wet, white latex dries clear and the final color is only that of the pigment you've added.

The drying times will vary depending on how thick you apply your layers of liquid rubber. What you're waiting on is for all of the water to evaporate out of the latex, leaving the rubber behind. I try to apply my layers thick enough that they take about 30-60 minutes to dry. It's important that you don't let your latex pool in any lower areas of your prop as these areas will take much longer to dry.

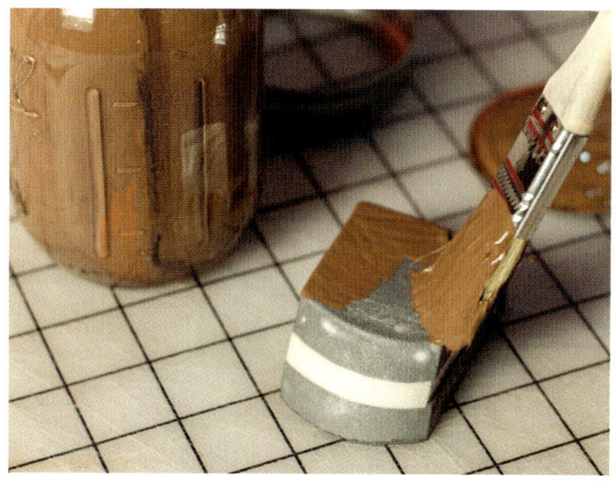

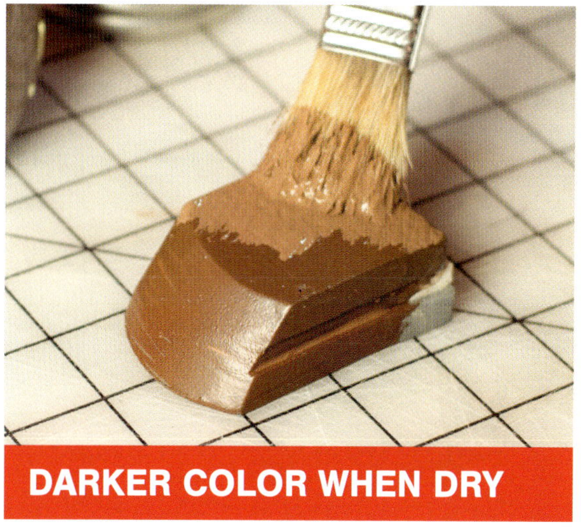

DARKER COLOR WHEN DRY

If you hang up multiple pieces to dry, make sure they don't touch one another. The latex will stick and pull away from your piece.

If you plan on brushing all of your layers, keep at it. I would give it at least 5 good layers, but probably more as it'll increase the durability of your prop a lot. If you're going to spray the next few layers, I would recommend adding at least 5 layers on top of what you've brushed down already. Make sure your layers are applied in even strokes. Also be sure to keep the layers thin enough that they don't drip and sag on the surfaces of your prop.

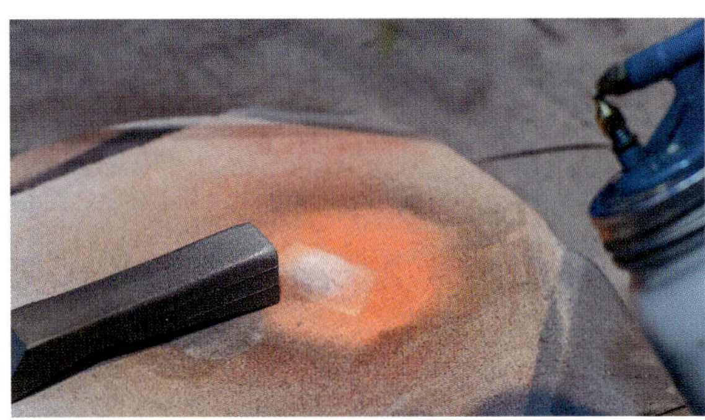

I highly recommend applying all of your latex rubber in one, long session. This means you'll have to carve out a good 3-5 hours to get it all done, so long as you get in a good rhythm. I like to be able to spray on a new layer every 45 minutes or so. I just plan my day so that I can work on something else when I'm waiting for the rubber to dry.

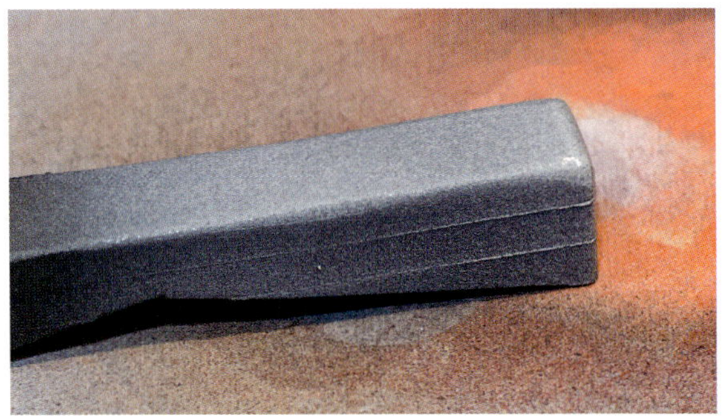

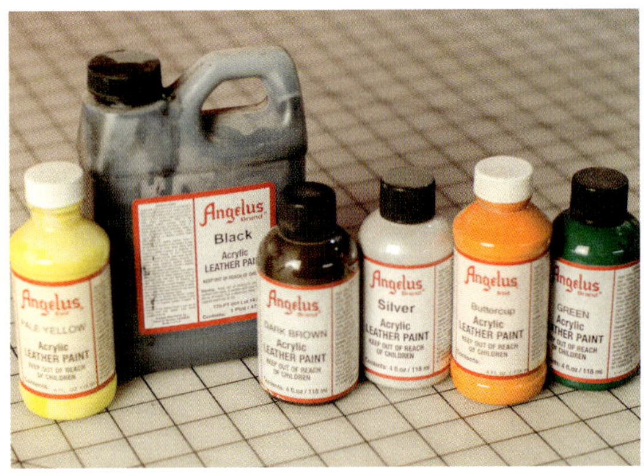

How does one paint rubber? There are a lot of options out there, like rubber cement paint, but I prefer to get as much of the base coat in the tinted rubber as I can. You can't really use masking tape with rubber, so you'll have to hand brush some of your differently colored layers. You'll see more of that in the example axe build later in the book. If I need to just use normal paint for some areas, I reach for flexible acrylic paints, like the stuff used for painting leather.

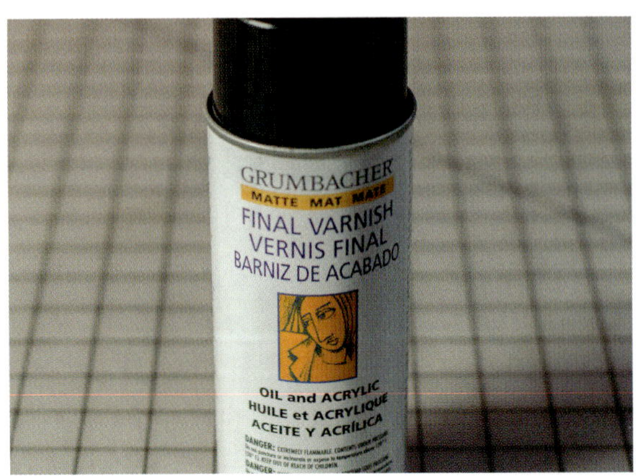

Varnish

Want to seal your finished paint job? Try varnish! You can find matte and glossy varieties in both brushable and spray can options. It dries really fast and is super flexible; a necessity for squishy foam props.

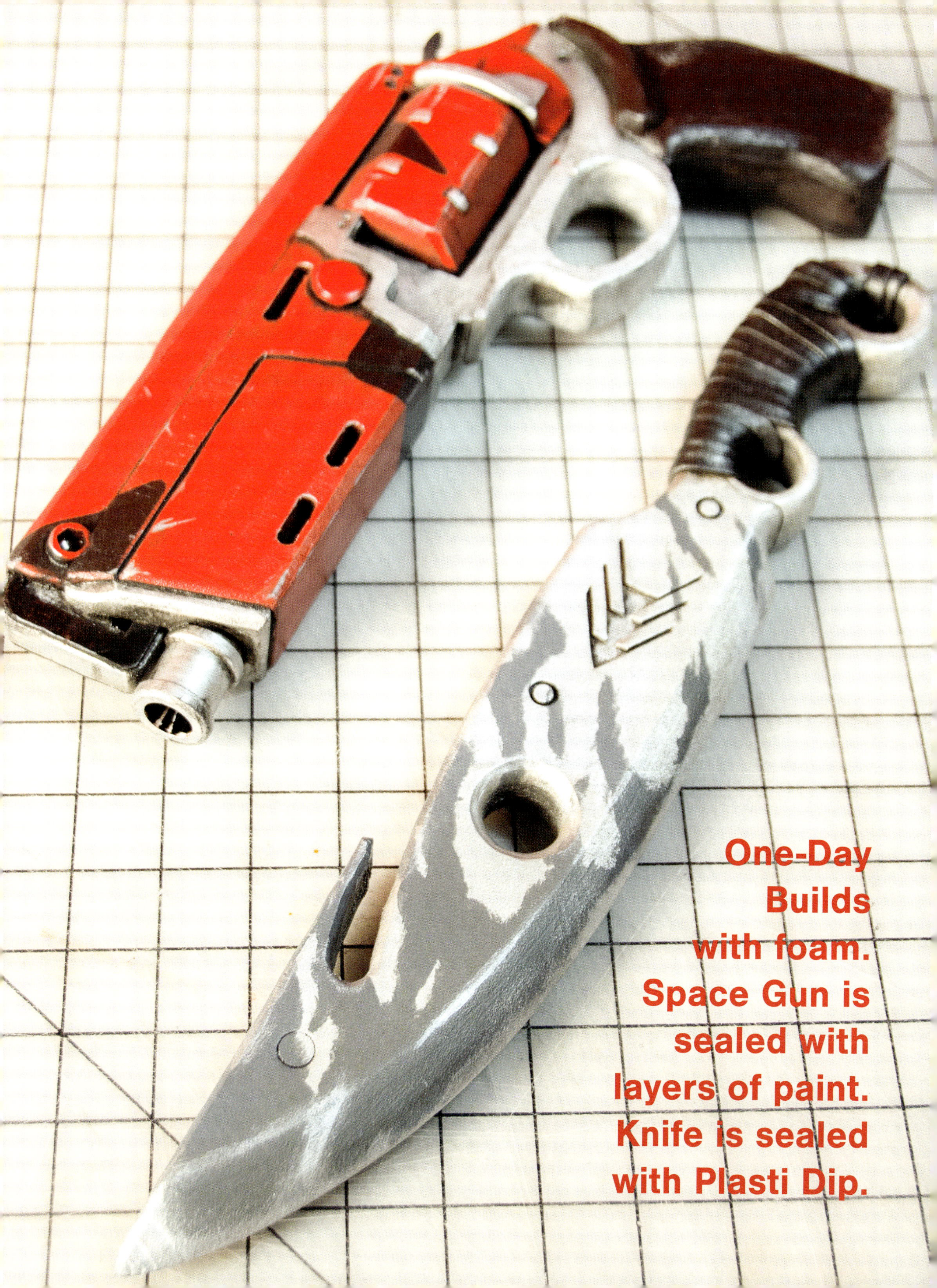

One-Day Builds with foam. Space Gun is sealed with layers of paint. Knife is sealed with Plasti Dip.

Fixing Seams

Filling Gaps and Making Repairs

Nobody's perfect, even the most practiced Foamsmith. No matter how careful you are, you may end up with unsightly seams and gaps in between your foam pieces. It happens to the best of us. If the gap is too severe, my preference is to rebuild the piece. Foam is fairly cheap, after all, and I try to get it as clean as possible in the first place.

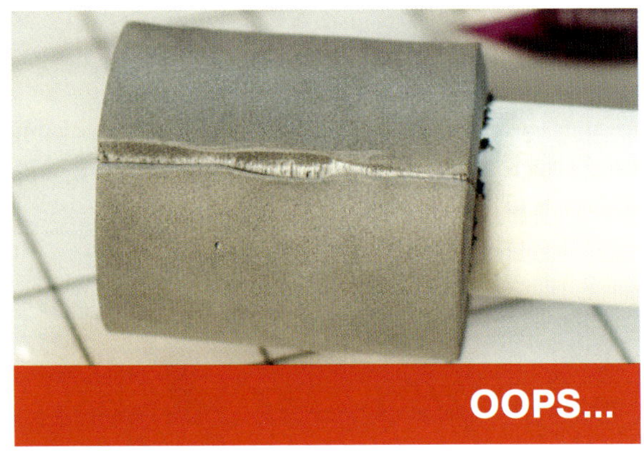
OOPS...

That being said, sometimes rebuilding a piece is simply not an option. Sometimes you just have to fill those ugly gaps and get on with the build. Prop makers who work in more rigid materials, like wood and plastic, would turn to any number of automotive body fillers to get the job done. Simply mix up some filler, spread it into the gap, let it cure, then sand it flush! Unfortunately, the same method will not work on foam. Body filler is a rigid material and foam is flexible, so any attempt to sand them flush would be met with failure and tears.

For EVA foam, we must turn to other materials to solve our woes. For smaller gaps, I would try and stick them back together with just a bit of super glue. Spread a little bit of the glue into the gap and then run your finger down the edges, pushing them together as the gap closes. Yes, you will get glue all over your finger. This is the price you pay for not getting it right in the first place. (Or, you could just wear gloves.)

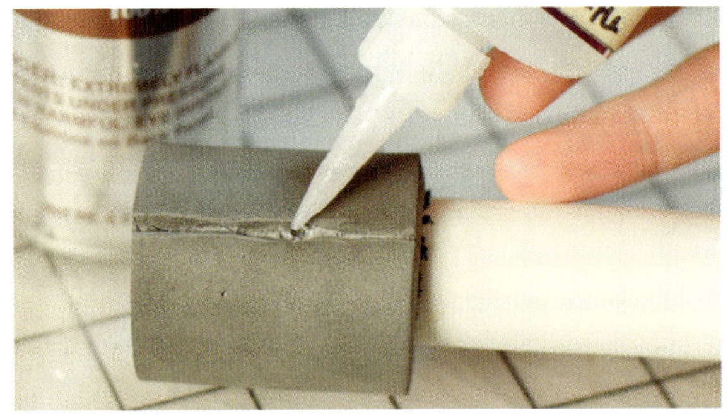

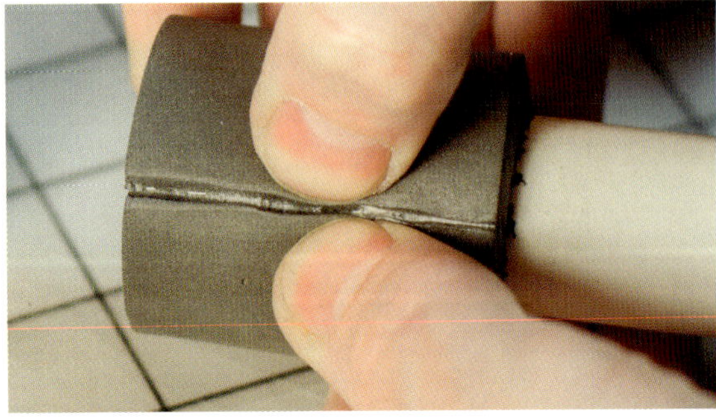

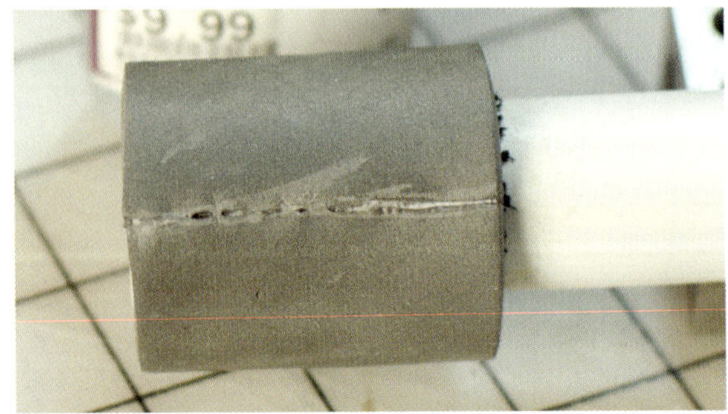

Adhesive Caulk

For larger problems, you'll want to fill in the offending gap with something that takes up that negative space. This is where a product like Kwik Seal really shines. Using a flat tool or popsicle stick, spread a little bit of the material into your gap. I like to use just a little bit more than I think I need to make sure it's going to take up all that space. Then, with a wet finger, smooth out your work, trying to get a nice even finish between your two pieces of foam. All that's left now is to let it dry.

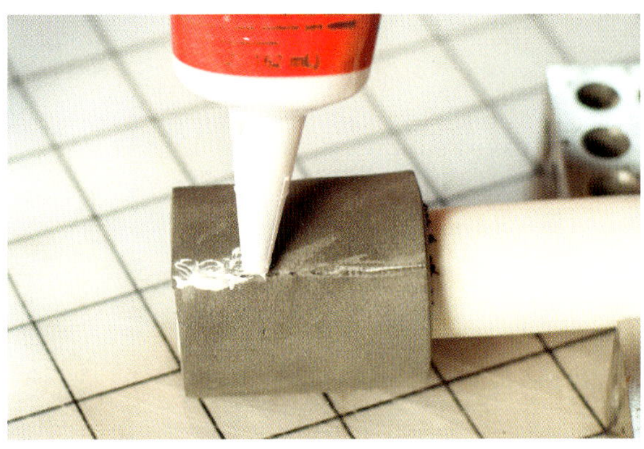

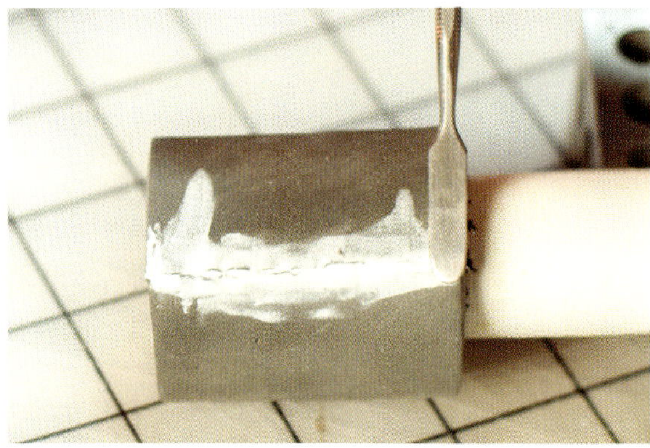

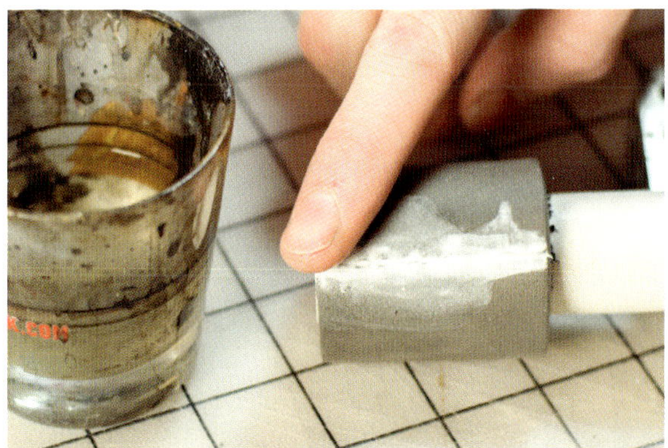

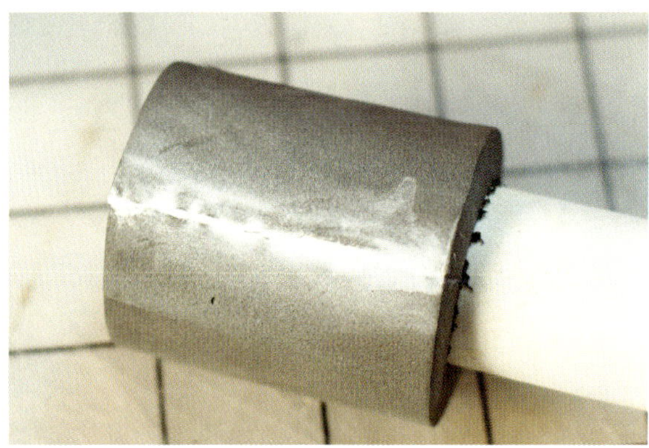

Will the finish be perfect? No, but it'll be a shy sight better than the hideous gap that was there before. Also remember that you can't sand this stuff, so get it looking as nice as possible before the Kwik Seal dries. When it does dry, feel free to add more layers if the gap persists!

Can't find Kwik Seal? It's a latex polymer "Tub & Tile Adhesive Caulk" found in most hardware stores.

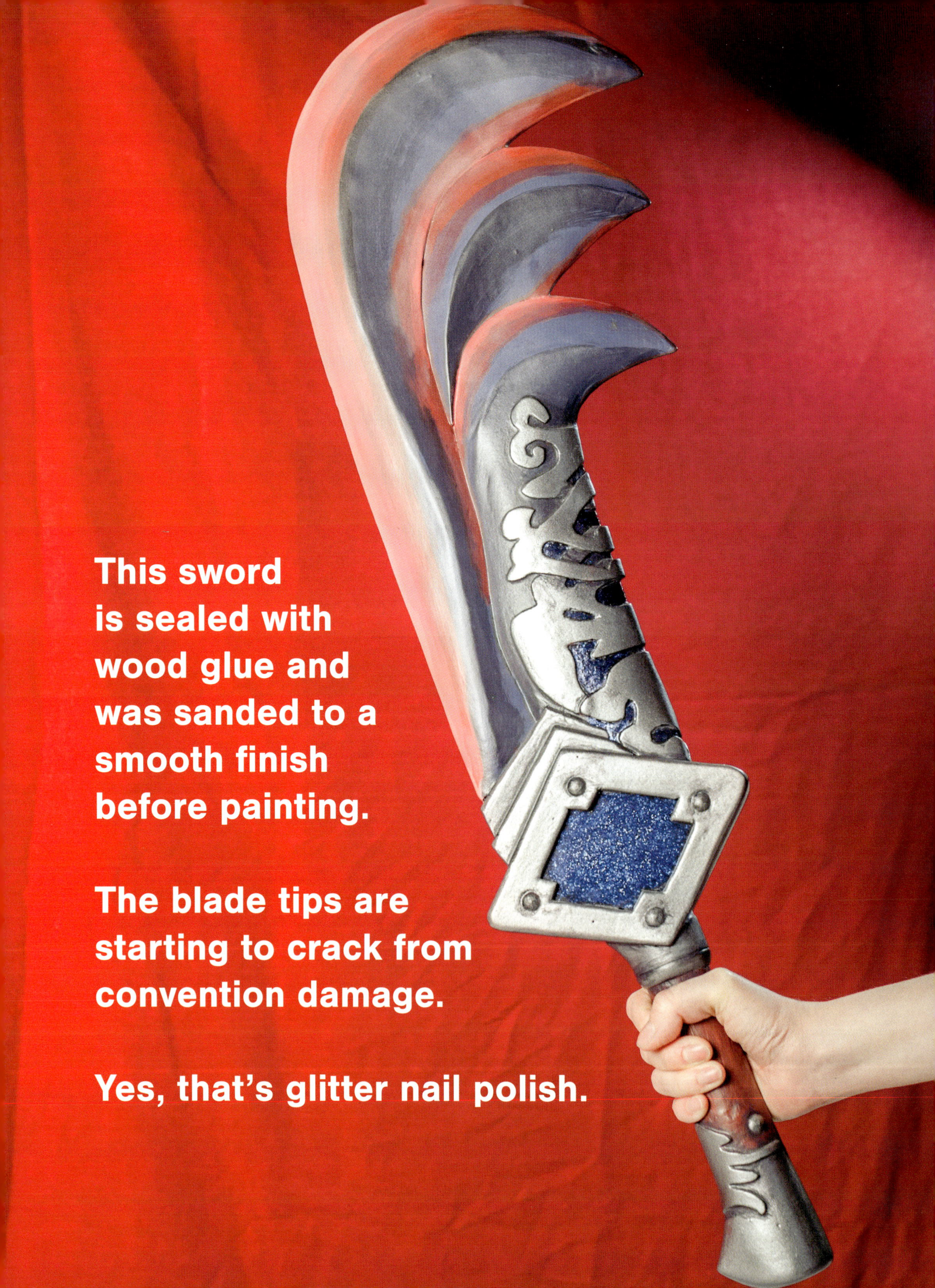

This sword is sealed with wood glue and was sanded to a smooth finish before painting.

The blade tips are starting to crack from convention damage.

Yes, that's glitter nail polish.

PAINTING

It's painting time!

Many of the painting techniques from the first Foamsmith armor book will apply to your prop weapons, but there are plenty of techniques specific to props that will help elevate your work to masterpiece status. Here are a handful of painting tips to augment your prop finishing game.

When you think you're nearly done building your prop, prime it. Most rattle can primer paints will do the trick. Primer does a couple of things for you. First, if there are any flaws in the finish of your piece, they will show up like beacons of failure on the surface of your prop. As you add pieces and layers to your foam prop, it may turn into several colors with the combination of foams, glues, and dust. Primer reduces the entire prop to one, solid color. This gives you an accurate indication of the surface finish on your prop.

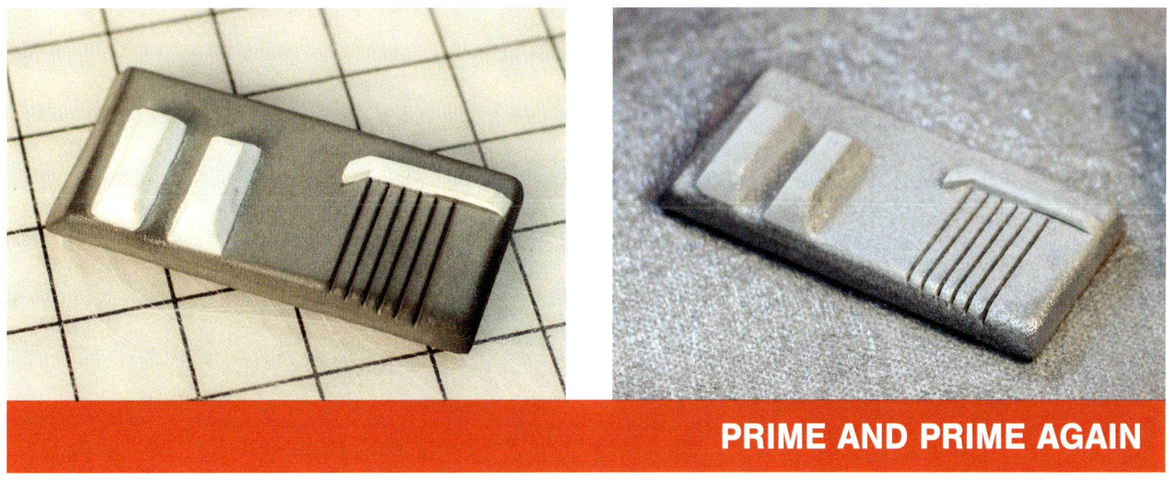

PRIME AND PRIME AGAIN

I like to use Krylon Fusion as a primer for my foam. It dries fast and bonds really well to EVA foam.

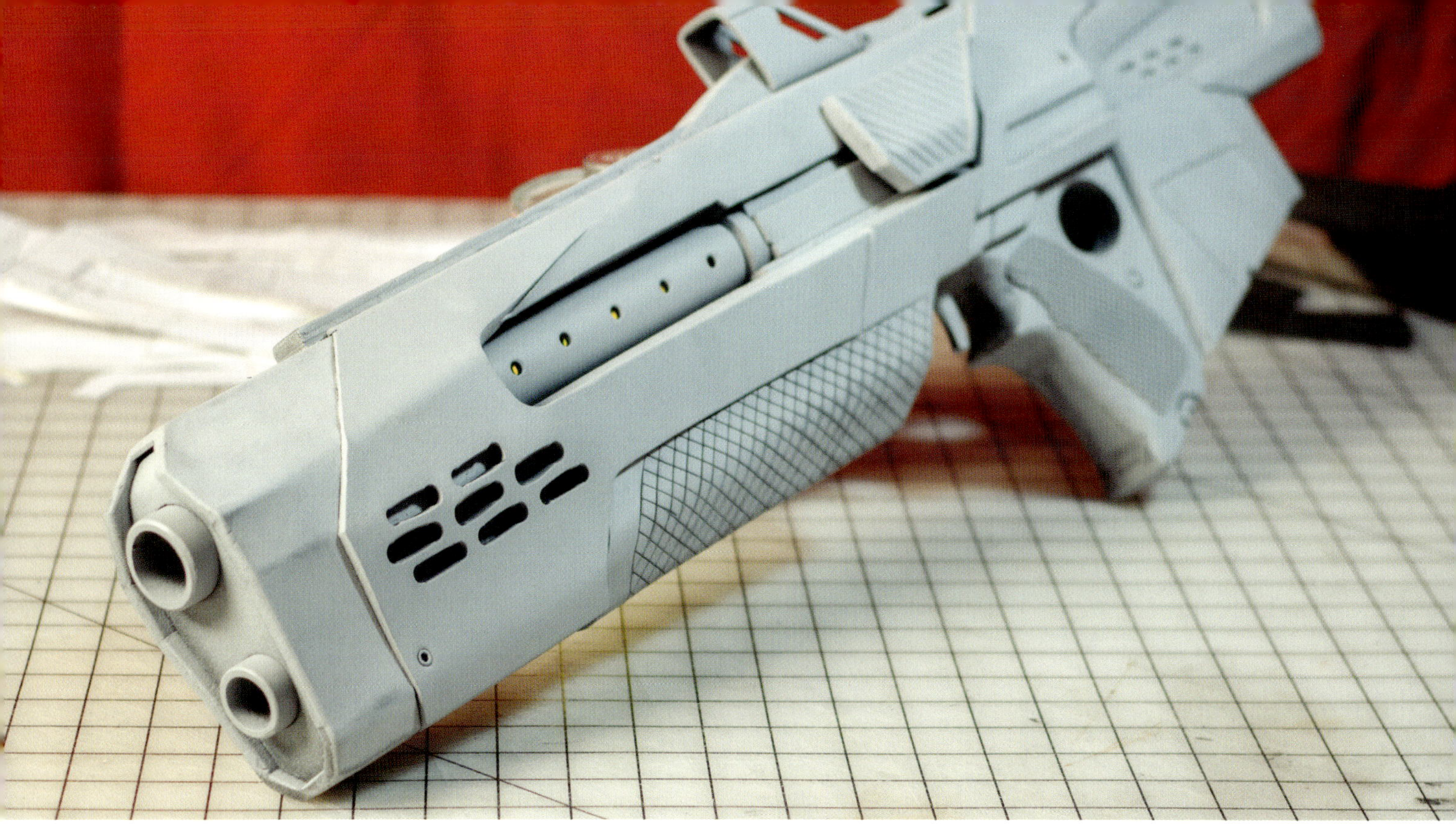

You may find areas that have unwanted gaps, weird textures, or gouges that should be repaired before painting. These areas can be fixed with some of the gap filling techniques mentioned earlier. You'll be happy to tackle these issues now rather than later when you've applied some of your final coats of paint.

The other thing that primer does for you is provide your base coat of paint a nice, even canvas to cover and adhere to. Primers are designed to work with just about any paint you can think of. Spray on a couple even coats of primer, letting them dry according to the directions on the can, and then your prop is ready to get some color!

Color Me Excited

There are about as many ways to paint your props as there are cosplayers at Comic Con, so don't get too bogged down in the specifics of nailing your finish, especially for your first build. Again, the first Foamsmith book dove deep into painting specifics, so I won't cover it all again here, but I will give you some prop specific tips. I will also provide you a couple of examples of how I like to finish my props in the example projects later in this book.

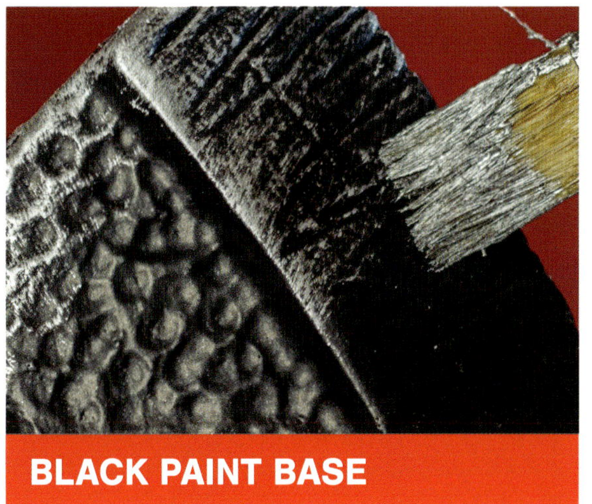

BLACK PAINT BASE

Metal Is Rarely One Color

If you're painting an axe or sword blade, you may be tempted to simply buy a rattle can of "metallic" paint and douse your prop with the stuff. This is a sure fire way to end up with a finish that looks flat and unrealistic. Especially for anything that needs to look grimy and rough hewn, you'll want to start with a dark base coat. You heard me correctly, paint your blades black. Then add your metallic paints over that, taking care to not cover up all of that black base coat. What does this do for you? It adds contrast. The type of contrast that you would see in a real, old metallic weapon!

More than anything, have fun and experiment with layering paints. I've always got a pile of foam scraps at the ready to try out my painting techniques on before I commit to my final piece. The more variations you try, the more likely you'll stumble on that finish that is absolutely perfect for your prop.

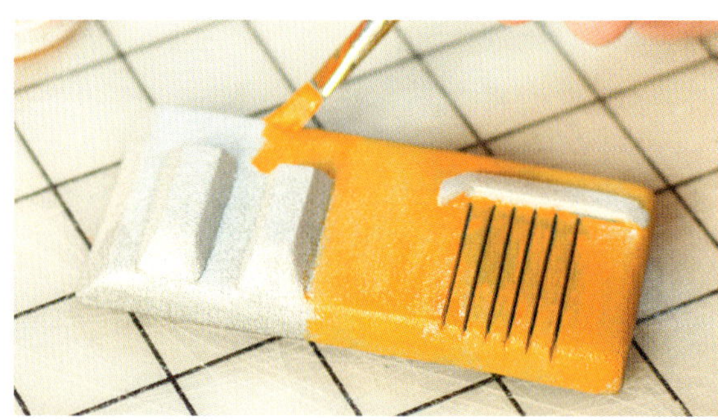

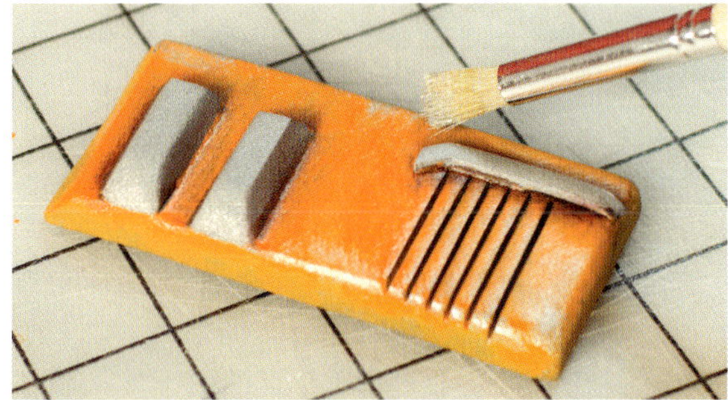

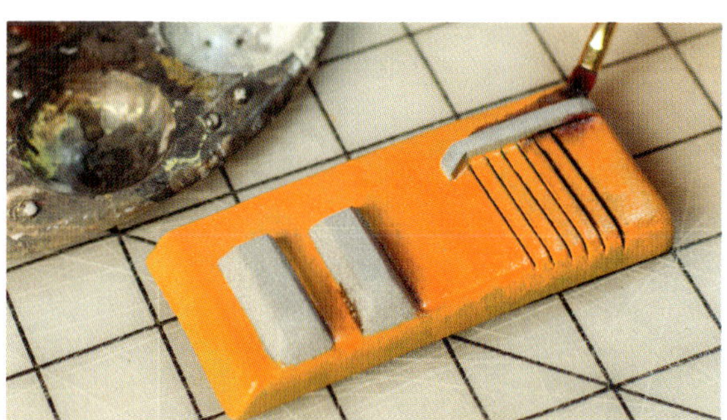

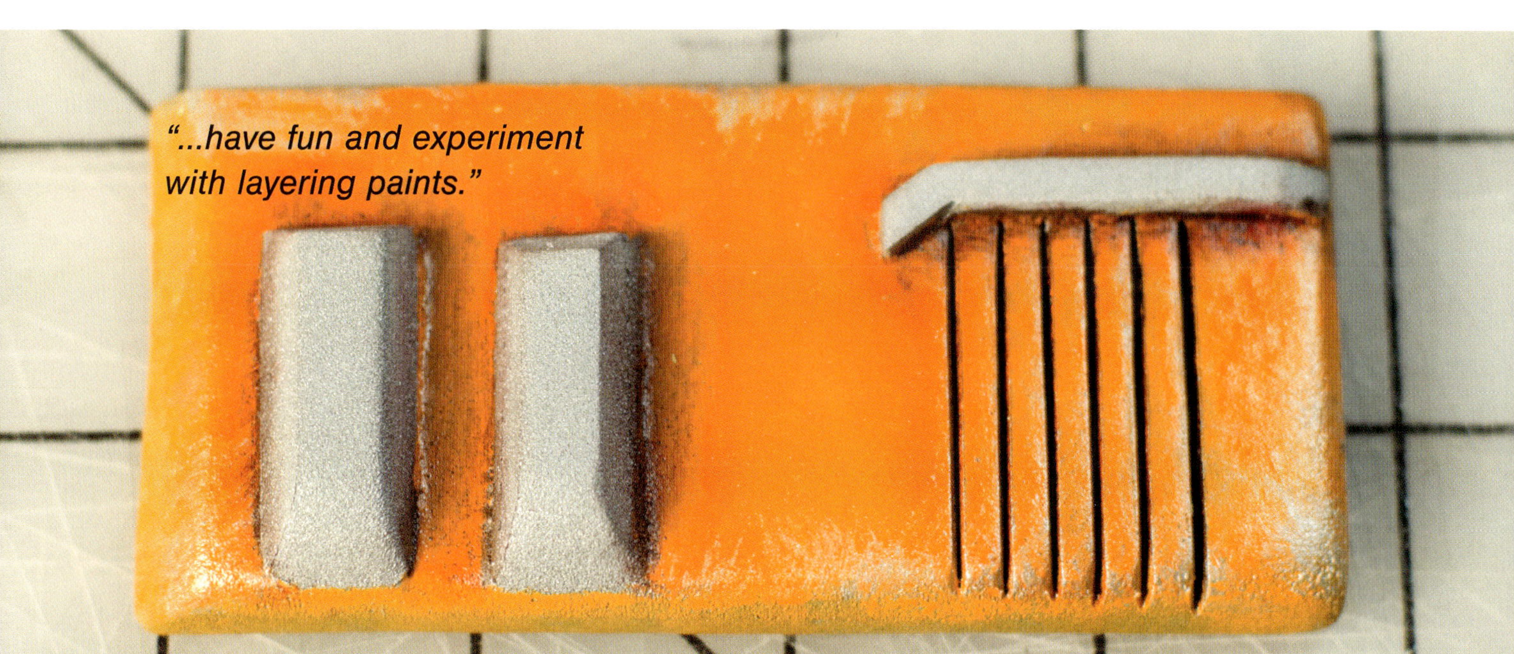

"...have fun and experiment with layering paints."

I covered just about all of my painting techniques in the first Foamsmith book and all of those methods apply to your foam weapons too! Here are a few of my past foam weapon projects with a quick rundown of the sealing and painting techniques used for finishing them. You can also look forward to a couple of highly detailed painting tutorials in the two full builds later in the book.

Finishing & Painting Examples:

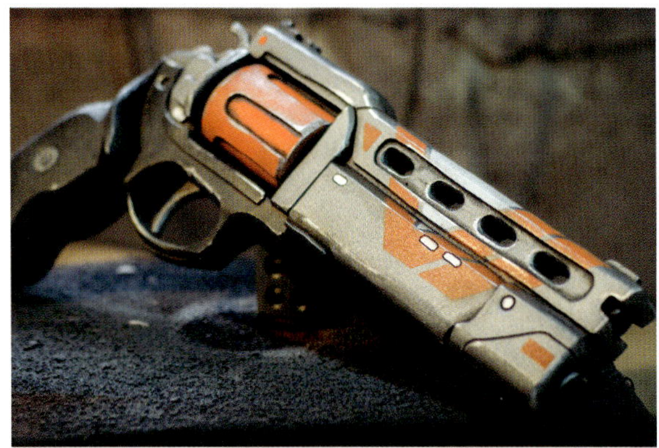

Destiny: Hand Cannon

- Foam Sealing: 5 layers of sprayed Plasti Dip
- Base Color: Metallic spray paint
- Handle: Black spray paint after masking off handle
- Decals: White and orange spray paint after masking off stencils
- Weathering: Black and brown acrylic paints
- Paint Sealing: Matte clear spray paint

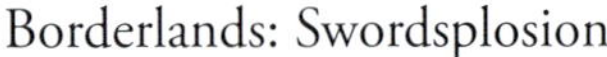

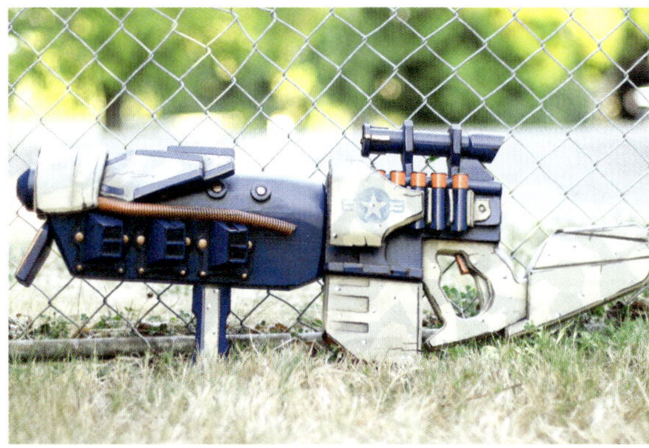

Borderlands: Swordsplosion

- Foam Sealing & Base Color: Several layers of Krylon Fusion tan colored spray paint
- Secondary Color: Blue spray paint after masking off base color
- Detail Colors: Brushed acrylic paint
- Star Decal: Acrylic paints brushed on with a stencil
- Dots & Black Edges: Paint pen
- Paint Sealing: Matte clear spray paint

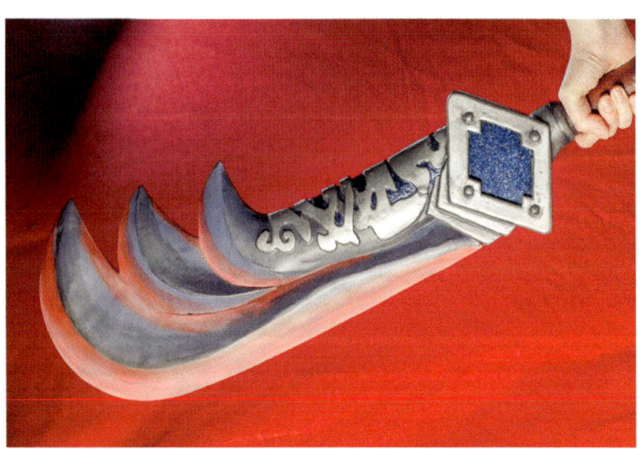

World of Warcraft: Vis'kag the Bloodletter

- Foam Sealing: Several layers of wood glue
- Primer: Spray paint primer
- Color Paint: Several layers of airbrushed acrylic paints
- Shiny Gem: Clear acrylic plastic painted from behind with shimmery nail polish
- Paint Sealing: Matte clear spray paint

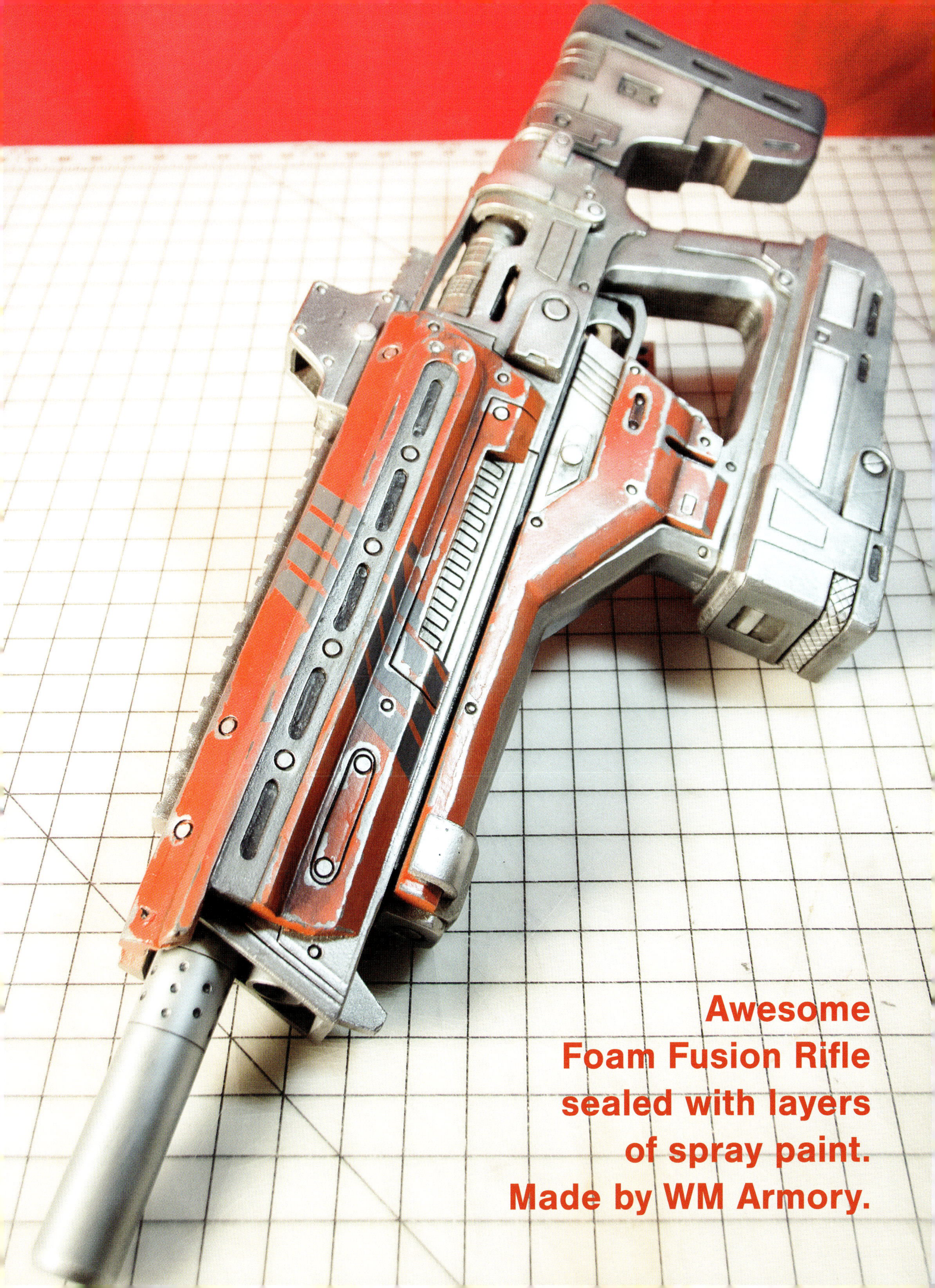

Awesome Foam Fusion Rifle sealed with layers of spray paint. Made by WM Armory.

Practical Application

I know I just threw a whole bunch of technical knowhow at your face, but don't worry, it'll all make sense shortly. The remainder of this book will follow along two in-depth prop builds. These build write-ups are designed to give you a look into how I plan, build, and finish my foam props with a variety of techniques.

The first build is a large axe. This build is meant to show you how to make something large that can be taken apart for travel. It also has a focus on making things with a more organic looking texture. Finally it details my specific techniques for finishing a foam prop using latex rubber. This guide will help you build nearly any fantasy bladed weapon.

Build number two is a sci-fi rifle. Everyone loves a good space gun and I'm no different. This build is meant to show you how to make a foam prop that looks clean and machined, like it came off the assembly line of a space aged arms manufacturer. It also showcases how to finish a prop using only spray paint. This should give you a good starting point for making any kind of space gun.

I've also included digital blueprint files for both of these prop weapons. You can download the axe and space gun from the link below. Feel free to follow along as I take you on a ride through my foam prop making process!

Download your Templates here:
http://punishedprops.com/foamsmith2

In these builds, I'll be using all of the power tools at my disposal, but as I mentioned earlier, just because you may not have those tools, doesn't mean you can't do the project. Except a rotary tool. You'll really need one of those no matter what, so make the investment!

Part 2
Foam Axe

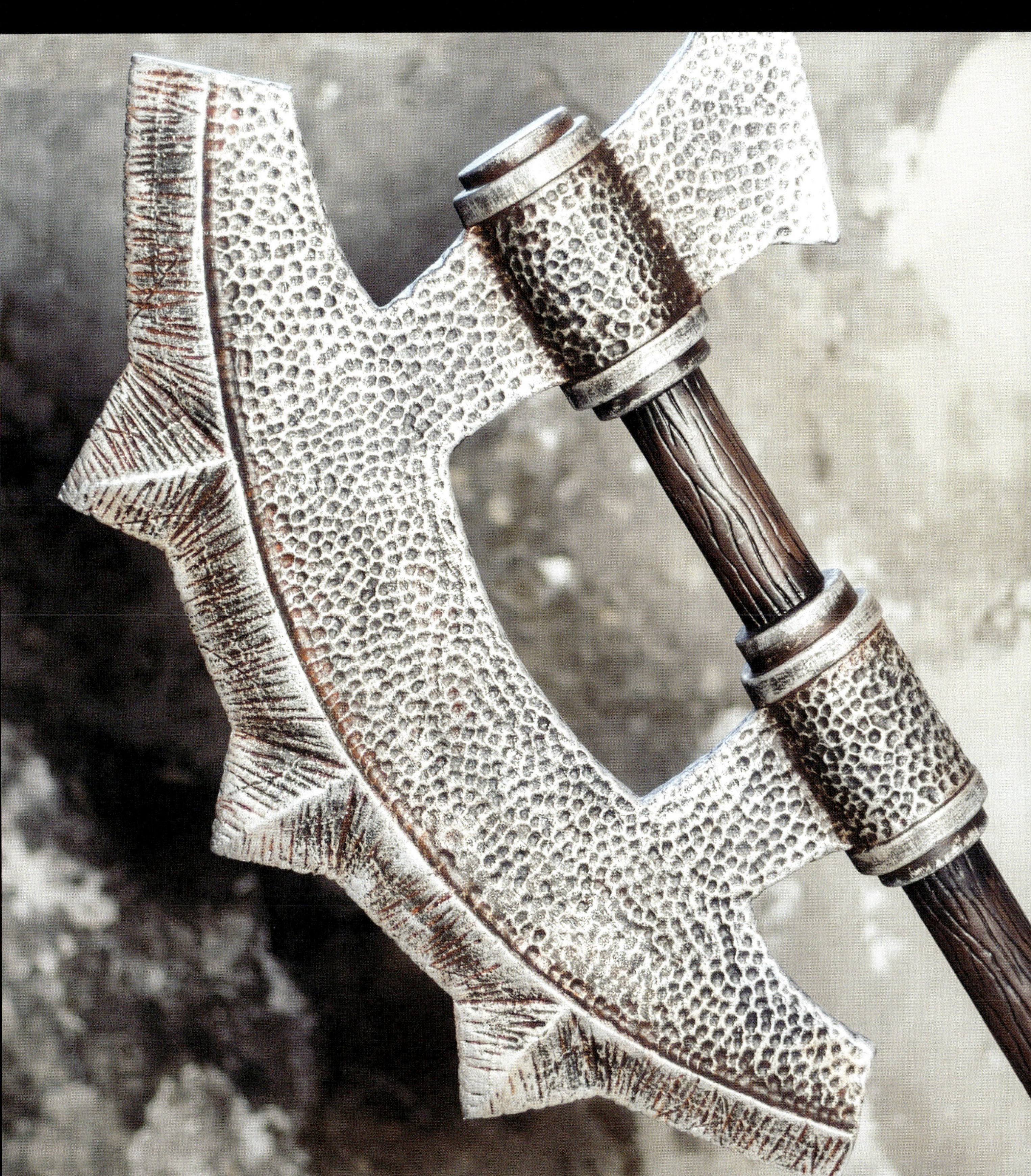

Foamsmith Weapon Build Example:
Diablo III Two Handed Axe

Materials

- ½" Thick Foam Floor Mats
- 6mm Craft Foam Sheets
- 2mm Craft Foam Roll
- PVC Pipe
- PVC Coupler
- Barge Cement
- Acrylic Paint
- Latex Rubber

Template

http://punishedprops.com/foamsmith2

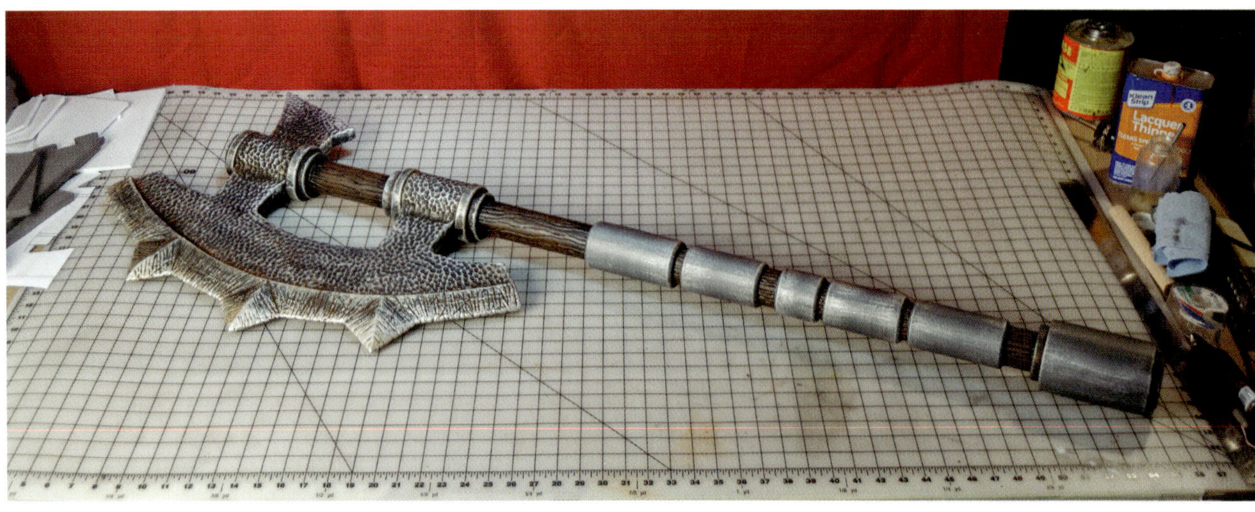

Axe Template

I printed out all of the template sheets on letter sized card stock. These were trimmed along the dotted registration lines on each sheet and taped together at the labeled seams. This was a lot like doing a big, easy puzzle!

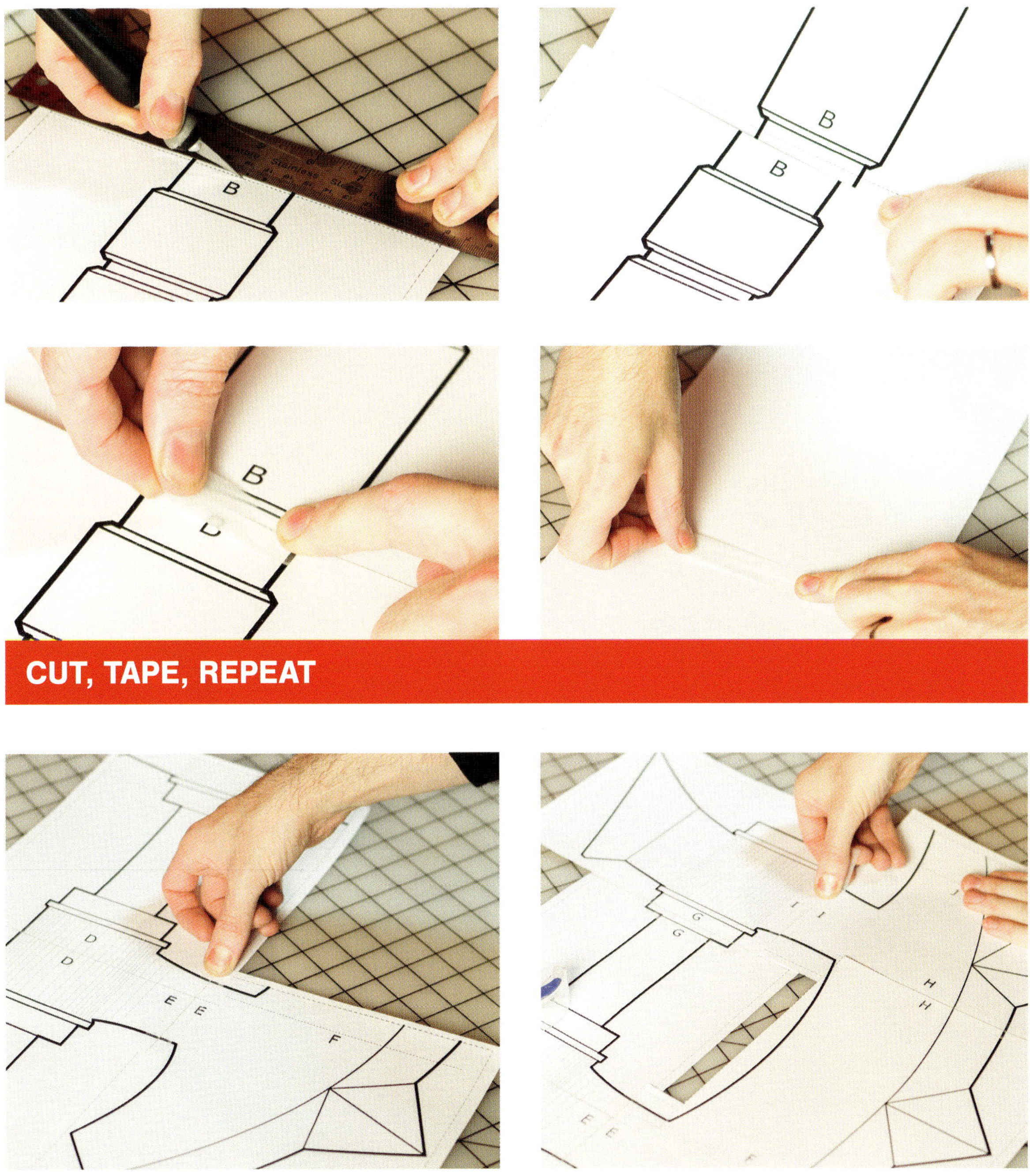

CUT, TAPE, REPEAT

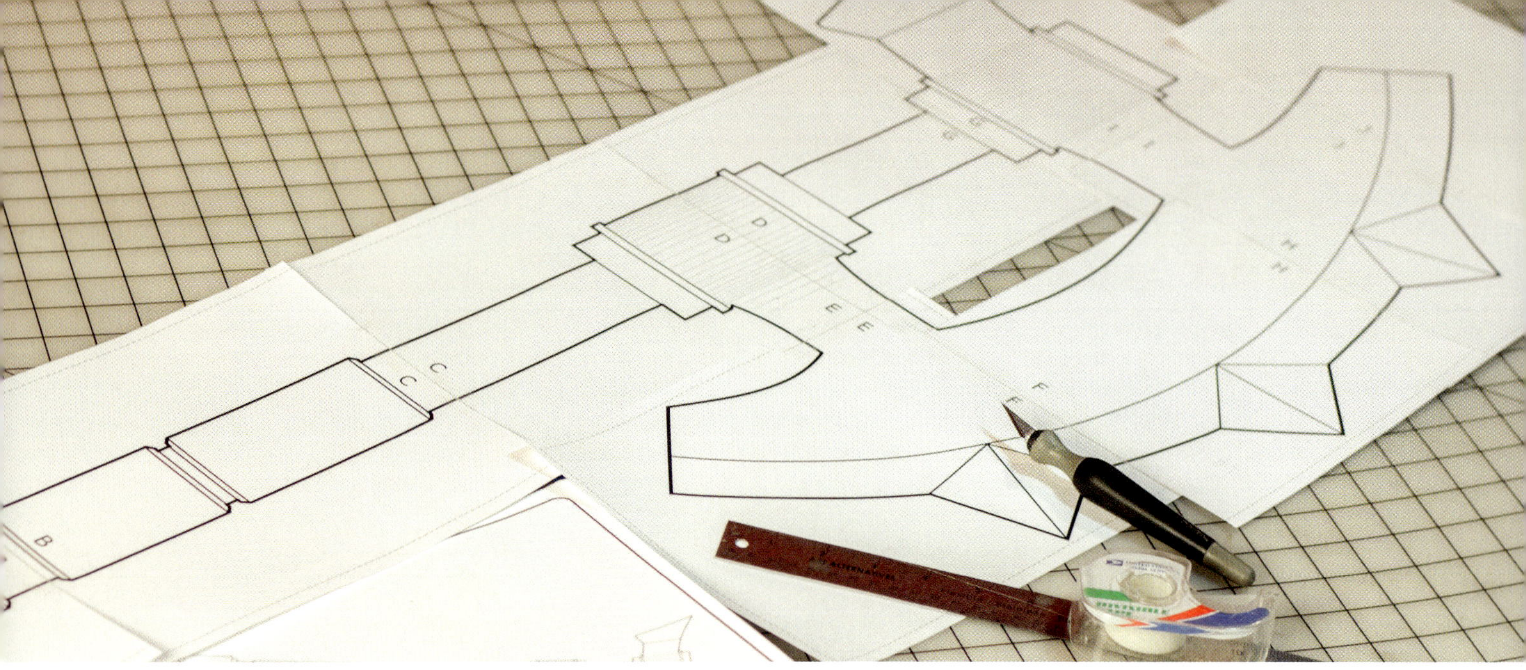

Plan The Disassembly

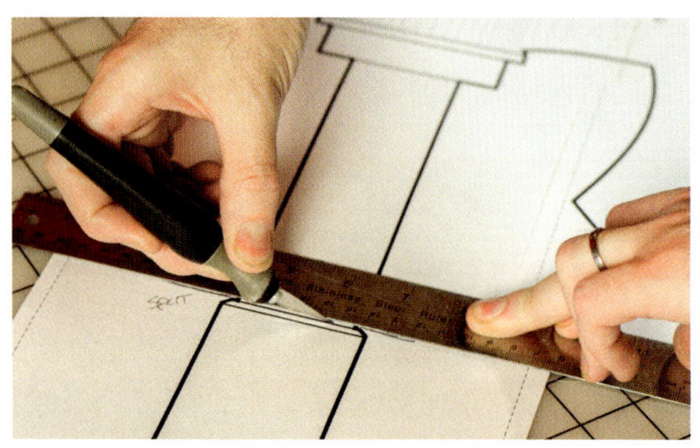

Then, I trimmed the template in half at the place on the shaft where I would be splitting the prop apart for transport. This way I could build each piece separately. I planned this seam along an existing line on the handle so that it could be disguised easily.

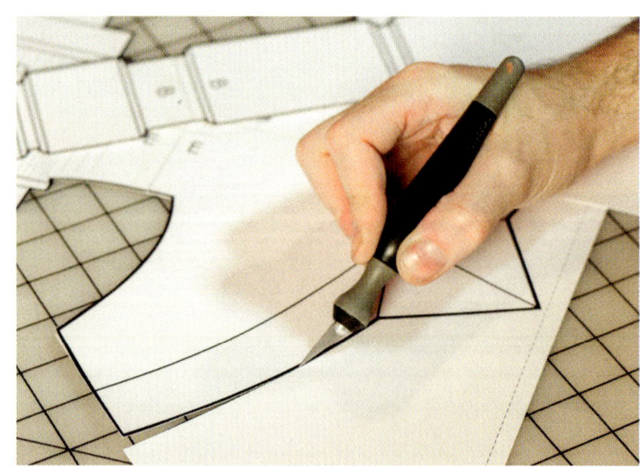

Next, the outline of the prop was trimmed and I was ready to start cutting foam!

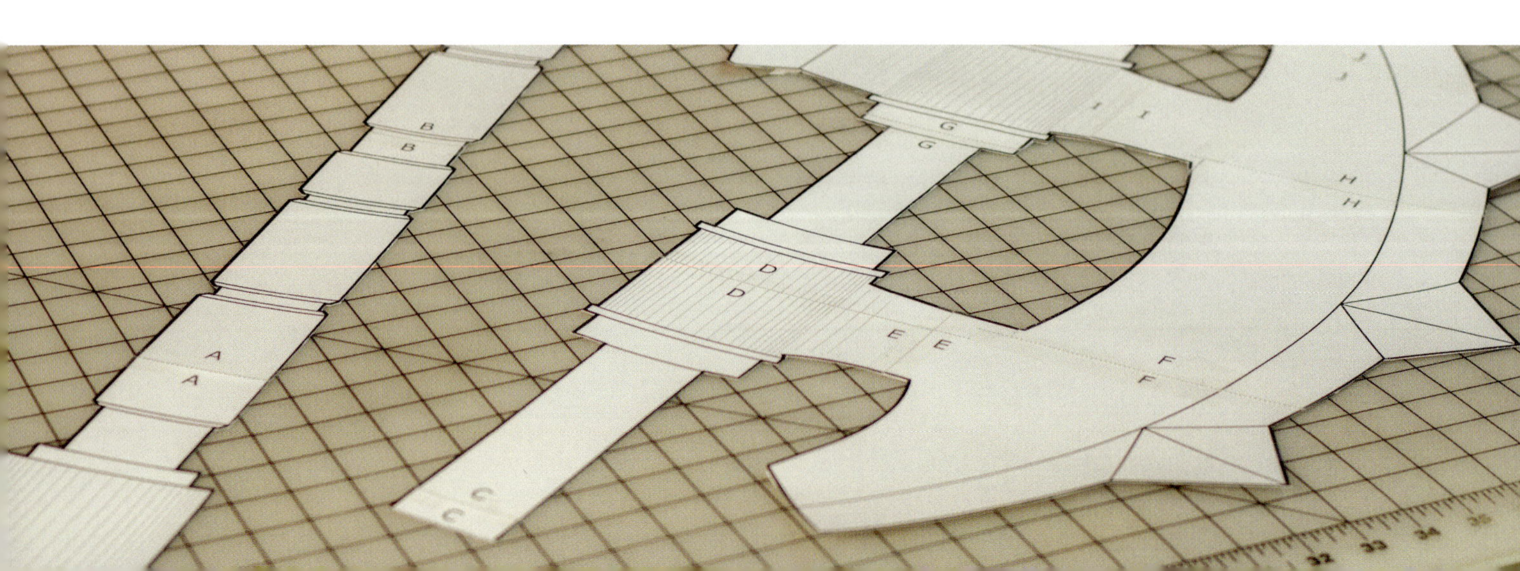

Handle

I started with the lower handle bit. The two parts of the axe would come apart using the PVC coupler. The pipe is snug enough in the coupler that friction would hold it together when I'm carrying the prop around, but the coupler needed to be glued to at least one side of the PVC pipe handle. So, I used PVC cement and glued the coupler to the pipe that I would use for the lower handle.

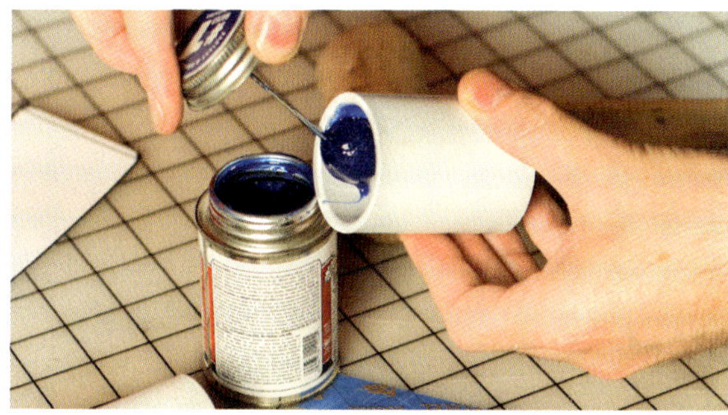

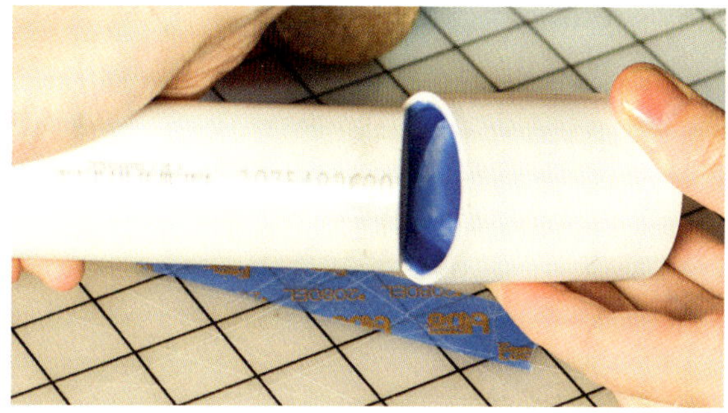

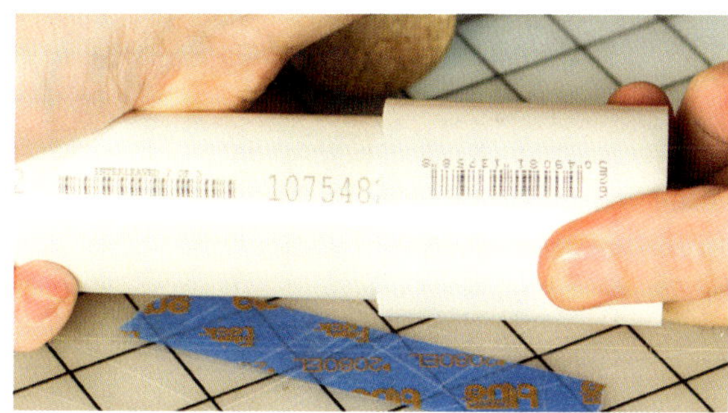

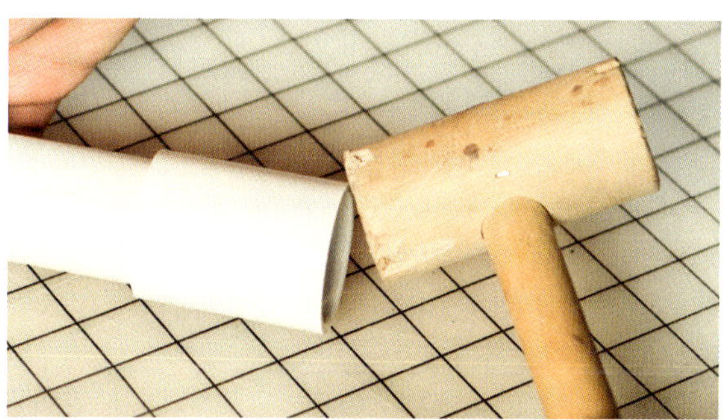

The PVC pipe was then cut to the appropriate length and sanded. I would be gluing foam to the pipe and I wanted to make sure there was some tooth in the plastic for the glue to grip.

Sanding sponges contour to curved shapes and come in different grits!

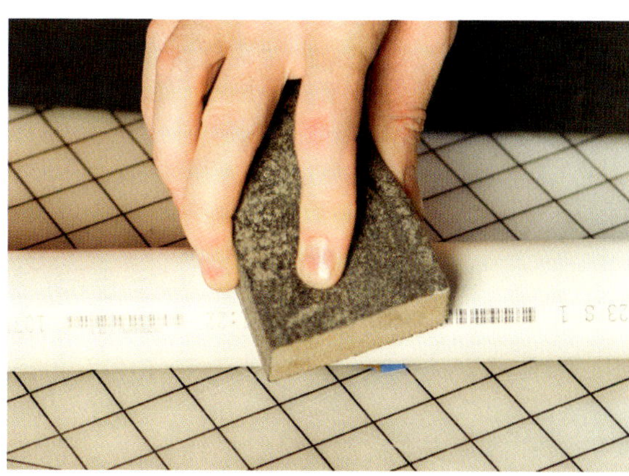

Foam Handle Thickness

Next I had to decide what thicknesses of foam to wrap around the handle. I decided that for the thinner "wood" parts, I would use 2mm foam and for the thicker "metal" parts, I would wrap 6mm foam on top of that. These layers of foam on top of the PVC pipe gave me the diameter I needed to match the template.

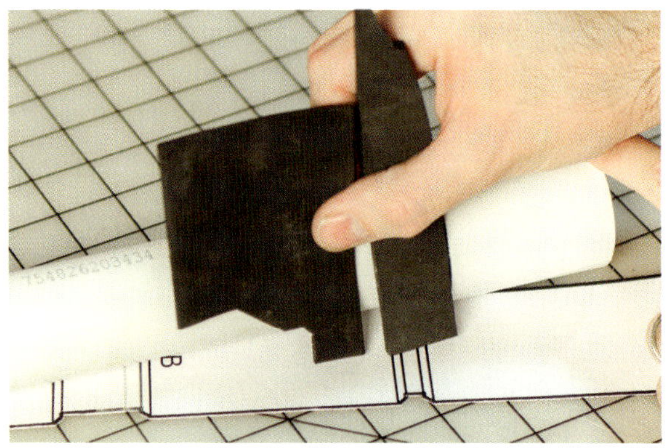

I measured the length of pipe and the circumference I would need to wrap around the handle and cut out a rectangle of the 2mm foam. Then, I coated both the PVC pipe and the foam rectangle in Barge cement and let it dry for 5 minutes.

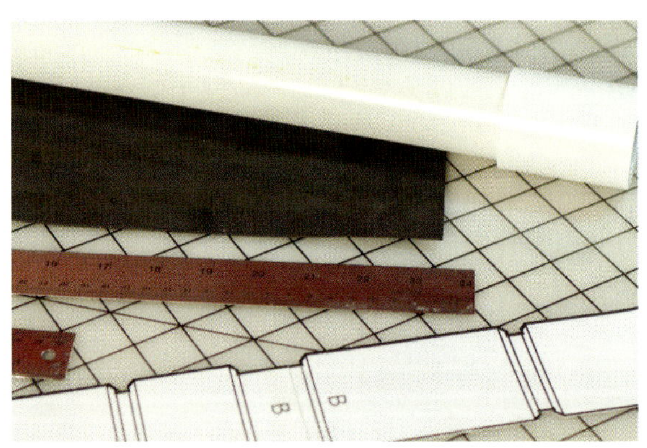

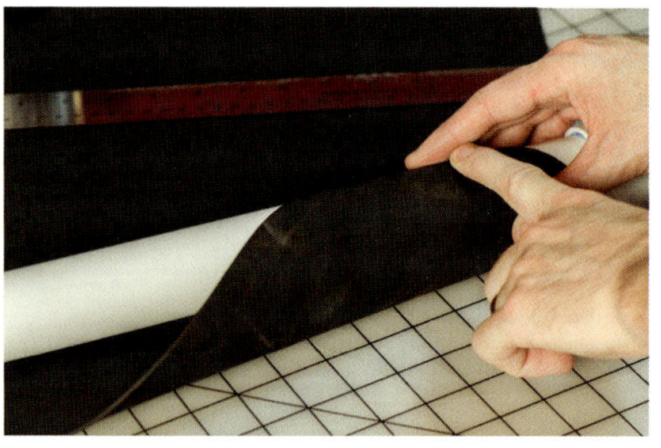

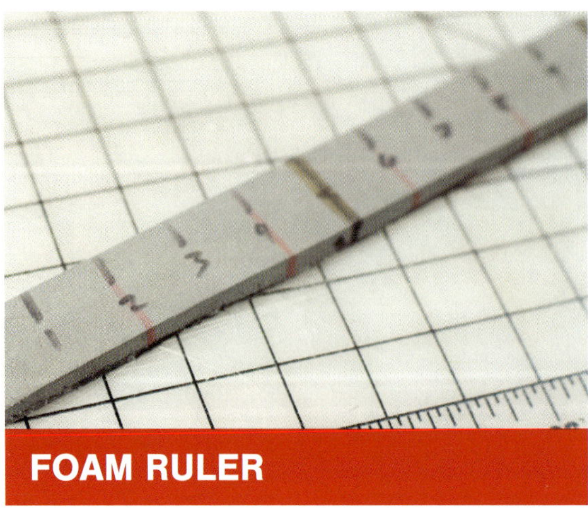

FOAM RULER

Make a "foam ruler" to get accurate circumference measurements.

Next I slowly and carefully laid the foam on the plastic, wrapping it around. The trickiest part of this process is getting the foam to lay down evenly and getting the edges to meet up on the other side of the pipe. Practice and patience are a real virtue here.

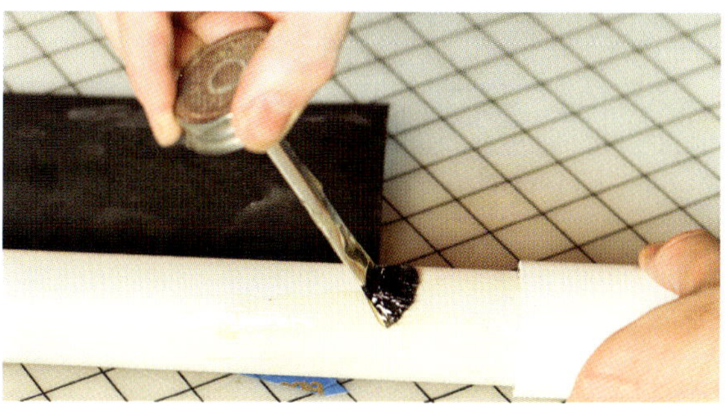

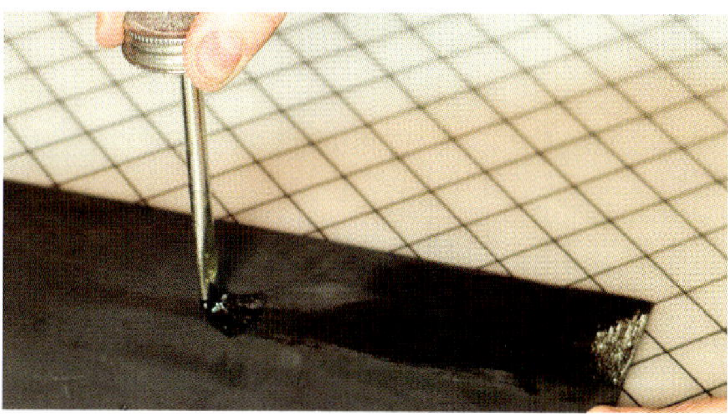

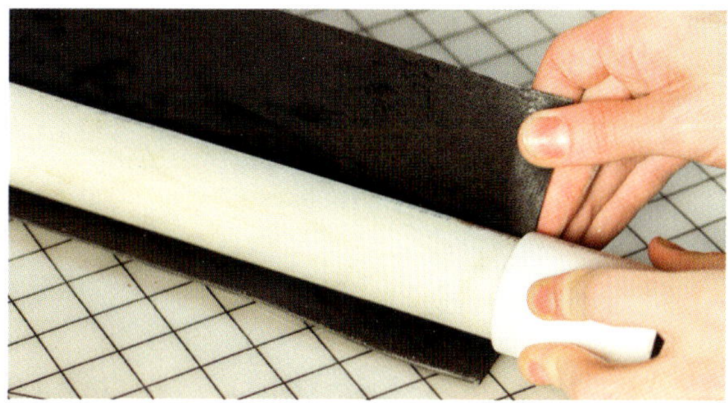

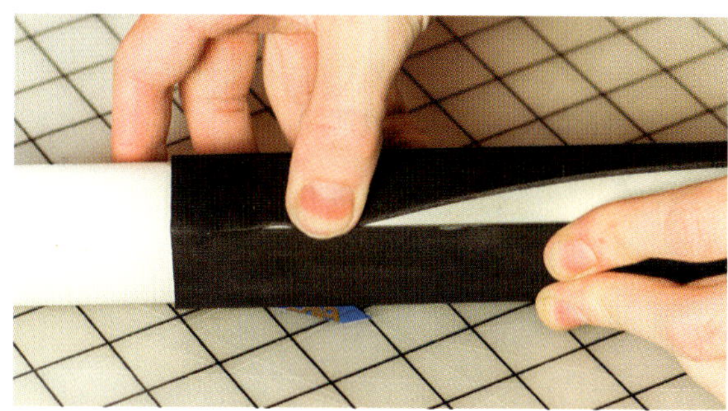

In my haste, I ended up with some gaps along this seam. Fortunately, this provided me with a chance to show you how to fix them using Kwik Seal! Using a craft knife, I smeared a bunch of Kwik Seal into the offending gaps. Then, with a wet finger, I smoothed out the mess. Bear in mind that you can't sand this when it dries, so be sure to get it as good as possible on the first try. Also note that this isn't a perfect fix, but is reasonably effective.

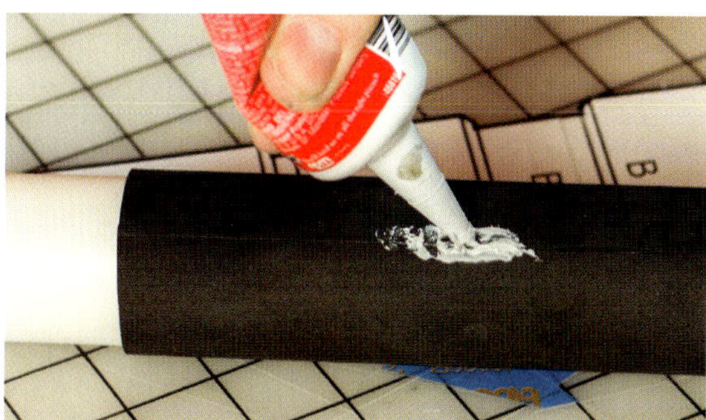

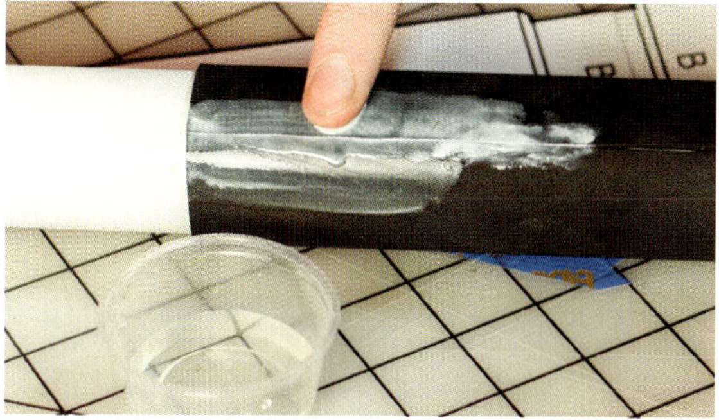

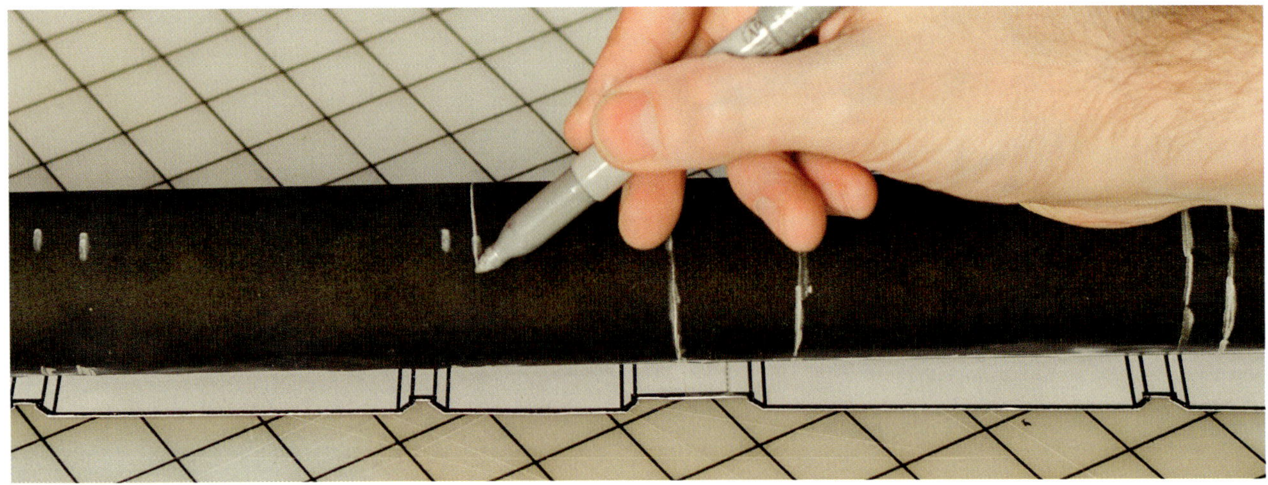

Wood Grain Texture

I wanted to add a wood grain texture to the handle, but most of it is covered by metal bands, so I marked off only the areas that needed to be textured with a silver marker.

Once I knew which areas needed the details, I used a hot knife to carve in the grain lines. I made sure to wear a respirator for this part because melting foam isn't great to breathe.

When I started this project, I knew I wanted to seal it with lots of latex rubber. That added surface coating will soften any kind of details that I cut into the prop, so I made sure to burn the wood grain in extra deep.

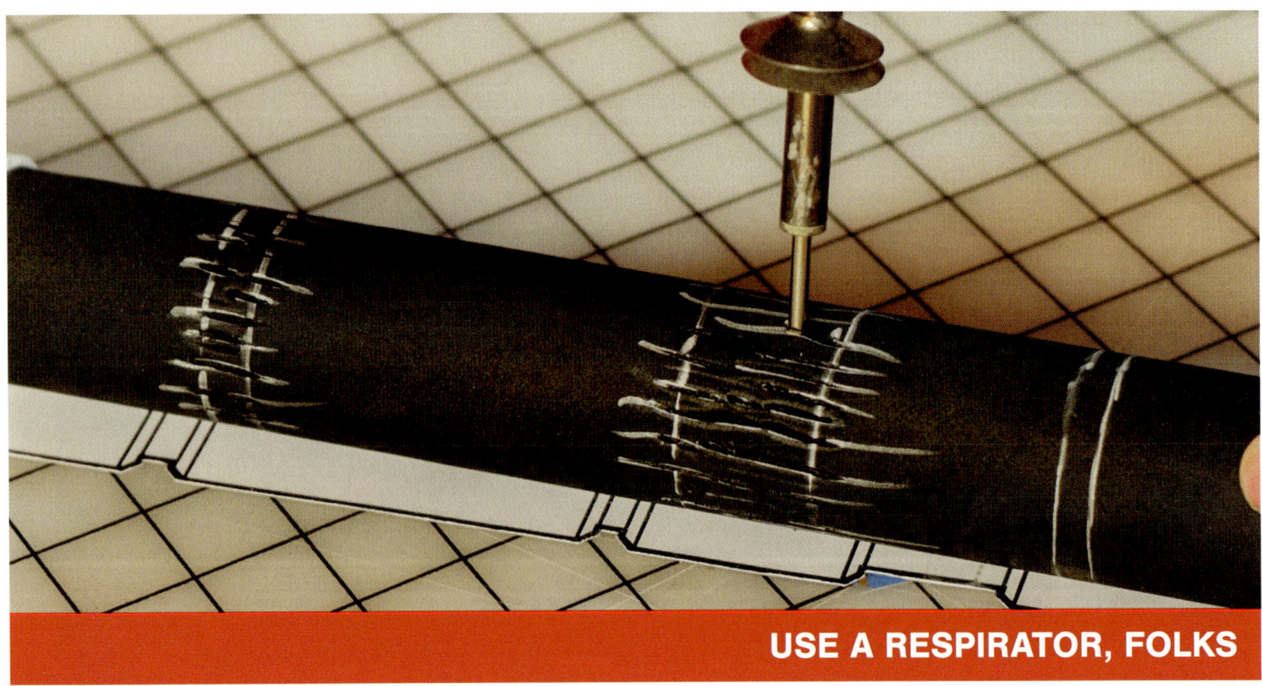

I planned on hiding the PVC coupler under one of the "metal" bands, but the coupler was shorter than the band. To solve this, I glued another piece of 2mm foam around the previous layer, making that part match the diameter of the coupler.

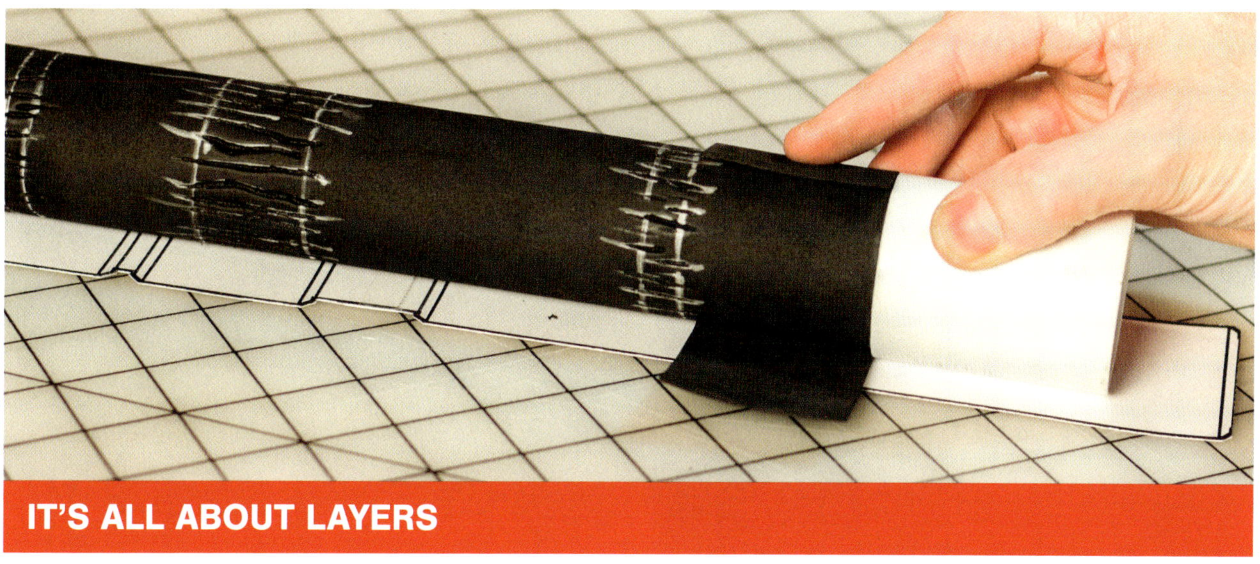

IT'S ALL ABOUT LAYERS

Bevel the Edges

The metal bands all had a bevel along their edges. This is where I used my handy-dandy band saw! I set the bed angle and fence, then zipped off a tiny shred of each piece. Boom. Perfect bevels.

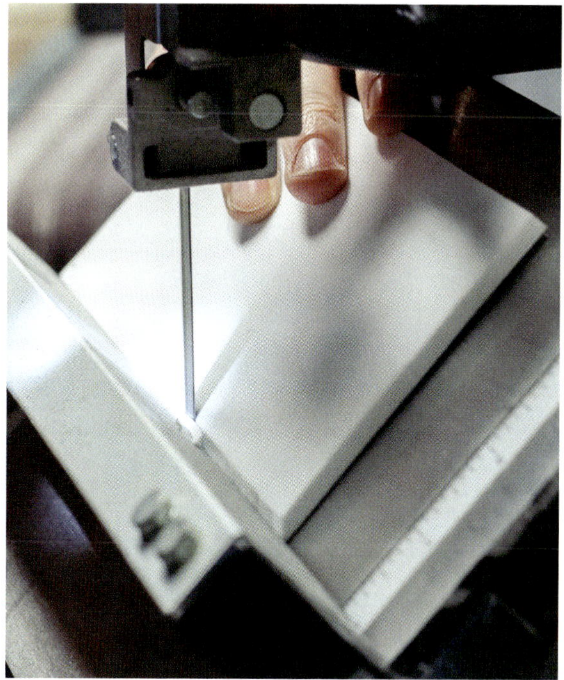

Just like the foam I wrapped around the PVC pipe, these bands were measured for length and circumference. Then I cut out rectangles, beveled their top and bottom edges on the band saw, and glued them around the handle. The edge of the 6mm foam is thick enough that I was able to put contact cement on the edges that would meet on the other side of the tube. When these edges met, I slowly and carefully pinched them together, trying to get the seam to match up as evenly as possible.

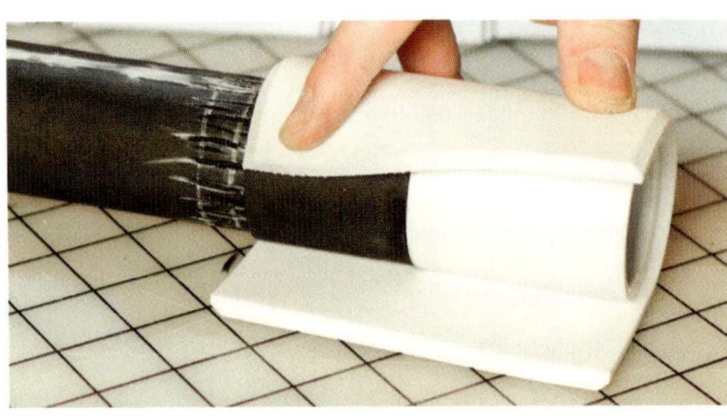

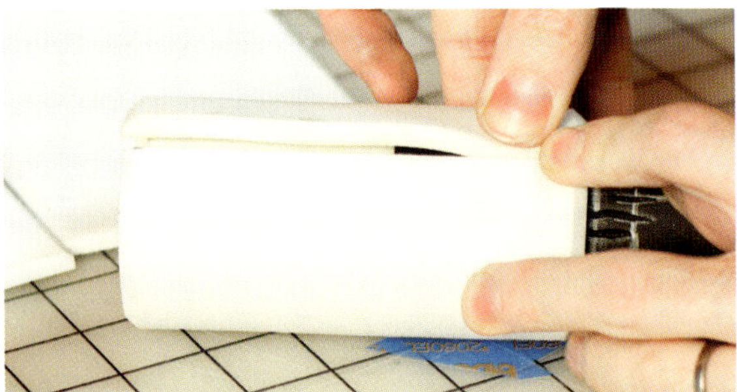

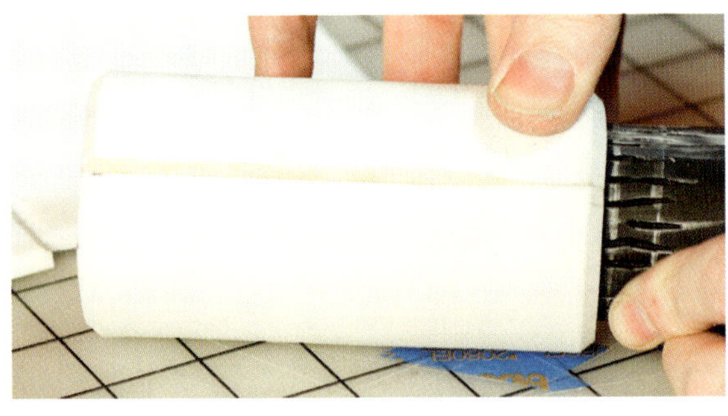

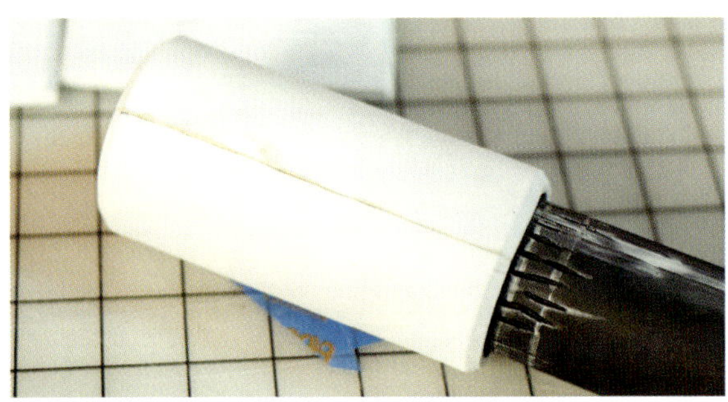

This process was repeated for all of our faux "metal" bands on the handle.

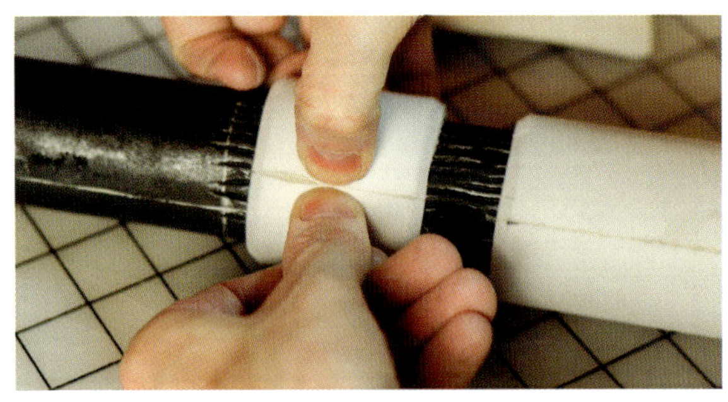

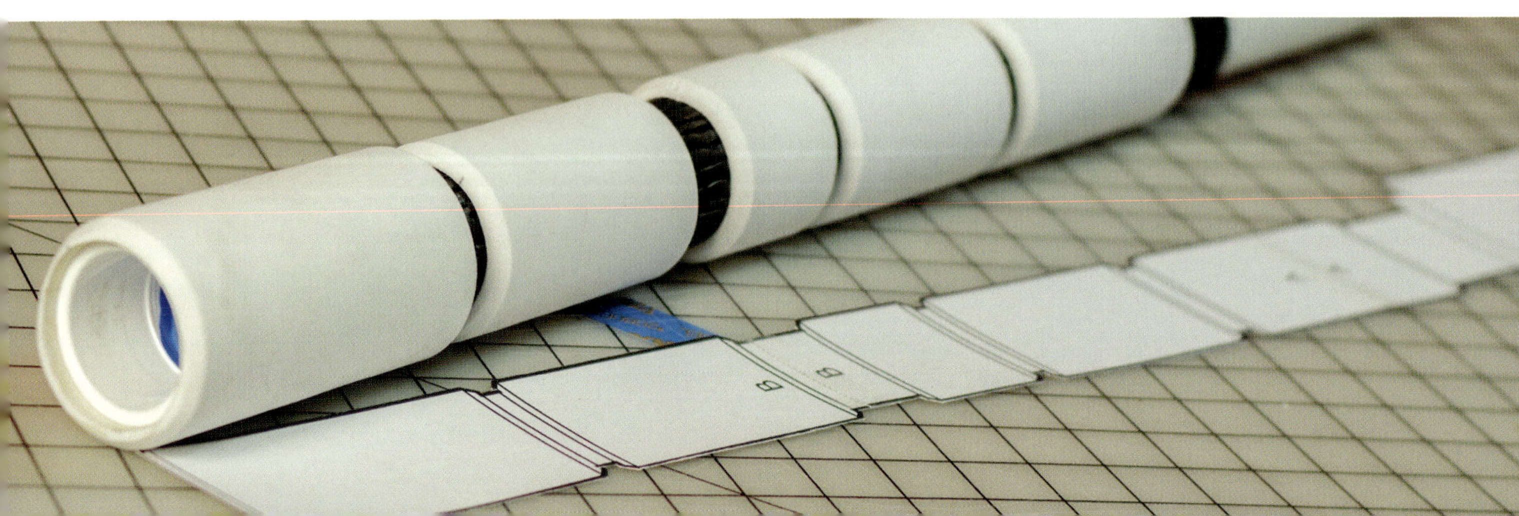

Thicker Foam Pommel

For the large pommel on the bottom of the handle, I knew I would need to use some of the thicker floor mat foam. Like with all builds, I checked for thickness, comparing what I wanted to use against the template.

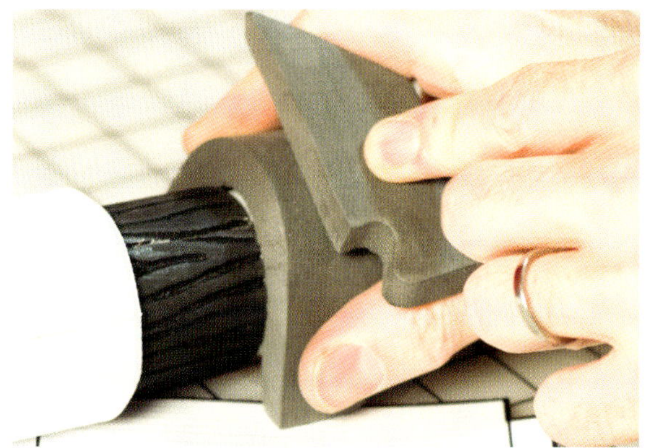

The main downside to the floor mat foam was is the texture. Once I had my foam cut to length, I ran the texture side against my belt sander. I didn't need to totally remove it, but I did need to rough it up enough so it would adhere to the glue.

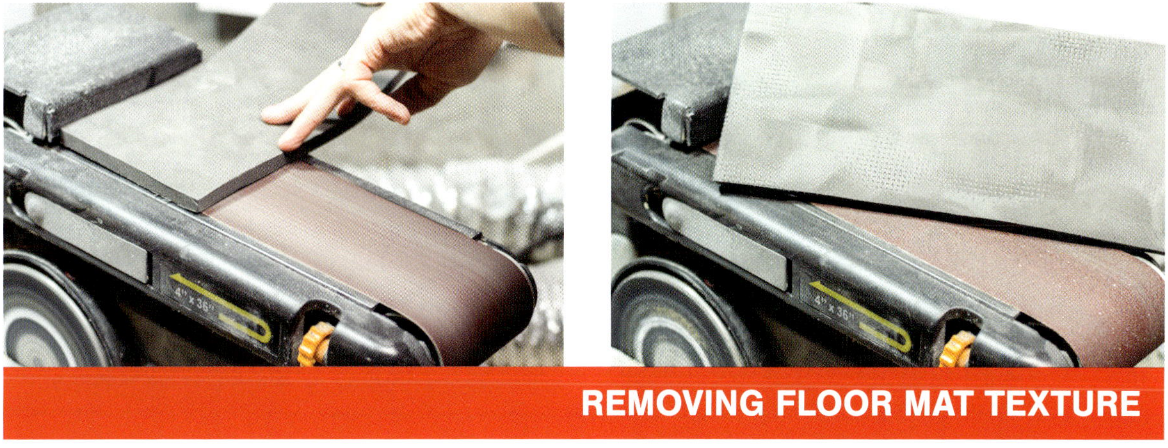

REMOVING FLOOR MAT TEXTURE

I also wanted to remove the texture *before* checking for the circumference on my PVC pipe. Removing the texture can change the thickness of the foam, changing the circumference.

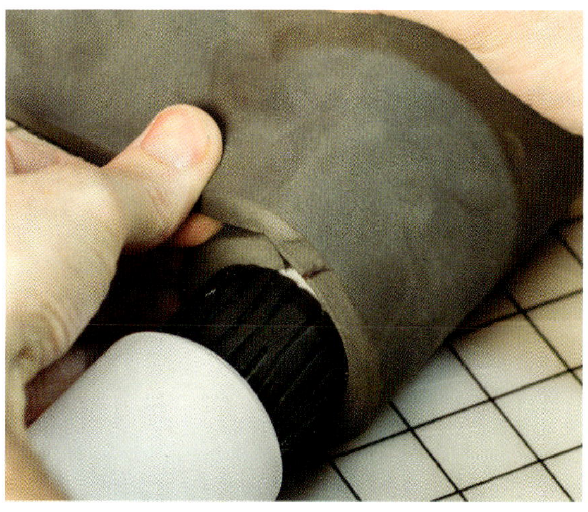

"Remove the texture before checking the circumference."

Getting perfect seams on this thicker foam can be really tricky. I like to cut a little bit of an inner bevel on one of the meeting edges. This makes it a little easier to push the edges together when you're wrapping them around the tube.

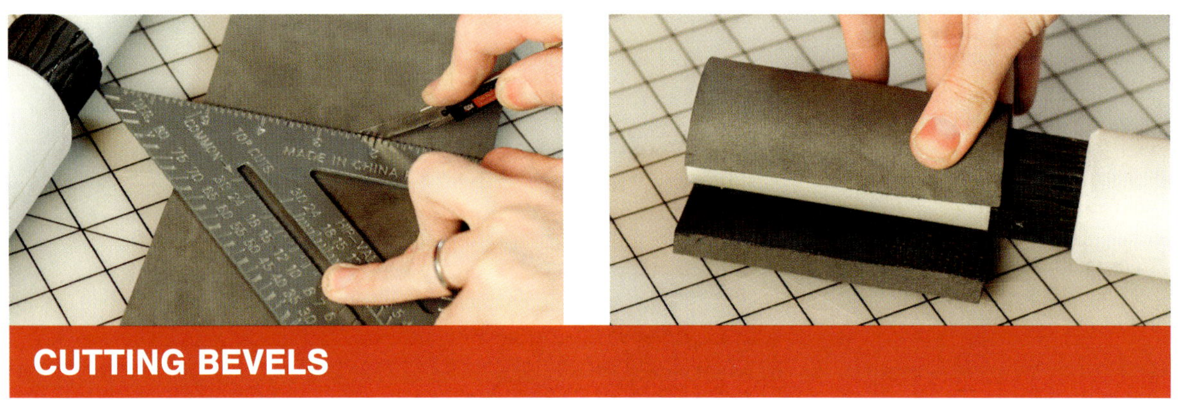

CUTTING BEVELS

Once the first pommel piece was glued down, it needed to be capped. So, I traced the perimeter of the tube end and cut out that circle with my band saw. This new cap piece was then glued down with contact cement.

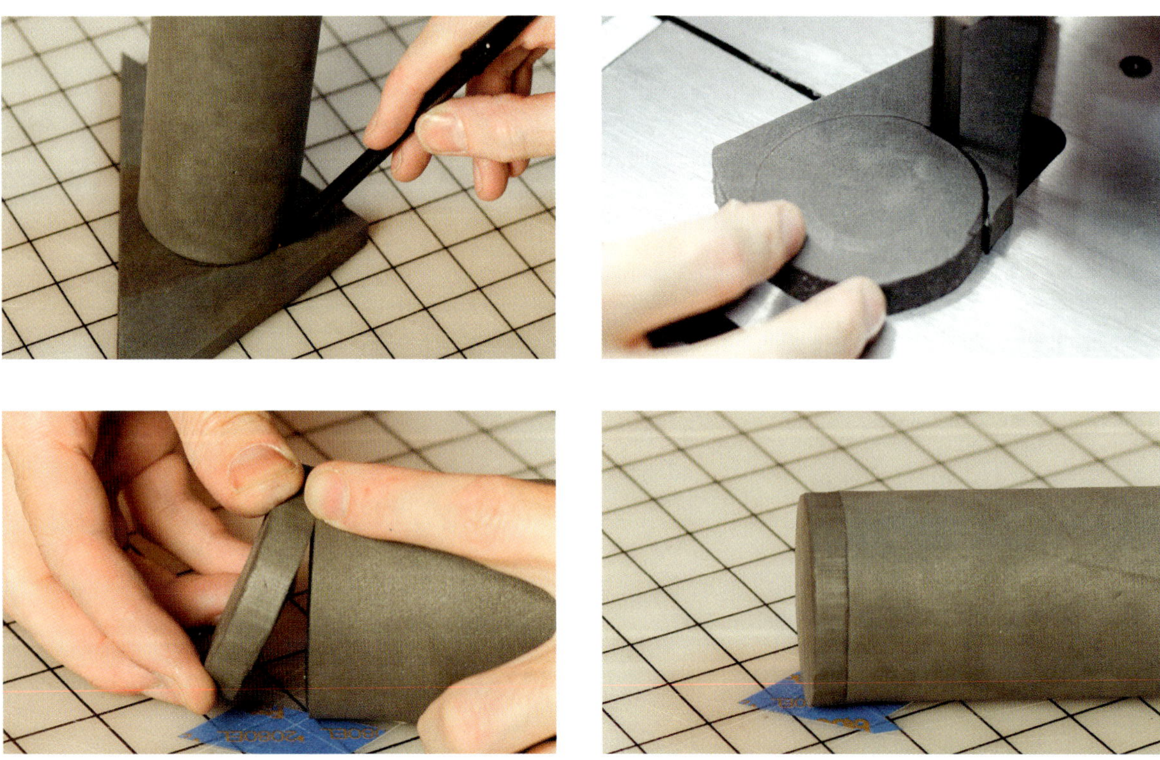

POMMEL

The pommel has one more layer, so I cut out another rectangle of floor mat foam and glued it around the previous one, completing the lower handle assembly!

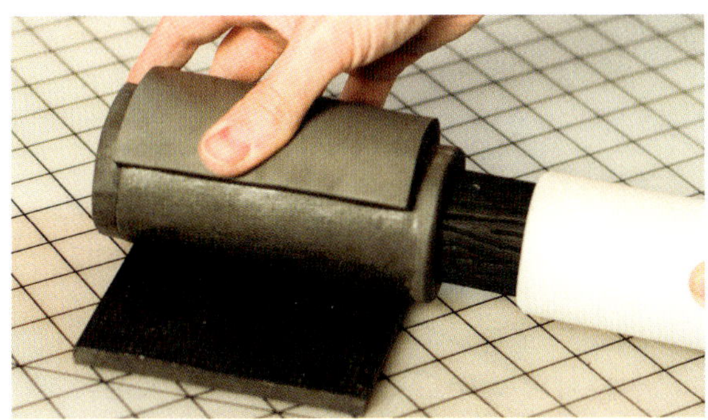

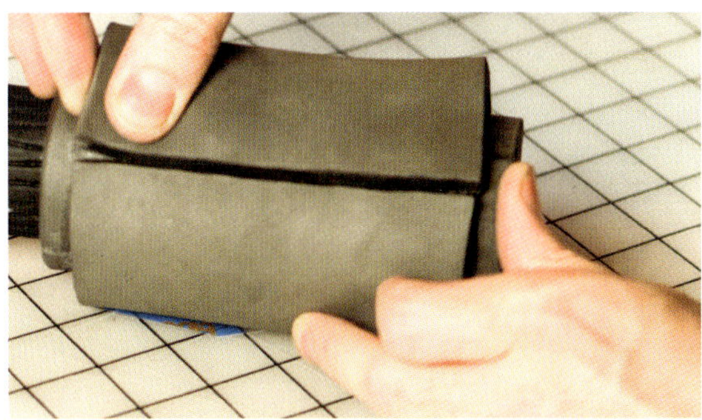

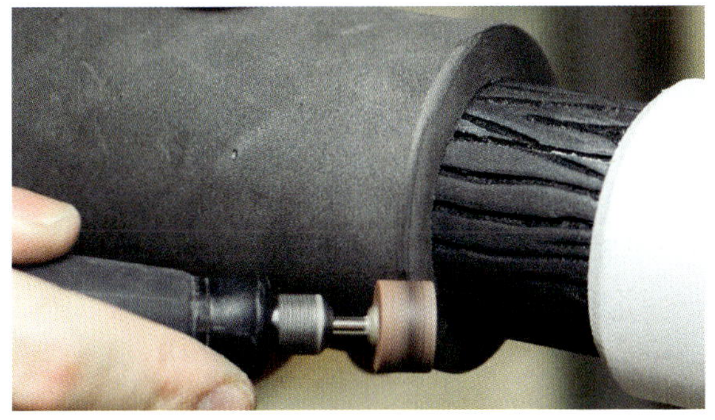

The good 'ole grinding bit is perfect for smoothing the edges.

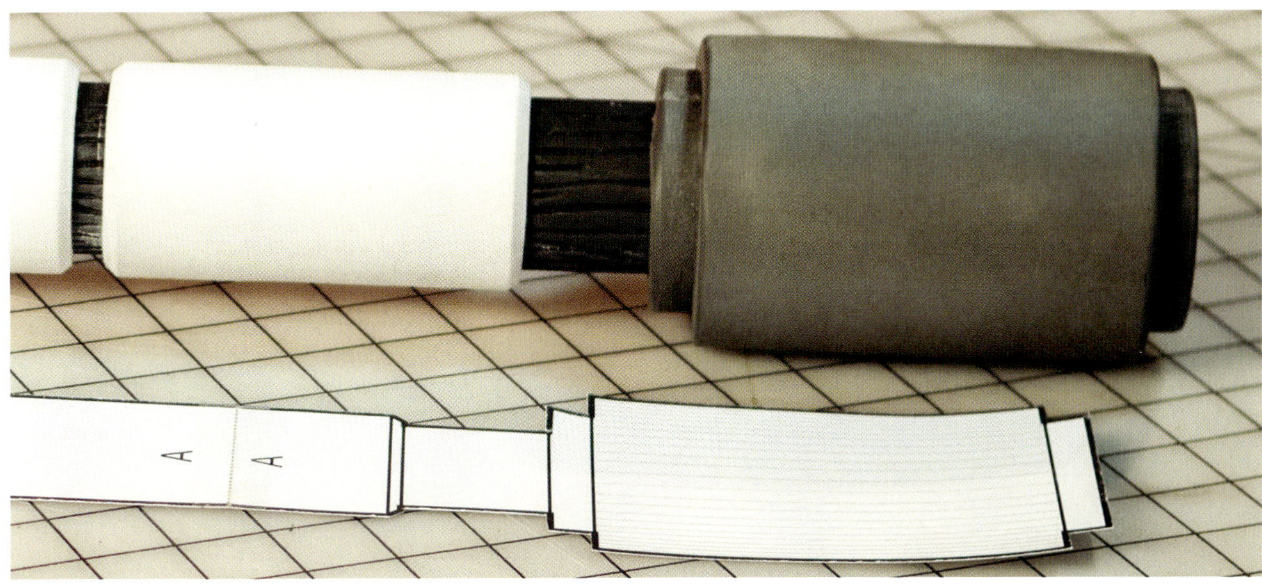

Upper Handle and Spike

The upper axe assembly started much like the lower handle part. Using the template, I judged how long the PVC pipe needed to be and trimmed it to length on the band saw.

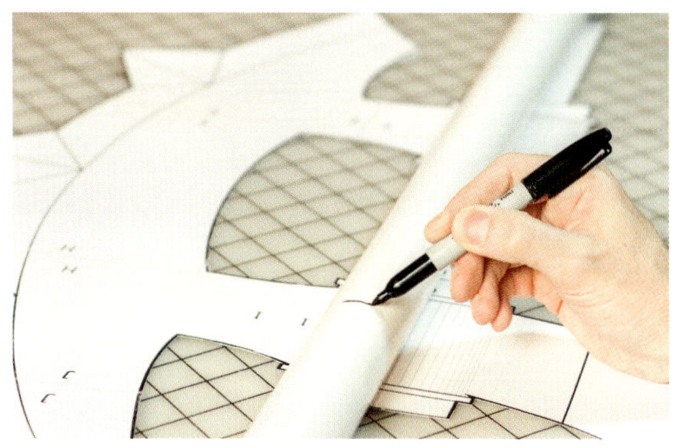

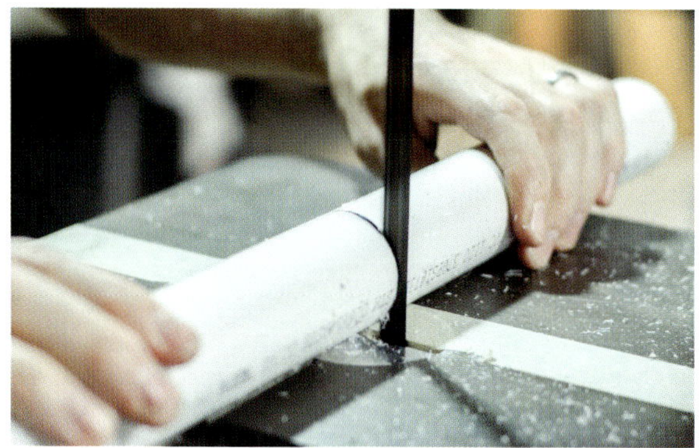

Just like the handle, I glued on a thin layer of 2mm foam and carved in wood grain lines to simulate the wooden shaft of the axe.

Hot Knives come with a selection of tips. Test them out on scrap foam to see what works best for your project.

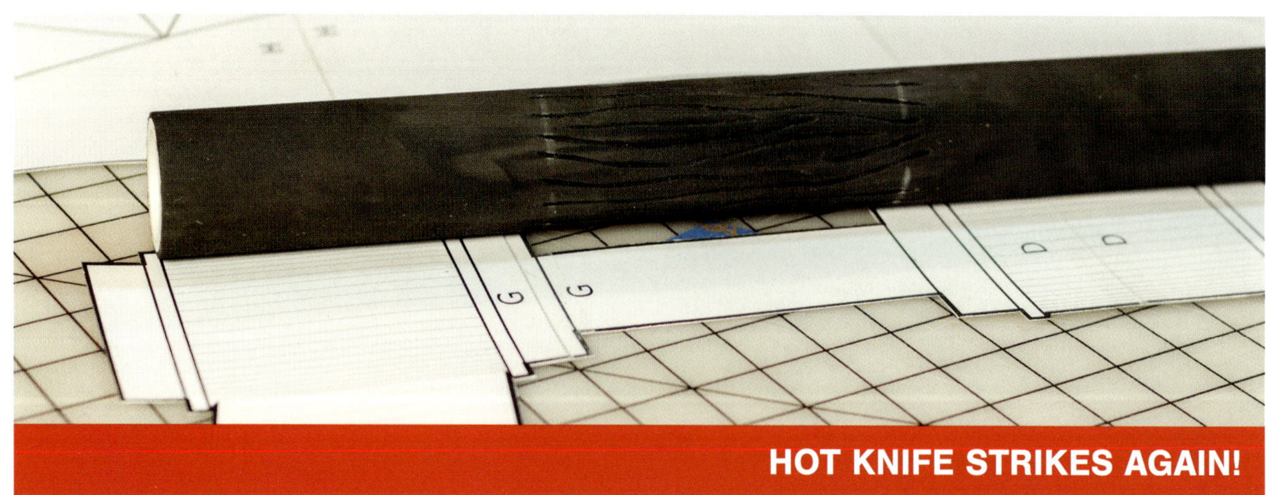

HOT KNIFE STRIKES AGAIN!

More Bands

Just like the pommel of the handle, I cut out rectangles of the thicker floor mat foam and glued them around the axe shaft, on top of the faux wood layer of foam.

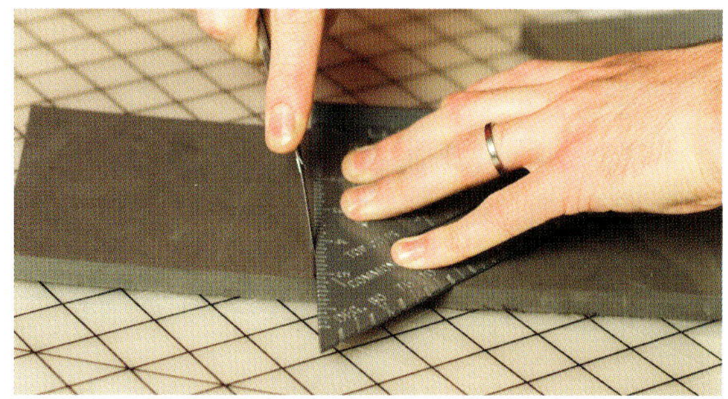

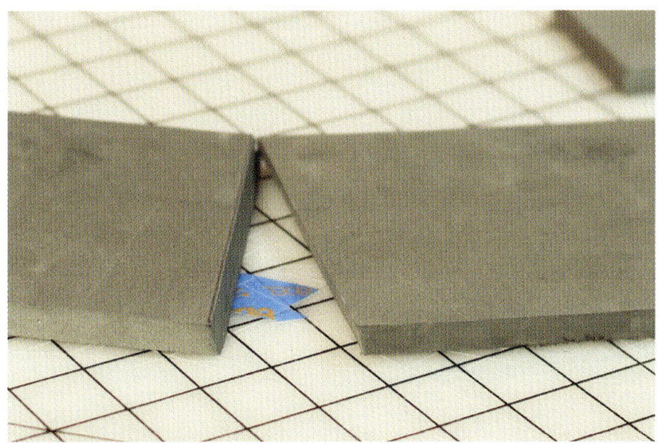

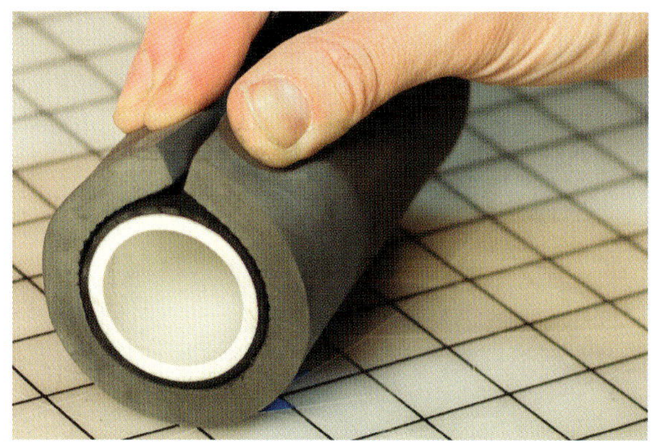

The templates for the blade and spike were removed from the main template piece. These are used to trace out parts to attach to the axe head shaft. For the spike, I decided it should be two floor mats thick and traced out the shape twice; once on each side of the paper template.

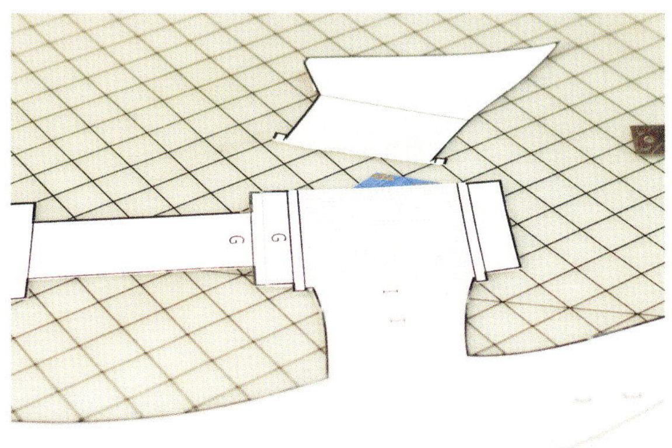

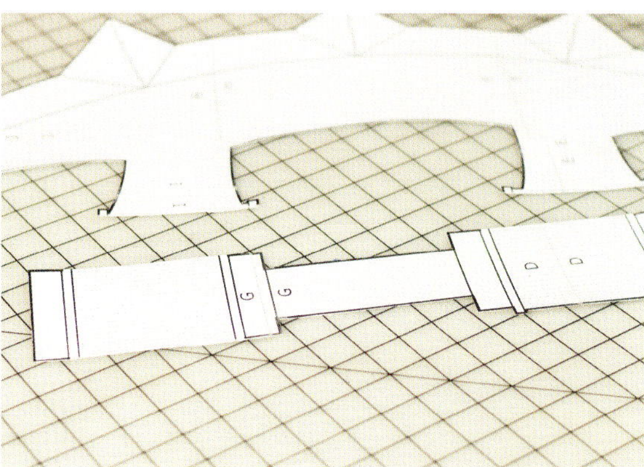

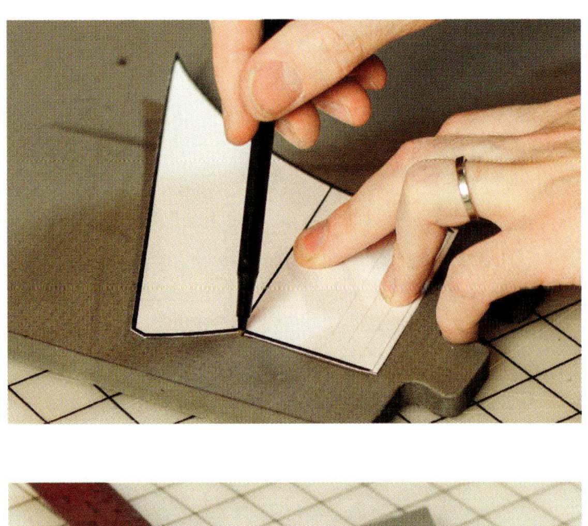

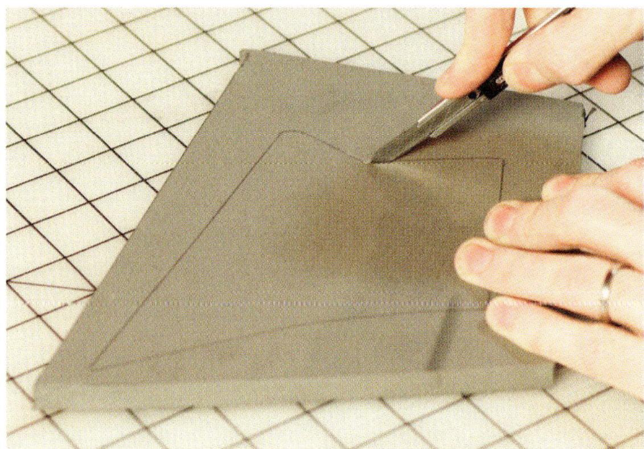

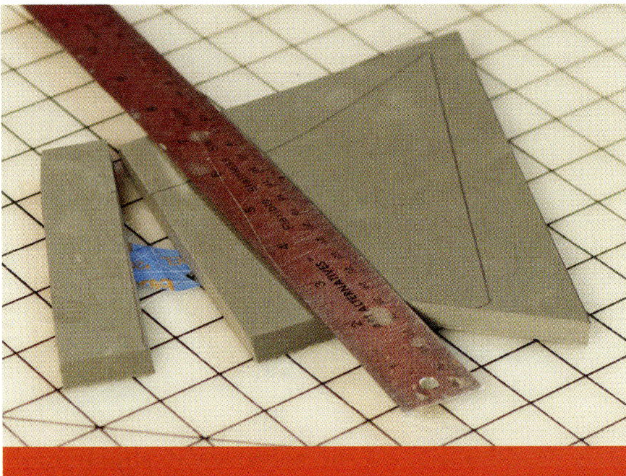

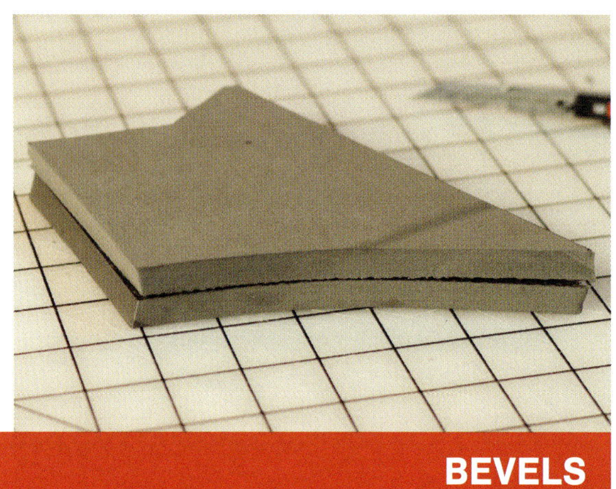

BEVELS

These two mirrored pieces were cut out from the foam. The two edges that would be attached to the round shaft were beveled in a little bit to better match the contour of the pipe. Then, the floor mat texture was sanded off and the two pieces were glued together with Barge.

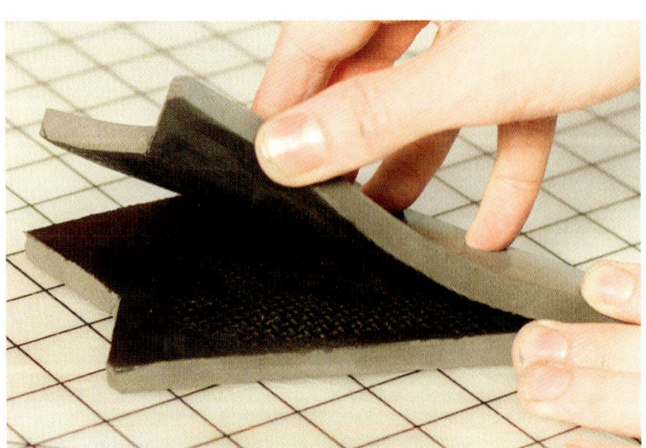

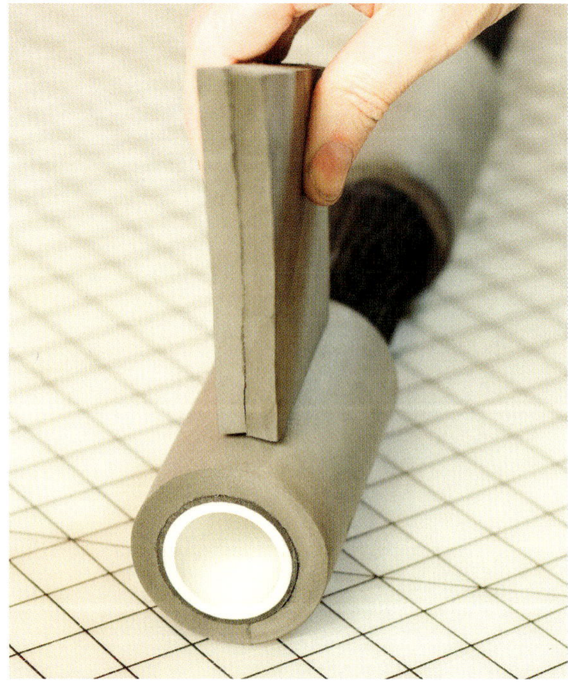

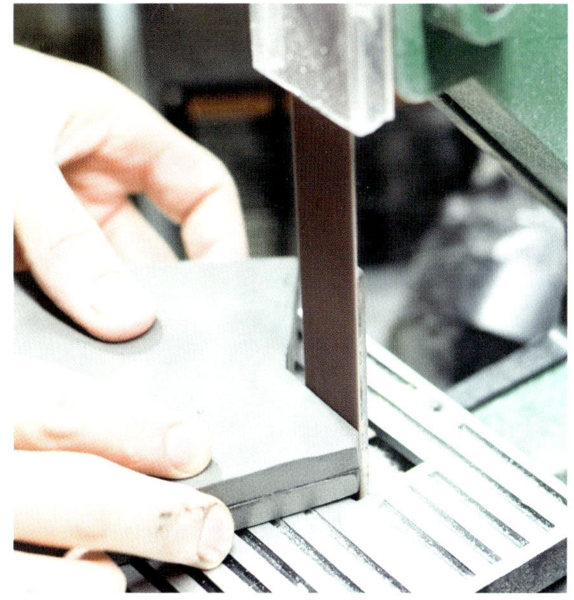

Clean Up!

The edges of the spike got cleaned up on the spindle and belt sanders. I may have a sanding tool buying problem...

I upgraded from the drill press drum sander to a spindle sander. I needed the extra sanding drum height when I made a wooden bow. The variety of drum sizes and grits works great for foam! Plus, the foam dust is sucked away by holes in the center disk into your vacuum system.

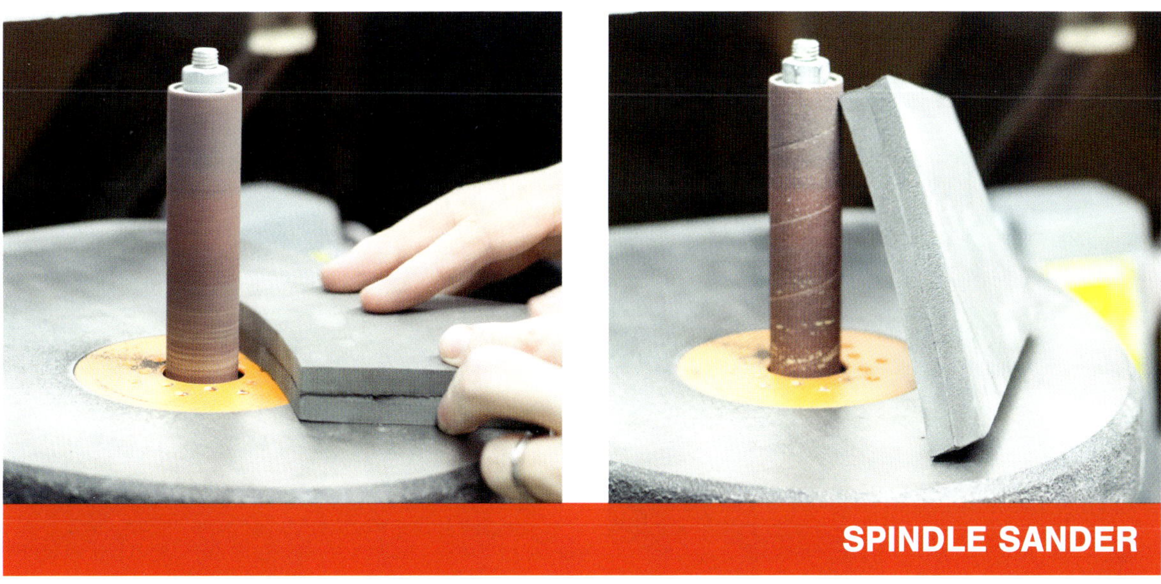

SPINDLE SANDER

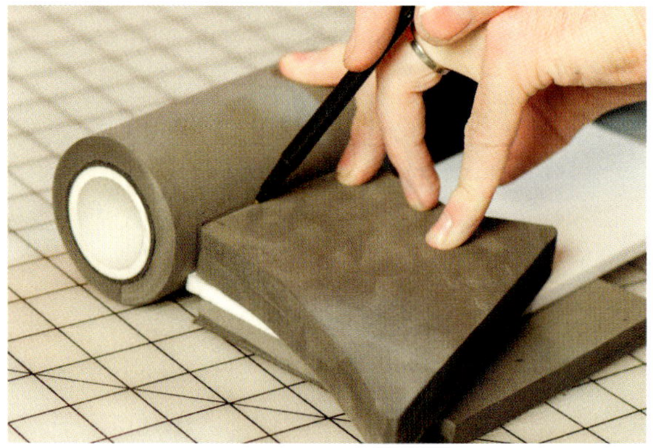

I needed to ensure that the spike would be attached to the main shaft at a perpendicular angle. So, I used some various thicknesses of scrap foam to lay the spike down at the right height so it would join correctly and I wouldn't have to guess come gluing time. Then, I marked off where I needed to glue up the pole, Barged up both sides, waited, and then stuck them together.

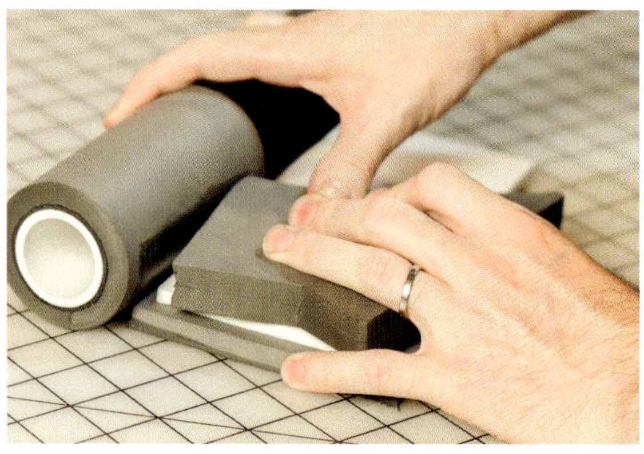

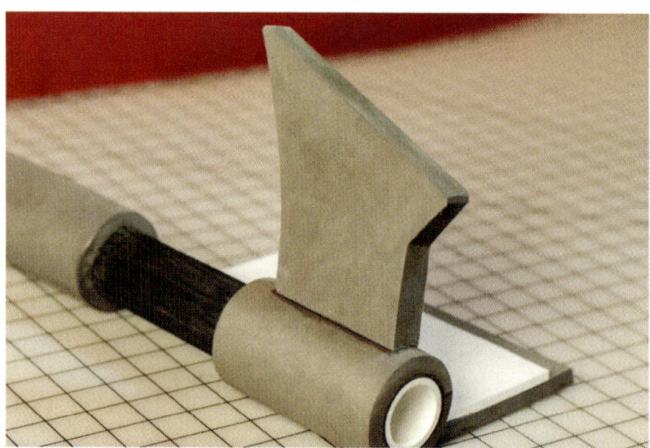

I messed this up on my first try. Fortunately, I keep Barge thinner on hand at all times! I was able to brush on some thinner and pull the piece off before it had time to set up forever. Then, I could give it a second try.

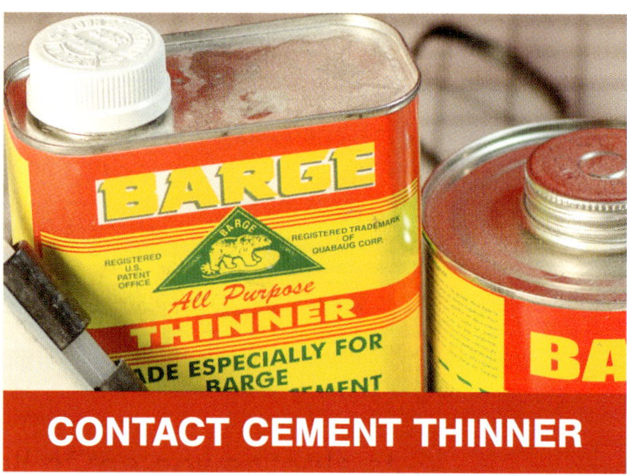

CONTACT CEMENT THINNER

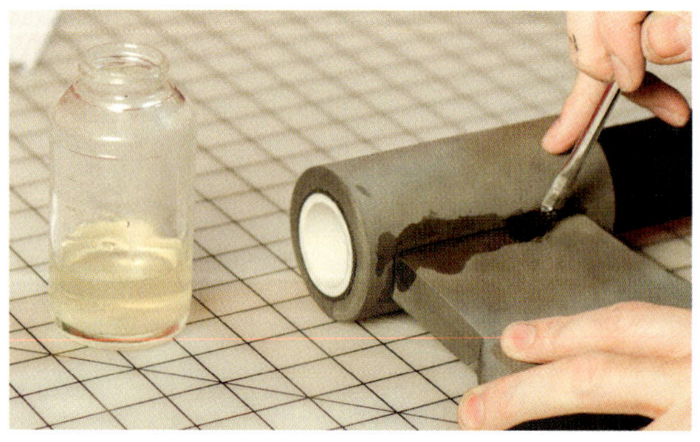

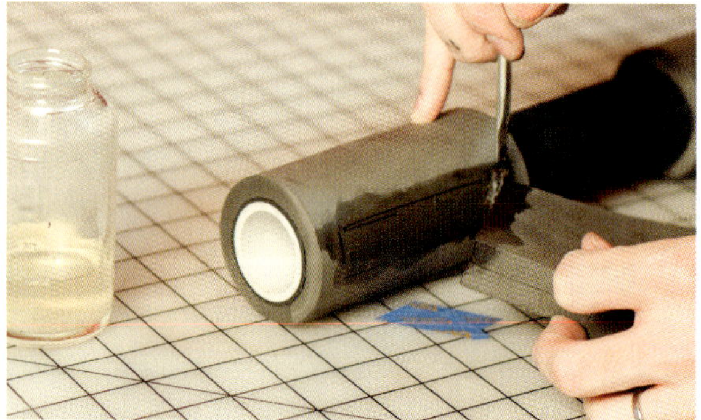

Axe Blade

Trace the Blade

The blade is easily the largest part of this entire build. I was crossing my fingers that its pieces would fit on a single sheet of floor mat foam and I lucked out. As I traced the pattern onto the foam, it pushed it right to the edges! Just like the spike I decided this part should be two floor mats thick, so I traced the pattern, mirrored, onto another sheet of foam.

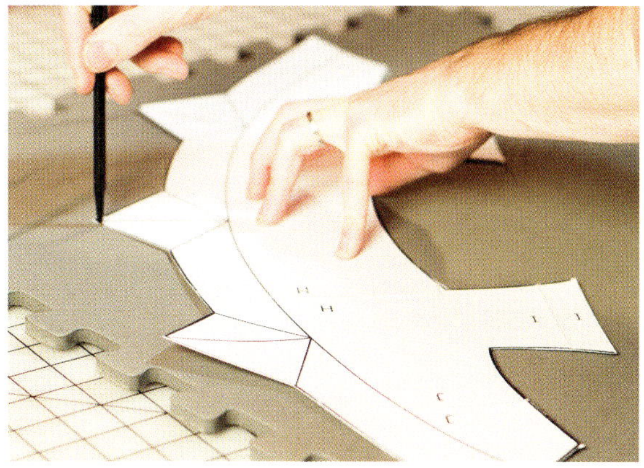

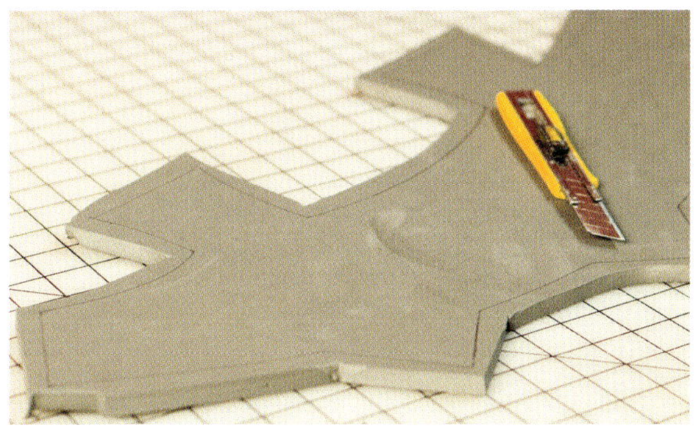

The blade pieces were rough cut, far away from the pattern lines. Then, I belt sanded the texture off and Barged them together. This way, when I cut the edges, there wouldn't be any clean up sanding, like there was on the spike. Most of the cutting on this guy was done with the band saw.

Also like the spike, the edges that meet the shaft were beveled in slightly to make appropriate contact for gluing. This was done before gluing the two rough cut halves of the blade together.

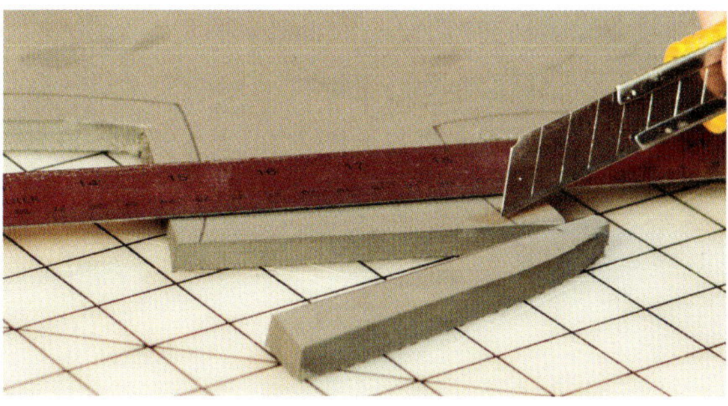

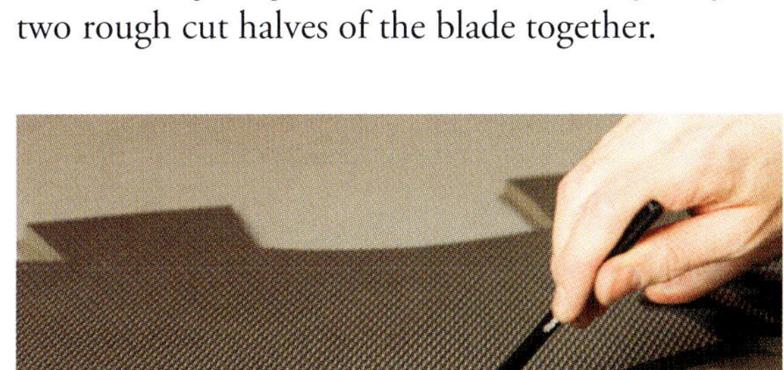

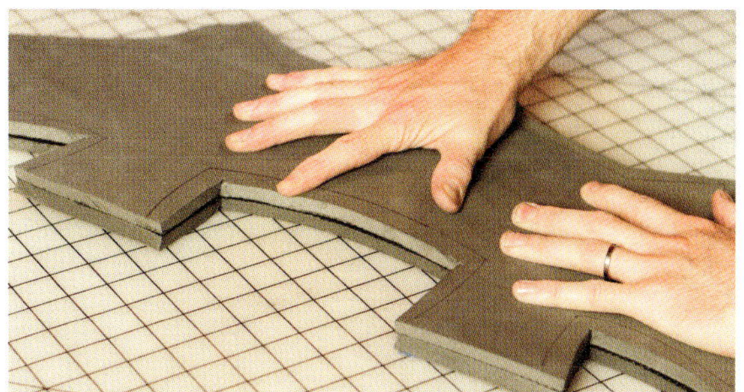

Due to the shape and size of this piece, I swapped between the band saw and the scroll saw for some of the cuts. It really pays to have both types of saw in your shop. Another bonus of foam is the ability to bend the piece you're working on if it doesn't quite fit into the choke of your machine.

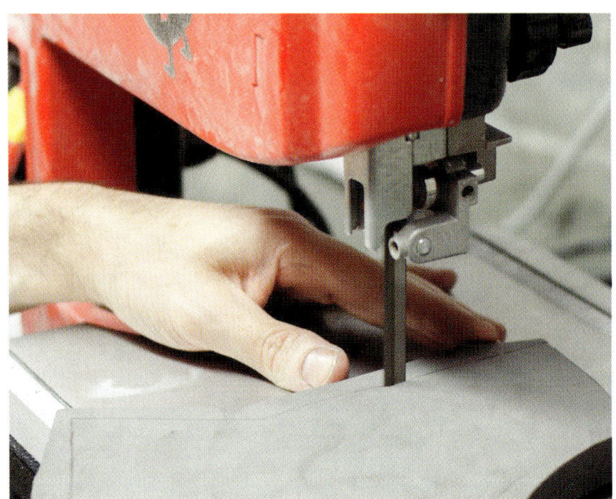

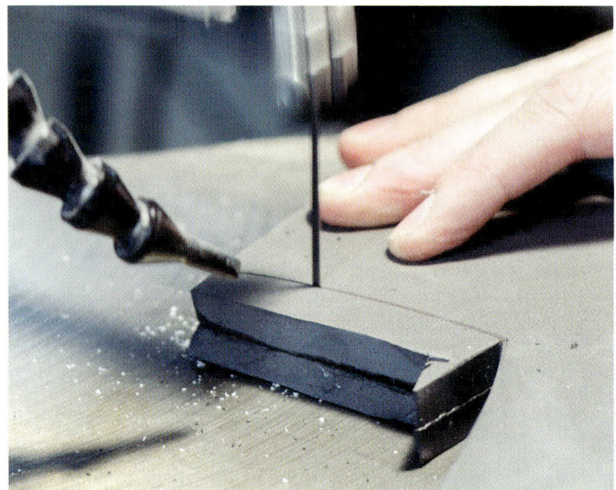

BEND TO MY WILL!

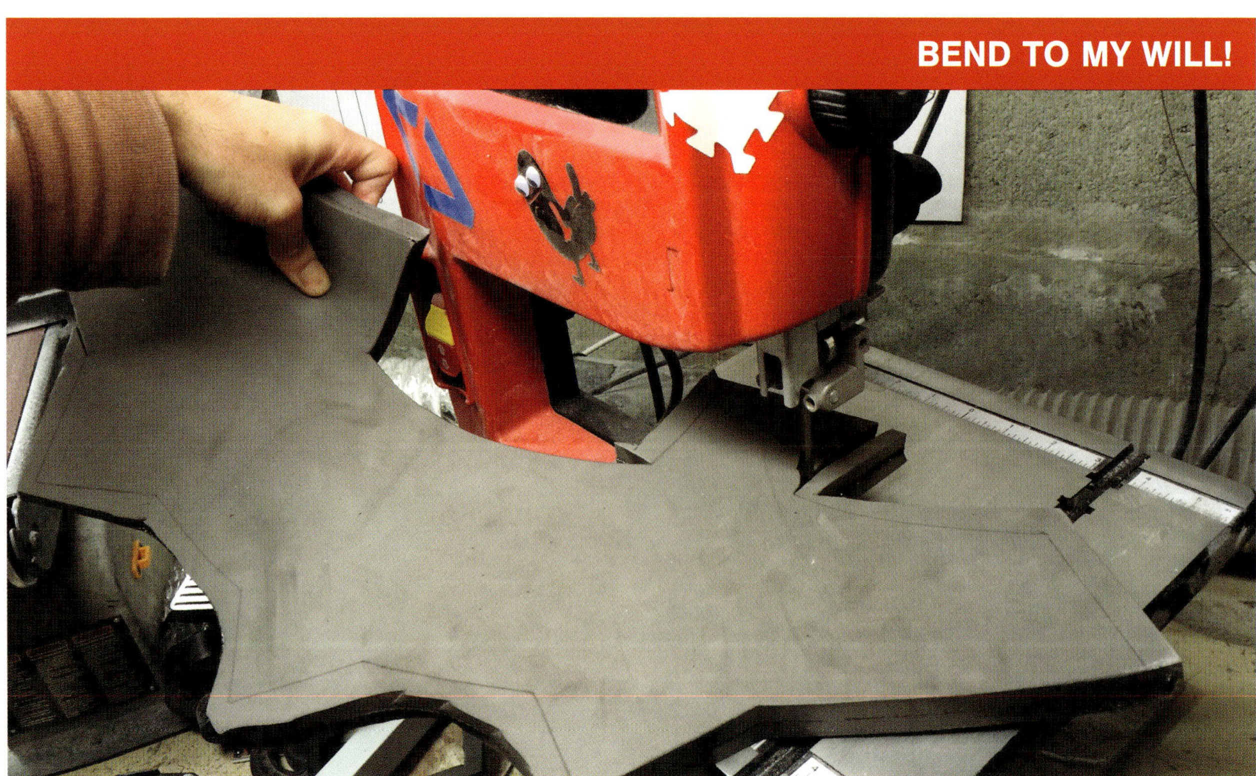

The edge of this axe blade is thicker than the rest of the form, so I trimmed off that part of the template and traced it onto some 6mm craft foam. Unfortunately, the small sheets weren't long enough to accommodate such a long pattern, so I had to glue together several sheets along their edges to make a piece big enough. This worked better than I expected!

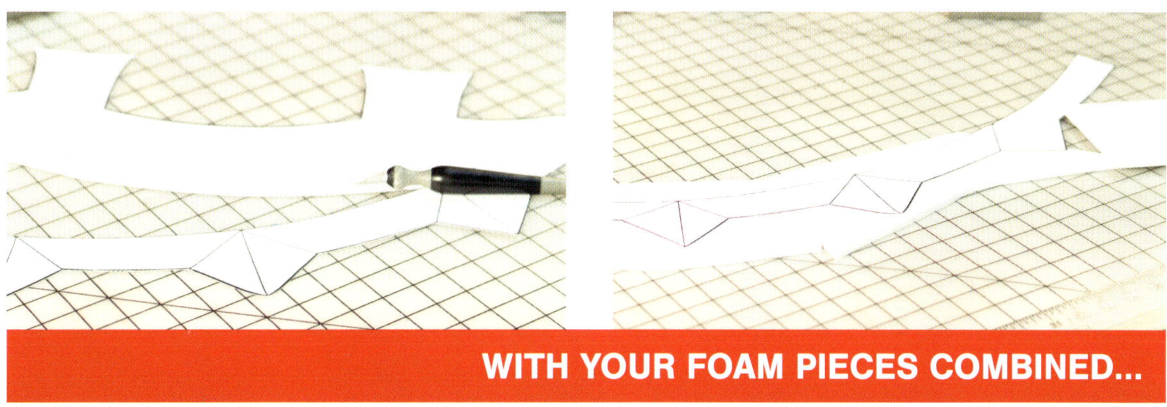

You can contact cement edges together to make big foam pieces.

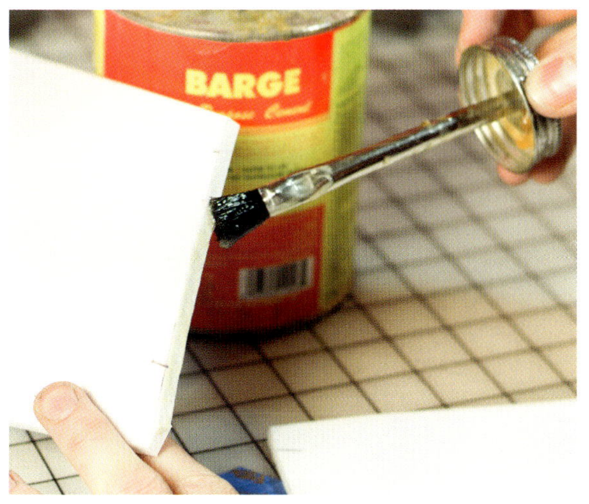

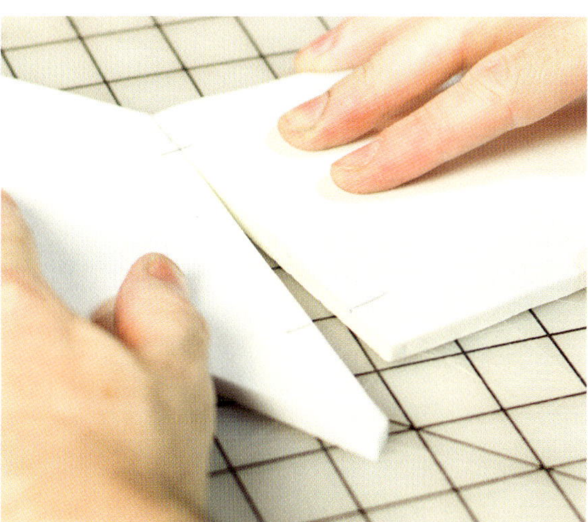

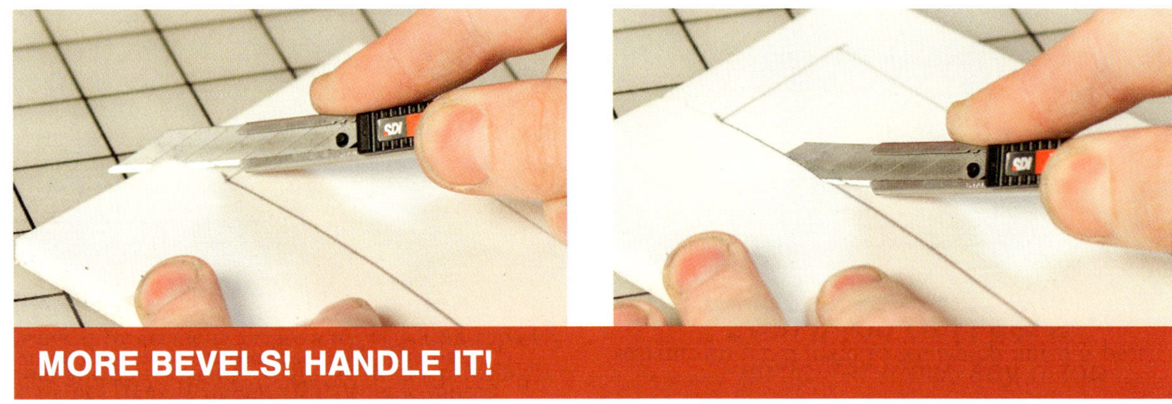

MORE BEVELS! HANDLE IT!

These 6mm edge pieces were cut out, taking care to bevel the inner edge before gluing it down. I wanted this part to have a nice chamfer and it would be difficult to add it once it was adhered in place. Once the pieces were cut out, they were Barged to the main blade part.

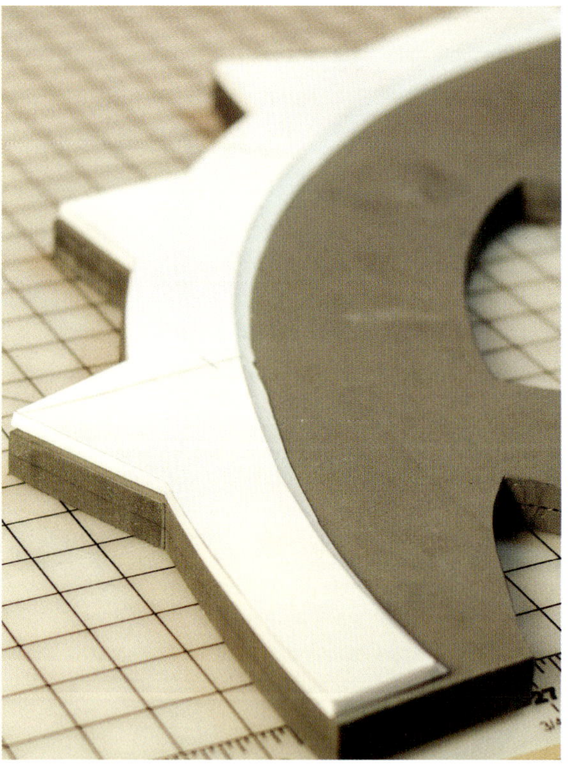

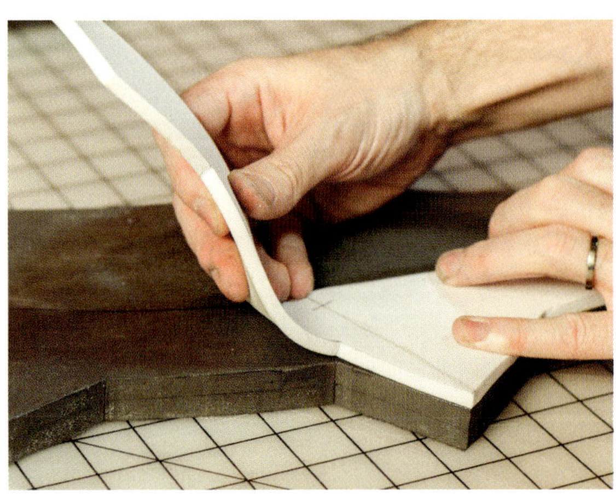

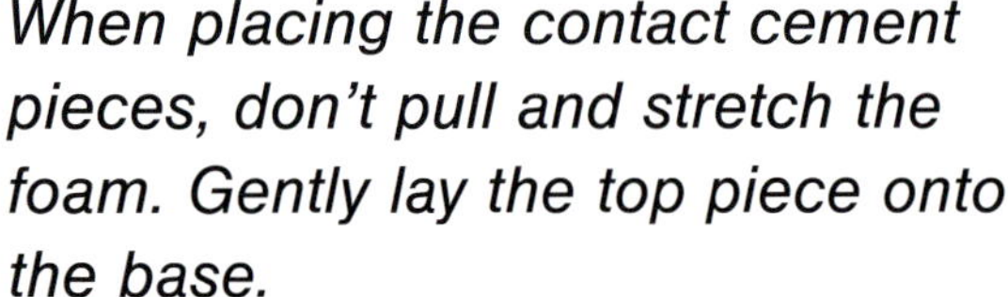

When placing the contact cement pieces, don't pull and stretch the foam. Gently lay the top piece onto the base.

Carve Away Extra Foam

The outer edge of the blade needed to be beveled down to a "sharp" edge and I had a lot of material to remove. I started by cutting into the inner corner areas with a knife to gauge how deep I needed to cut. Then, I started hacking away foam.

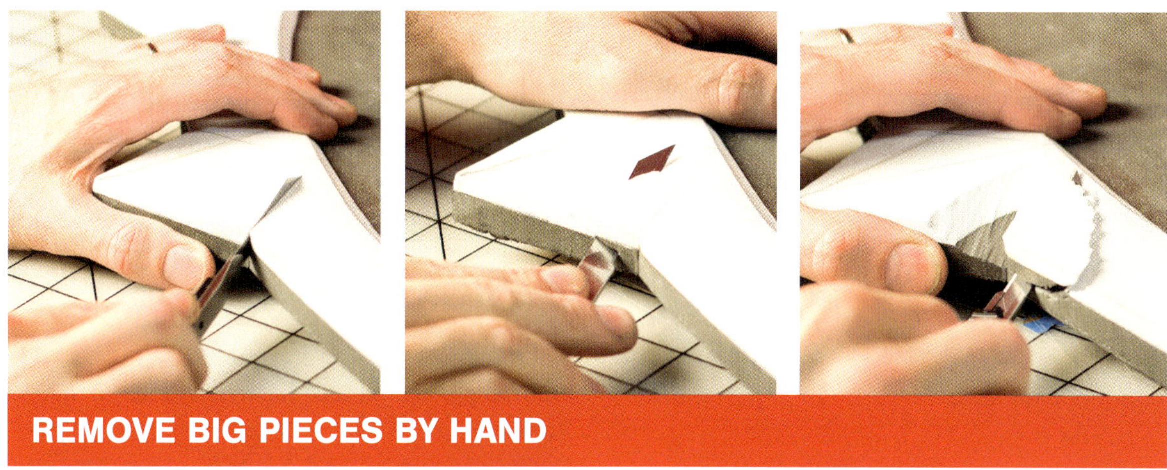

REMOVE BIG PIECES BY HAND

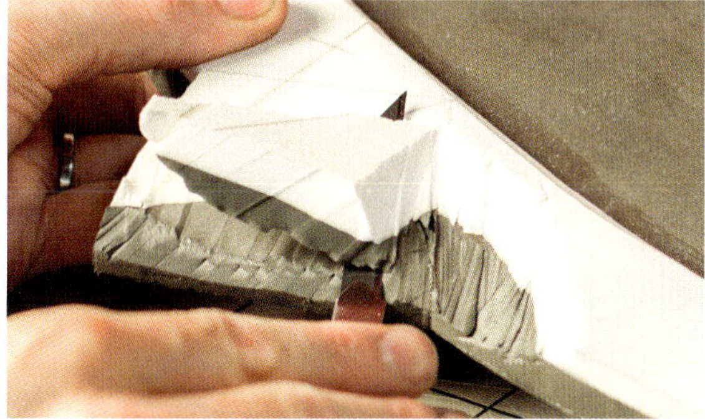

This took a good amount of time, but my patience paid off. I also had to repeatedly sharpen my blade to make sure my cuts were clean and true.

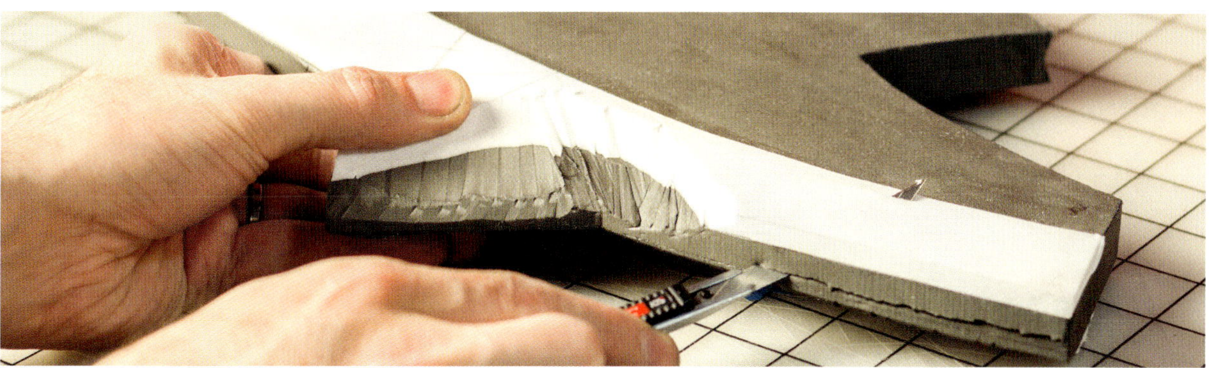

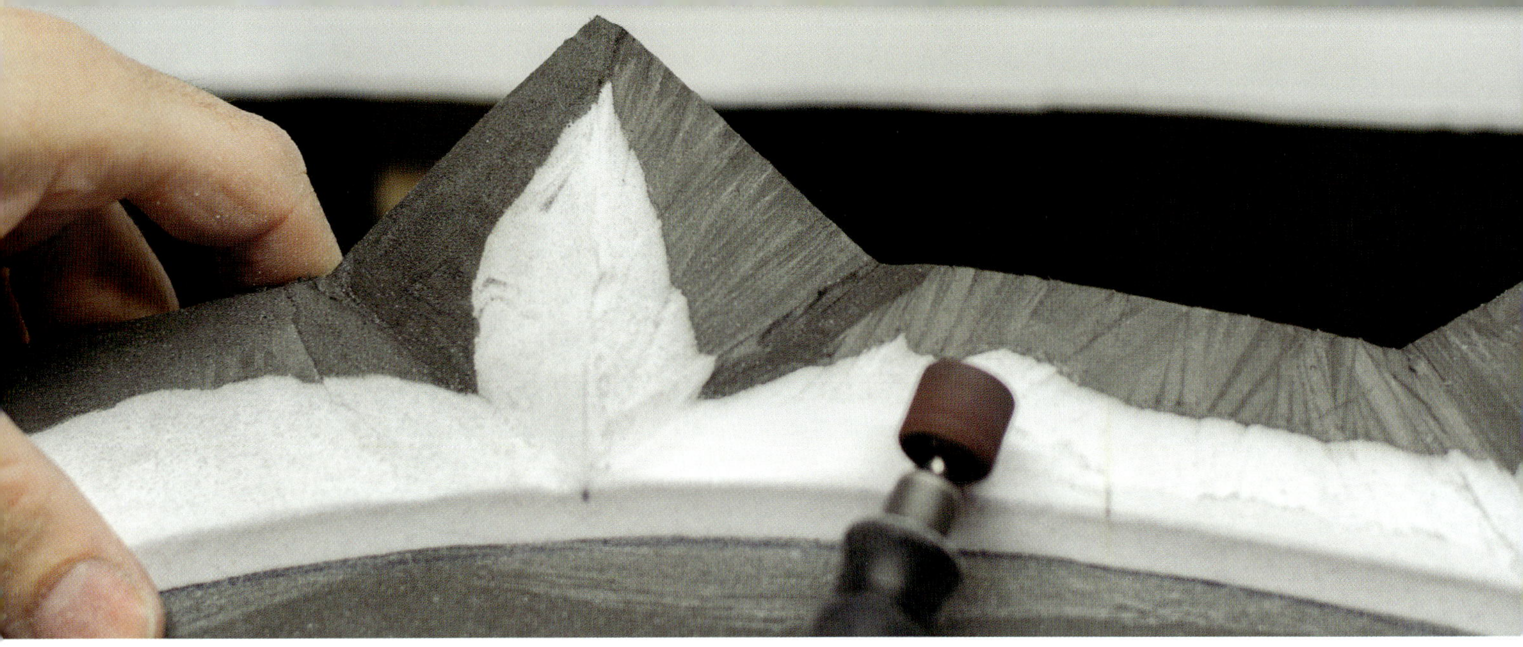

Foam Sculpting

Once the bulk of material was removed, I went back in with the sanding drum in my rotary tool and cleaned up my work. This is still a pretty rough process, but it refined the bevel much better than the initial pass.

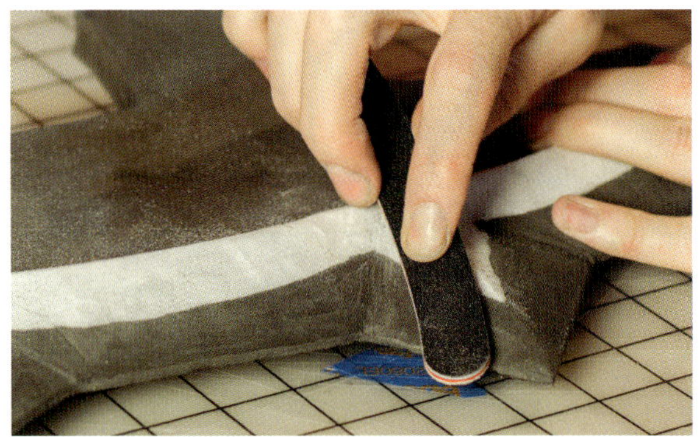

Next, I sanded the entire edge with a nail file to clean up any remaining rough areas. Once I was happy with the finish, I used the corner of a grinding bit in my rotary tool and started carving in a bunch of rough gouges in the edge. I imagine these are meant to make the axe look like it was sharpened with some kind of super rough grinding wheel or stone.

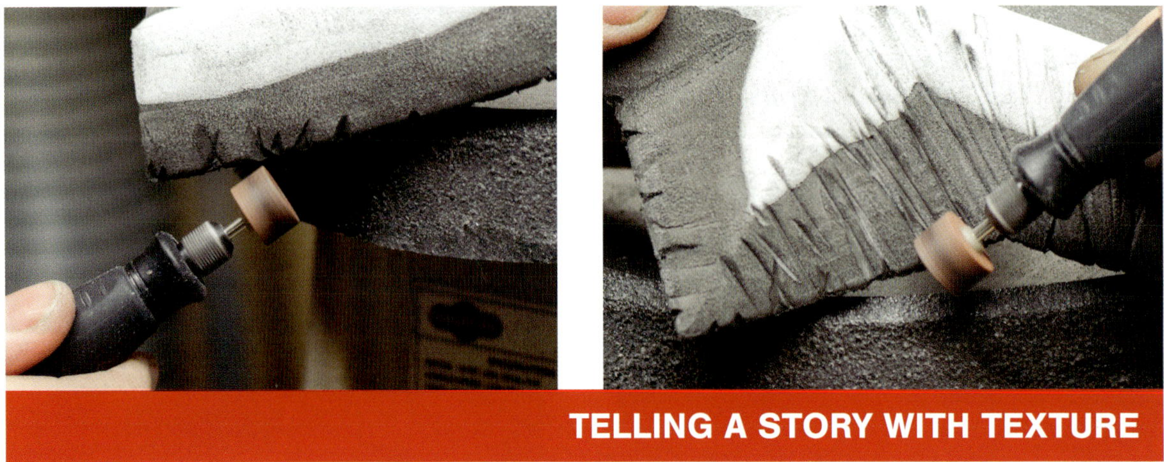

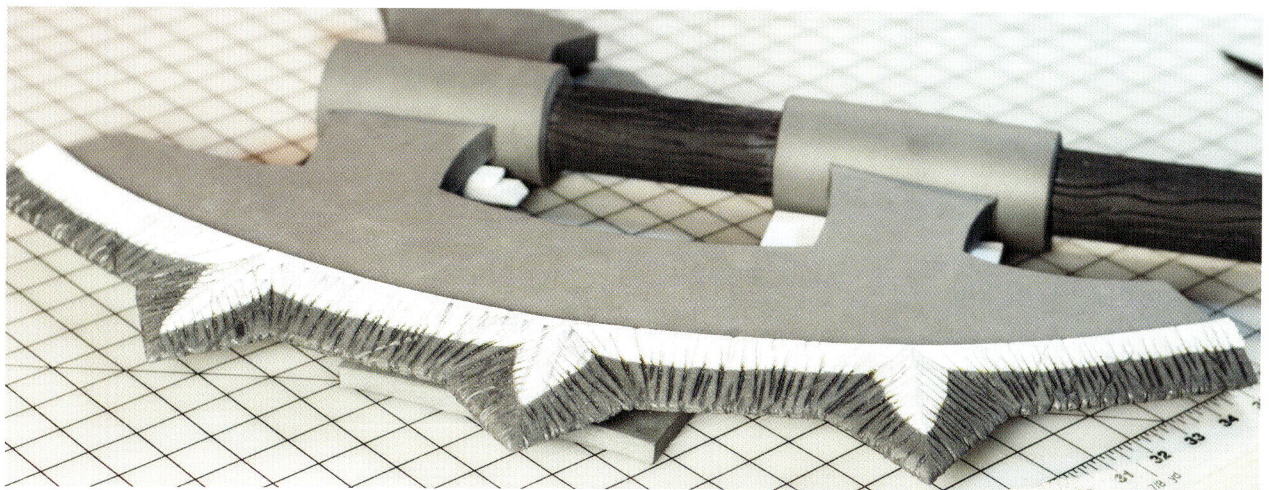

Assembly

Happy with how the axe edge turned out, I decided it was time to attach it to the axe shaft. Just like the spike, I stacked up layers of foam to ensure the blade would be placed correctly and then I Barged it to the pole. I also added a cap to finish off the top of the pole.

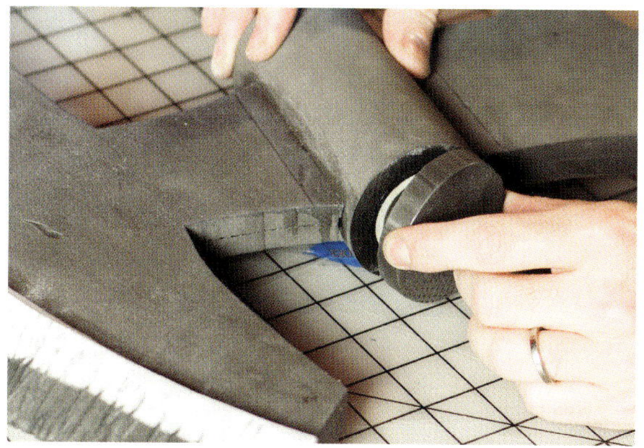

I wanted the blade to blend seamlessly into the shaft parts, like they had been forged together, so I needed to wrap some foam around the shaft that didn't meet up with the blade at a right angle. So, I cut out some 6mm foam rectangles and tapered their edges to a nice thin edge using a piece of wood and the belt sander.

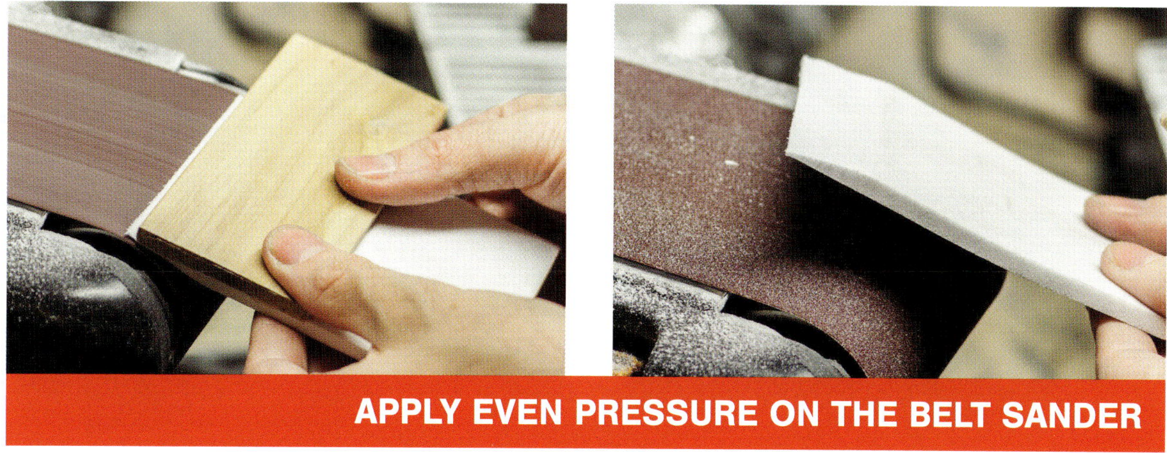

APPLY EVEN PRESSURE ON THE BELT SANDER

These tapered foam pieces were then glued down to the blade and shaft, pushing the tapered edges down into the crevasse between the two parts, forming a nice smooth transition.

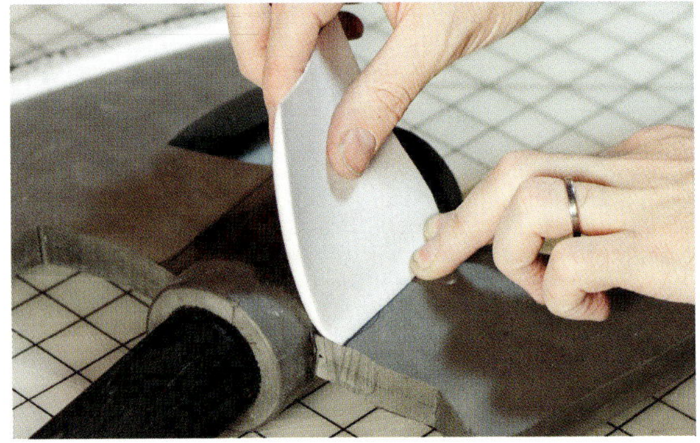

The last parts to add were a few bands of foam around the thicker shaft pieces, just above and below the parts I had just glued down. These were cut from floor mat foam and Barged in place.

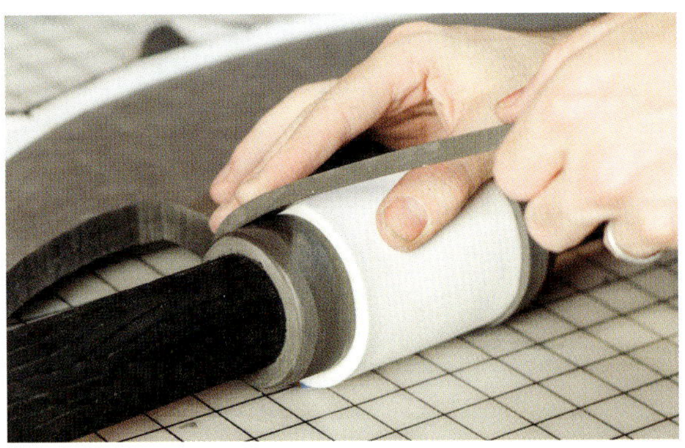

With all of the foam pieces attached, I could go over the entire axe and round over any rough or squared edges. I like to use a grinding bit in my rotary tool for this. It isn't as aggressive as a sanding drum and will give a little bit of polish to the foam.

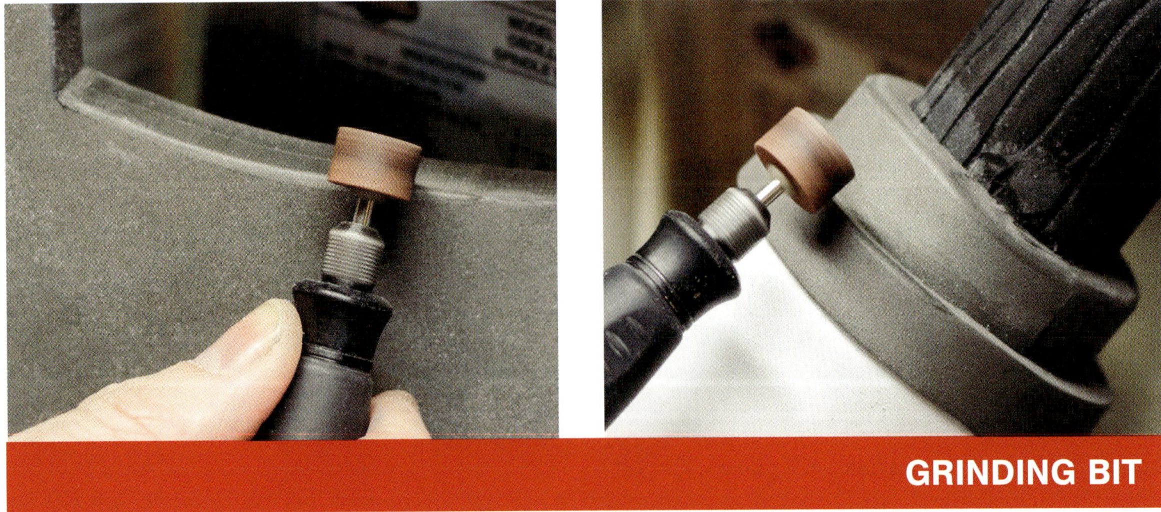

GRINDING BIT

Adding Texture

Next, I needed to texture the axe blade. In my opinion, good texturing can make or break the believability of a really good prop. For this one, I needed a "hammered metal" look. So, I used my spherical grinding bit and started carving away. The grinding bit scoops out little rounded divots in the foam, leaving a really convincing hammered texture.

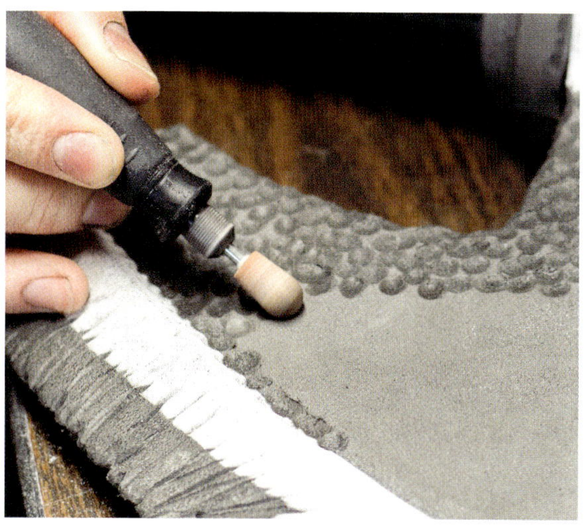

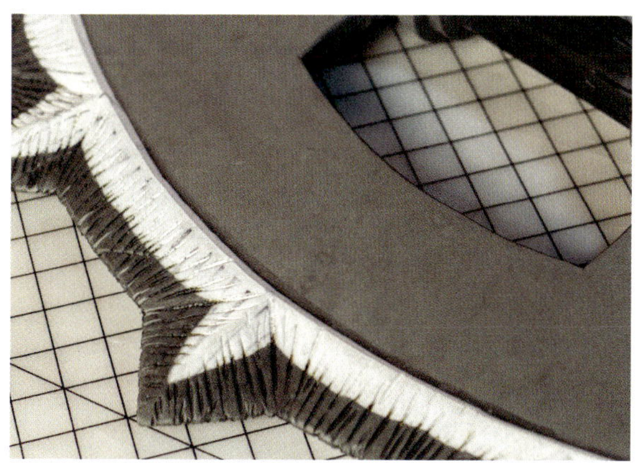

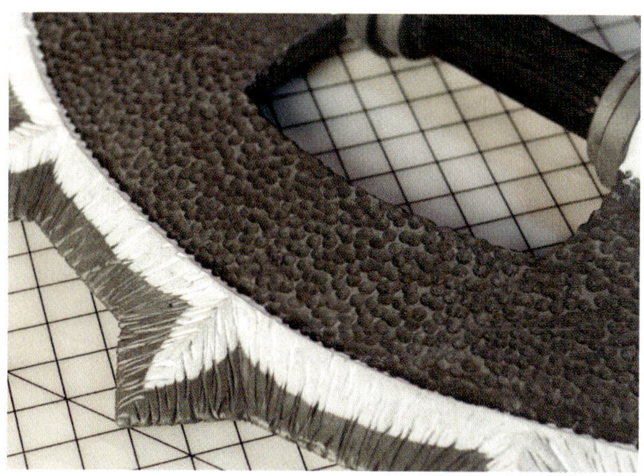

You can see what a difference some texture makes!

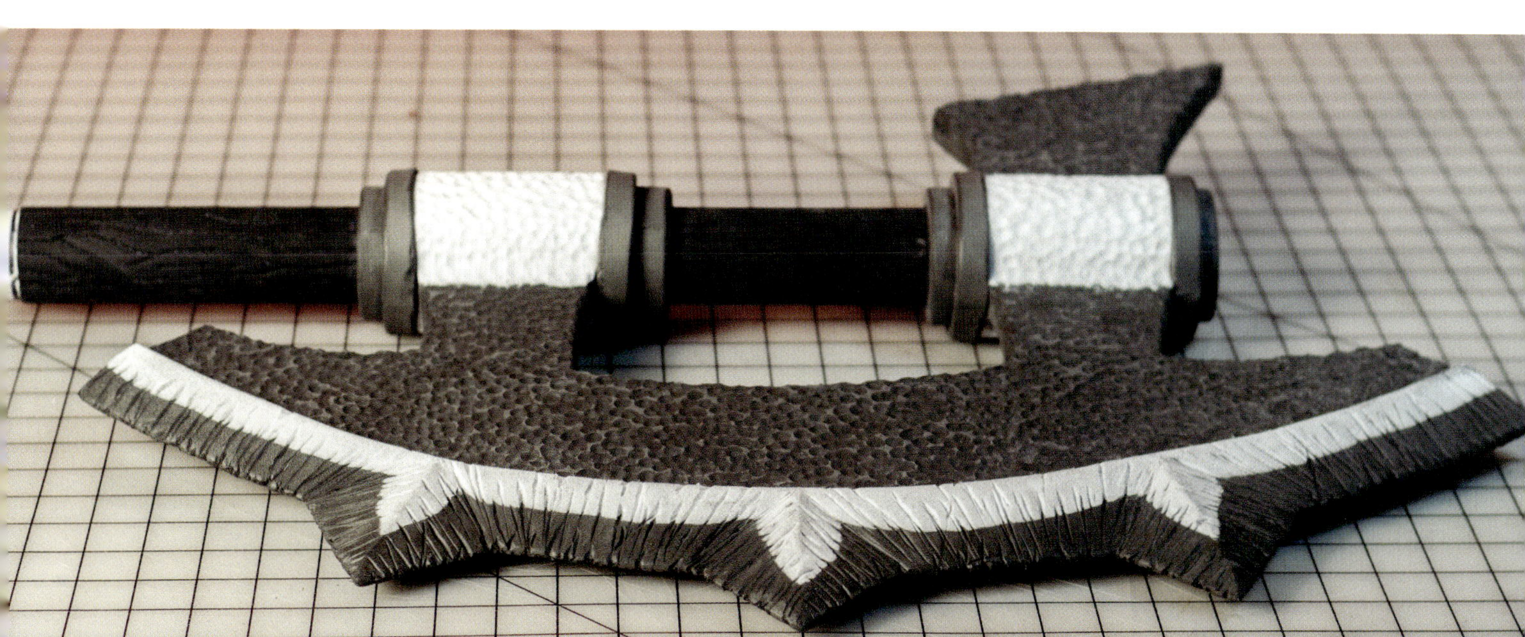

Sealing and Painting

With the construction completed, it was time to consider how I was going to finish this beast! I decided on sealing it with latex rubber to make it super durable. To make sealing and painting a breeze, I built a couple of stands from PVC pipe that my axe parts could rest on during the process. This kept the pieces safe from falling and the vertical angle made application easier.

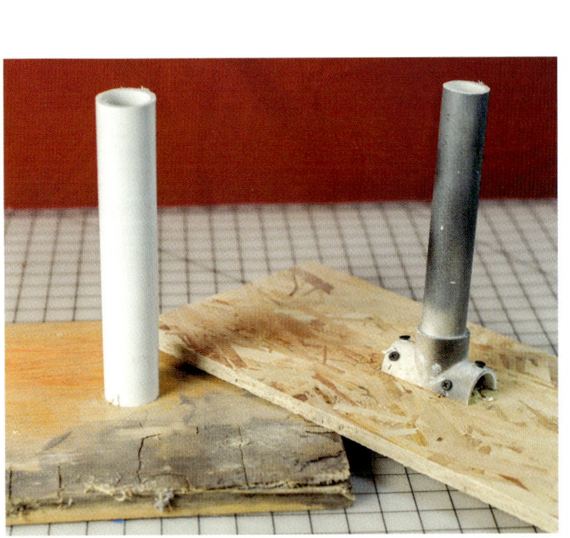

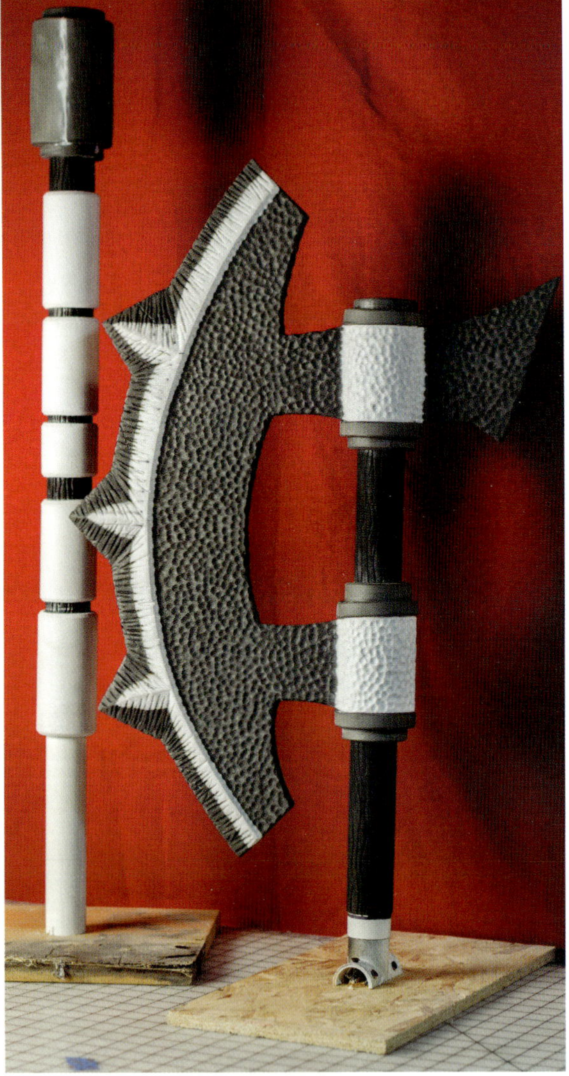

Build custom painting stands for large props.

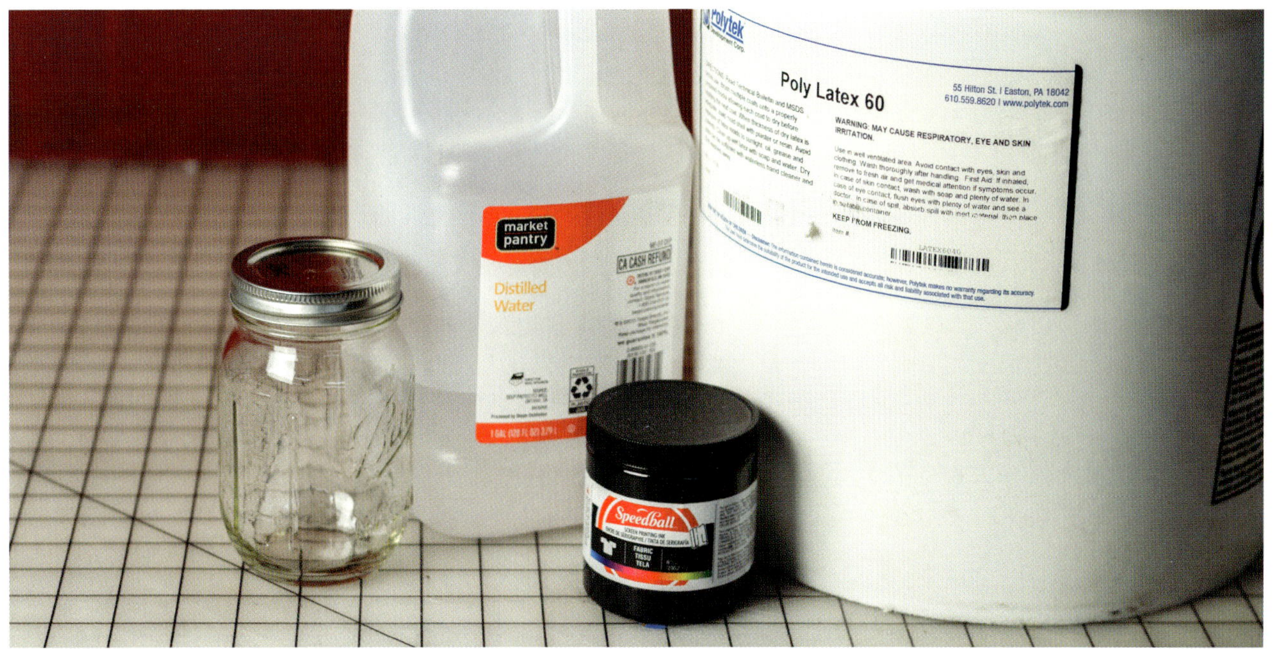

Most of the base coloring would be done in the latex. Some of the best pigment for that is acrylic based screen-printing inks, though any acrylic paint will do. Using a mason jar, I mixed up my latex rubber with distilled water and the pigment. The latex I use (Poly Latex 60) comes in a thick paste and I like to thin it 1:1 with distilled water for ease of spraying.

This latex dries transparent, so I didn't need to add much pigment. The ratio was maybe 20:1, water/latex mixture: pigment.

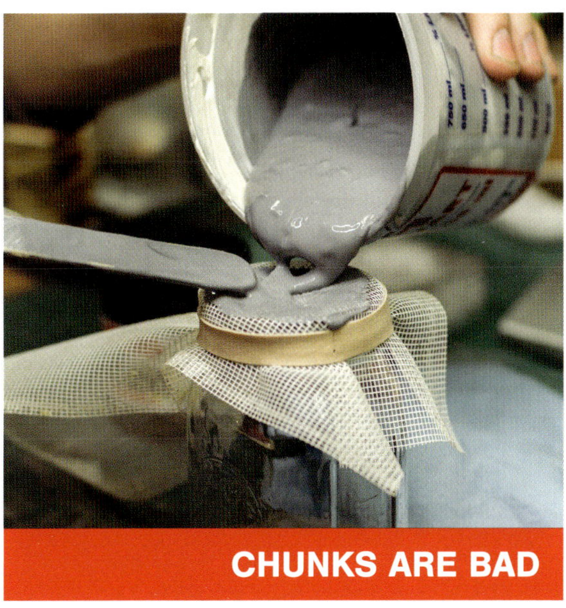

CHUNKS ARE BAD

I'll usually mix up the latex, water, and pigment in a small bucket and then strain it through mesh to remove any lumps. The mixture gets strained into a mason jar so I can attach it to my Critter sprayer and also cap it when not in use. For most of the base color, I mixed in a black pigment. It looks gray when it's wet, but the latex dries transparent, so it'll dry black.

Brush on Latex

I planned on applying many layers of latex and spraying is the easiest way to add lots of rubber, but I wanted to make sure the first couple layers got all the nooks and crannies. So, I used a chip brush to apply the first couple layers of black latex rubber to the axe head. When the latex turned black, I knew that layer was dry and I could brush on another. I did the same thing for the handle, but it was tinted with a silver acrylic paint.

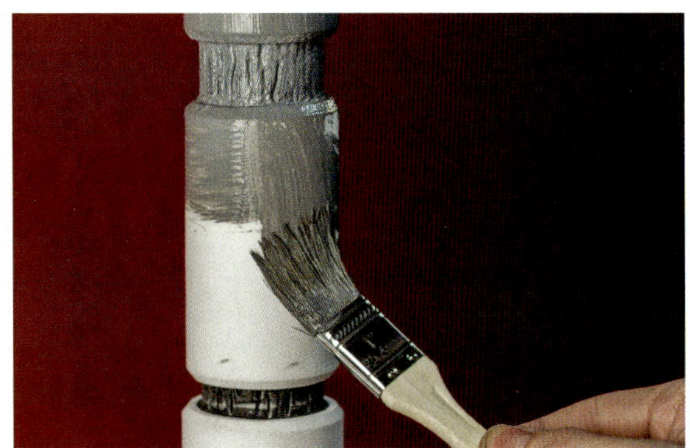

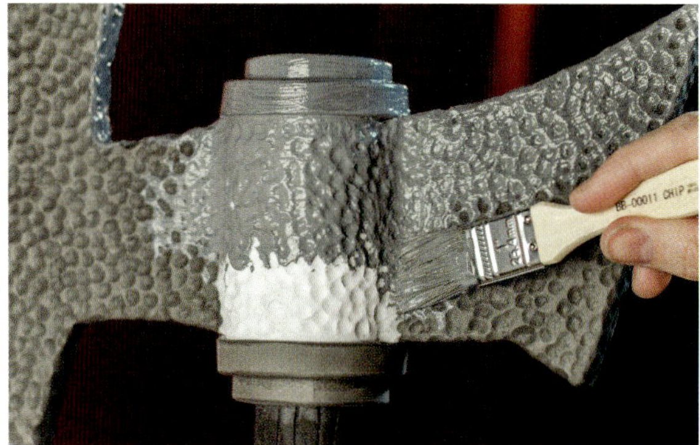

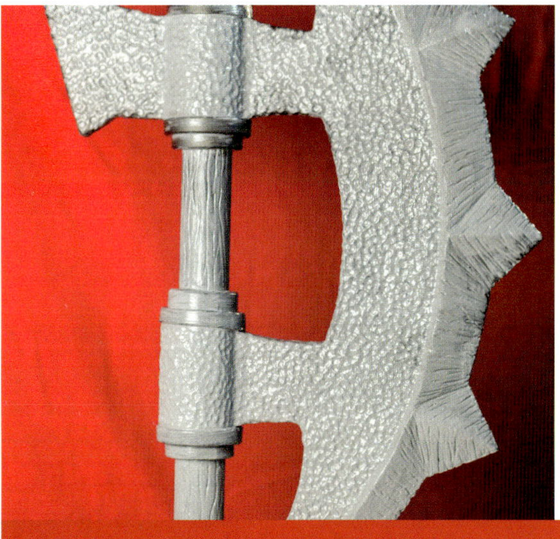

WET LATEX

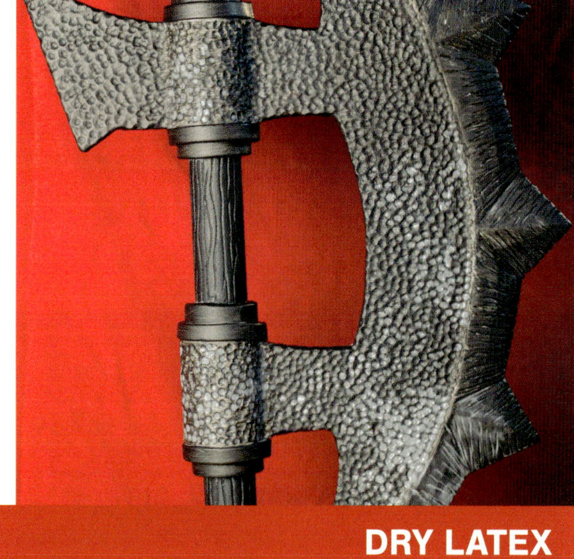

DRY LATEX

Spray on Latex

The remaining five layers of latex were applied using my Critter sprayer with an air compressor. The Critter attaches to mason jars, so I used the same jars I used to mix my pigmented latex. With the right tools, the process couldn't be easier. I simply sprayed on a light layer of latex, let it dry for about an hour, then sprayed on the next. I focused on getting good coverage without applying too much of the liquid, so as to create drips.

Wood Color

After two brushed and five sprayed layers, the axe was perfectly sealed and base colored! All that I had to do next was add the rest of the detail colors.

I mixed up a batch of brown latex to simulate the wood colors on the axe. The easiest way to apply the brown to specific areas was with a smaller brush. This was especially necessary for the "wooden" areas between the "metal" bands on the handle. It took two or three brushed on layers to obscure the color below.

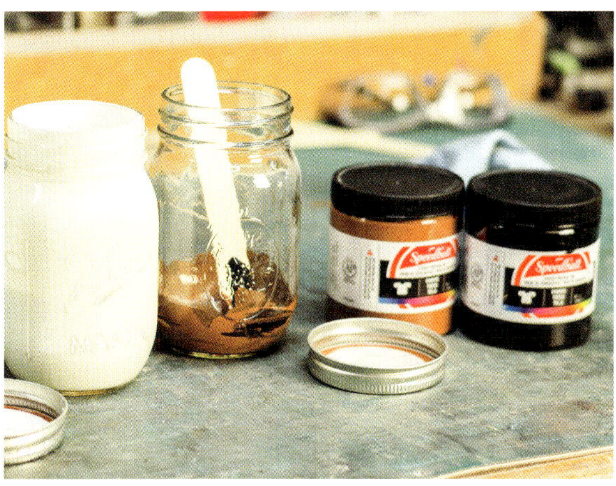

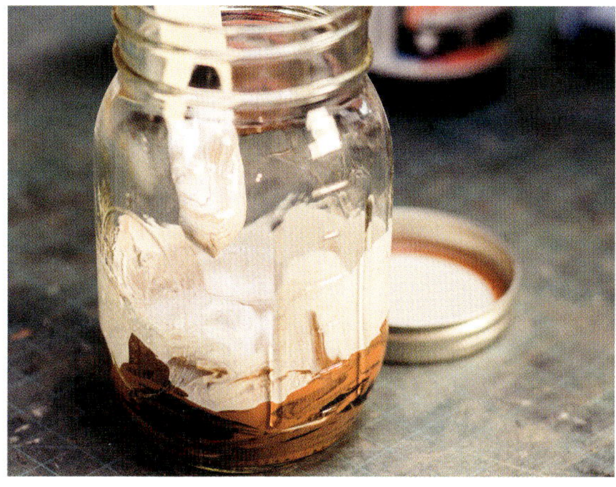

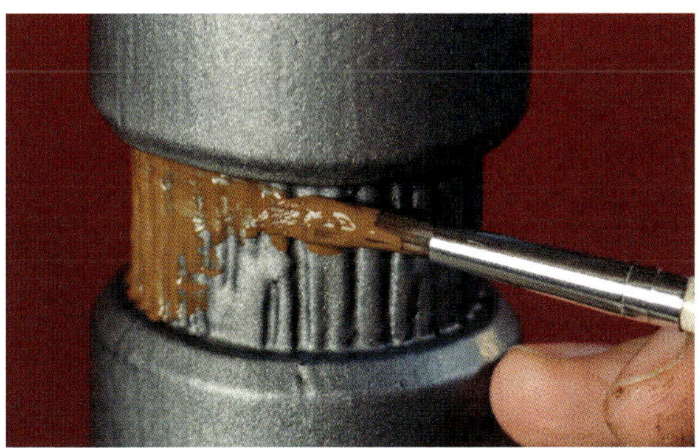

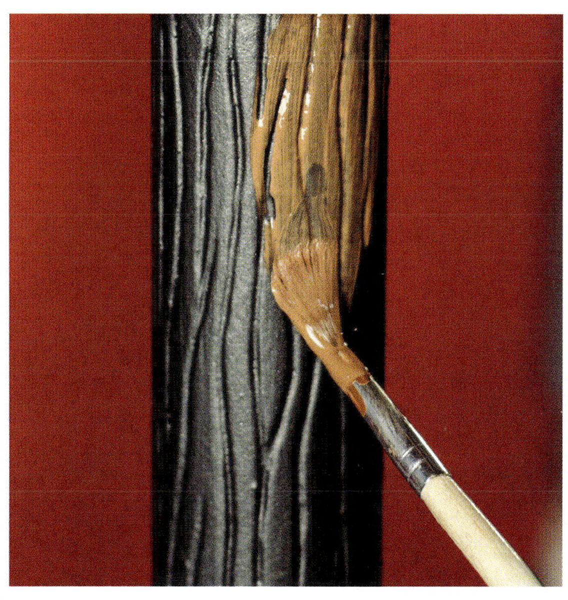

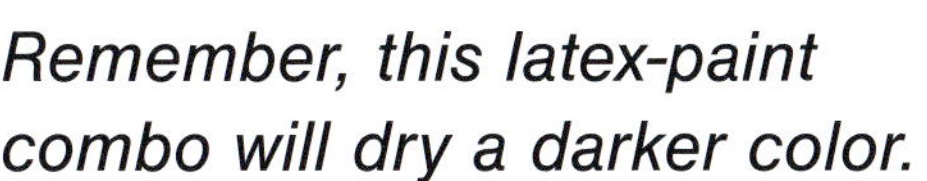

Remember, this latex-paint combo will dry a darker color.

Dry Brush Silver

In between waiting for layers of brown to dry, I added silver highlights to the rest of the axe. For this, I just used a silver acrylic paint with no latex. I went with a heavy dry brush technique using a chip brush. I didn't want to completely cover the black or gray colors below, so I just grazed the high spots with the silver paint, creating some good contrast. This contrast adds some really nice depth to the axe head, showcasing all of that texture work and helping pull off the hammered metal finish.

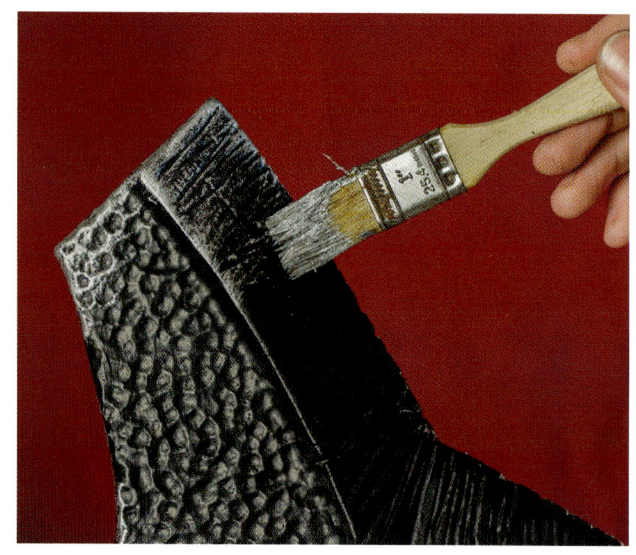

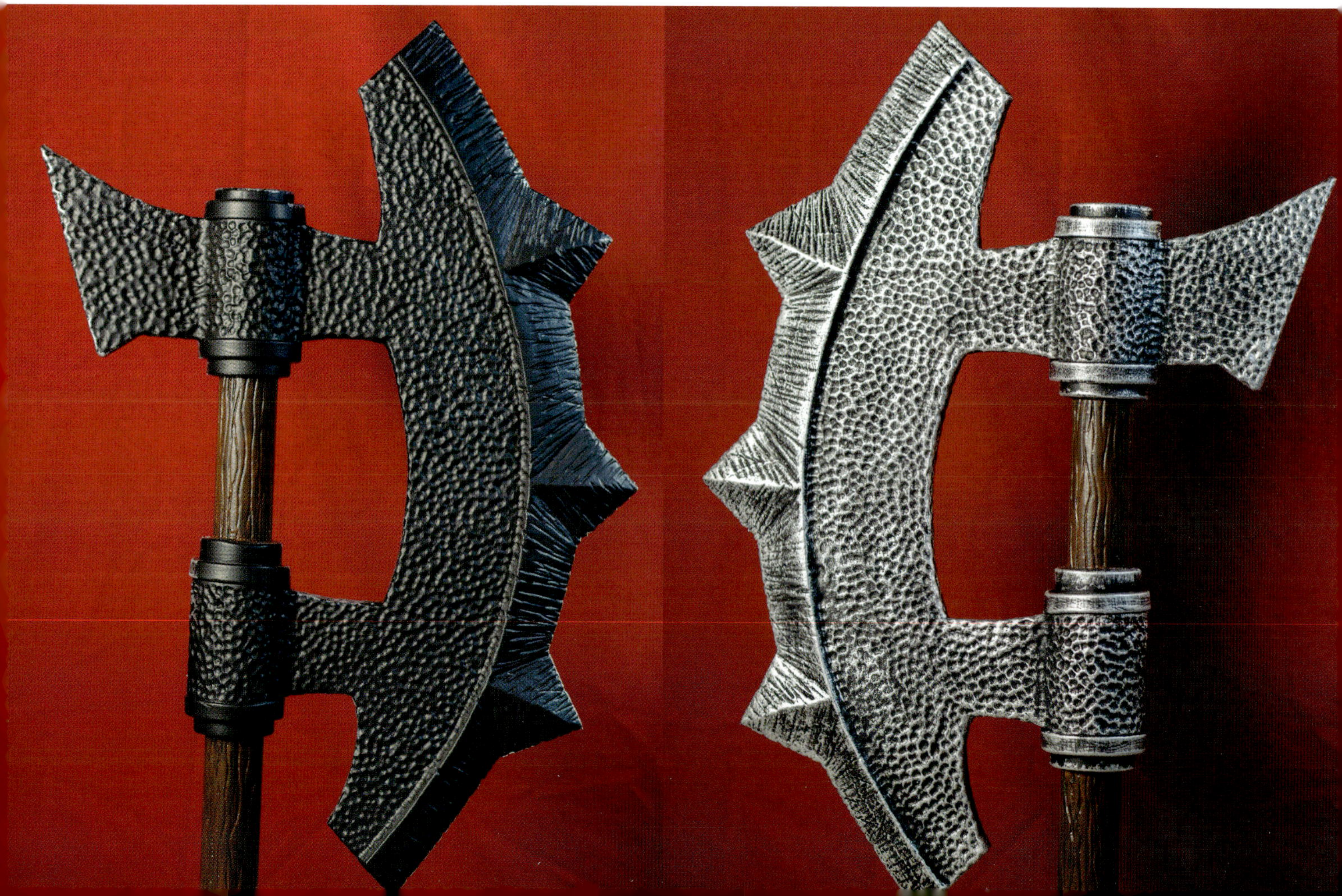

Prevent Latex Peel

I didn't want the latex to peel off the PVC pipe where it connected the two pieces of the axe together, so I had to glue it down. To do this, I trimmed the edge of the latex off, leaving a nice clean edge between the PVC and the latex rubber. Then I glued down a strip of leather with contact cement, overlapping both the plastic pipe and the rubber. This will keep the rubber from peeling off. I did the same thing for both the axe head and inside the PVC coupler on the handle.

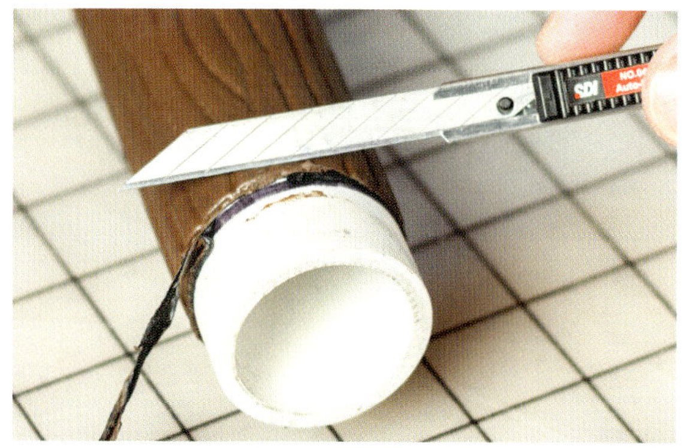

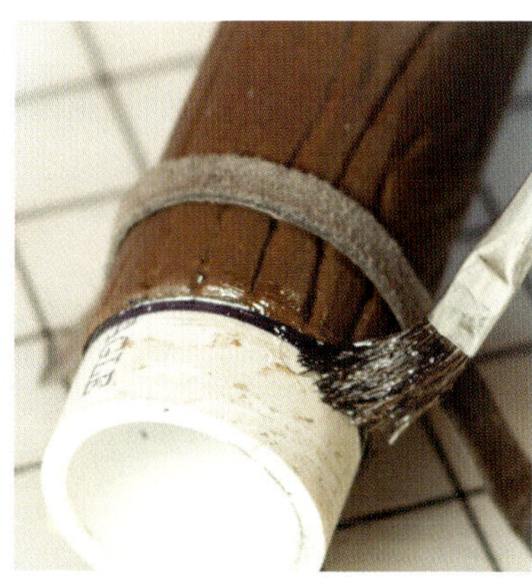

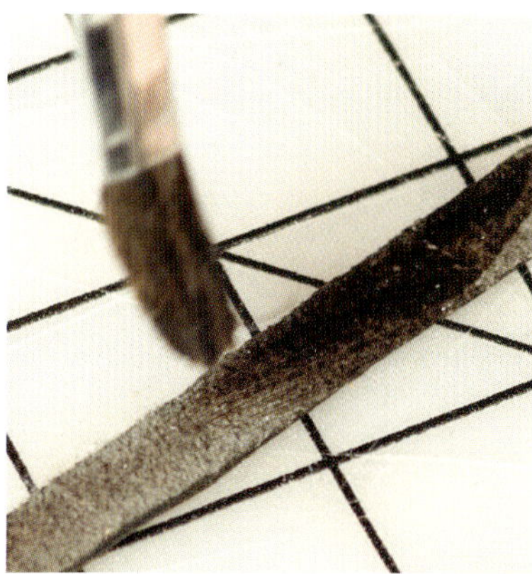

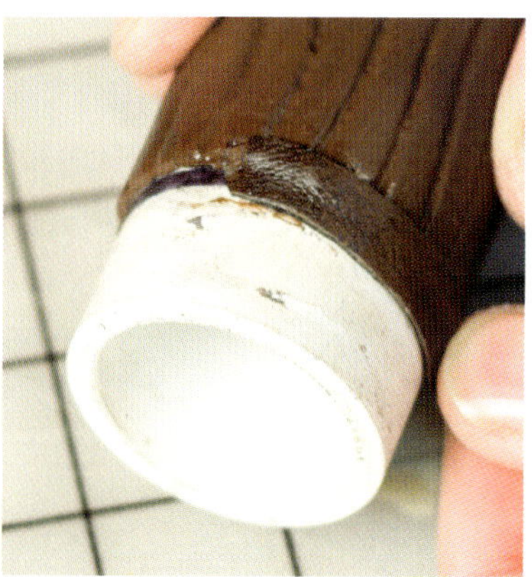

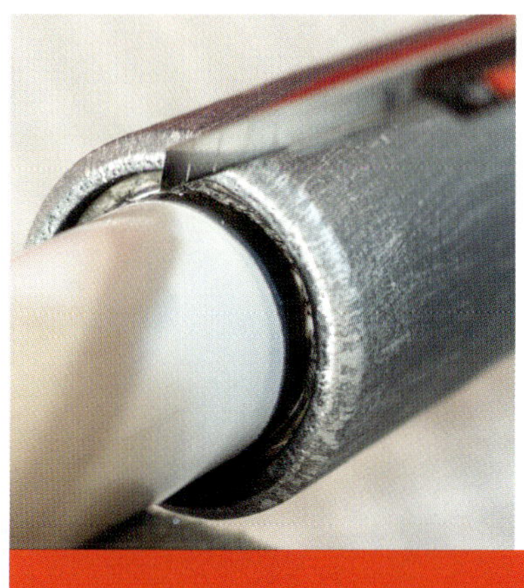

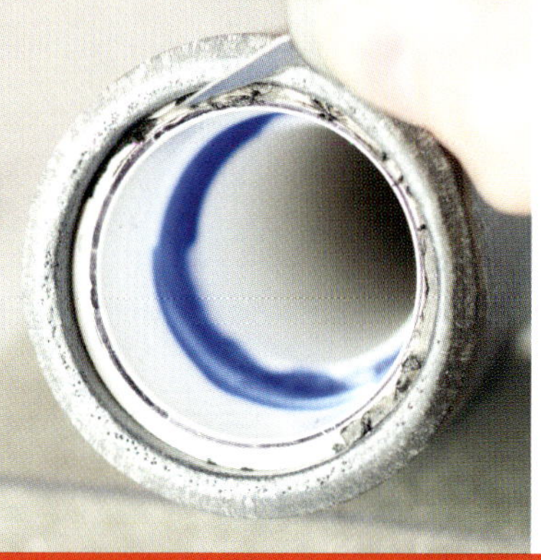

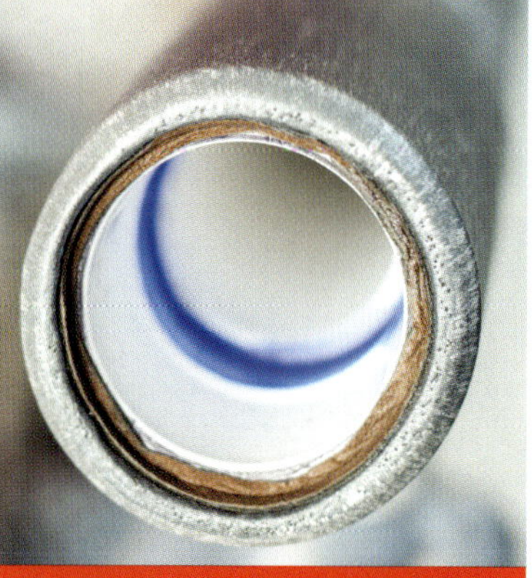

LATEX PEELING? COVER THE EDGE.

Weathering

The last thing I needed to do to really sell the look of this axe was to weather it a bit. I really wanted it to look dirty and a little rusty. So I mixed up some acrylic brown, black, and burnt sienna paints and started messing it up.

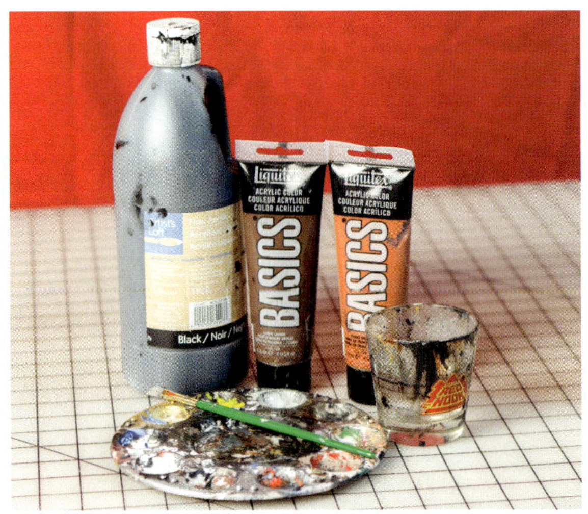

The weathering process for this build was fairly straight forward. I would brush a bunch of my dirty looking paints into the crevasses on the axe and then wipe most of the paint away, leaving some "grime" behind.

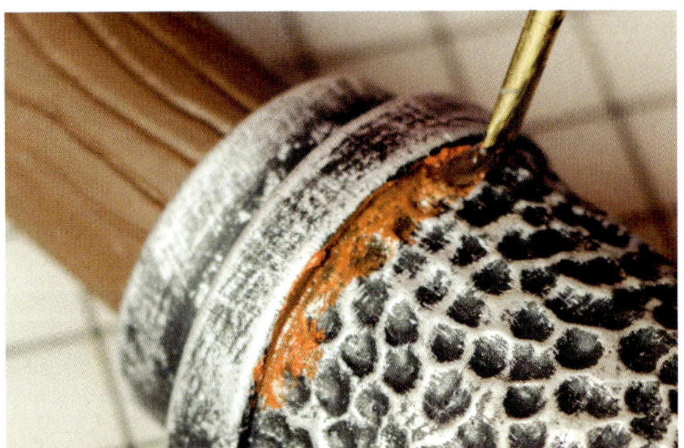

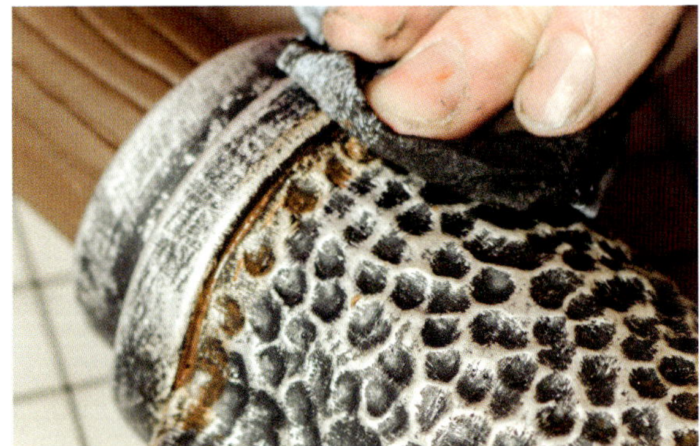

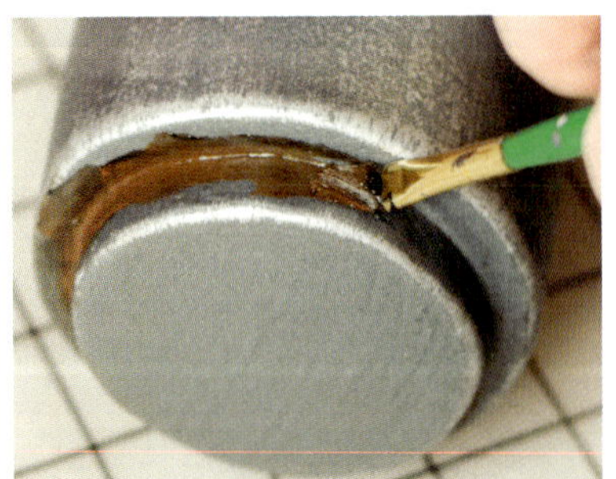

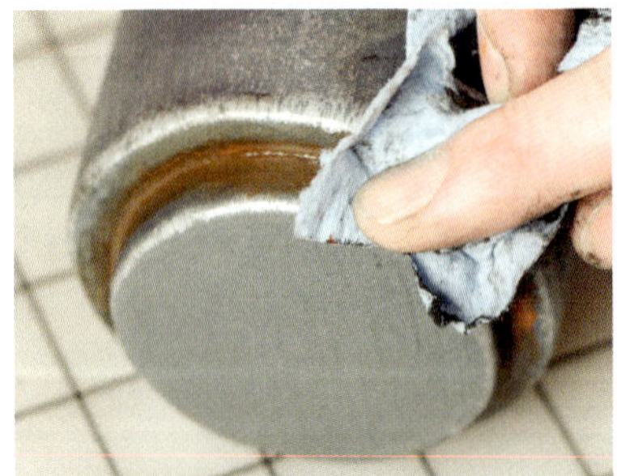

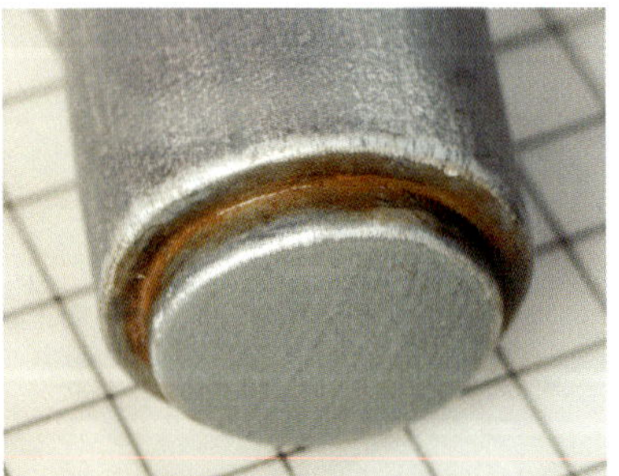

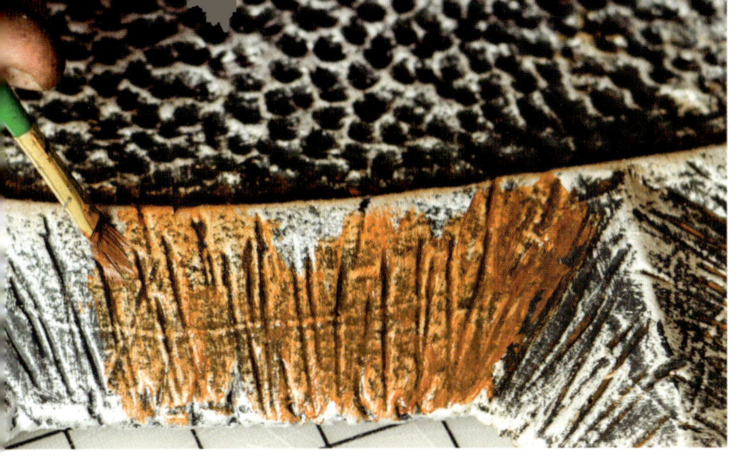

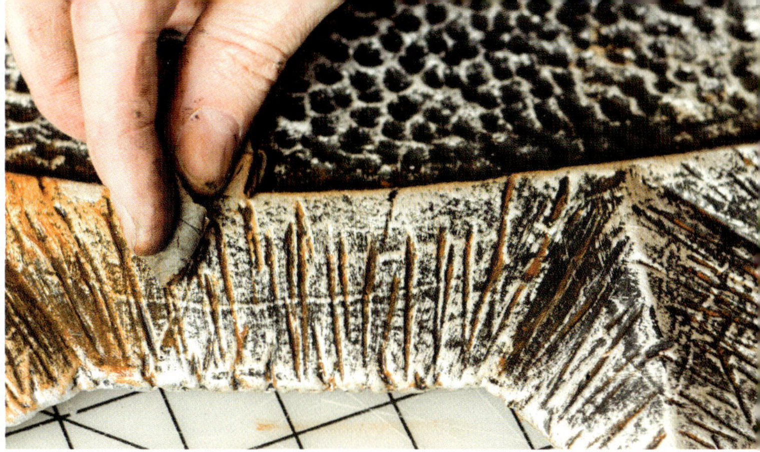

On some of the "wooden" handle spots, my black paint darkened the raised areas a little bit more than I wanted. So, I used some lacquer thinner and a paper towel to wipe the black paint off of the high areas, leaving it in the deeper wood grain. Since the brown pigment was mixed into the rubber, the lacquer thinner did not take the color off, like it did with the black.

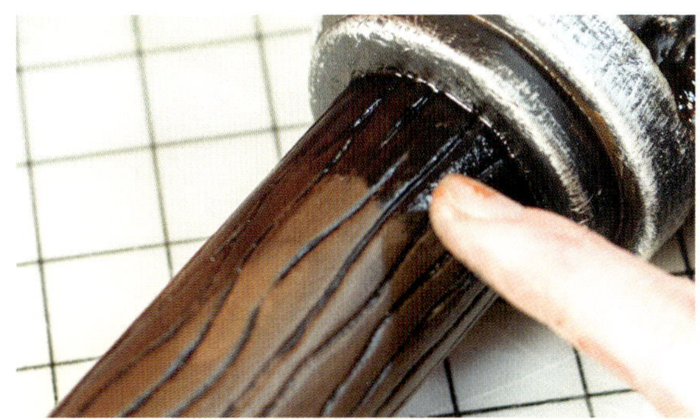

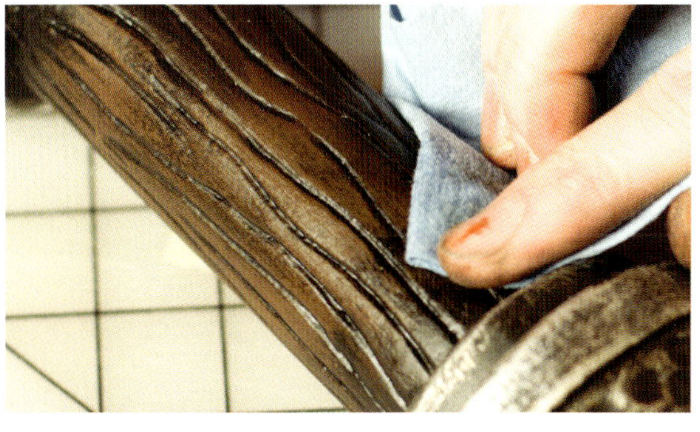

Seal with Varnish

After several passes of weathering paint, the axe was finally done! To seal in all of my hard work I sprayed on a couple layers of matte varnish.

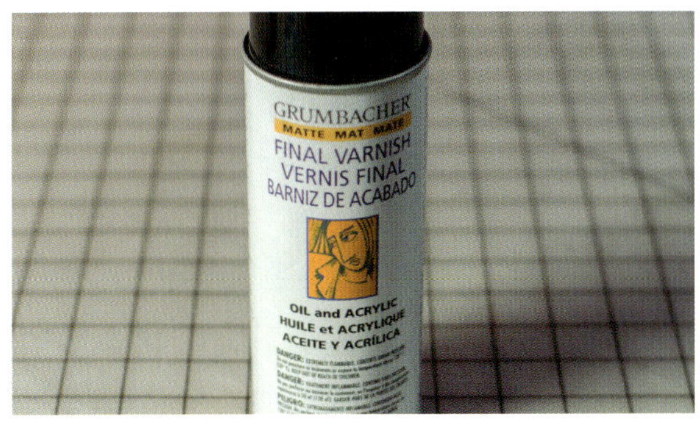

Don't spray on varnish right before the convention! The smell of varnish takes a few days to dissipate.

This axe was a really fun project! I took it to BlizzCon to use with my Crusader costume and it performed marvelously. Not only was it lightweight and durable, but it also traveled very well to and from Anaheim! Good on you, Mr. Ripper Axe. Welcome to my arsenal.

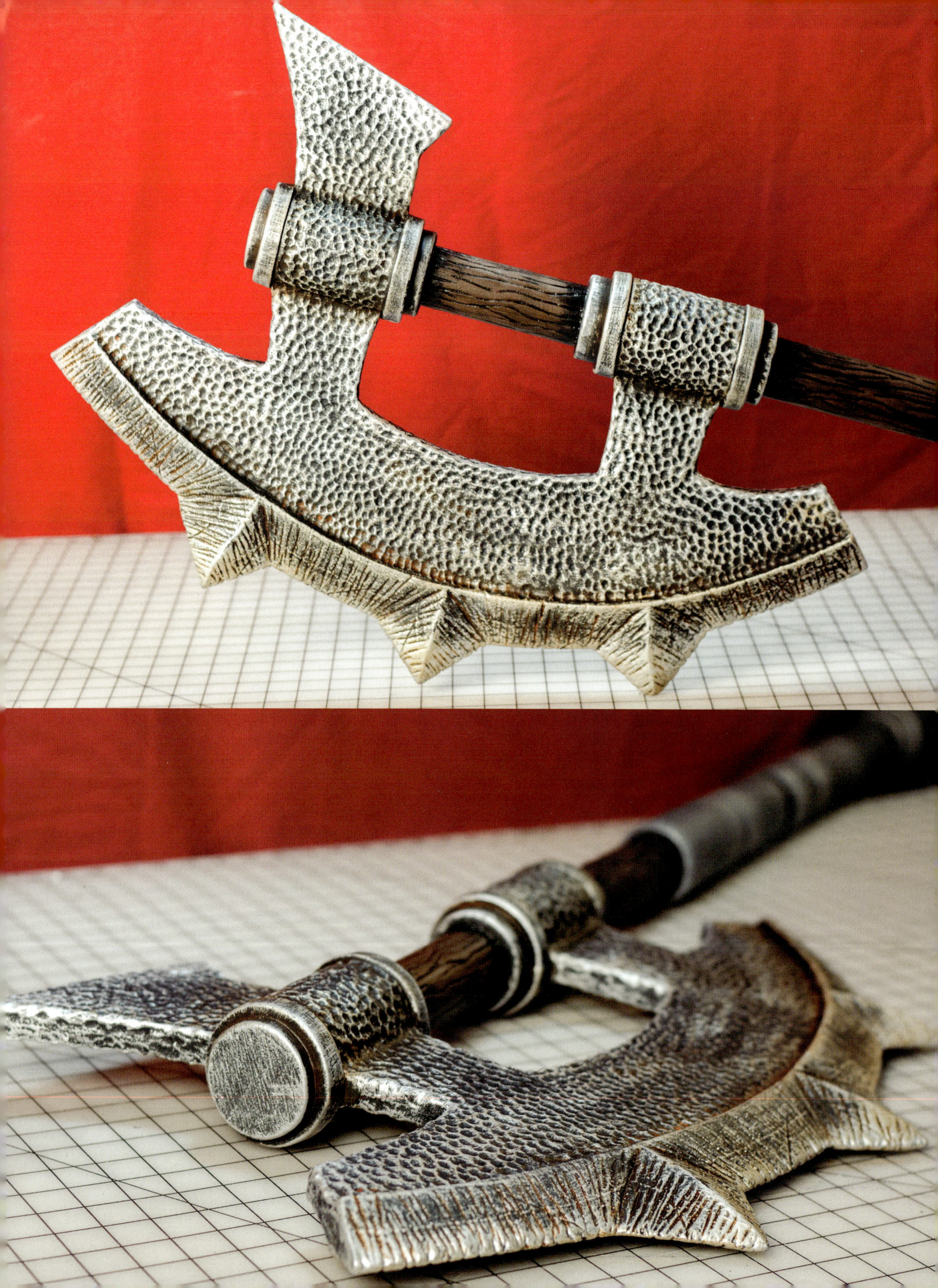

Part 3
Foam Space Gun

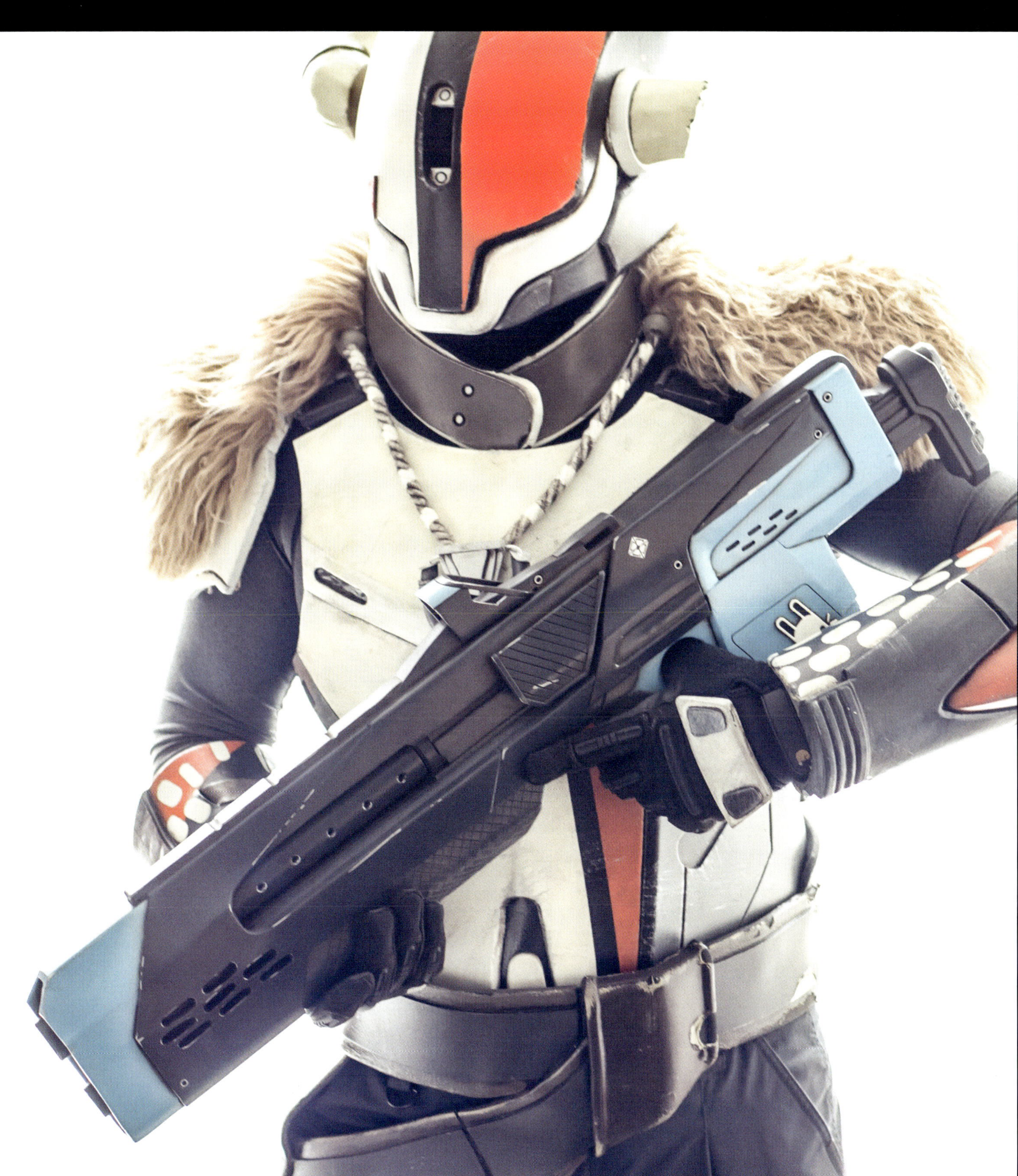

Foamsmith Weapon Build Example:
Destiny Jade Rabbit Scout Rifle

Materials

- ½" Thick Foam Floor Mats
- 6mm Craft Foam Sheets
- 2mm Craft Foam Roll
- PVC Pipe
- PVC Foam (Sintra)
- Barge Cement
- Krylon Fusion Spray Paint
- Acrylic Paint
- Water Mixable Oil Paint

Template

http://punishedprops.com/foamsmith2

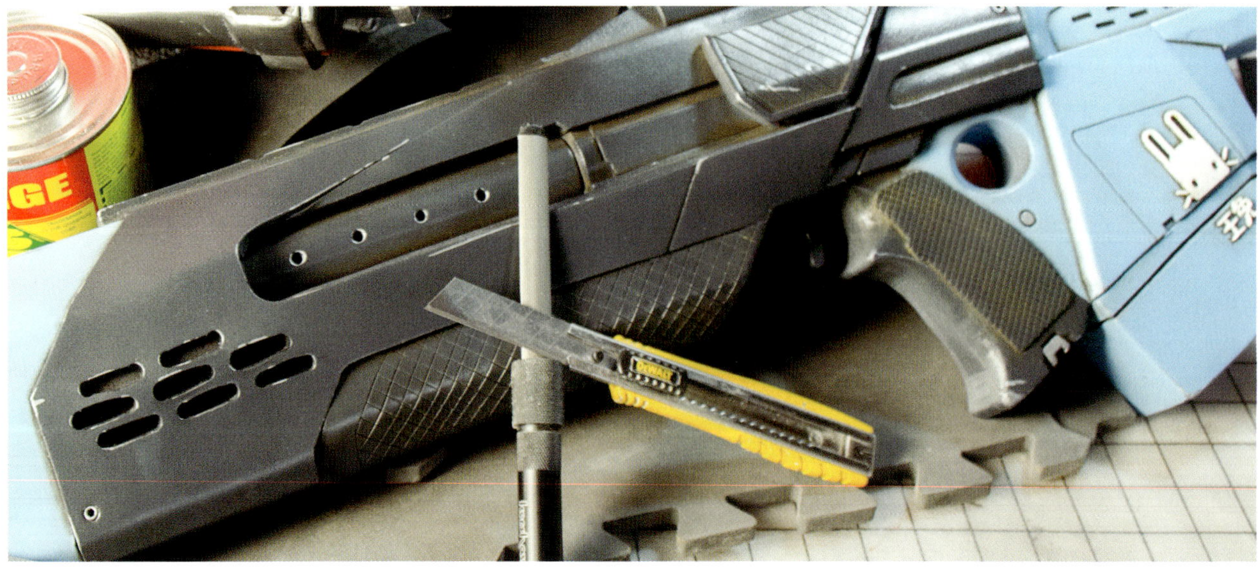

Gun Template

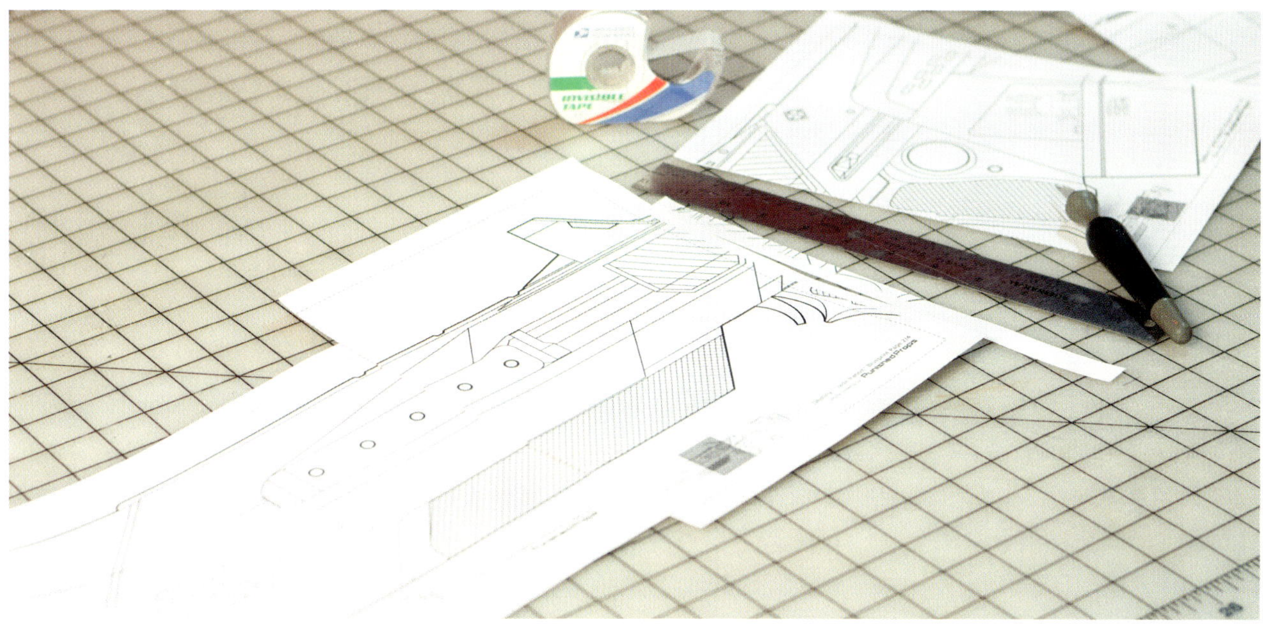

Just like the axe, I printed out all my template files on thick card stock and taped them all together. I actually ended up printing out two copies of the blueprint because the first one had to be cut up a whole lot in the first step of the build. I trimmed out all the gun parts, taking care to remove some of the parts that would be built separately, like the stock and the magazine.

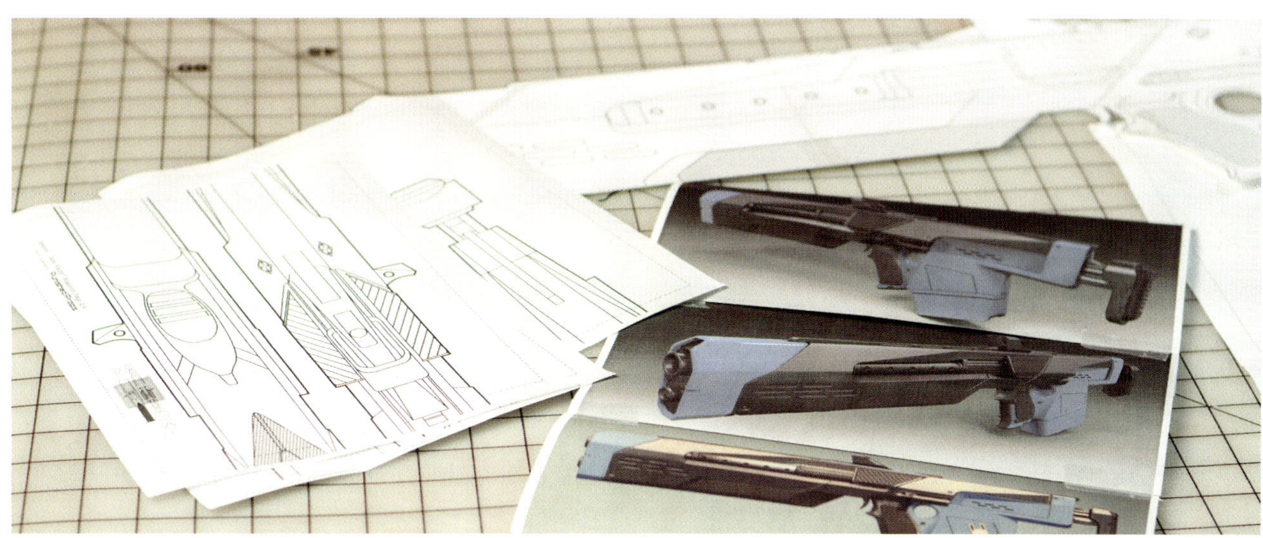

Base and Structure

Adding Structure

Next I needed to figure out the internal structure for the rifle. I used a couple of PVC pipes that would run the length of the gun, sticking out the front as the top barrel. It would provide both mechanical and aesthetic functions. The plan was to make one large middle layer of foam that I could embed the PVC pipes in.

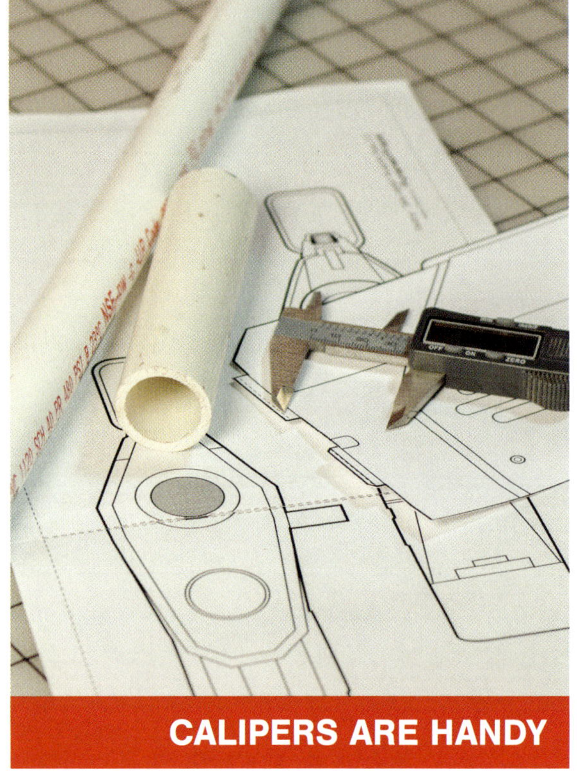

CALIPERS ARE HANDY

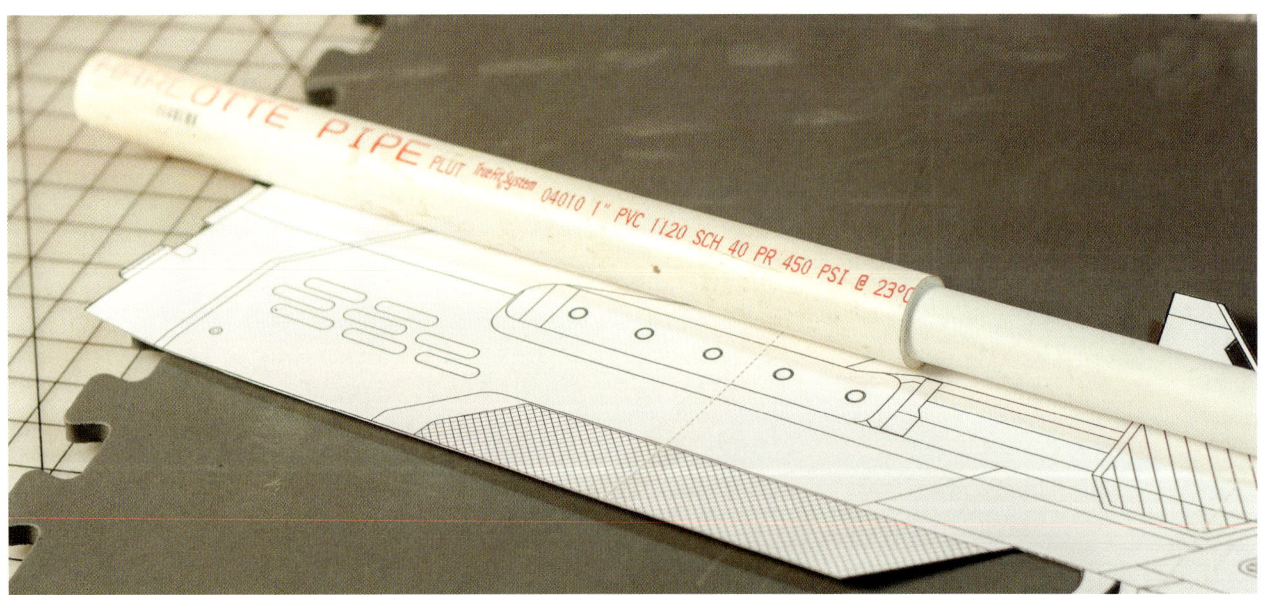

With the pipe location squared away, I could cut up my foam to shape. After figuring out the thickness of the gun, I settled on making the main body part from four pieces of foam sandwiched together. I rough cut several sheets of floor mat and used my belt sander to remove the texture from one side.

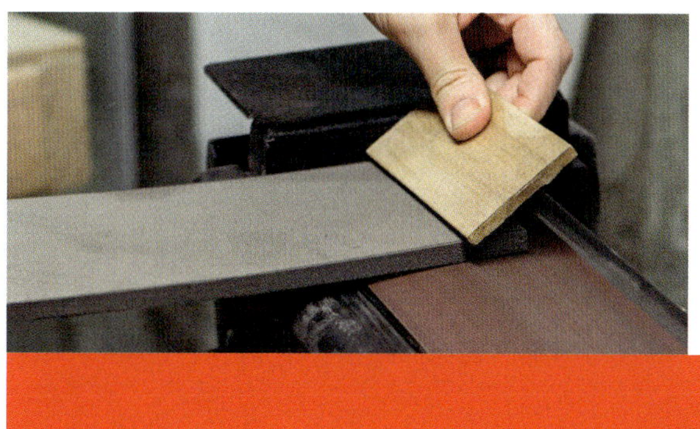

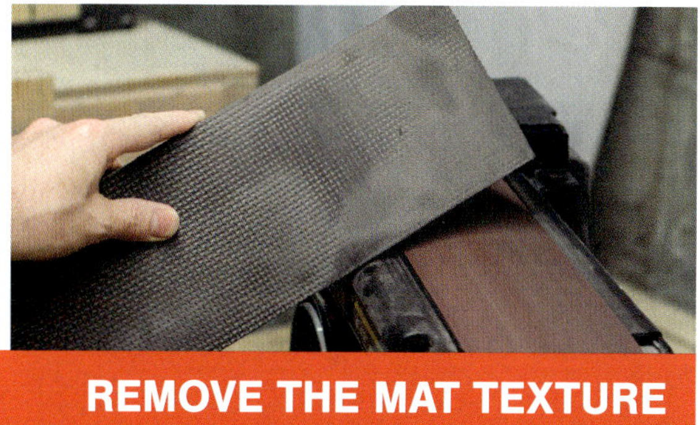

REMOVE THE MAT TEXTURE

Foam Layers

Then I was free to glue all four layers together using contact cement. My container of Barge was getting old and gooey, so I mixed in some Barge Thinner to make the goo easier to spread.

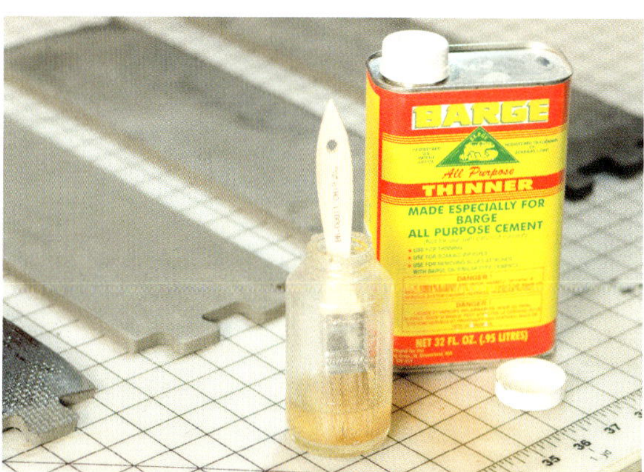

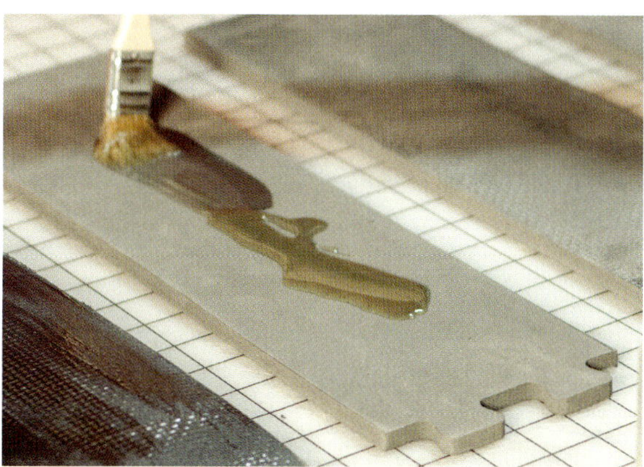

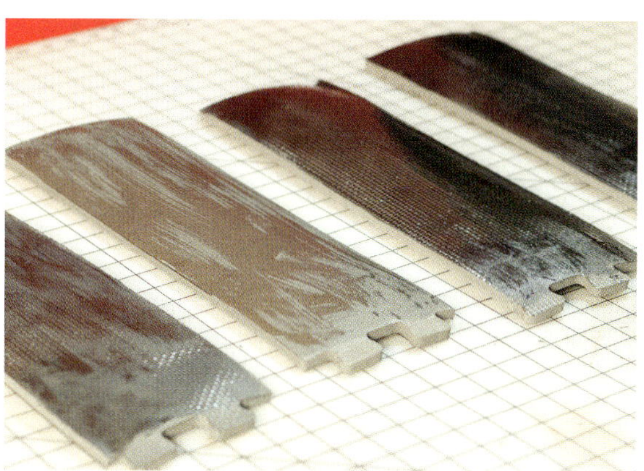

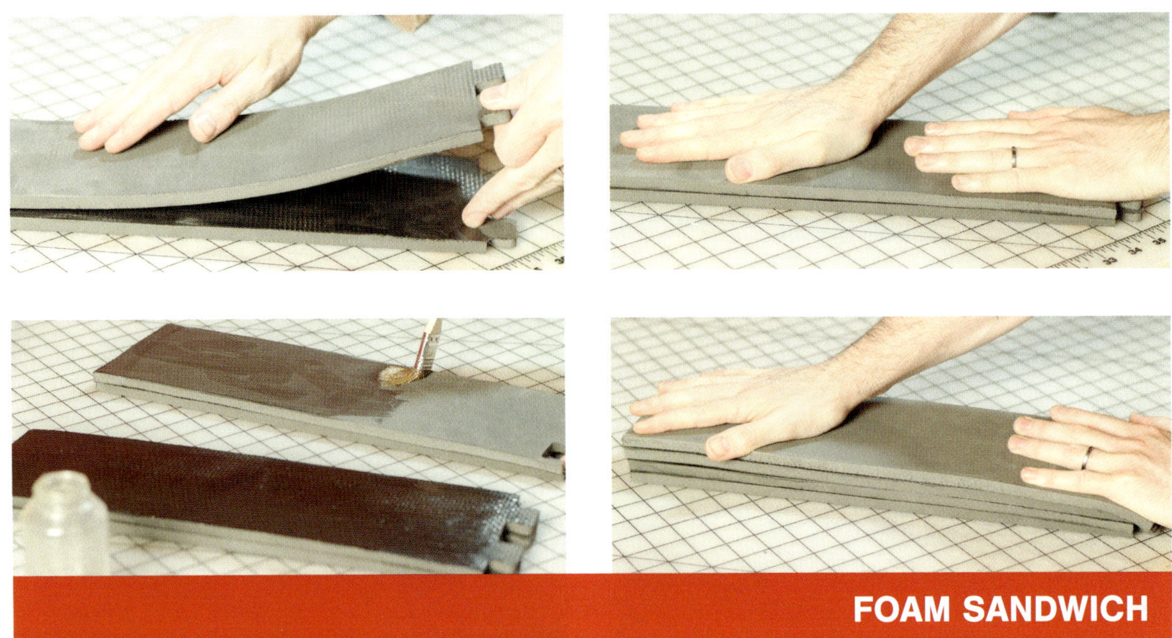

FOAM SANDWICH

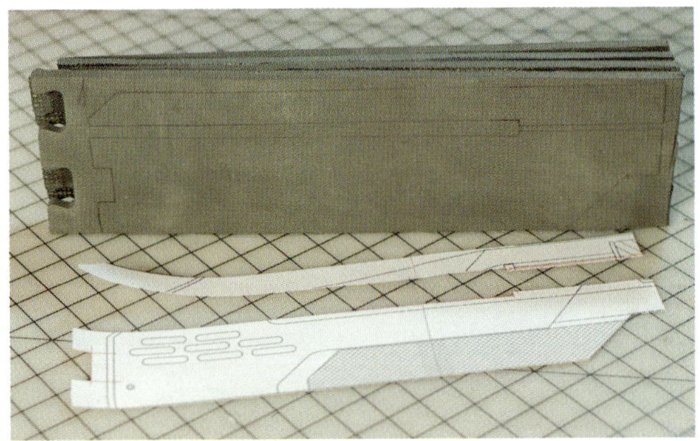

With my delicious foam sandwiches prepared, I traced out all of the main body shapes onto them and got to cutting. This is where it really paid to have both a band saw and a scroll saw. The machines made quick work of the foam and I was able to rapidly prepare to attach the PVC structure.

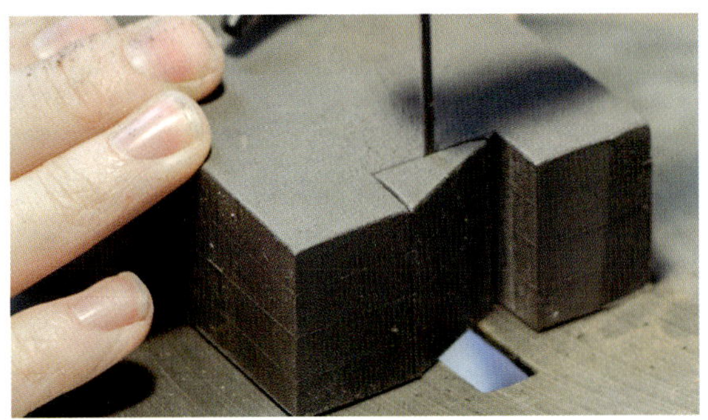

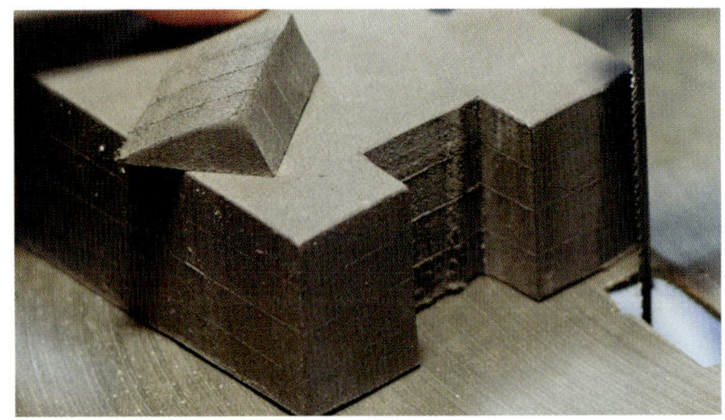

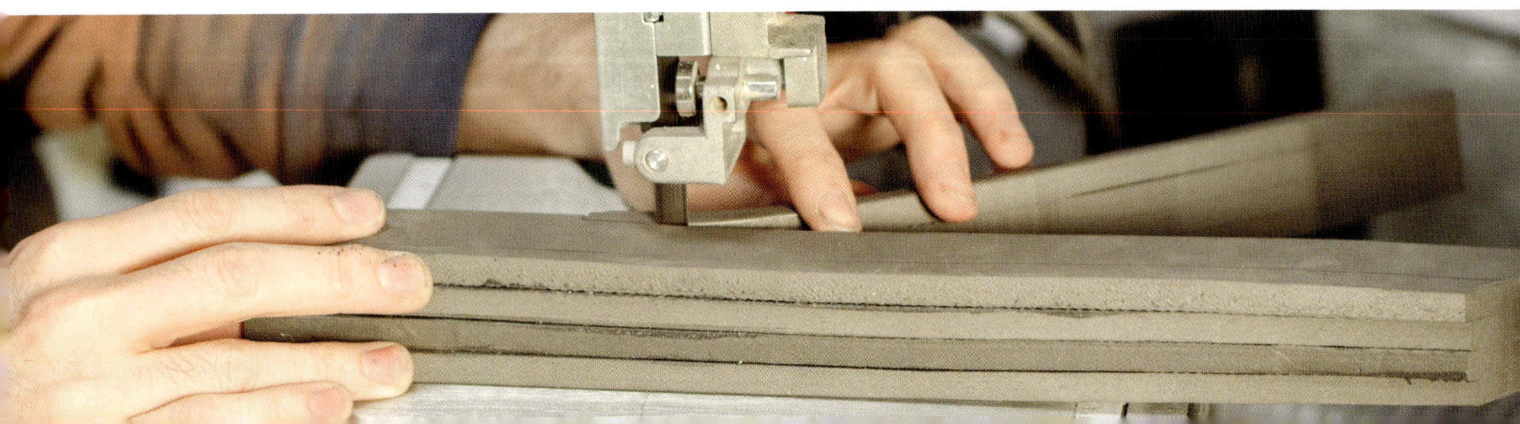

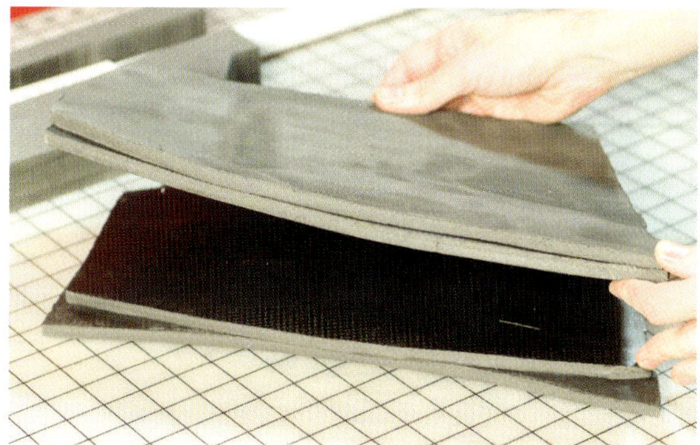

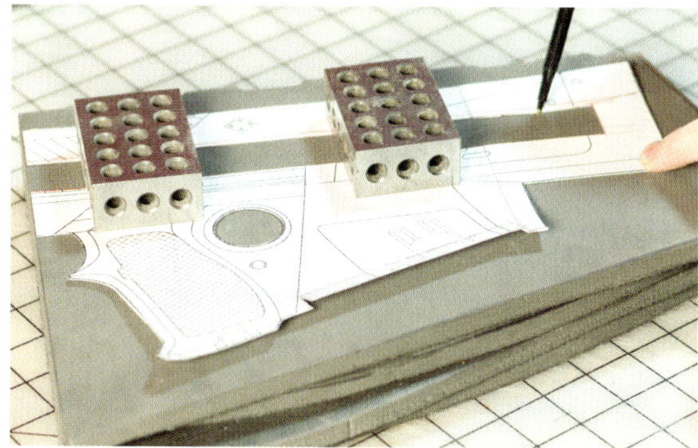

More Layers

The main part of the gun had to be made from two main sections since my floor mat foam wasn't long enough to accommodate the gun length. So, the same thing was done for the rear of the gun. The main difference with this piece was the thumb hole, which I made using the drill press and a forstner bit.

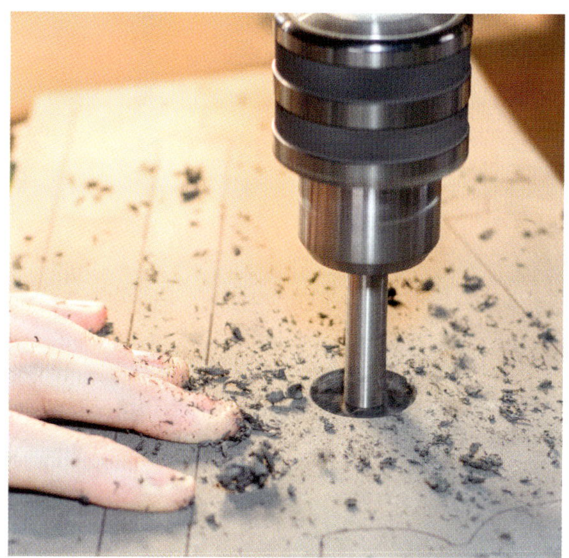

While these parts were cut out with mechanical means, I still went in with a belt sander to clean up any reachable surfaces to get it looking clean. When I was happy with the finish, I glued the front and back parts of the gun together.

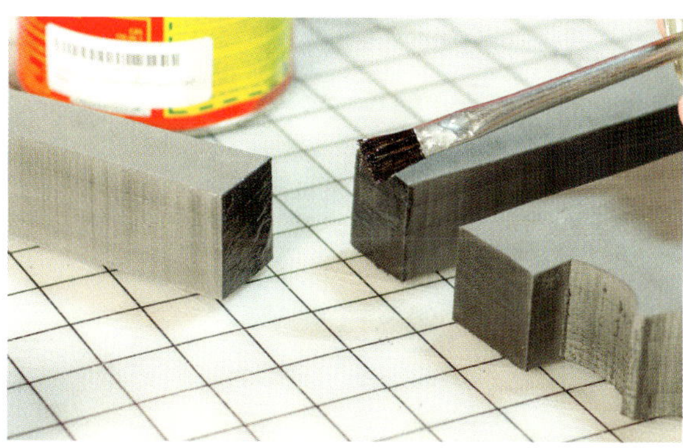

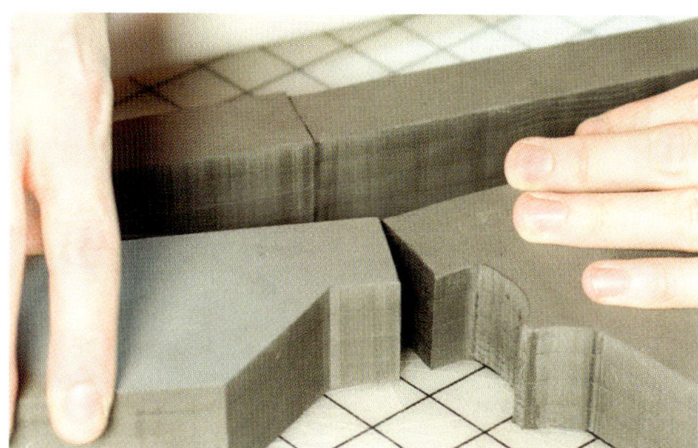

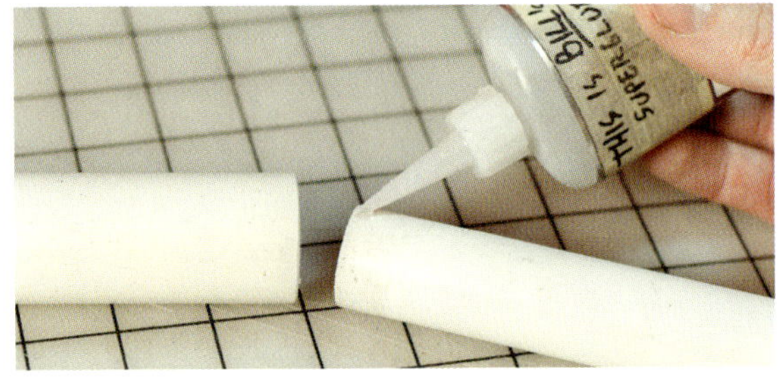

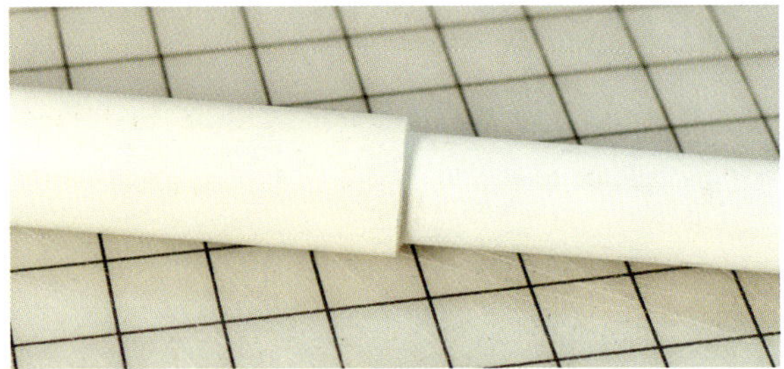

Adding Supports

The thicknesses of pipes snugged into one another, so I glued them together using super glue. I did this before cutting each piece to length so that I could figure out the distances after the glue had dried. Once I knew where I planned to place the pipe inside the structure of the gun, I cut it to length on the band saw and cleaned it up on the disc sander.

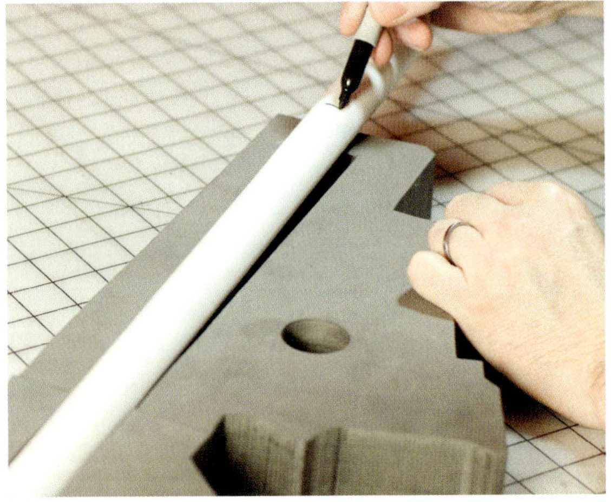

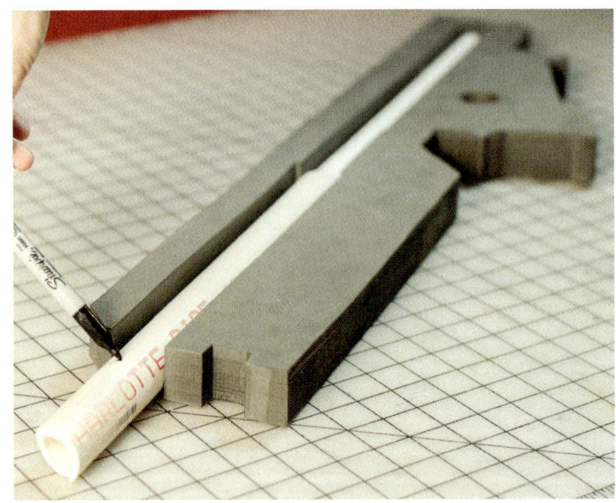

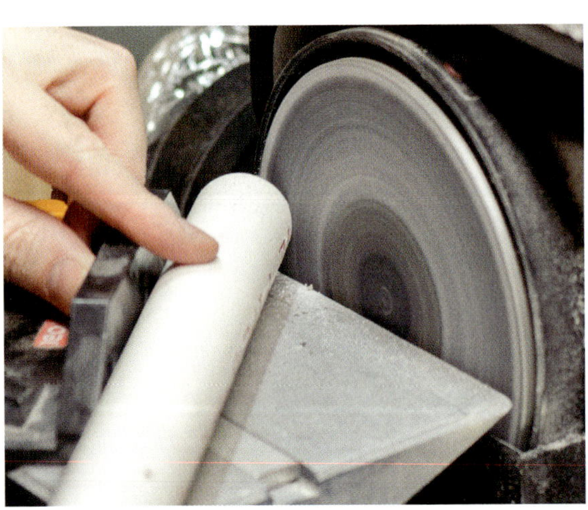

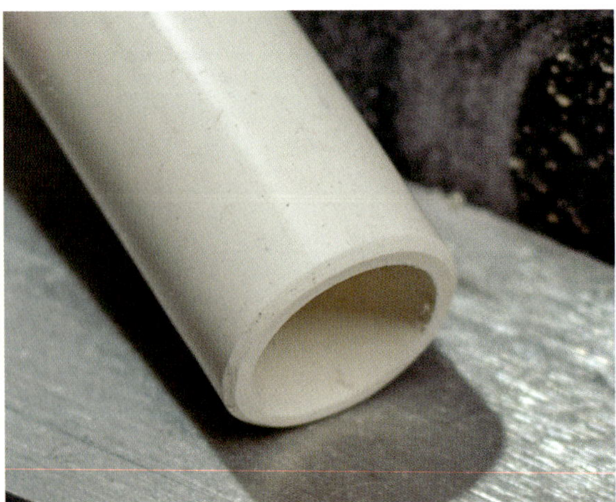

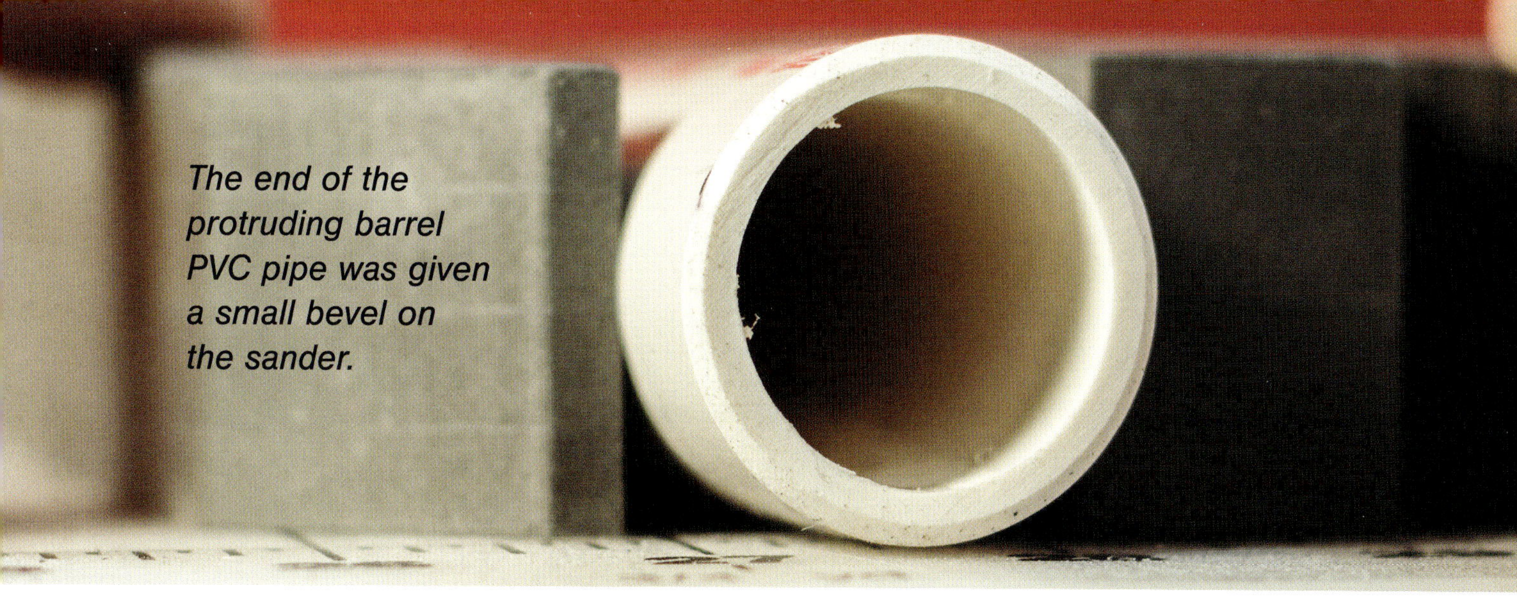

The end of the protruding barrel PVC pipe was given a small bevel on the sander.

Exposed Holes

The exposed portion of the barrel along the side of the gun has several holes drilled into it. Using my template, I marked the hole locations in the PVC using an awl. Then I was able to drill out the holes using the drill press and a clamp.

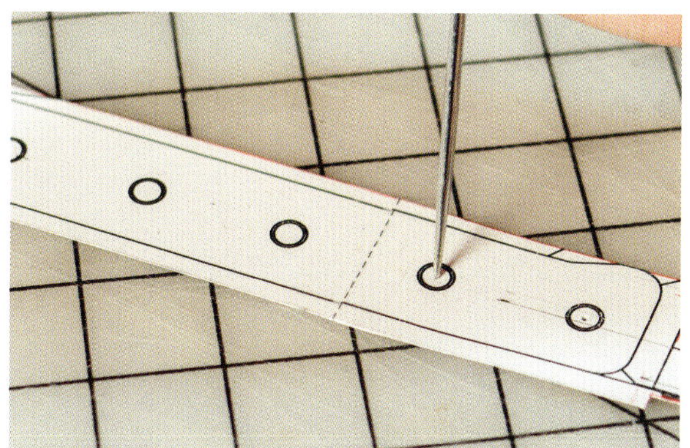

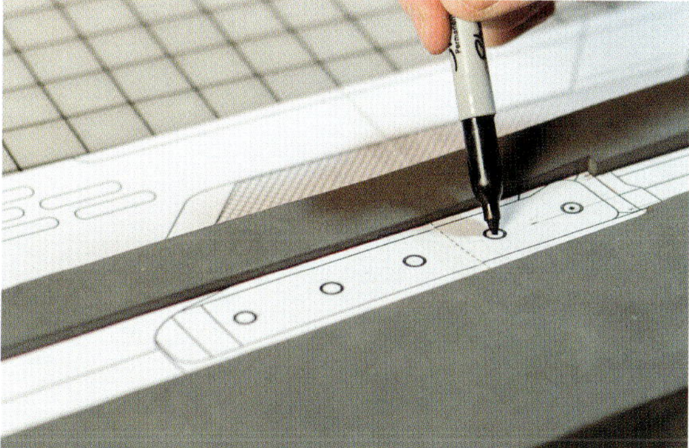

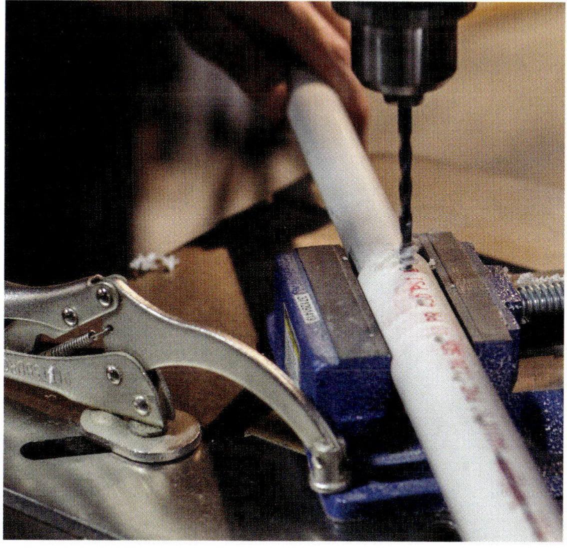

Use clamps on the drill press bed to prevent materials from catching and dangerously spinning into your hands.

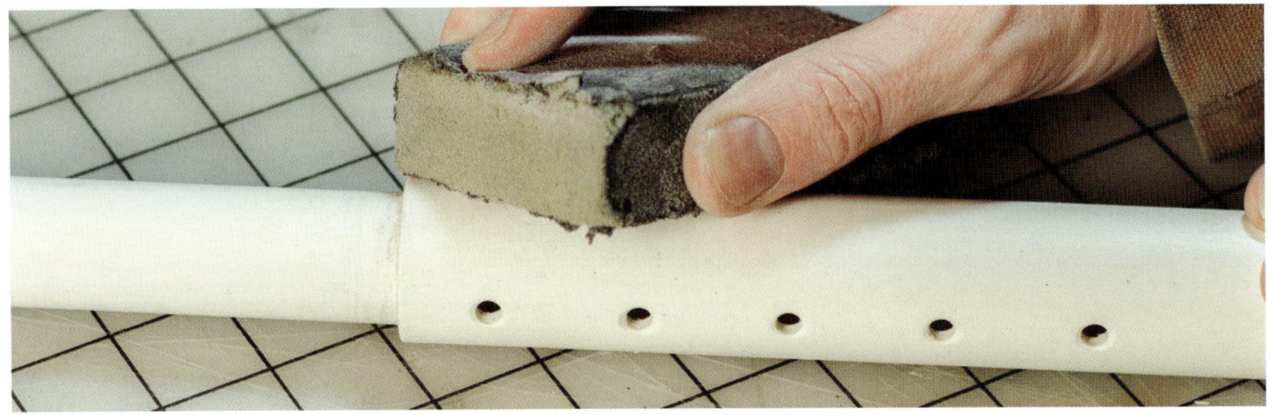

Hot Glue

With the bulk of the work done on the barrel PVC pipe, I hot glued it into the main foam portion of my gun body. I made sure to only put glue in areas where it would later be covered by further layers of foam. For the areas that would be obscured, I went hot glue crazy! I didn't want this thing falling apart at such an important structural component.

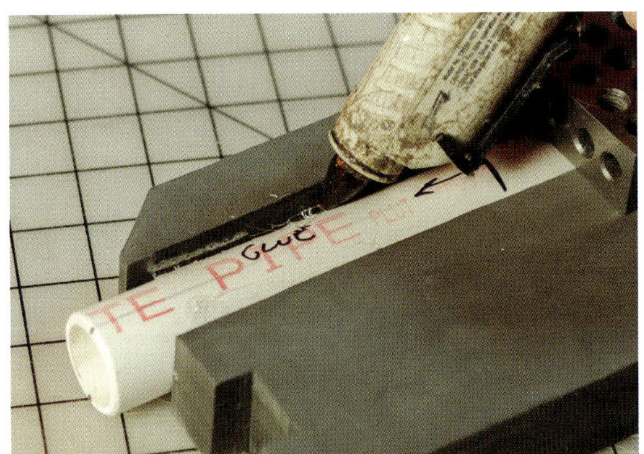

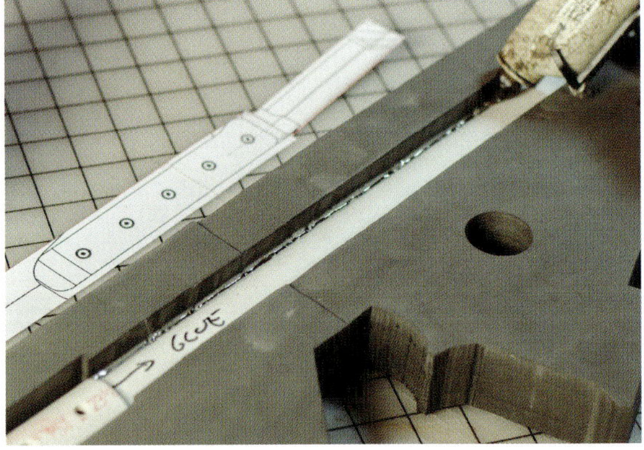

The hot glue was applied to both sides of the PVC pipe and gun. I also cut out a smaller section of pipe to serve as the lower barrel. This tiny fella was hot glued in place too.

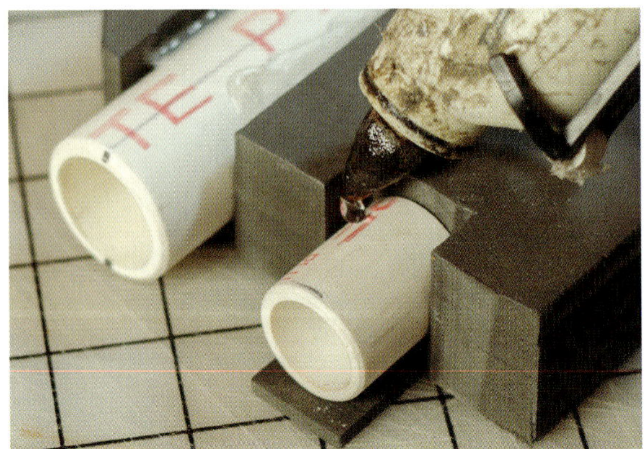

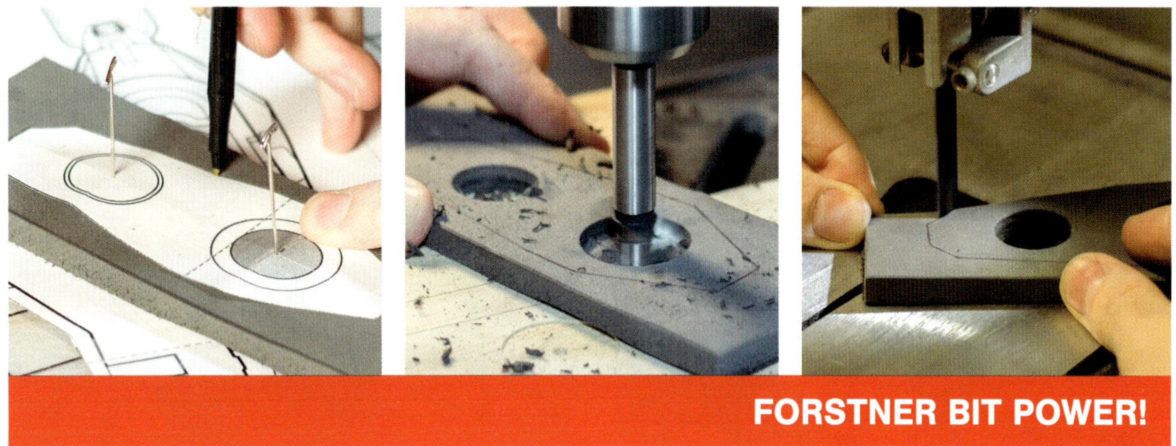

Cover Your Front Bits

To clean up the front barrel area, I drilled and cut out a panel that would attach to the front of the gun. This panel had a small bevel at the top, so before I glued it in place, I cut out a valley behind the bevel so that the foam could be folded back a tiny bit.

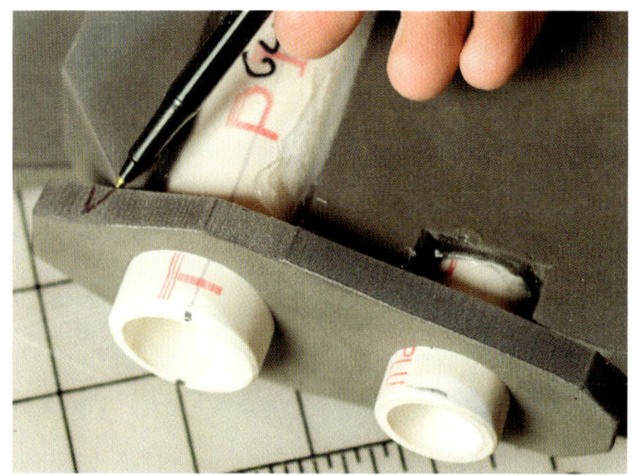

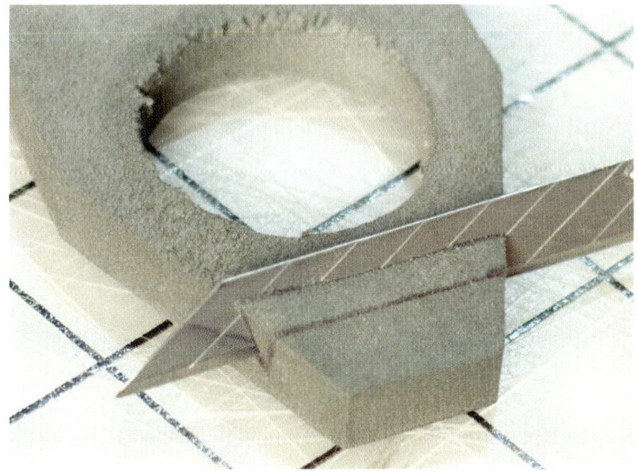

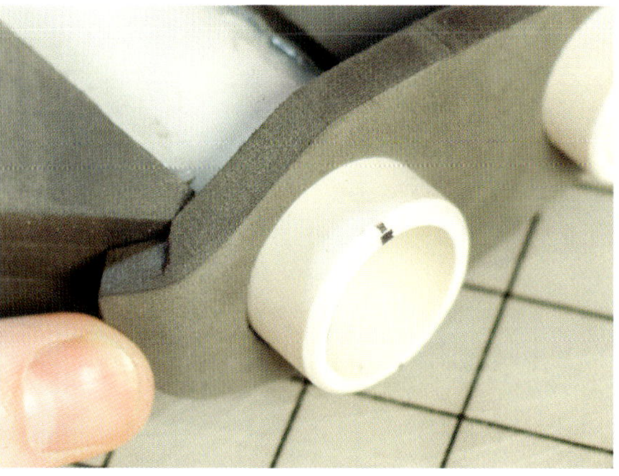

Use super glue to quickly attach small foam pieces together.

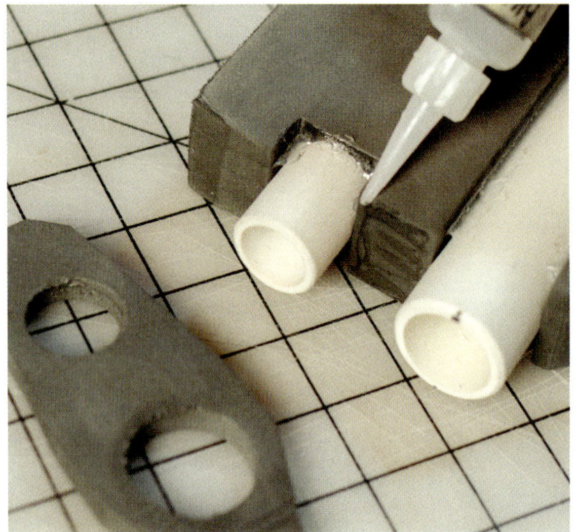

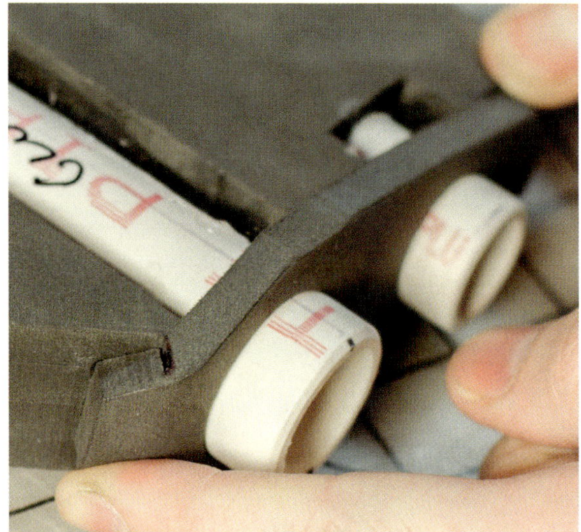

When I confirmed that this front panel would fit over my barrels, I glued it in place using super glue. I also glued in a small triangular piece of foam to complete the top part of the bevel. This piece was glued into place and then trimmed to shape.

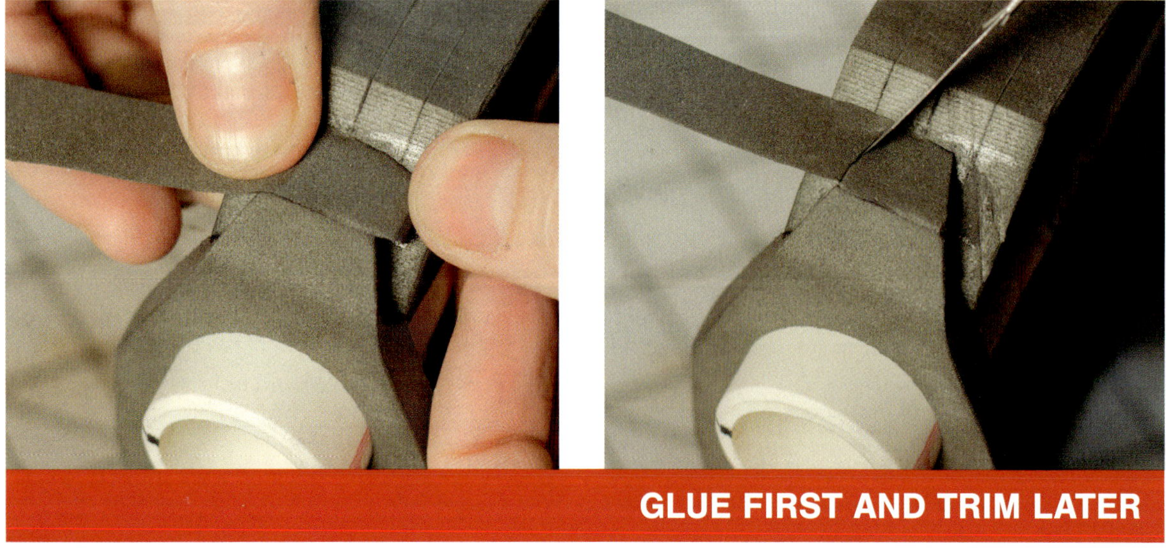

GLUE FIRST AND TRIM LATER

Contoured Forms

I decided it was time to start adding some contoured forms to my main body shape. The fore grip had some large beveled edges that matched up with the front place I had just installed, so I started there. Using a sharp knife I trimmed the bevel by hand. It didn't need to be too pretty because I knew it would all be covered by subsequent layers of foam.

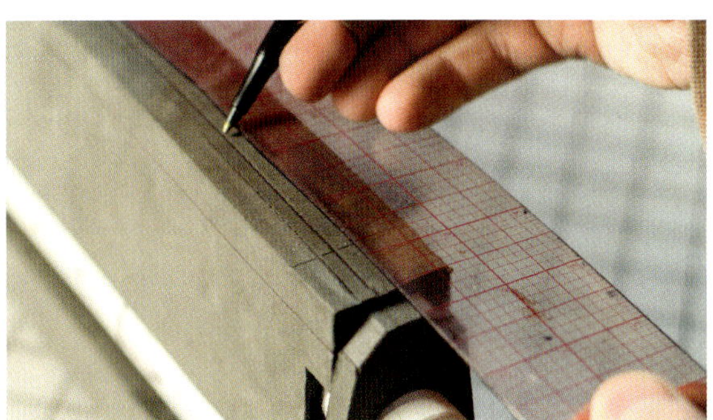

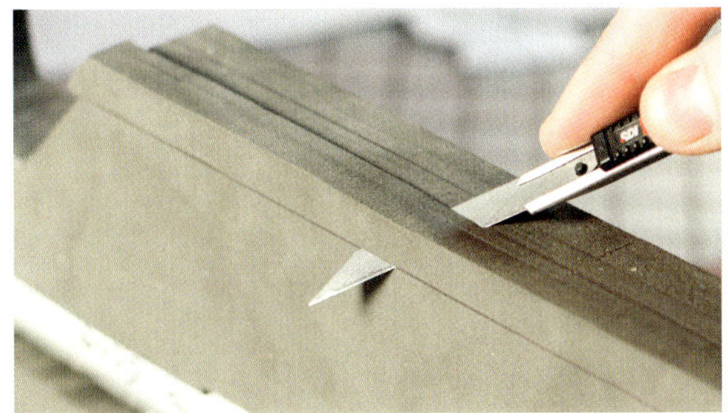

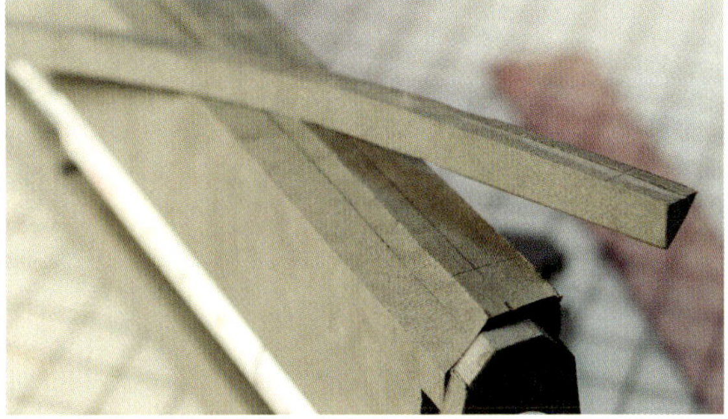

Just about all of the next steps were done twice. Once for each side of the gun, simply mirrored.

Along with taking some material away, it was also time to add more material. The shroud on the front of the barrel area was angled following the profile of the front panel, not flat like the main body piece. I glued down some foam rails to support the layer that would be glued on top of them.

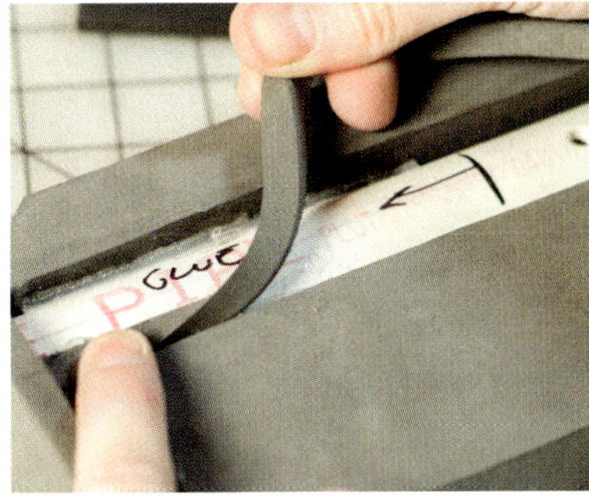

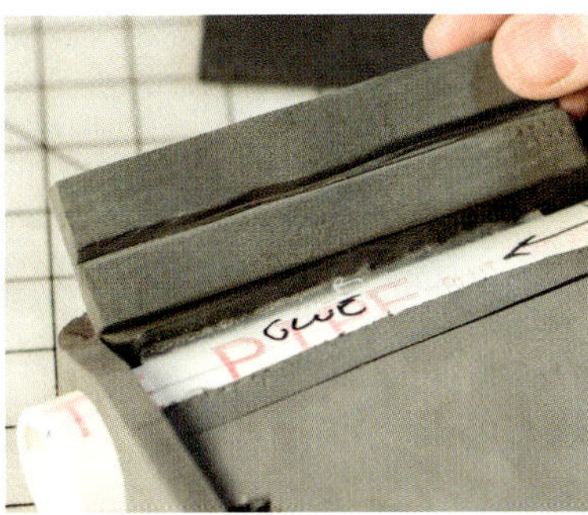

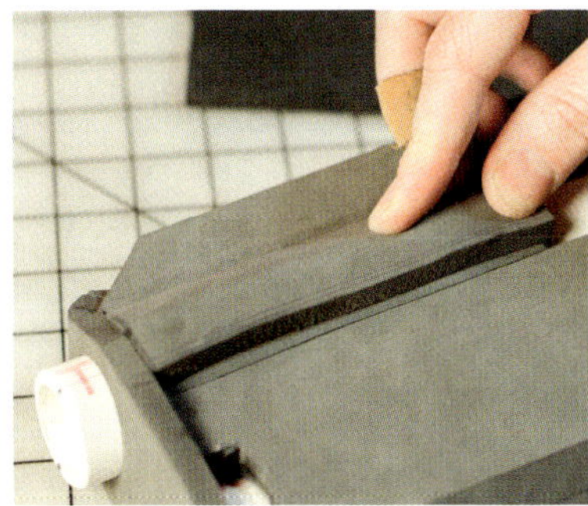

Always Be Bevelin'

I rough trimmed a bevel along the top, front section of the rifle. This bevel led back towards the main body of the gun and cut off at an angle.

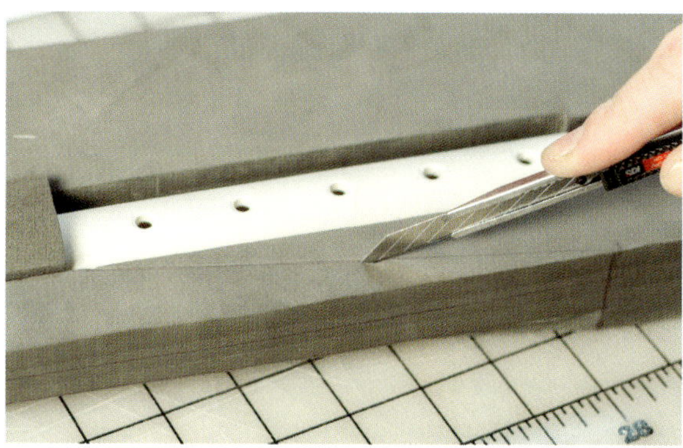

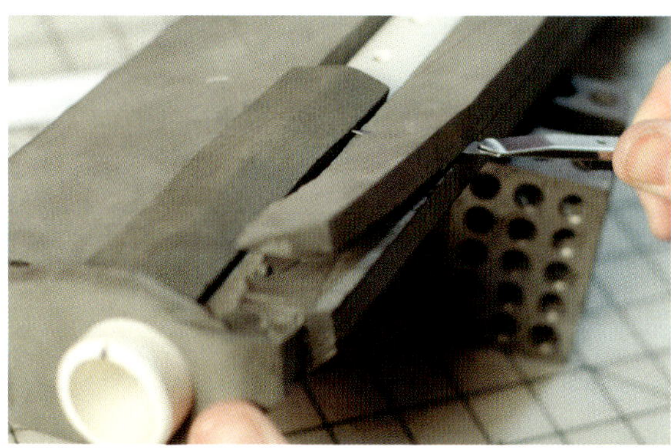

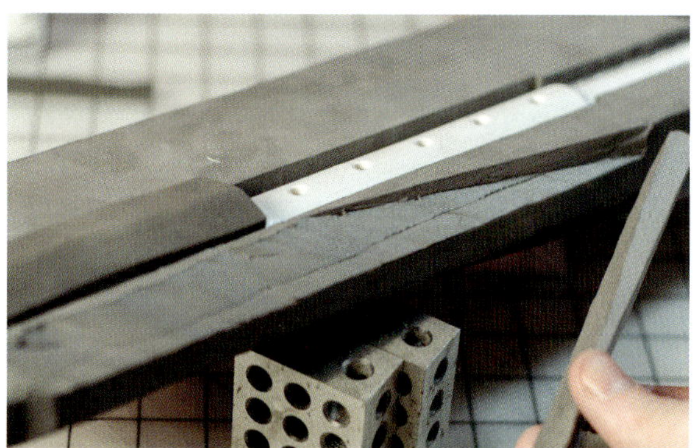

Additional foam parts were glued in place to extend the top and bottom bevels beyond the front plate. These were cut from 6mm craft foam and adhered with super glue. I made them longer than needed so I could trim them to shape once the rest of the front shroud was attached.

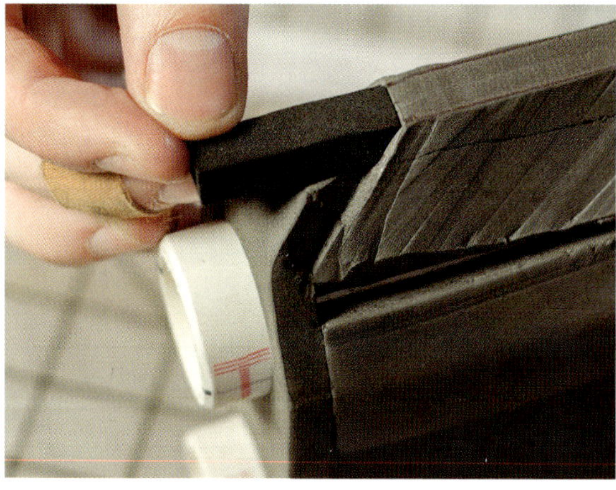

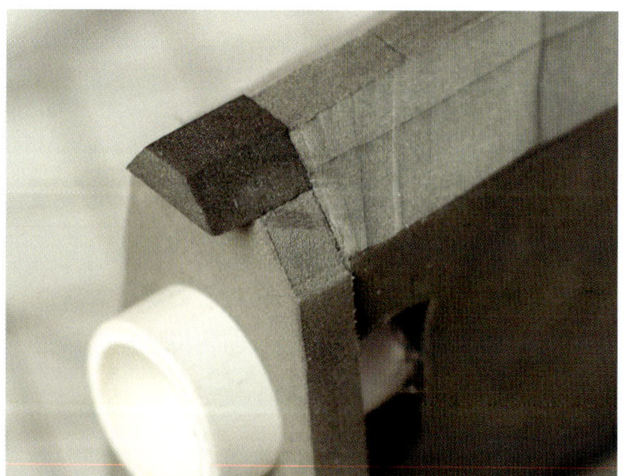

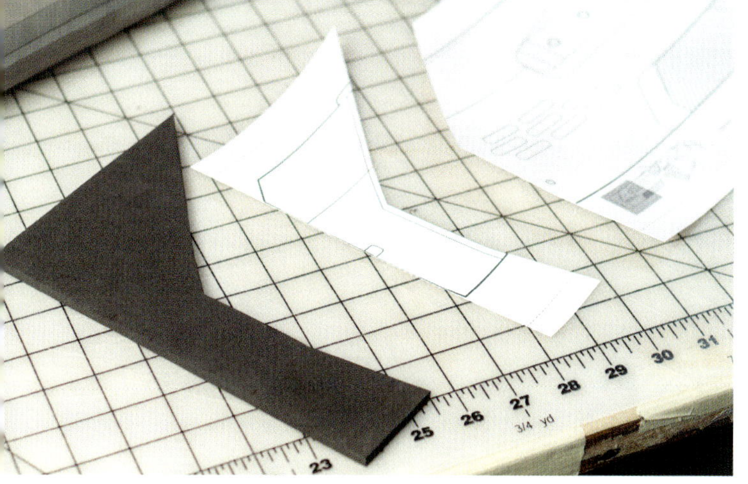

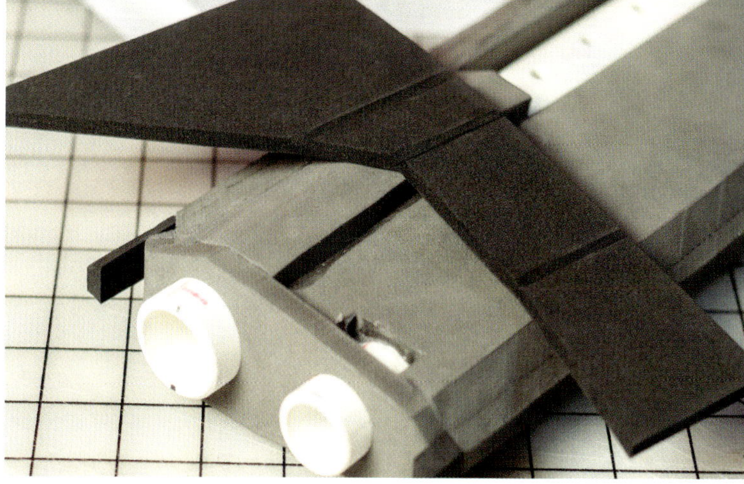

Front Shroud

With all of the underlying structures in place, I could finally cut out my front shroud pieces. These parts were made from 6mm craft foam and the top and bottoms were cut long on purpose. I wasn't exactly sure how long they needed to be to accommodate the surface angles, so I hedged my bets. I cut out small trenches on the back sides of these parts where I knew they needed to fold along the rails below.

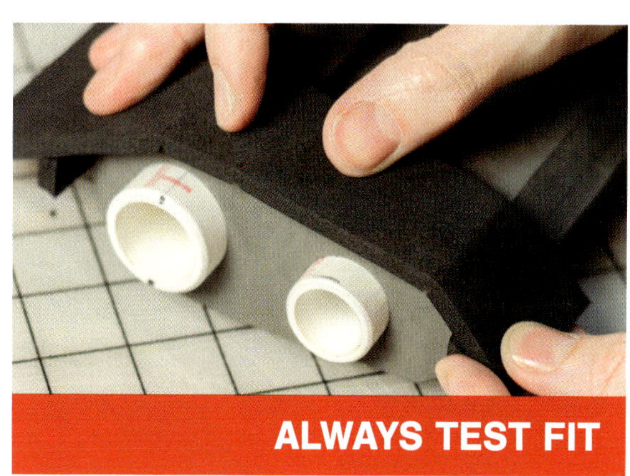

ALWAYS TEST FIT

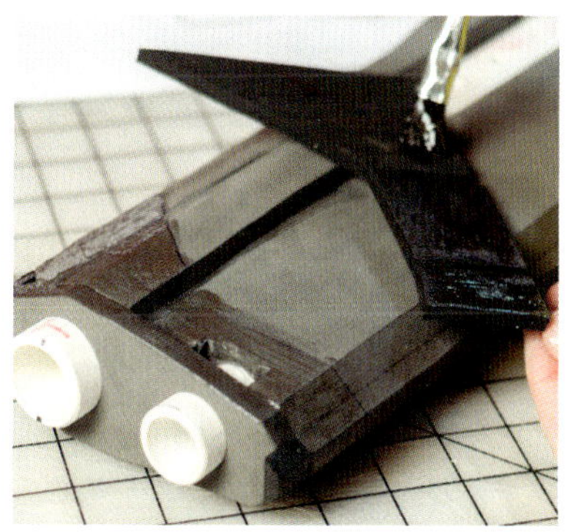

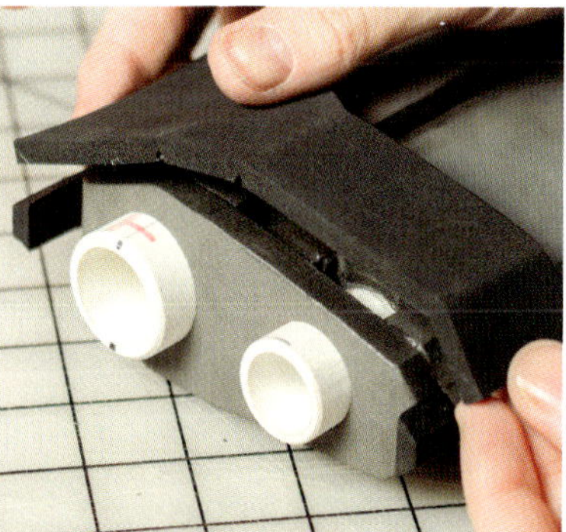

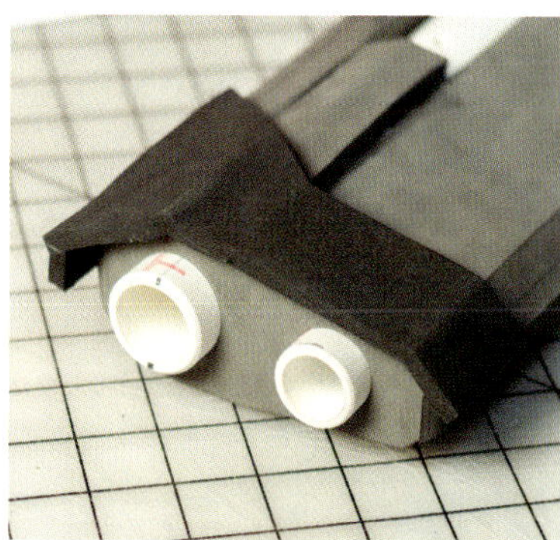

After some test fitting, I glued the shroud parts in place using Barge. They folded nicely over the front body, with extra material extending beyond the top and bottom of the gun. Once they were glued in place, I trimmed the foam to match the contours of the gun.

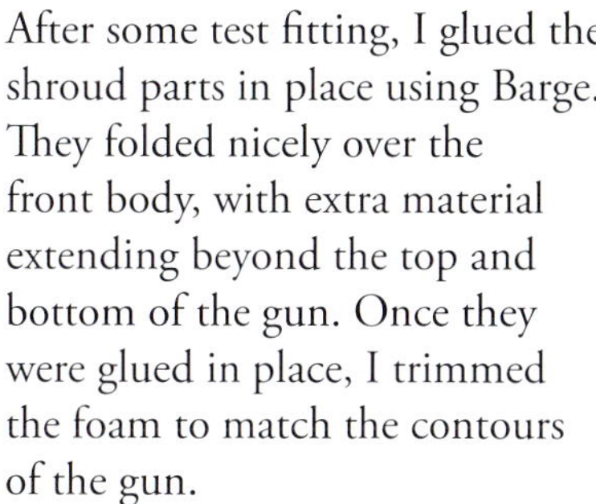

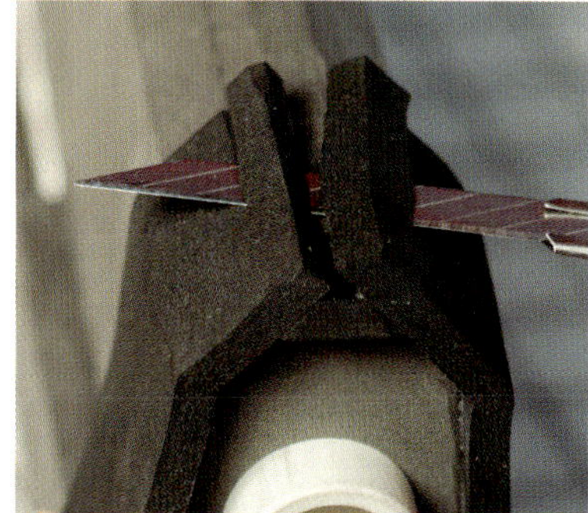

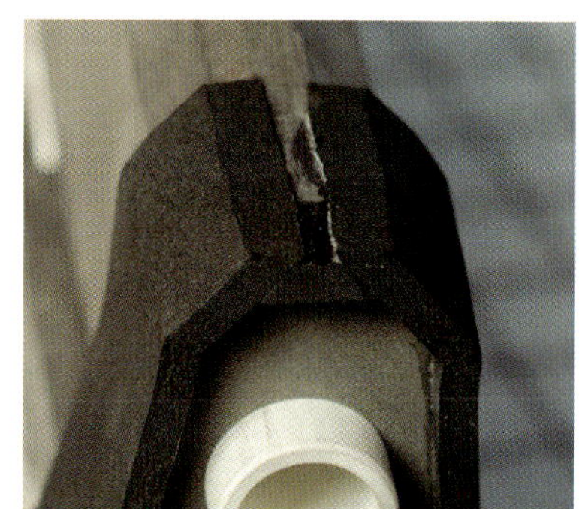

I cut in the last angled bit on the tip of the barrel shroud. Then I took the whole gun over to the belt sander and cleaned up the seams.

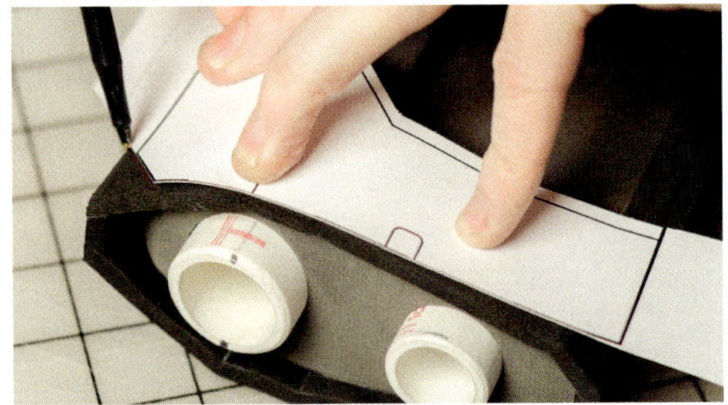

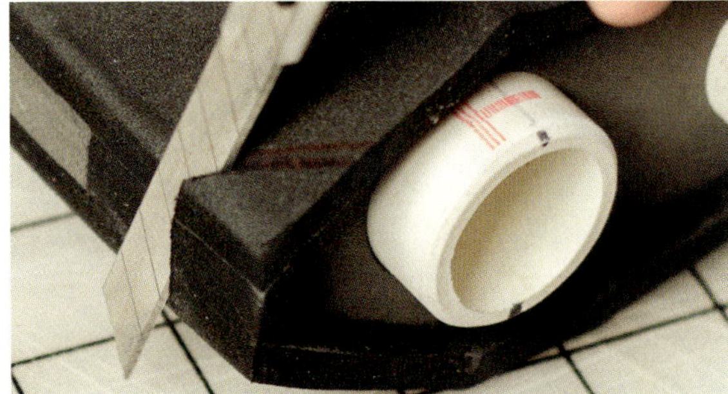

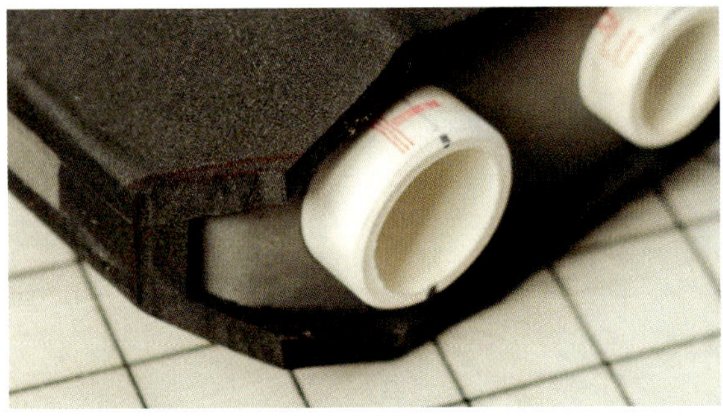

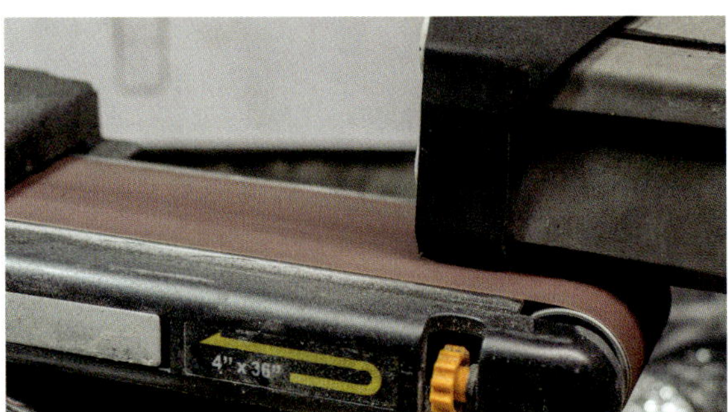

The form of this forward shroud piece continued back along the body of the gun, so I got to cutting out more foam parts. I wanted these parts to be a little bit thicker than the front of the gun, so I got my hands on some 8mm EVA foam. These parts were traced from the template and cut out in a similar fashion as the forward part, leaving extra material on the top and bottom.

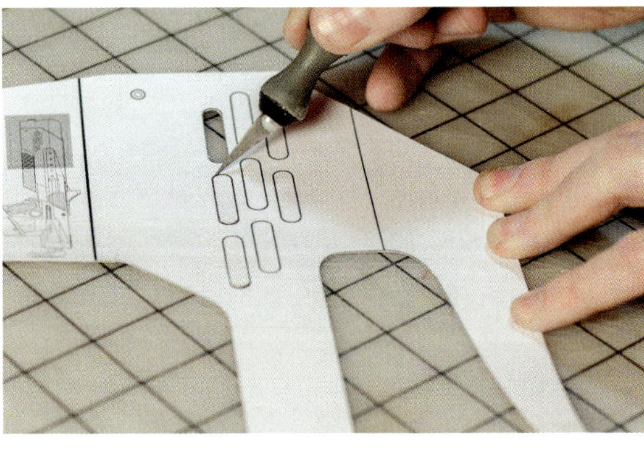

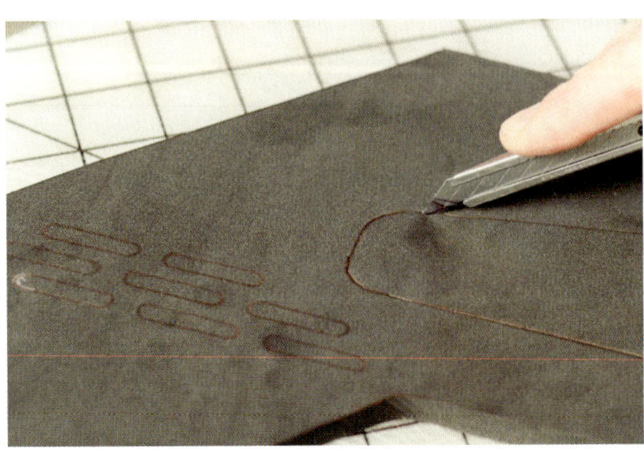

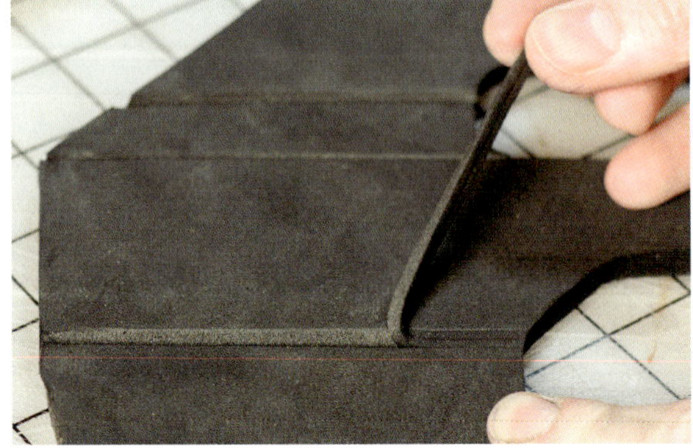

Side Vents

The forward shroud pieces had the added bonus of some sweet looking vents along the side of them. Once the main parts were cut out, I started the vents by drilling the ends using a small forstner bit in the drill press. This ensured that they would be nice and circular. Then I cut out the area between each set of drilled circles using a knife and cleaned them up with my rotary tool.

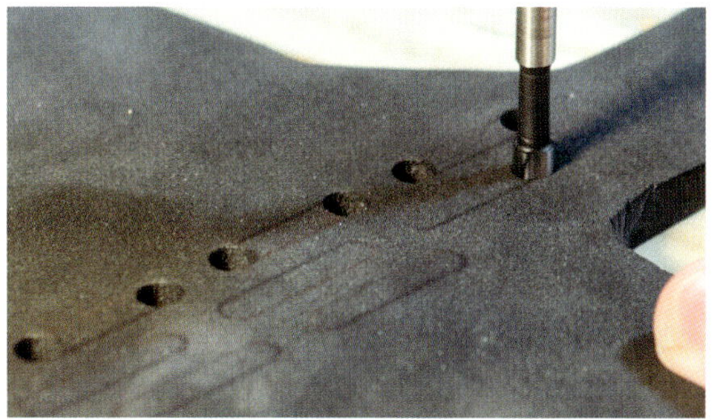

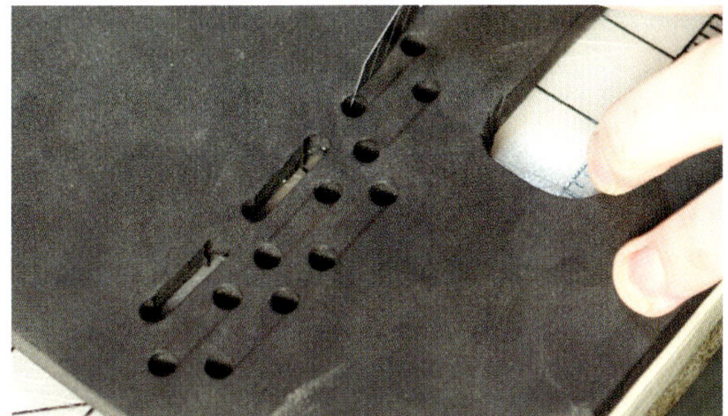

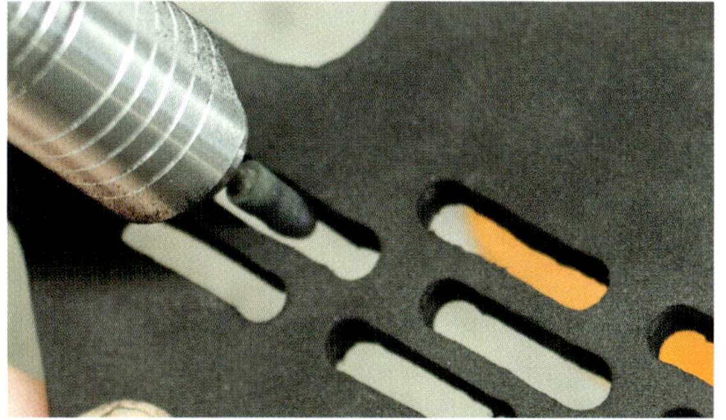

Our five-year-old rotary tool died during this build. He was such a trooper! This is our most-used tool, so we invested in a fancy Foredom, seen in the picture above.

Before I could glue these side panels to the main gun body, I had to glue down another long foam rail down the side of the rifle. This piece would ensure that the sides of the gun would maintain the form I was trying to achieve.

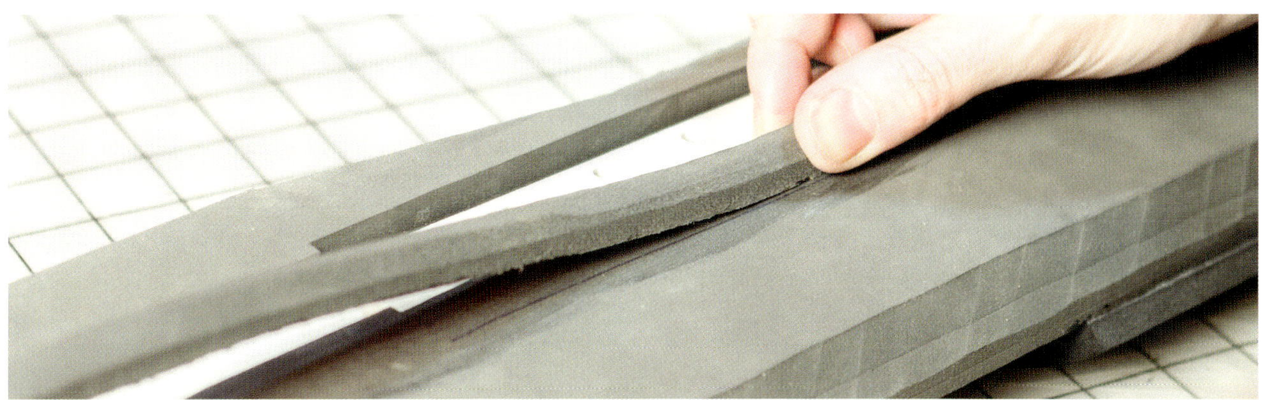

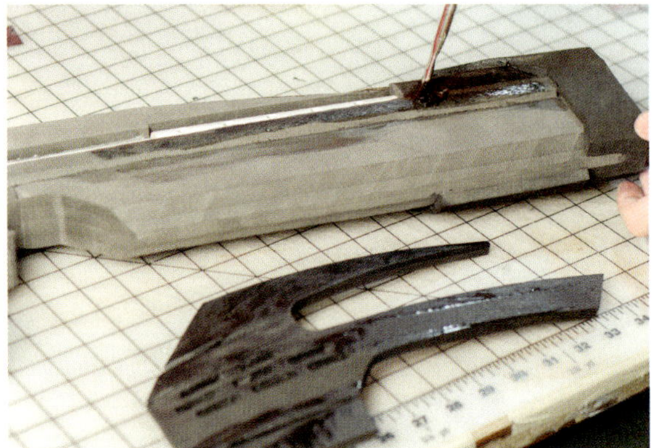

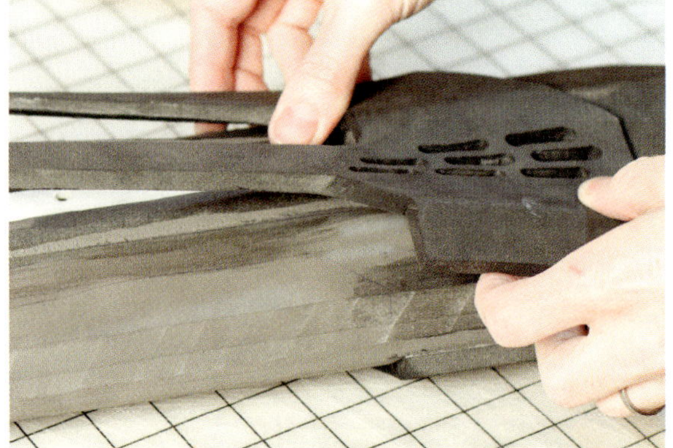

With the foam rail in place, I could happily glue down my fancy new side panel pieces with contact cement. Again, once the pieces were glued down, I trimmed the extra material on the top and bottom of the gun.

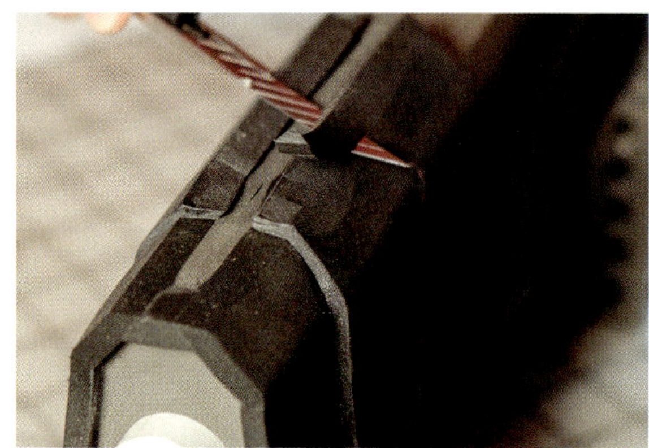

These side panels left room on the bottom of the gun for the fore grip. It wasn't quite as thick as I wanted it, so I added another layer of 8mm foam to bulk it out. As with most parts on this gun, I made this layer slightly oversized and then trimmed off the excess.

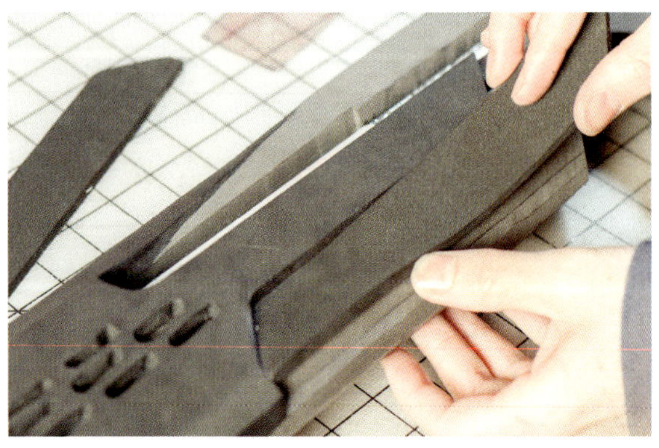

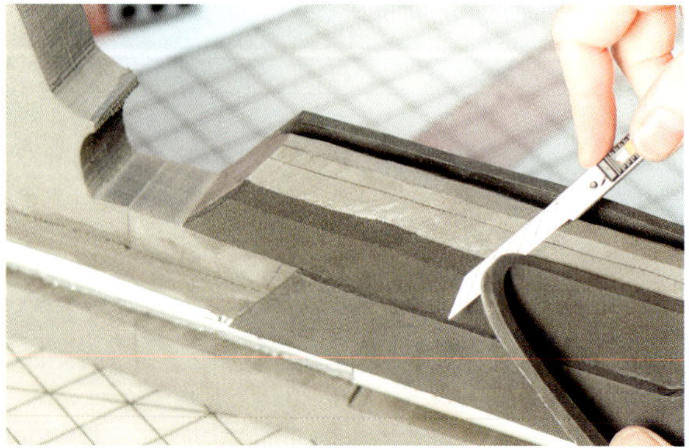

Knurling Texture

Before I could add the super neat, knurled texture to the fore grip, I wanted to smooth out the area where it would be glued down. I used a grinding bit in my rotary tool and gave it a good once over. This smoothed out the sharp angles and ensured the next layer wouldn't look lumpy.

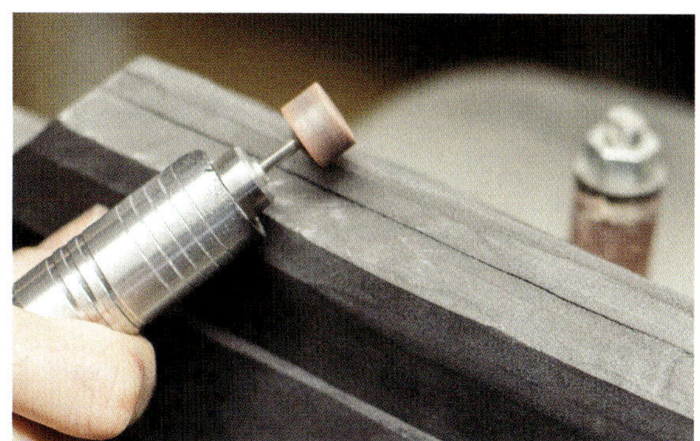

Using my template and some masking tape, I figured out how big the fore grip texture needed to be. This new and improved template was used to cut out shapes from my thin 2mm craft foam. Once I had my shapes cut out, I drew all of the surface details using a pen.

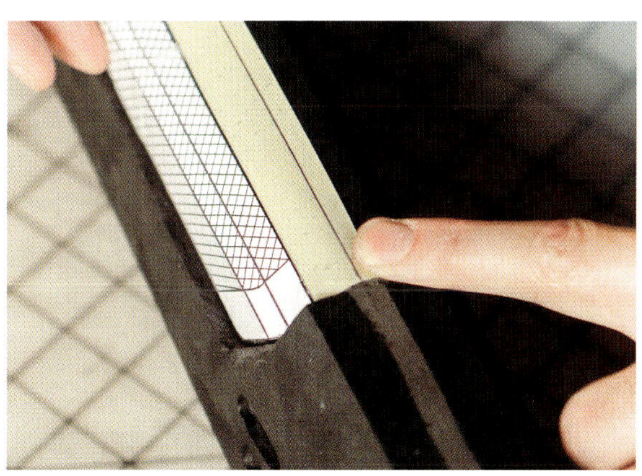

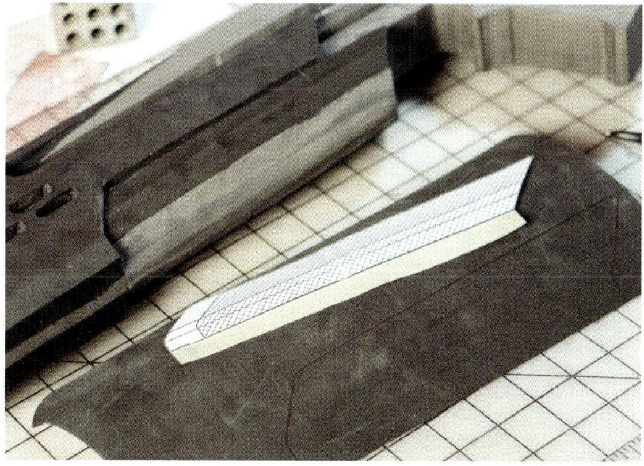

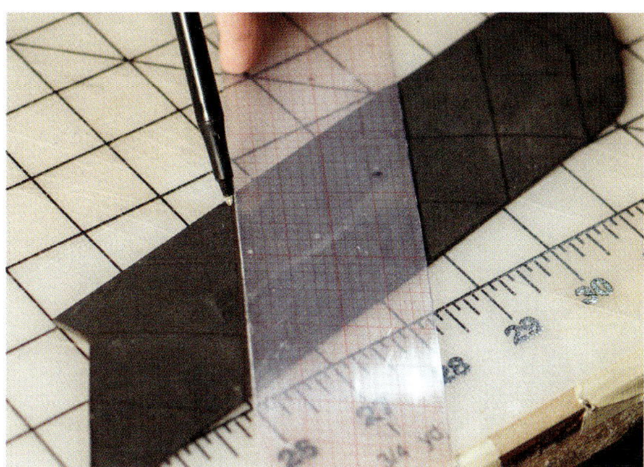

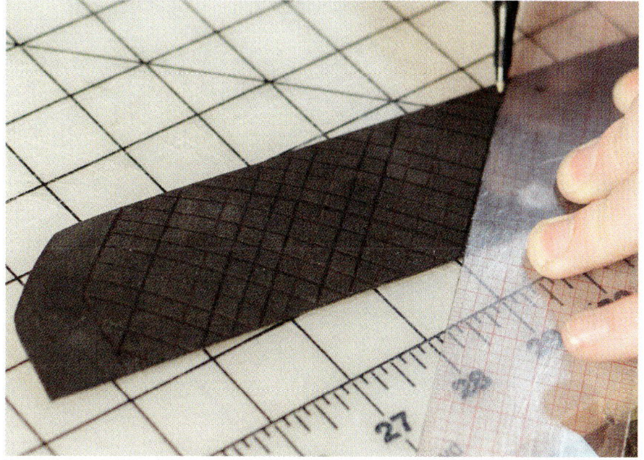

Scoring Foam

To make all of the texture on the fore grip, I needed to score a lot of lines into my 2mm foam. The challenge was to cut into the foam a little bit without cutting all the way through. This is one of the reasons why I like using knives that can extend out from their handles at a variety of lengths.

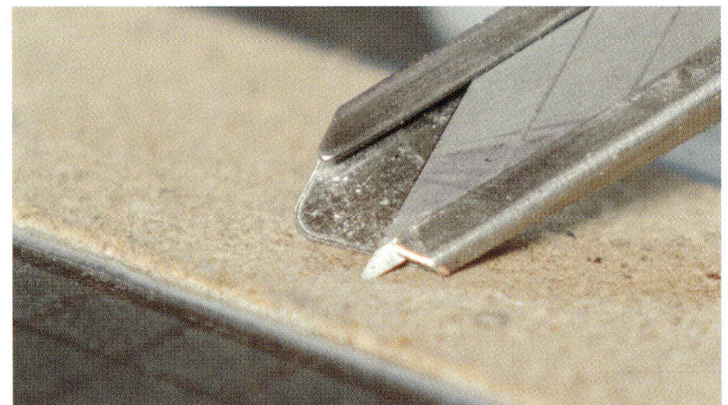

Using one such knife, I extended just the very tip of the knife out of the handle and used that, along with a metal ruler, to score the surface of my foam.

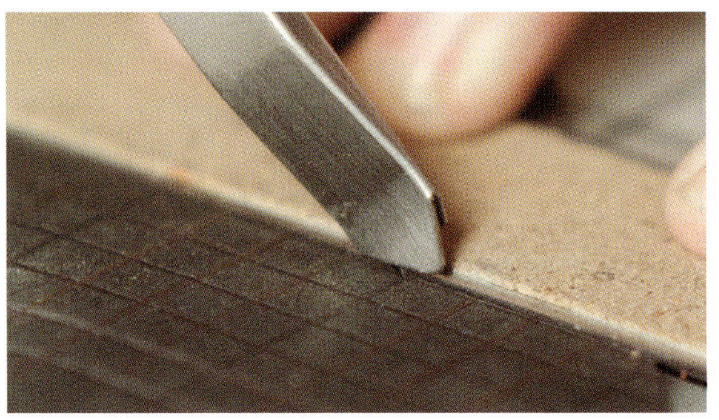

Cutting these lines was extremely tedious, but well worth it. Once all the details were cut, I hit the foam with a heat gun and the cut marks opened up, making the knurled texture appear like magic! When I was happy with these fore grip detail pieces, they could be glued down with Barge cement.

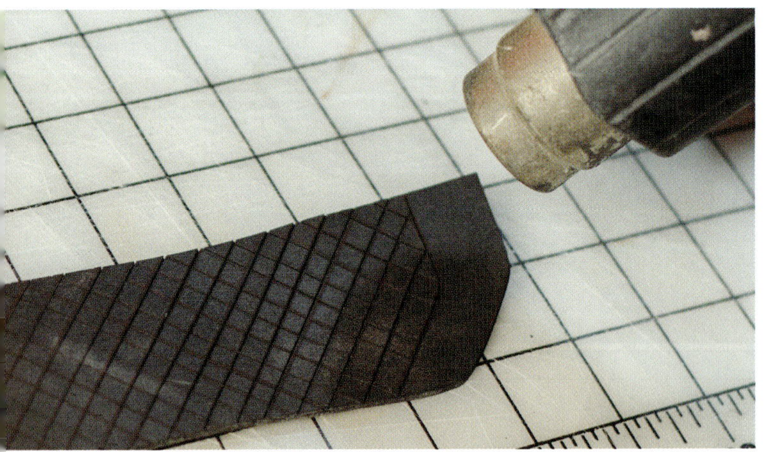

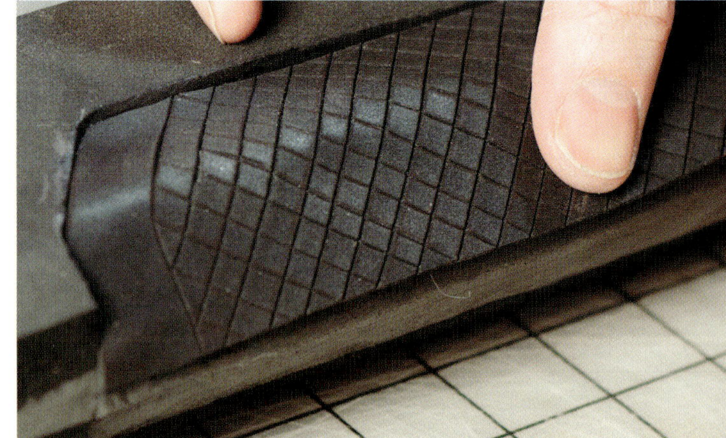

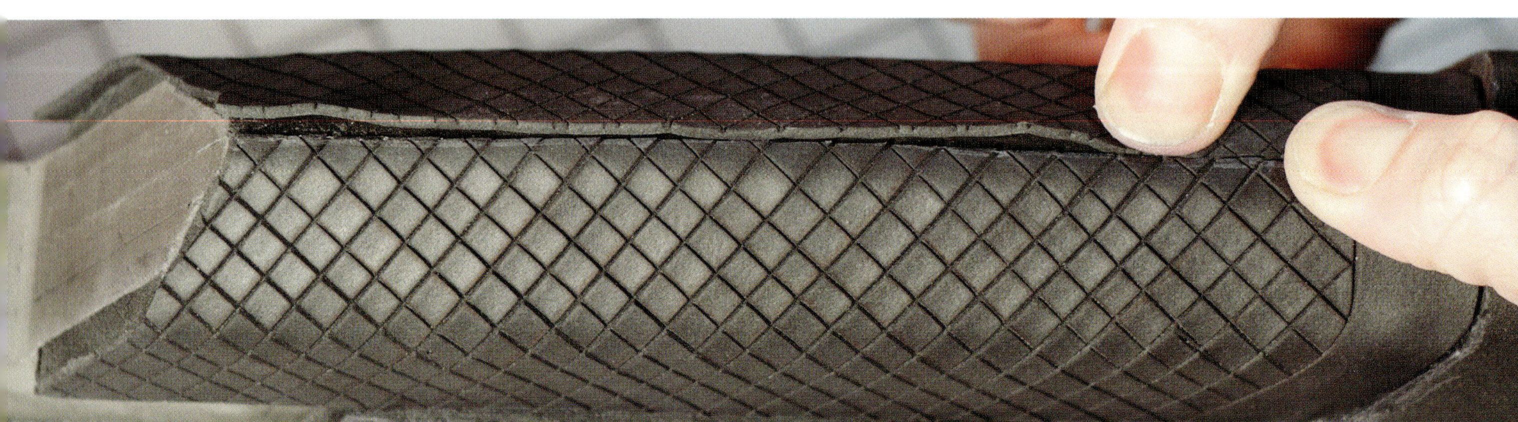

Side Panels

The PVC pipe behind the exposed barrel section needed to be covered up. In the original design there were some more detail pieces in this area, so I cut out several pieces and strips of craft foam to both conceal the pipe and add those greebles.

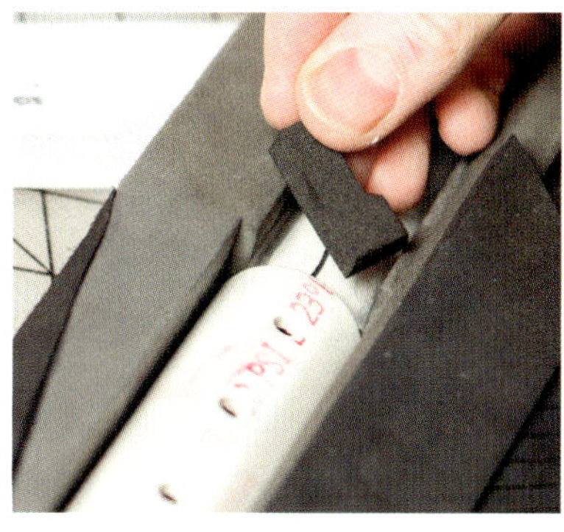

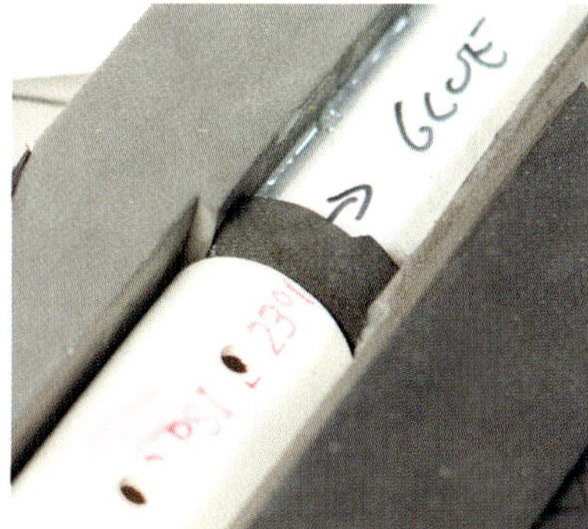

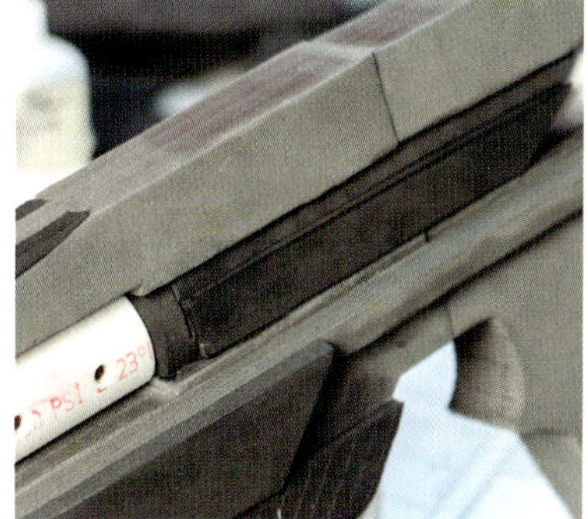

Way back when I glued the front and rear main body parts together, there was a seam left behind. To hide that seam I cut out a piece of 2mm foam and Barged it in place. Nothing to see here!

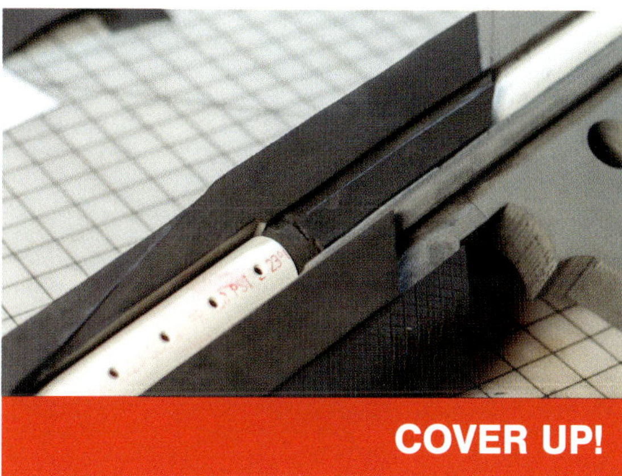

Then I kept working my way backward, adding more layers of foam where they made sense according to the template.

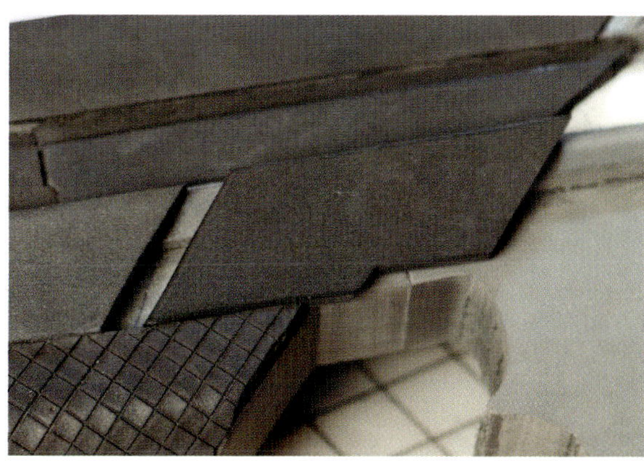

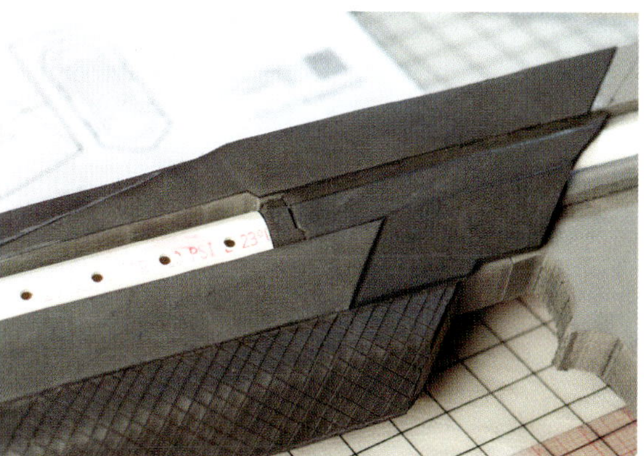

"Cosmic Radiator"

I have no idea what this side piece is supposed to be, so let's call it the cosmic radiator. The cosmic radiator has parallel lines cut into it, so I scored lines into the 8mm foam piece, just like with the fore grip.

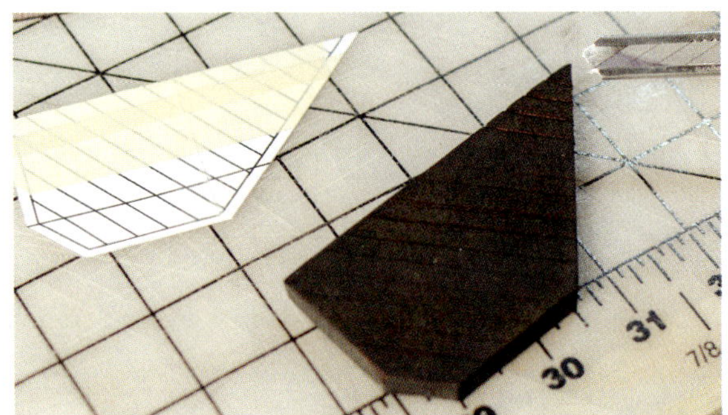

After opening up those lines with a heat gun, I trimmed some really thin strips of 2mm foam with a knife and a ruler. These strips were then super glued in place to provide some trim on our fancy pants cosmic radiator. I glued down each piece of the strip before cutting it off and gluing down the next part.

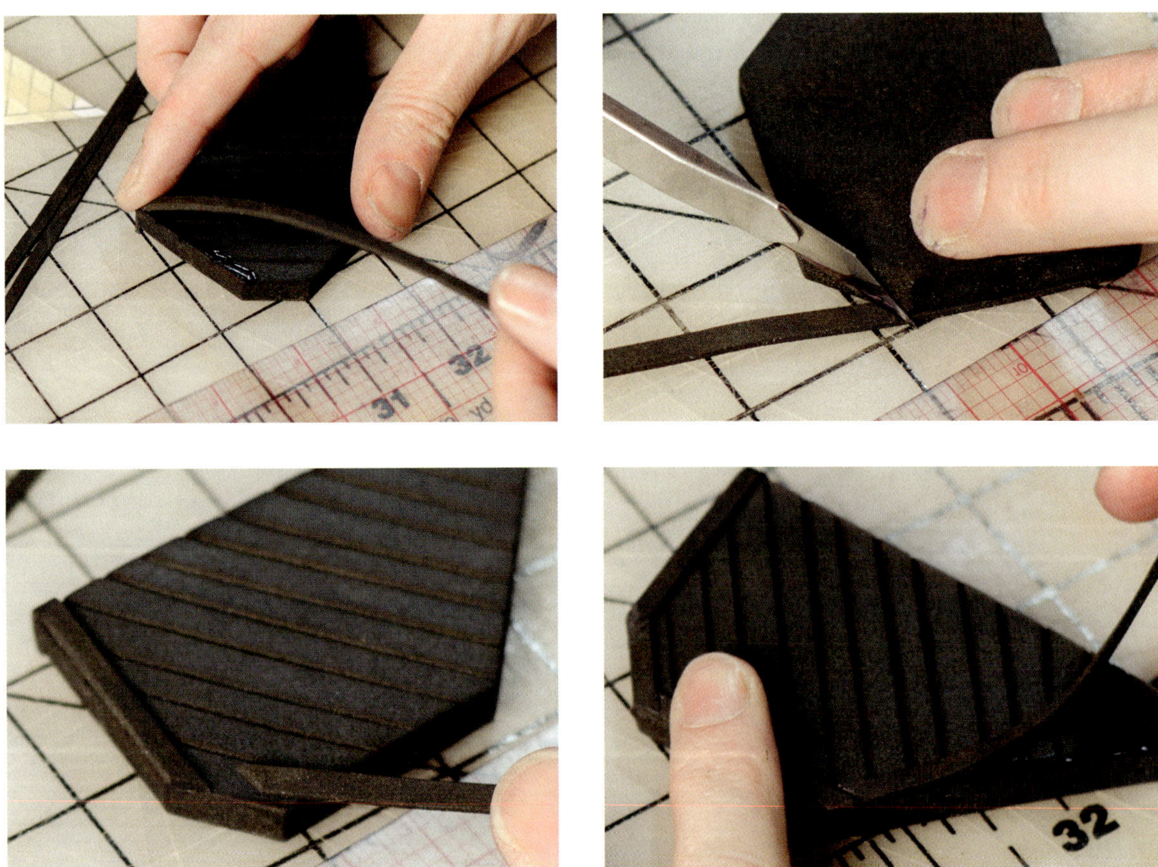

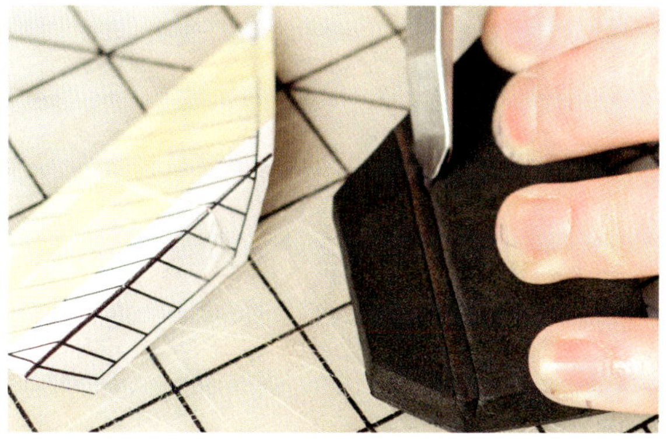

Foam Wedges

With the trim completed, I could carve out a trench in the back of the cosmic radiator and fold it a little bit to create an angle along the outer surface. This trench was filled with super glue and squeezed together so that it would hold that angle for all time.

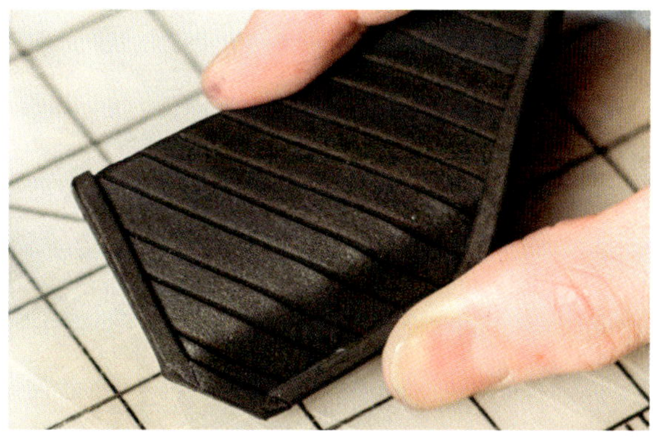

Use a super glue accelerator spray to speed up the process.

I added a small chunk of 8mm foam to the back of the cosmic radiator and used that chunk to glue it to the body of the gun. This way the radiator would be attached to the gun, but held slightly away from the main surface.

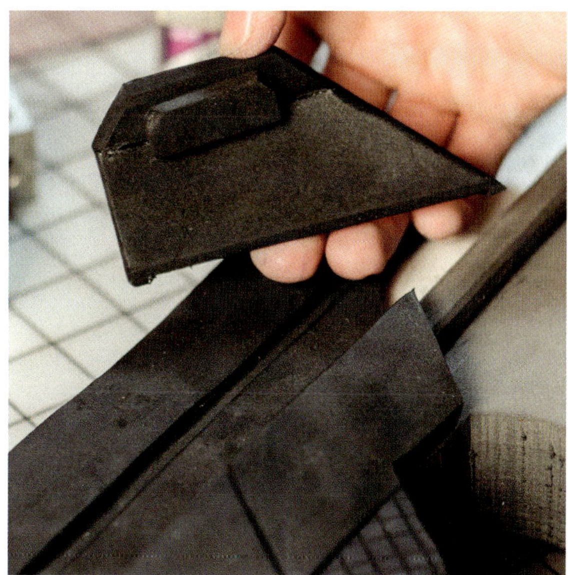

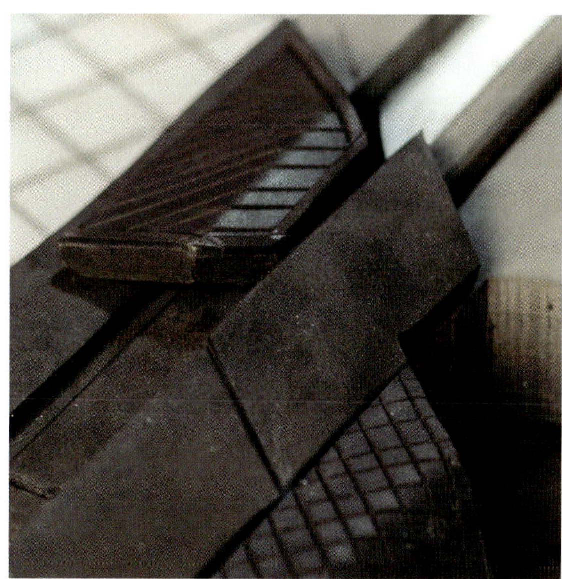

Trim The Rail

Earlier I had glued down a long foam rail along the length of the gun that served as a support for layers above it. I intentionally left it long because I wasn't sure how far down the gun it needed to be. When I cut out the last rear panel layer I knew where that rail needed to end, so I trimmed it away from the gun.

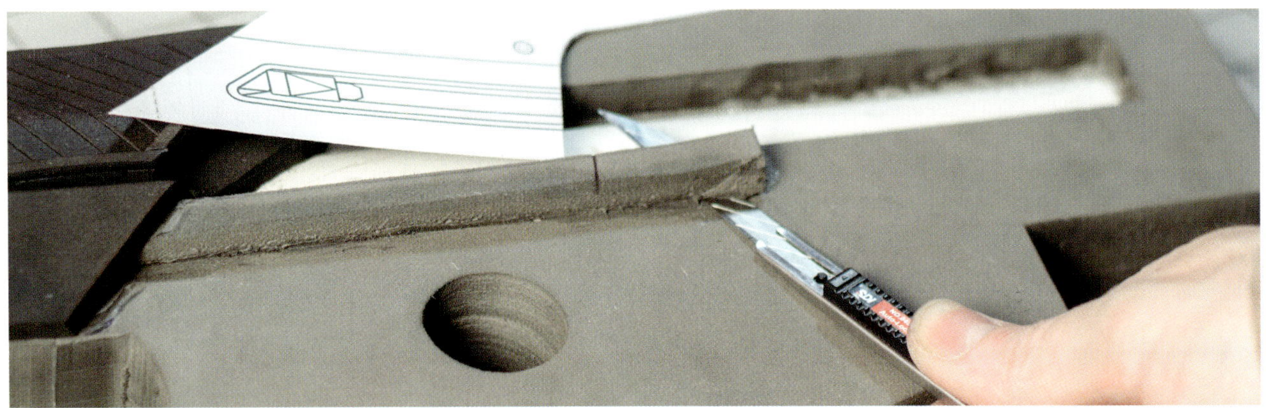

Assembling The Rear Panel

The top portion of the rear panel was done in a similar way as the front portions, cutting it a little taller than it needed to be. I also carefully trimmed out the area where the charging lever would go. After cutting out this area, I rounded over the edges of it and then glued the cutout back in place, slightly recessed.

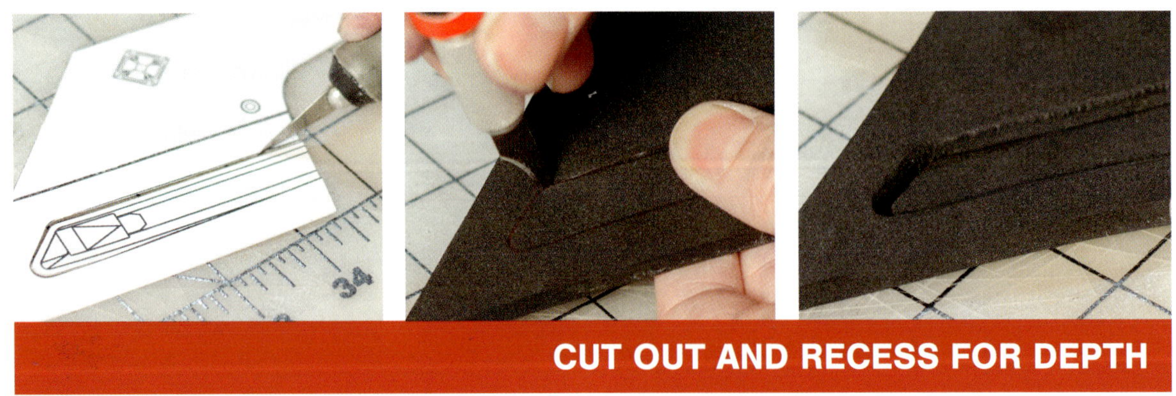

CUT OUT AND RECESS FOR DEPTH

The rear side of these pieces were then cut flush with one another to ensure they would lay down on the gun evenly. I also cut trenches in the rear side where I knew the piece would need to fold.

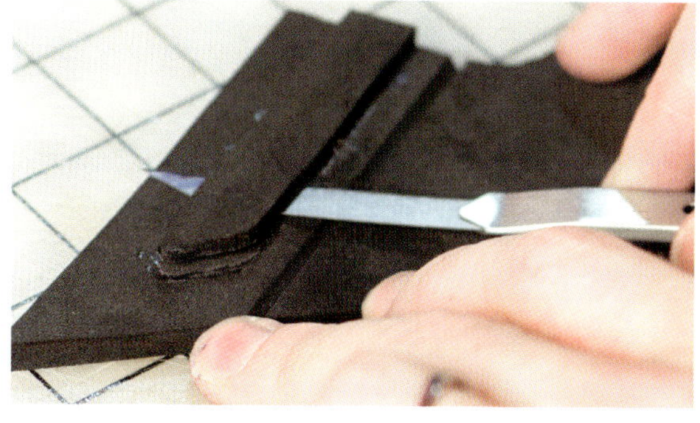

I extended the support rail down a little bit using more 8mm foam. This would support the bottom part of this rear panel, just above the handle.

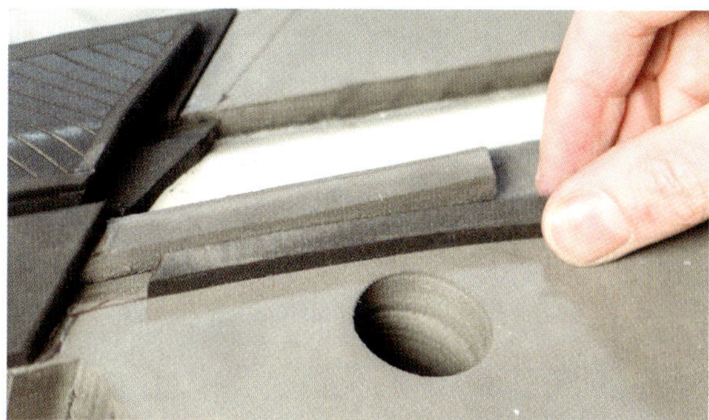

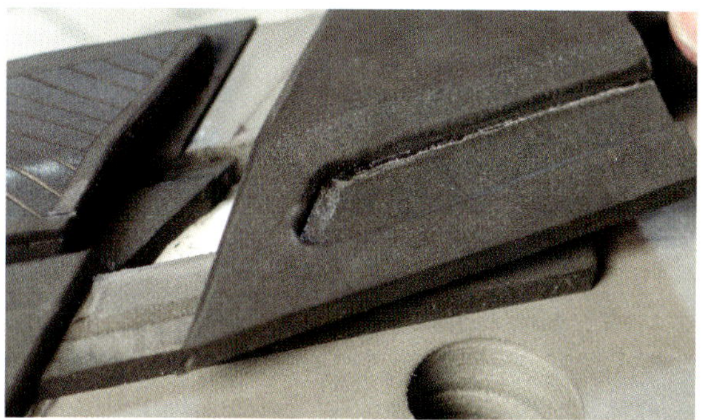

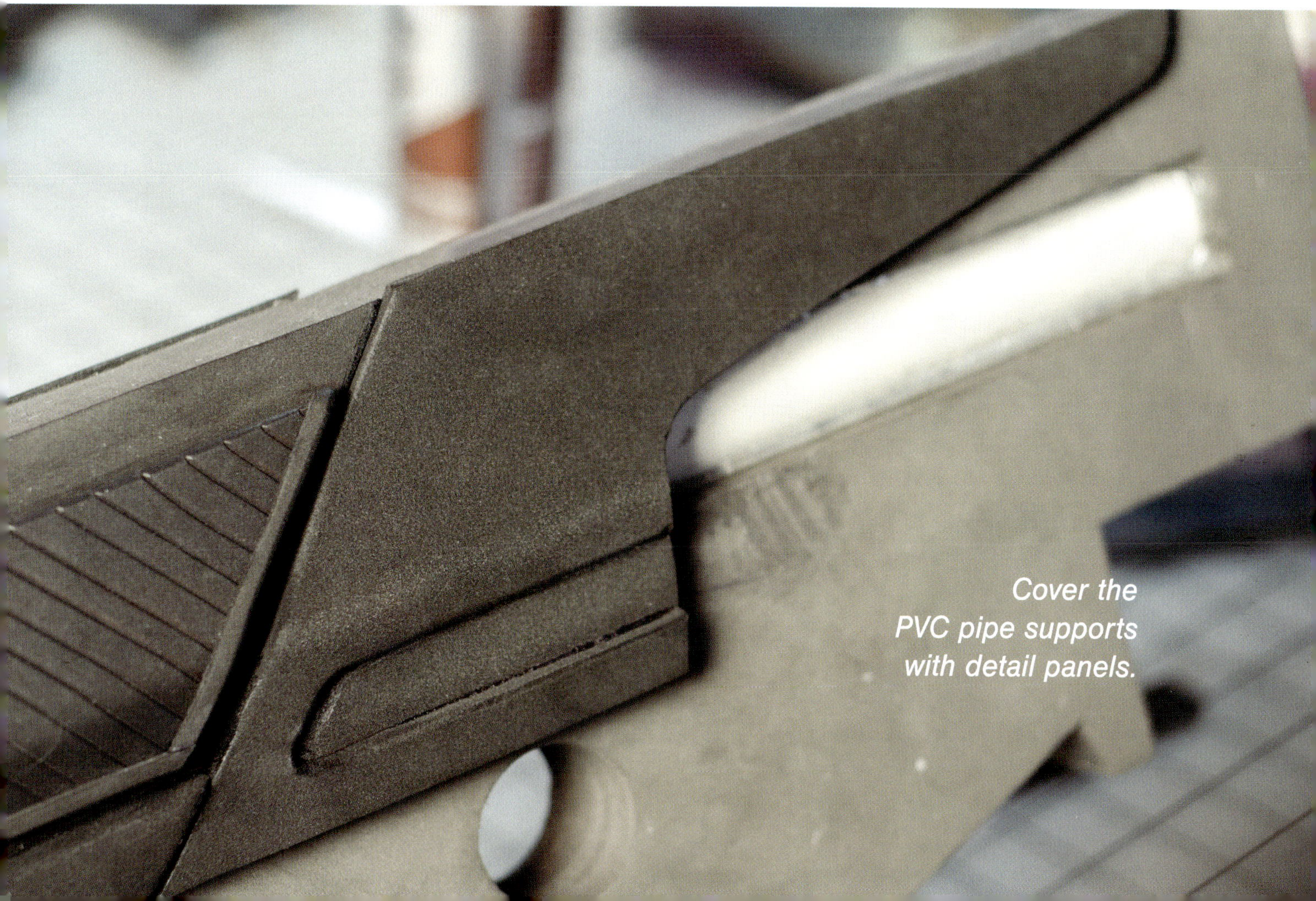

Cover the PVC pipe supports with detail panels.

MAGAZINE

I decided this was as good a time as any to make the top part of the ammo magazine. I also wanted to make the magazine removable with magnets, so I modified my templates to provide a cavity in the gun body and a protrusion on the mag. The cavity in the main body was cut out with a band saw and then I planned to cover it with additional layers of foam.

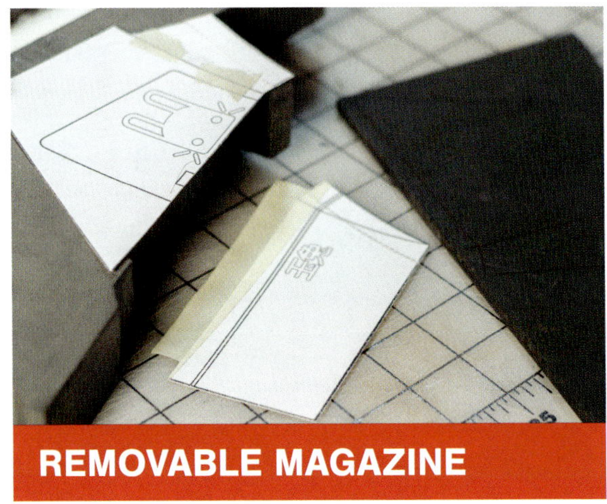
REMOVABLE MAGAZINE

The magazine covers were cut from 6mm craft foam. They have some large bevels on the rear of the panel, so I roughed them out with a knife and then cleaned them up with a belt sander. The forward edges of these panels had a bit of a bevel too, so they were shaped with my rotary tool and a sanding bit.

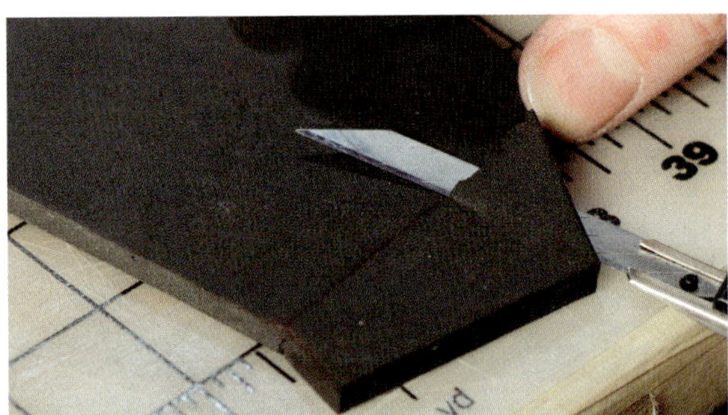

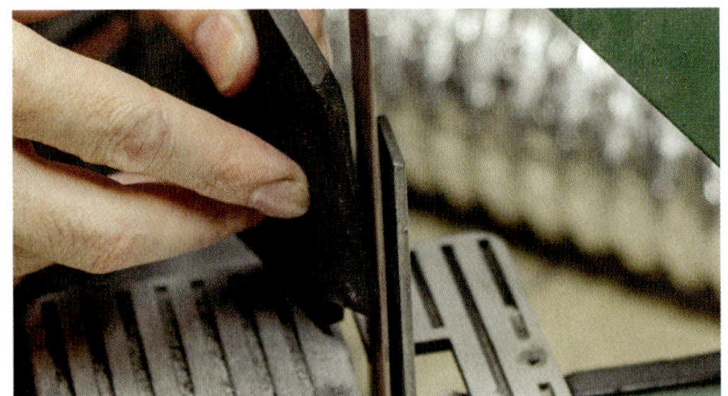

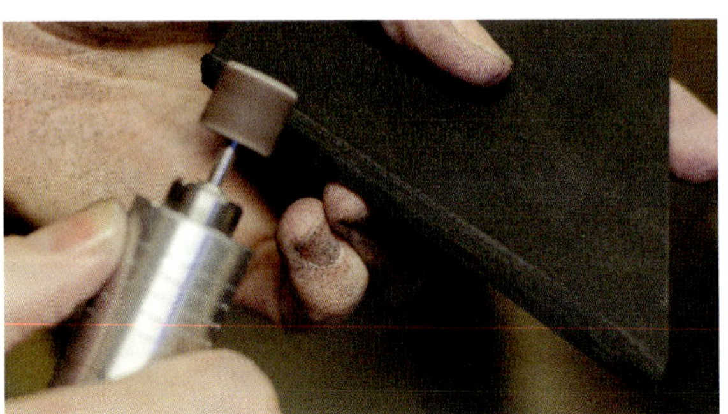

For the detail lines on these magazine cover panels, you guessed it, I scored the lines with a knife and used a heat gun to open them up. This trick never gets old. When the details were all cut in, I glued the magazine covers in place with Barge, making sure to keep the areas that overlap with the magazine protrusion free from any glue.

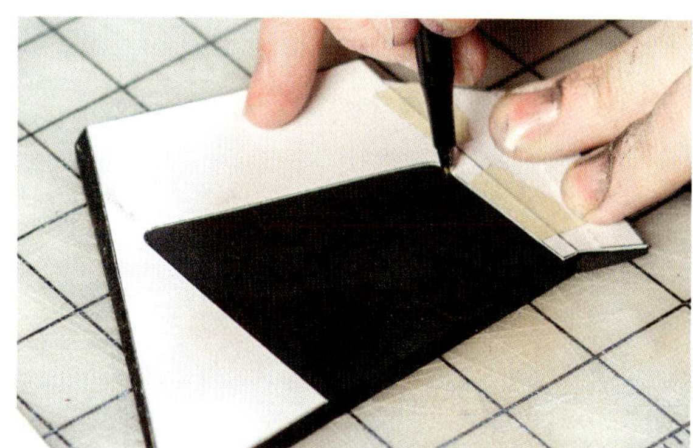

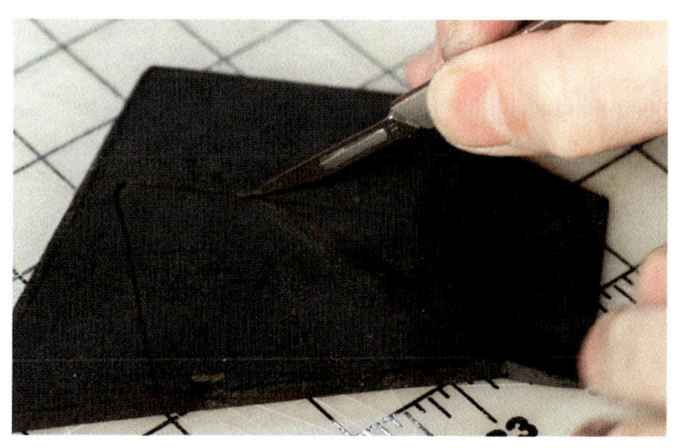

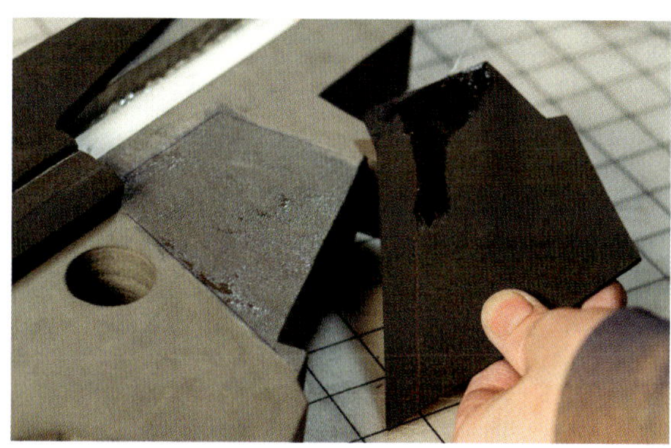

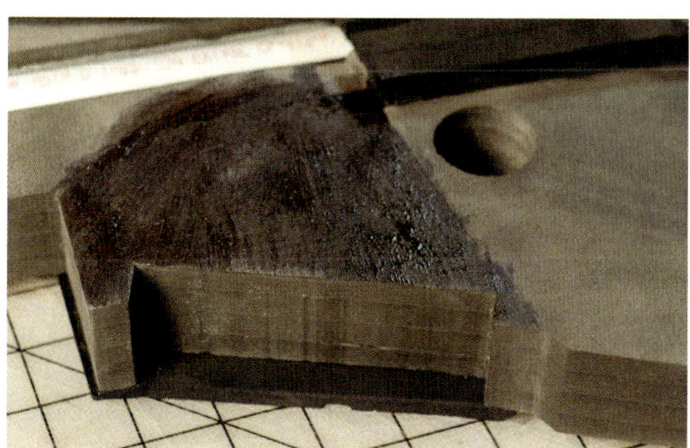

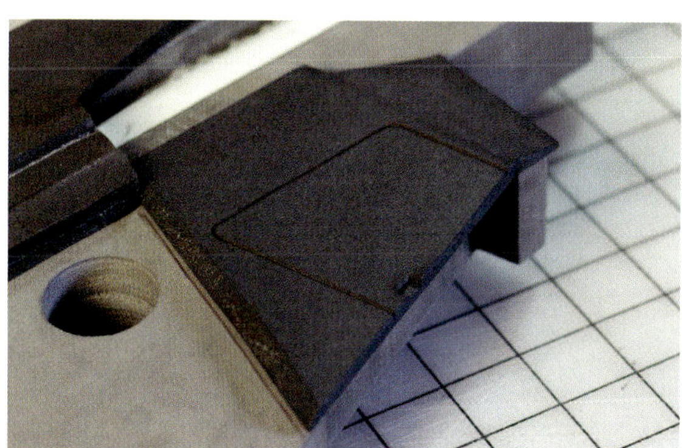

The magazine itself was made in a similar fashion as the main body part. I started by laminating four layers of floor mat foam together to achieve most of the thickness I would need. These were cut to shape with a bit of a protrusion at the top for attaching it to the gun body.

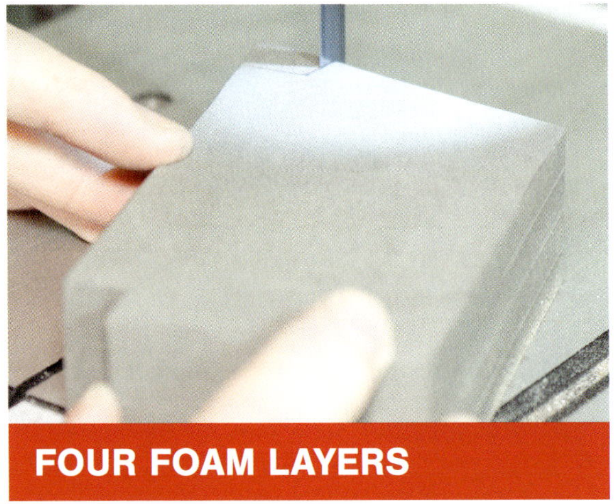

FOUR FOAM LAYERS

To get the magazine to the final thickness, I cut out another layer of 6mm foam. I trimmed off the top part of this layer so when it was glued down to the bulk of the magazine it would leave a protrusion. This protrusion should fit snugly into the cavity on the main gun body. I also beveled the rear edge of the magazine with my rotary tool.

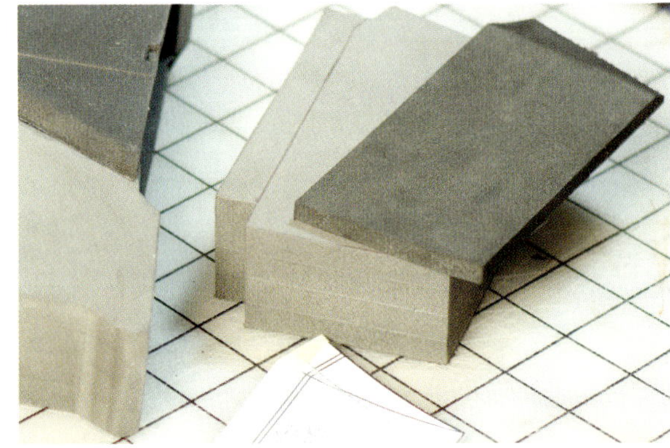

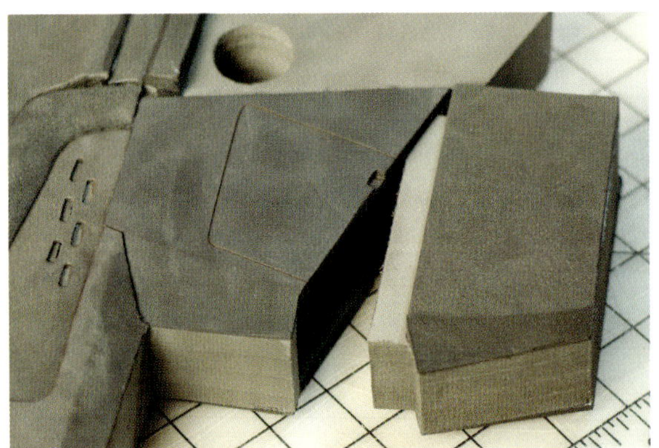

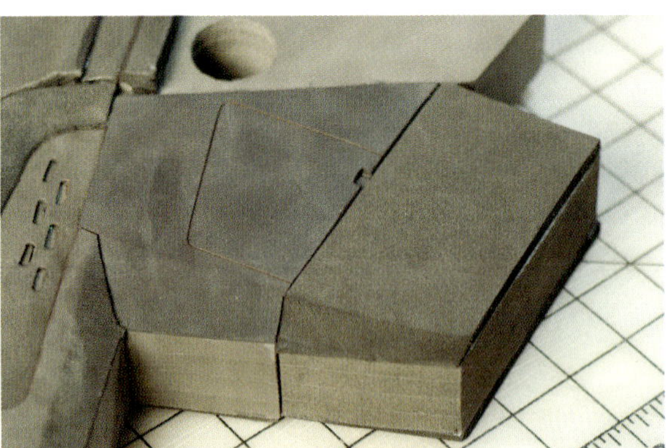

Magnets!

To get the ammo mag to stay attached to the gun, I decided to use some small rare earth magnets. I happened to have some square shaped magnets lying around, so I cut three square shaped holes in both the gun and the magazine. To be sure they would line up, I made a quick template from card stock. Since these holes wouldn't ever be seen, they didn't need to be pretty. I simply hacked the square-ish holes with a sharp knife.

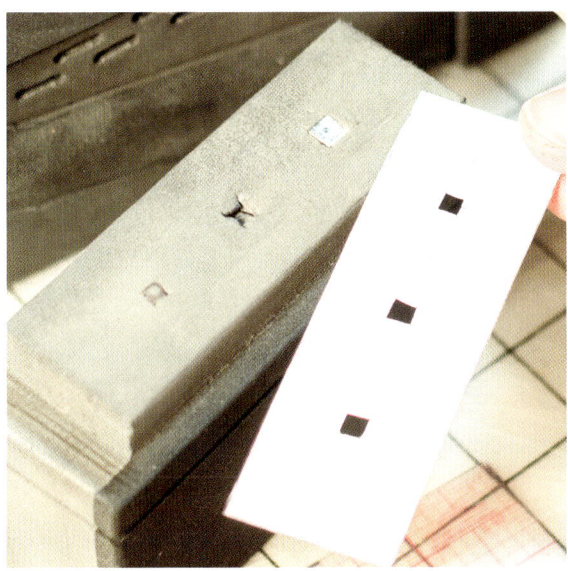

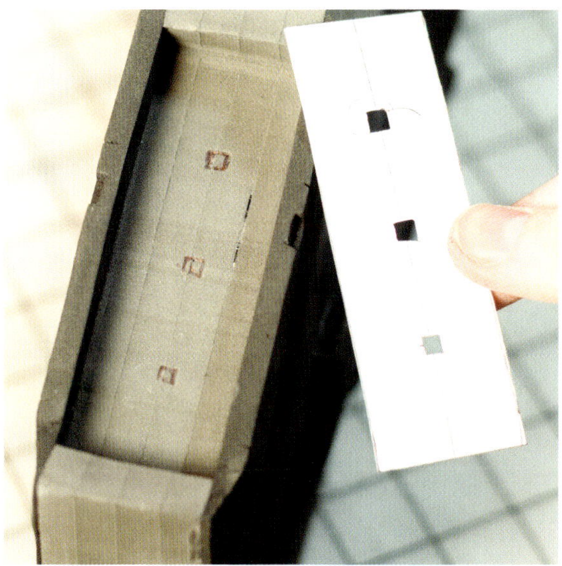

With the holes all cut, I used some super glue to secure the magnets to the foam. The magazine could then slide easily into the gun and be held in place with science!

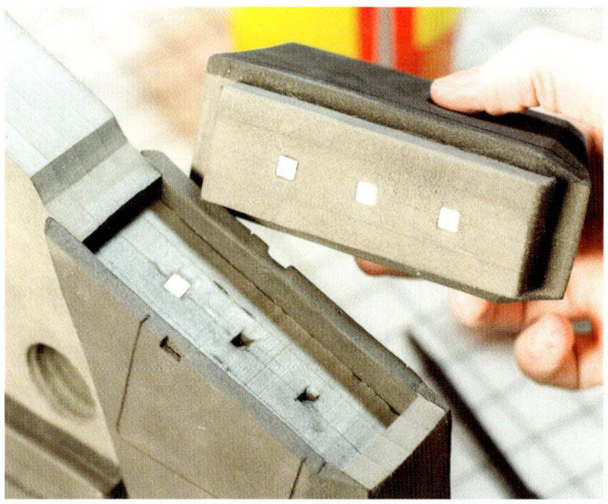

Details and Handle

The top, rear section of the rifle had some goofy geometry, so I had to get creative. I started by cutting a thin panel from 2mm foam and adding more vents to it. To make the starter holes for these vents I used a leather hole punch and then cut out the middle sections with a knife. Then this thin panel was glued into place.

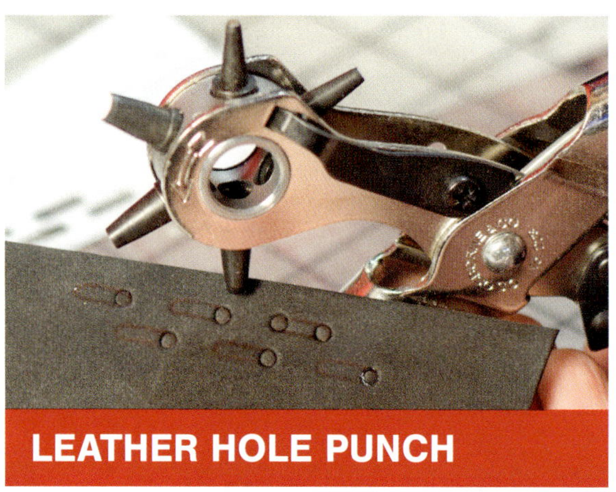
LEATHER HOLE PUNCH

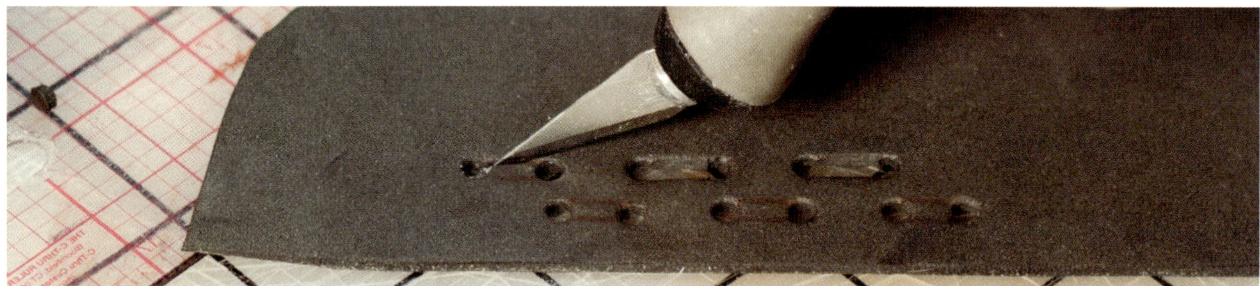

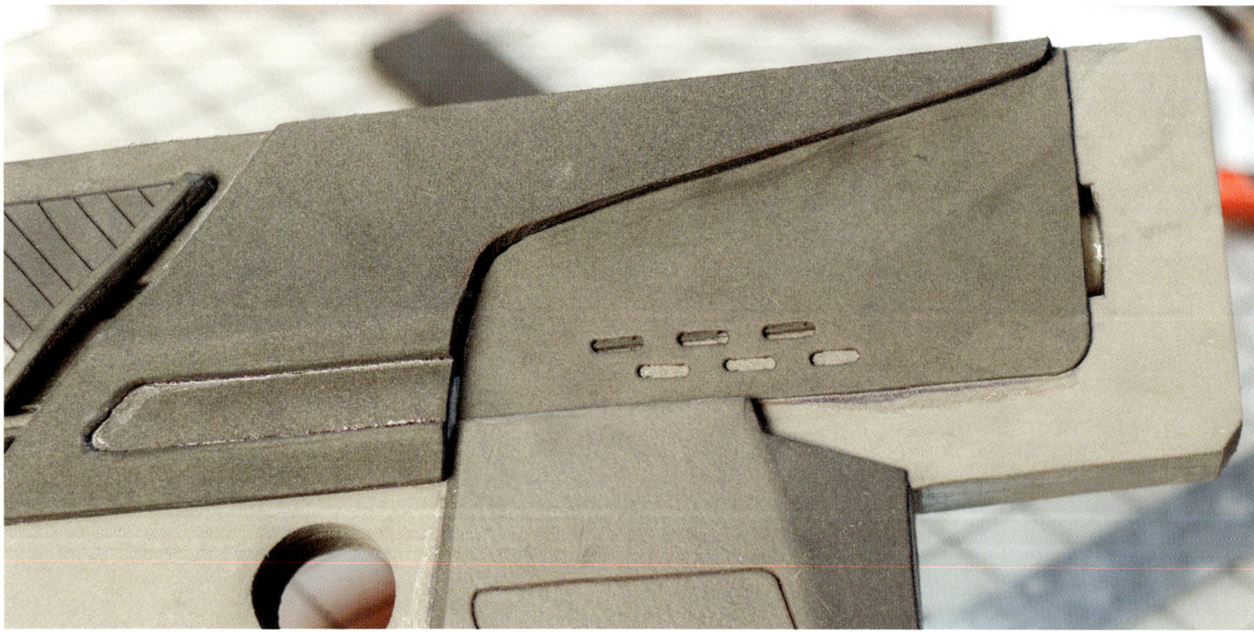

The contoured part that runs above the vents was a tricky beast. I started by cutting some 6mm foam to shape and then tapering it with my belt sander. This got it most of the way, but I had to freehand some more bevels with the rotary tool. Once I achieved the form I wanted, it was glued into place above the vents. Another piece of 6mm foam was cut and glued in place just behind the previous two parts, completing the rear part of the gun body.

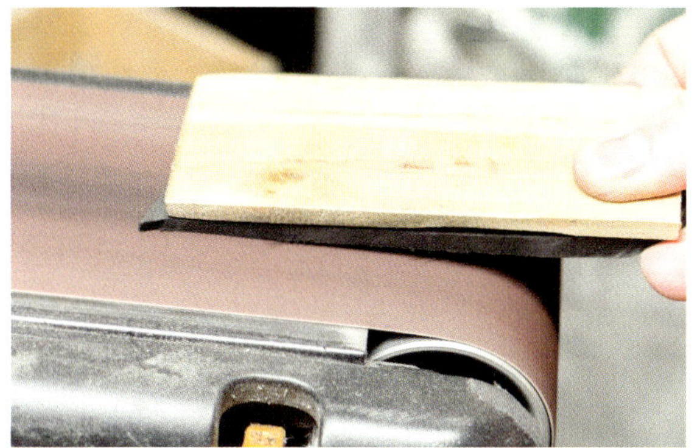

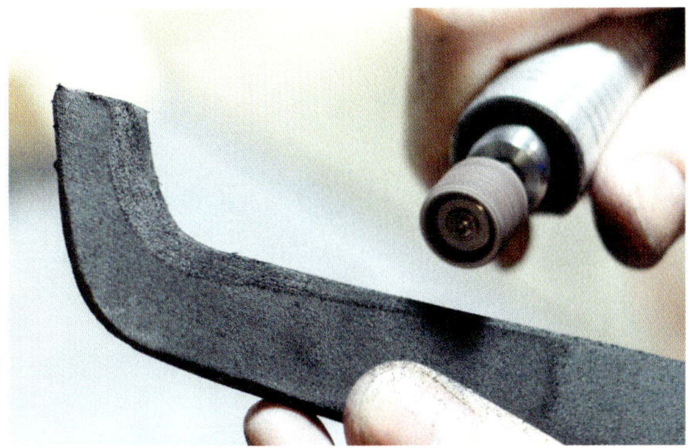

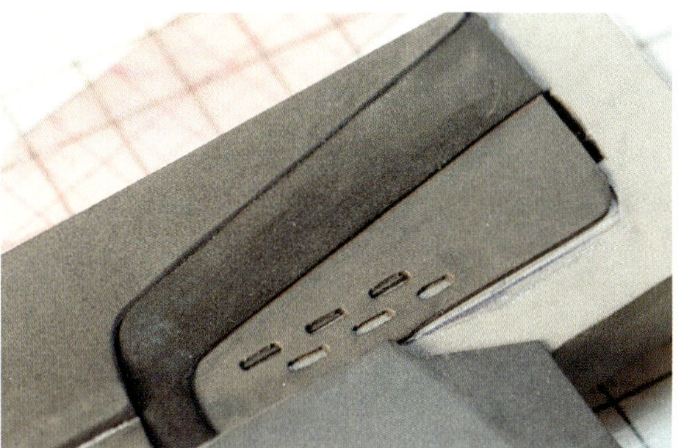

Rounding The Handle

Gun handles tend to be the most contoured part of a build like this, so I ended up doing a fair bit of sculpting. And by "sculpting" I mean "making a lot of foam dust with my rotary tool." Using a sanding drum, I removed more and more material until the handle felt good in my hand. This included the wacky thumb hole, which is a really neat looking design, but ridiculously impractical. When I was happy with the form, I went back over the handle with a grinding bit to tidy up my work.

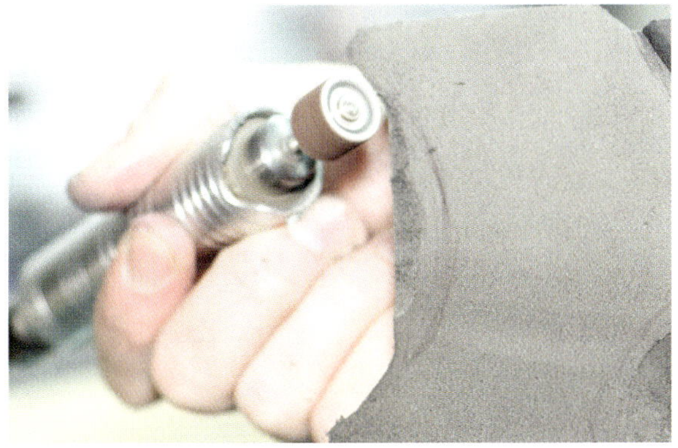

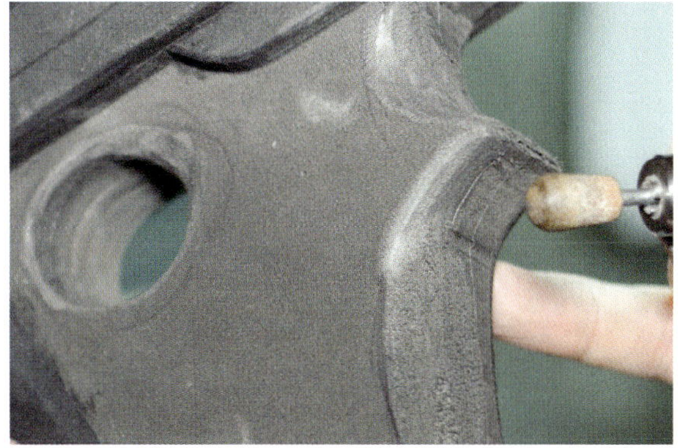

Handle Greeble

There was also a goofy bit of greeble detail on the bottom of the handle for some reason. Maybe this was the USB charging port for the space gun? Ethernet adapter? Either way, I ended up going with as simple a solution as possible and just cut out a bunch of material with a knife to make room for the details. Then I added the raised bits using cut pieces of 2mm foam.

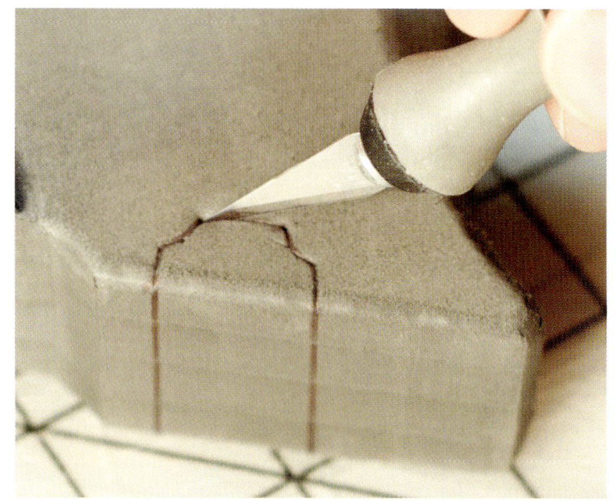

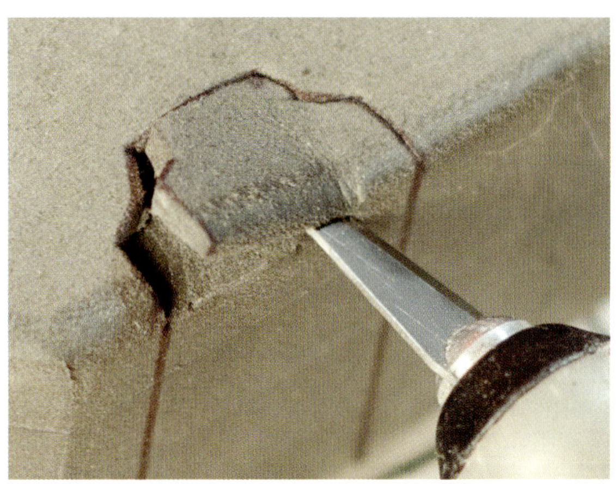

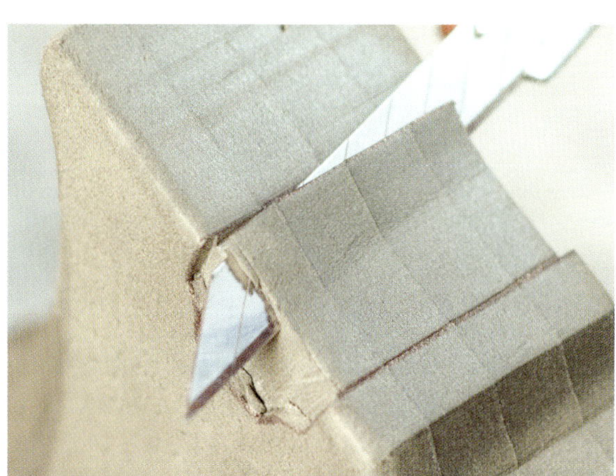

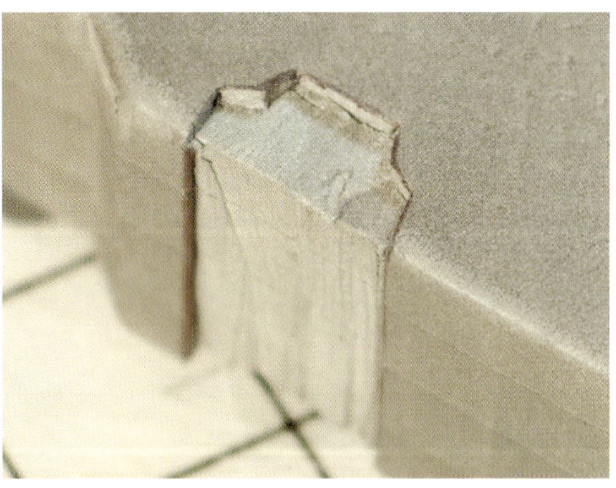

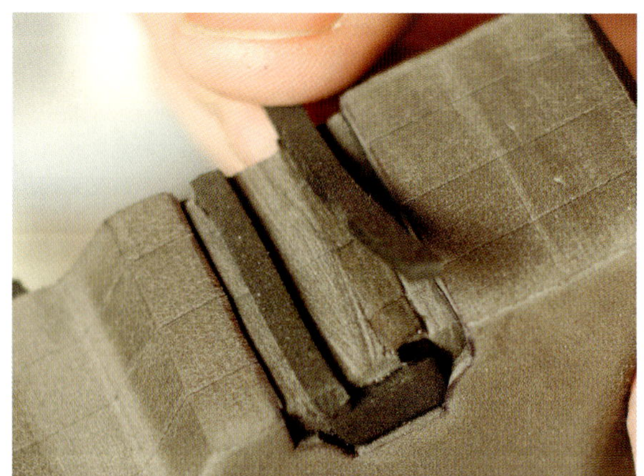

The grips on the handle were very similar to the fore grip, so I could have cut them out the same way using a knife and a heat gun. On the other hand, I do own a laser cutter. Now, I know most other makers don't have immediate access to a tool like this, but it is really cool, so I figured I'd show you how it works with foam.

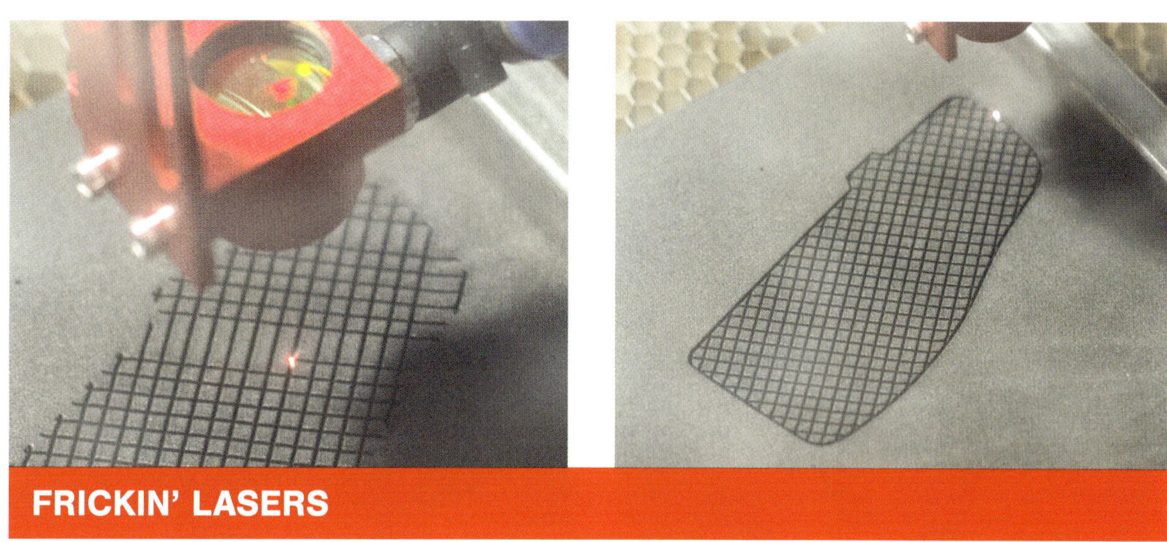

FRICKIN' LASERS

I took the vector files for my gun and fed the handle grip section into my laser. It was able to quickly, and perfectly, cut out and etch the knurled pattern on the grips from some 2mm foam. I took those grips and Barged them to the handle, piece of cake. I realize the robots will take over the human race some day, but so long as they're still domesticated, I really like having them around to do my bidding!

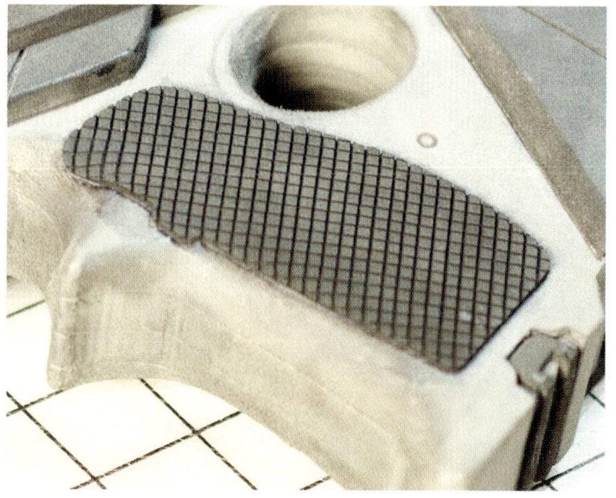

Want to experiment with foam and lasers? Look for laser cutters to use at local maker spaces or university workshops. Start with a low power setting and a high speed, with multiple passes. Make sure there's ventilation, since the laser vaporizes the foam!

Rear Stock

The shoulder stock of this gun was a really fun bit of engineering, starting with a block of floor mat foam made from three laminated layers. I used the front and side views of my template to trace out and cut the general shape from this block of foam using the band saw.

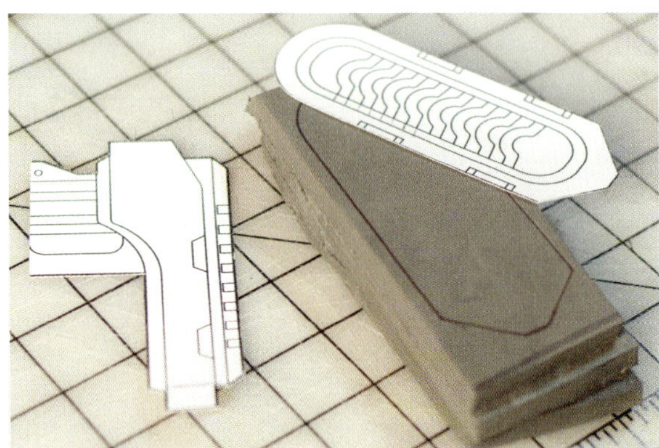

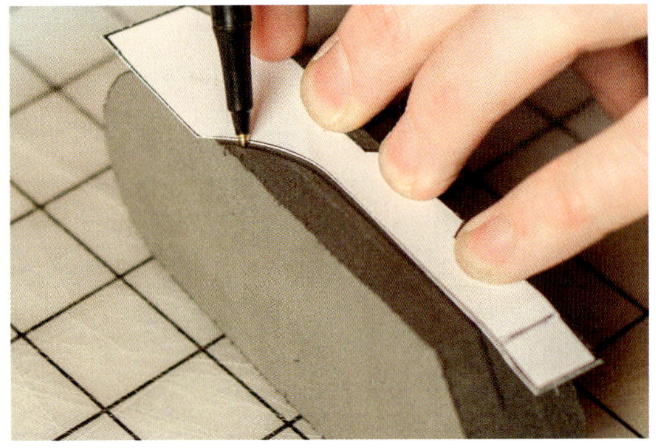

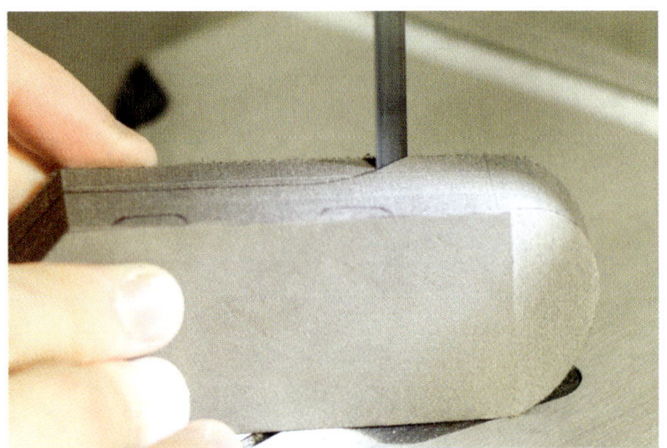

I trimmed a layer of 6mm foam to go behind the first part and glued it into place with Barge. This added another layer of detail to the piece.

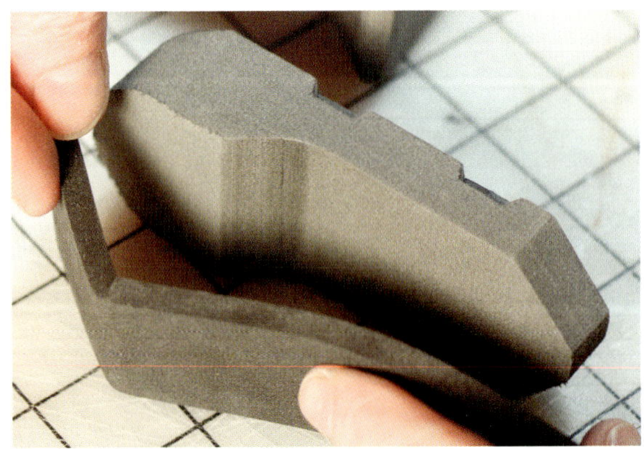

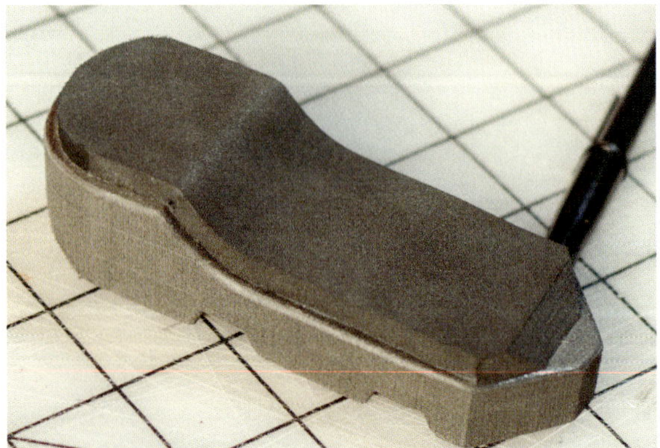

The portion of the stock that connects it to the rifle body was cut from four laminated layers of floor mat foam, again on the band saw. This piece has some greebles along the side, so they were achieved with 2mm craft foam cut out with a knife and secured with super glue. This whole part was glued to the stock with Barge.

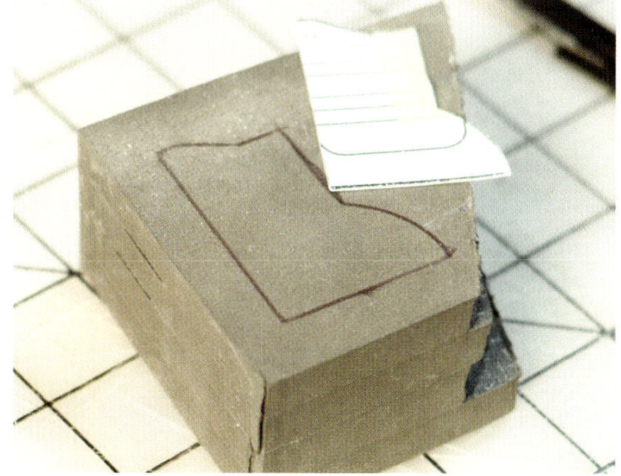

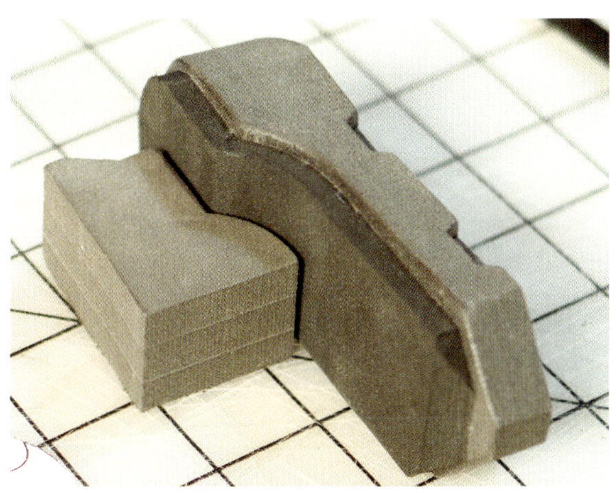

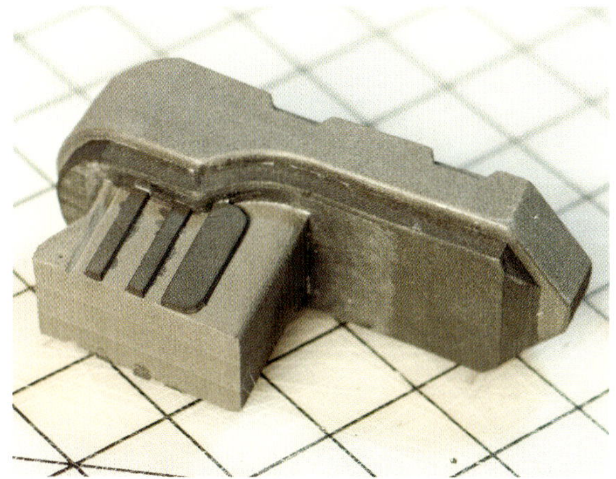

The rear portion of the stock had some really intricate details. Using the template, I definitely could have traced out each of these pieces and cut them out by hand with a knife or with my scroll saw...
But, I used my laser.

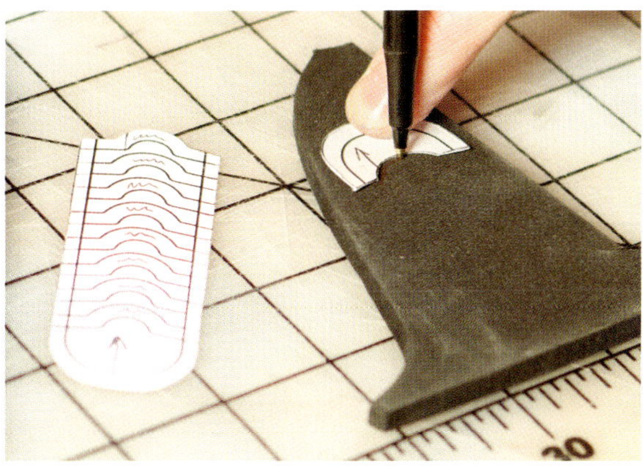

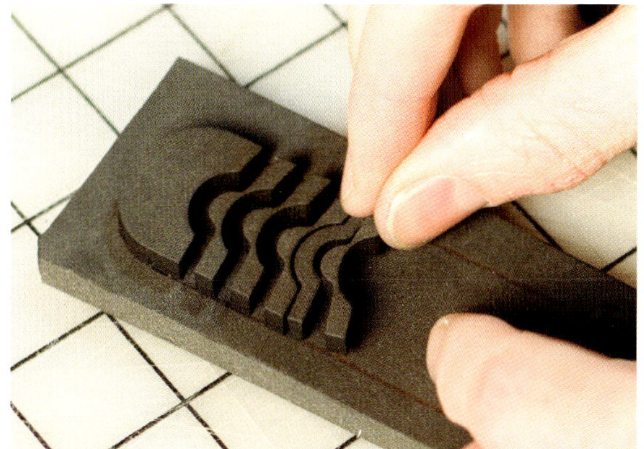

I traced out the base shape for the rear stock piece on some 6mm foam and then glued down all of these tiny detail parts with super glue. Then I cut out the perimeter of this piece with the band saw, cutting as close to the edges of the detail parts as possible. I tilted the bed of the band saw and cut a bevel along the edge of this piece and cleaned up my work with a knife and rotary tool.

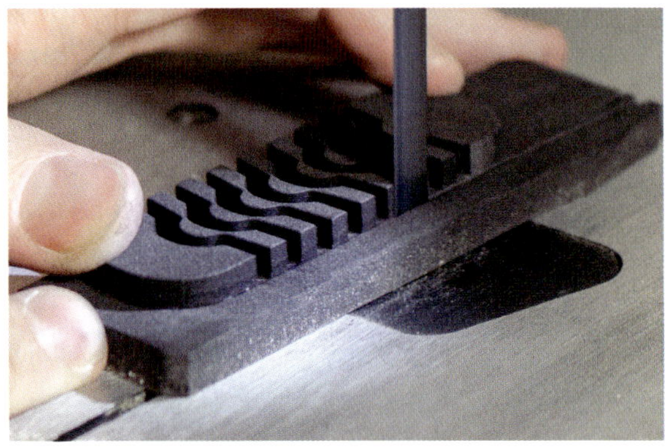

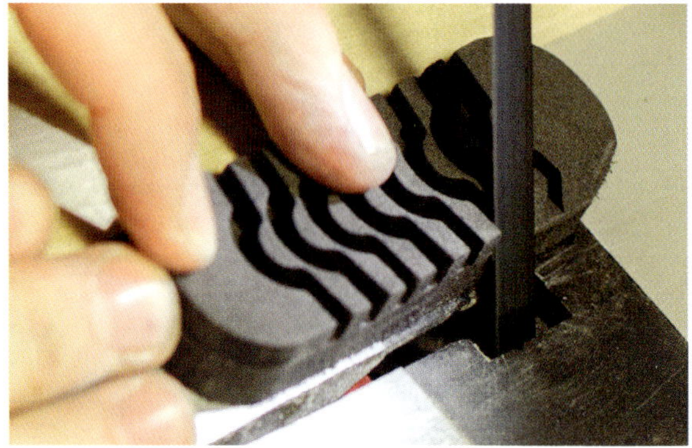

I turned this piece ninety degrees and used the band saw to cut off a section of its back side. This was done to make it fit nicely on the main stock part. All parts were glued together and there was much rejoicing (yaaaaay).

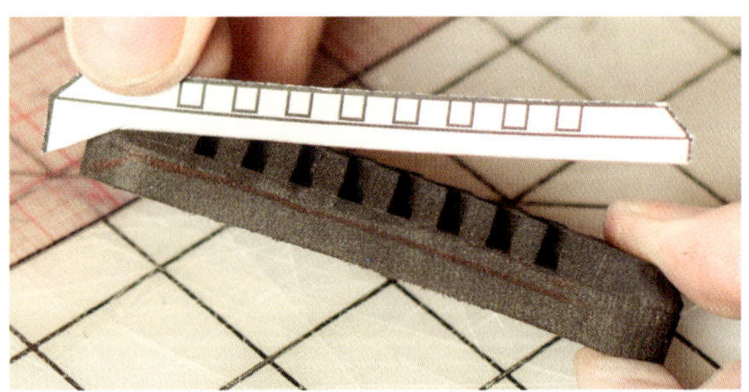

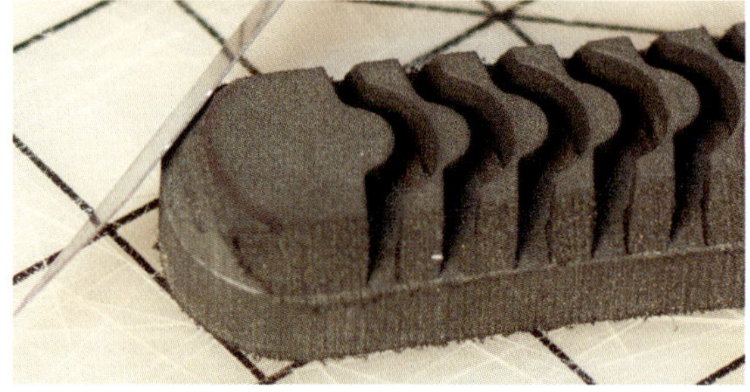

I kept this stock piece apart from the main body to make it easier to paint. It would be attached later on in the build.

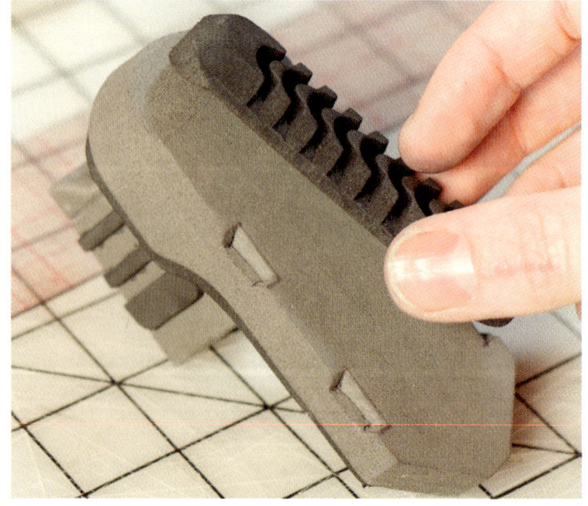

Rail, Sight, and Trigger

Something that was nagging me was how sloppy the top rail of the gun had become over the duration of the build. So I glued a large piece of 2mm craft foam to the top of it, overlapping all of the edges. Then I trimmed the edges all nice and clean with a knife and did some tidying up with my rotary tool.

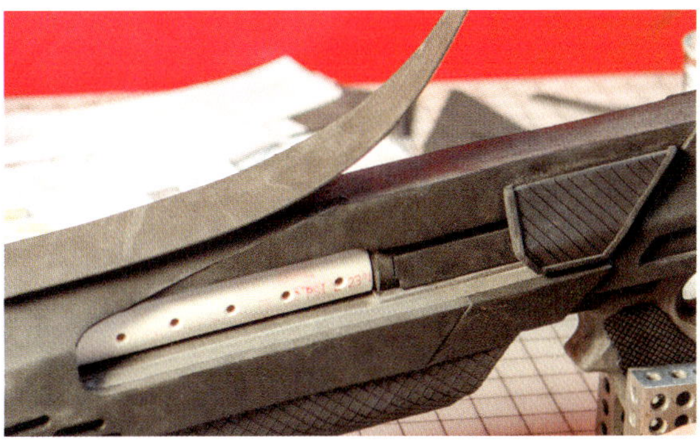

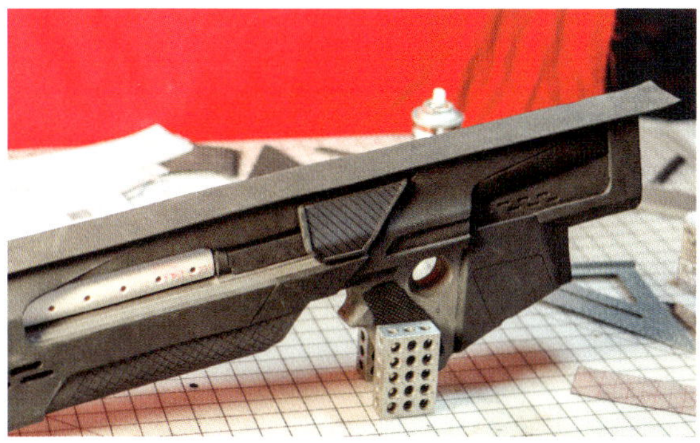

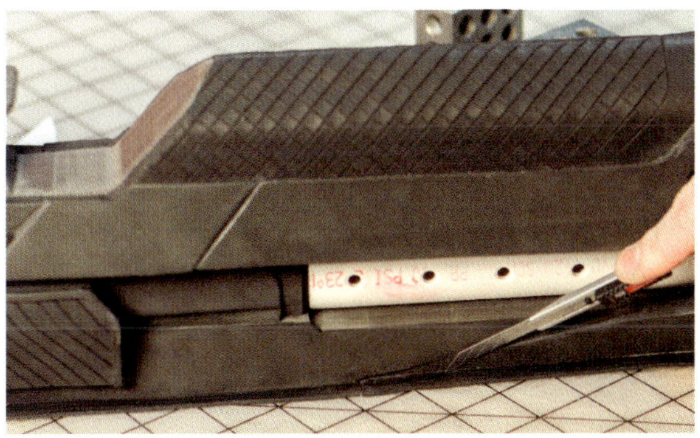

With the top of the gun looking nice and clean, I cut out a strip of foam to use as the rear rail. The piece got bent around the back corner of the gun. This is one very important reason why I like working with foam so much!

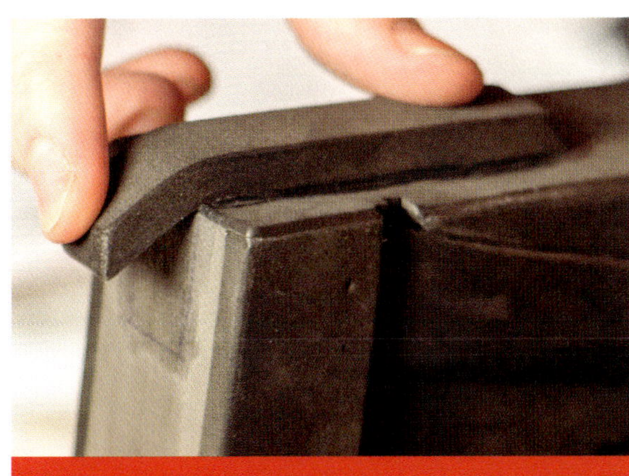

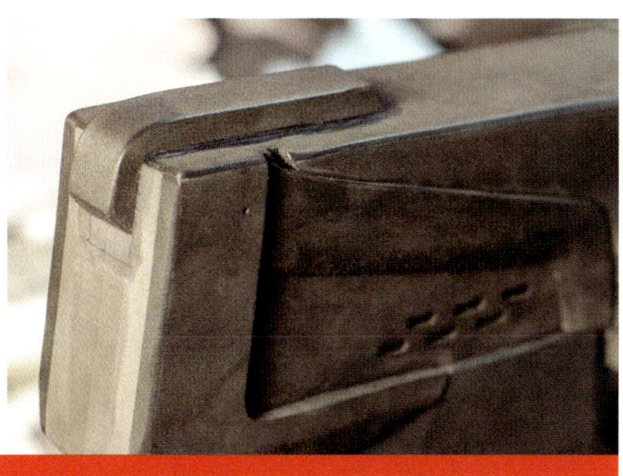

Gun Sight

The sight for the gun was made from some very thin material so I opted to use something other than EVA foam. What I used instead was a foamed PVC plastic. Yes, technically it's still foam! I got some sheets of this stuff at a local plastic distributor. It's really great to use when you need something a little bit more rigid than your EVA foam.

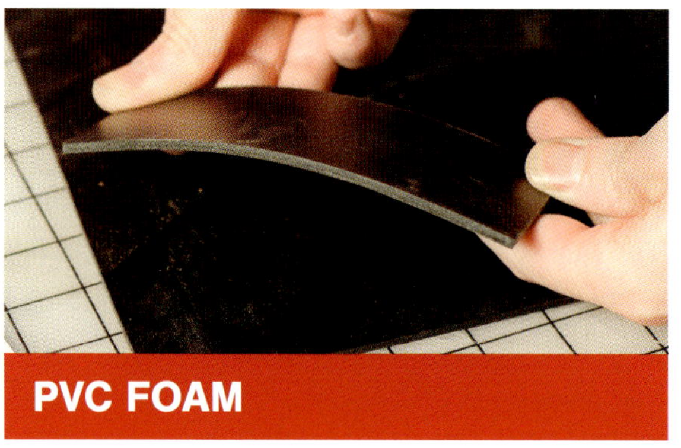

PVC FOAM

I started by making a form out of a piece of MDF on my band saw. This was used to heat form the PVC into the rough shape of the sight. I glued one edge of the sheet to my MDF form and then heated each bit with the heat gun until it was pliable enough to roll around the wood.

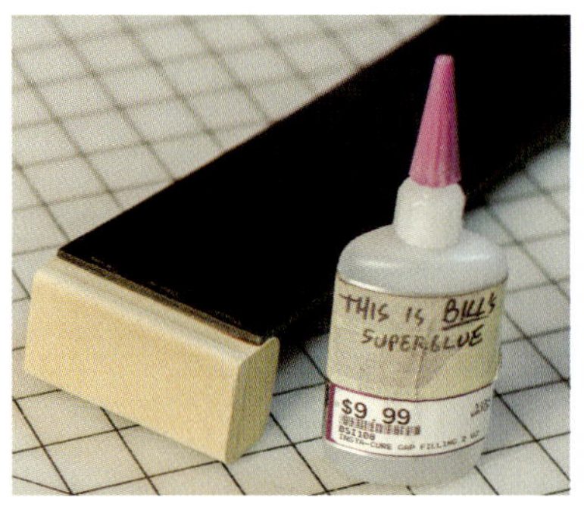

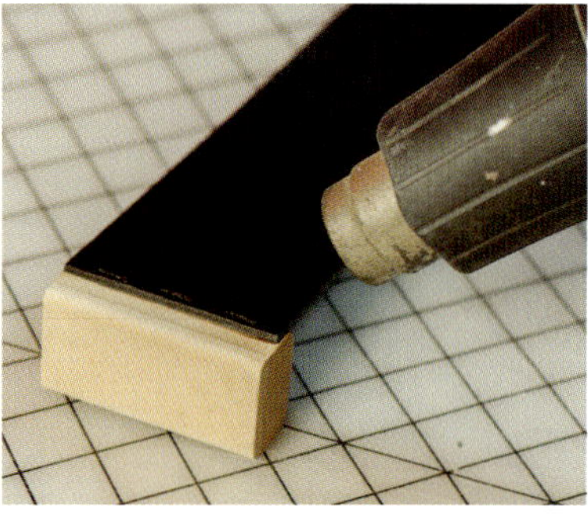

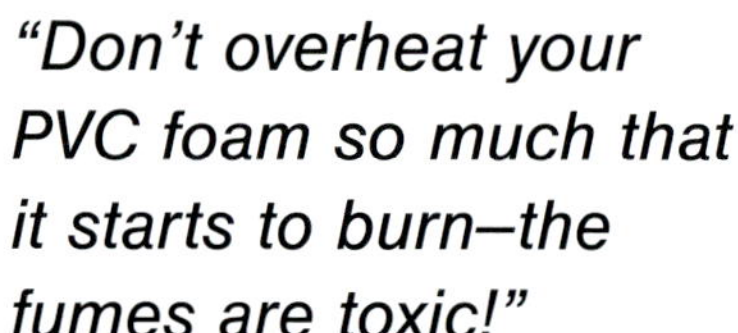

"Don't overheat your PVC foam so much that it starts to burn–the fumes are toxic!"

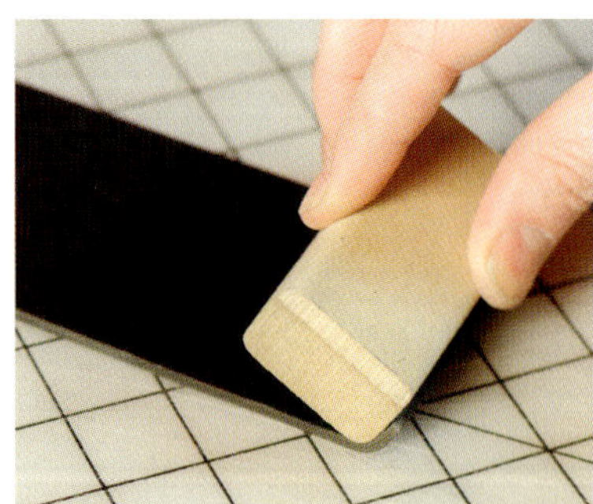

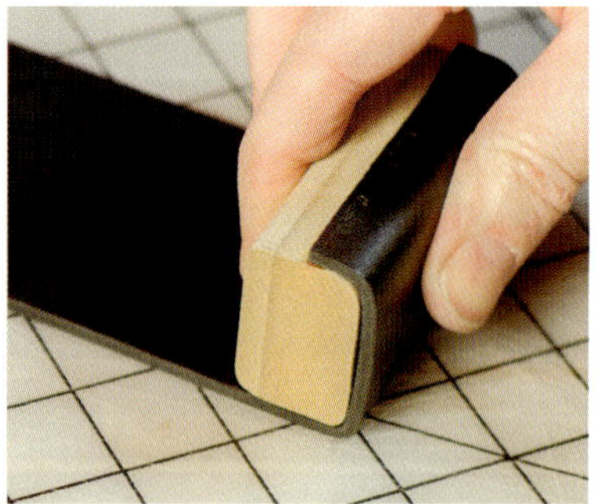

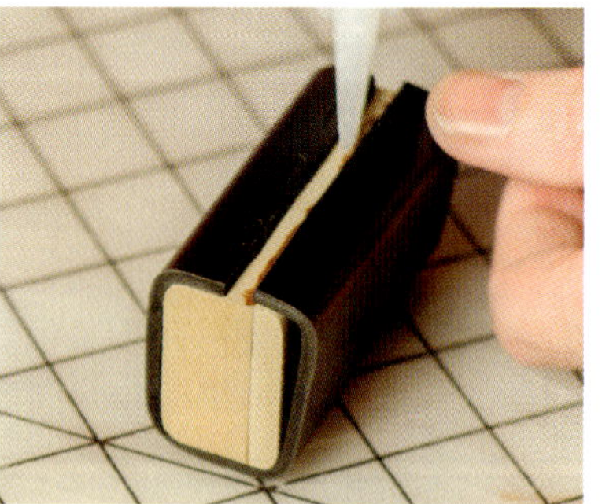

Don't overheat your PVC foam (also called Sintra) so much that it starts to burn. The fumes released from burning PVC foam are extremely toxic. Take your time and work slowly with the material. It will become nice and malleable with just a little bit of heat. If it does start to burn, put the material down and leave the area. As always, it pays to work in a well ventilated space.

With the plastic sheet wrapped all the way around the MDF form, I glued it all in place to keep it together for the next few steps. After sanding the whole surface, I cut out the profile shape of my gun sight with the band saw. Then I finessed the edges on the disc sander.

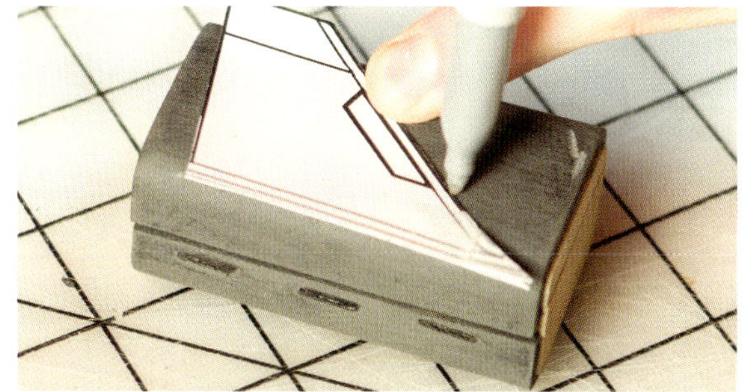

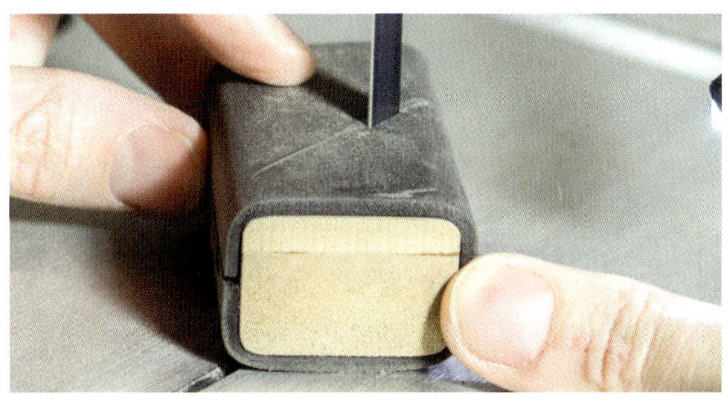

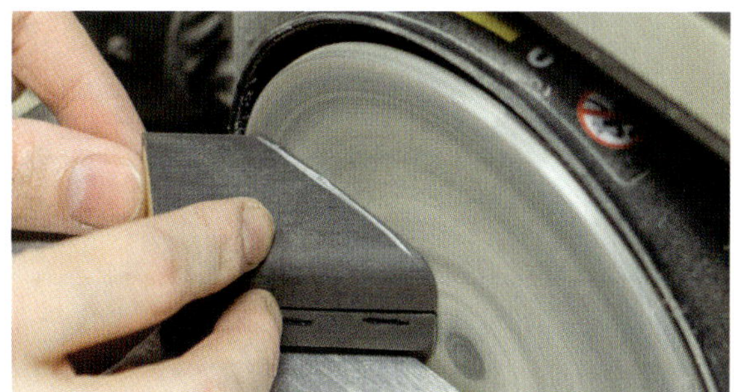

The sight has some other detailed shapes that needed to be cut in. The thin strip on the back of the sight was cut off again with the band saw. The other details were cut into the plastic by hand with a hobby knife. When I was happy with all of the shapes, everything got a good once over with some 220 grit sandpaper and I removed them from the MDF form.

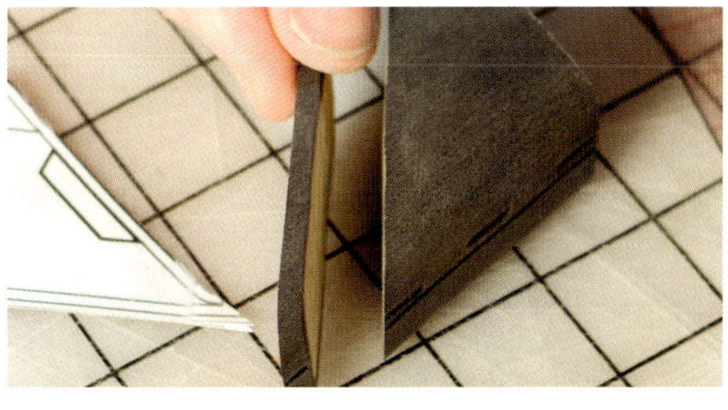

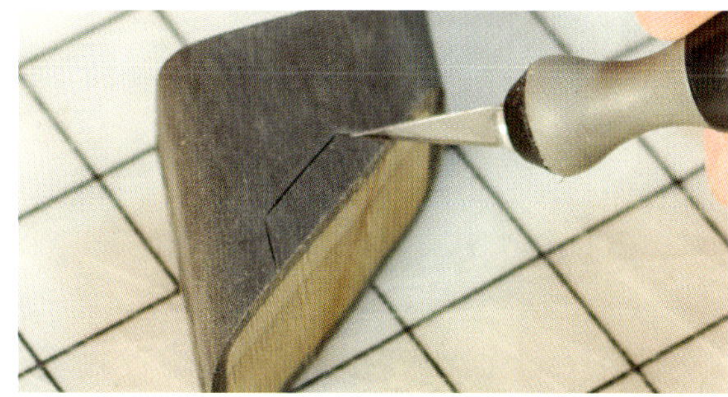

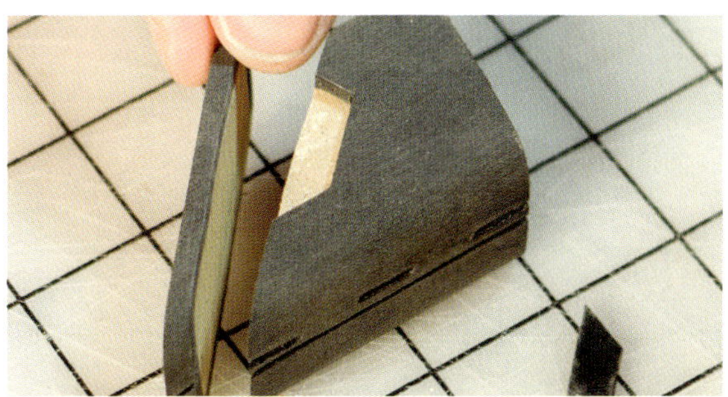

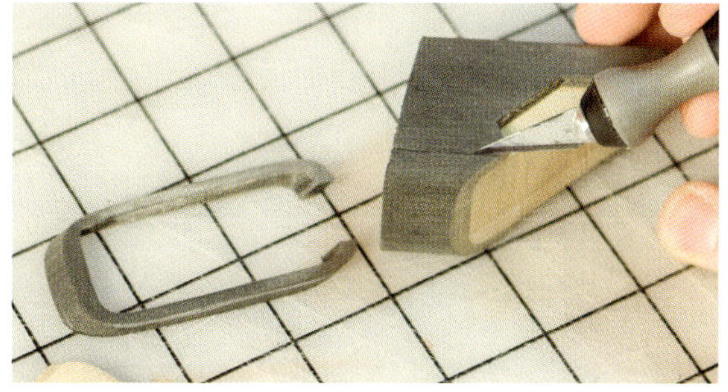

The thin rear part of the sight was glued back onto the main sight part to complete the assembly. Then the whole part was glued down to a portion of foam that would serve as the base for the sight. All of these assembled pieces got glued down to the gun body.

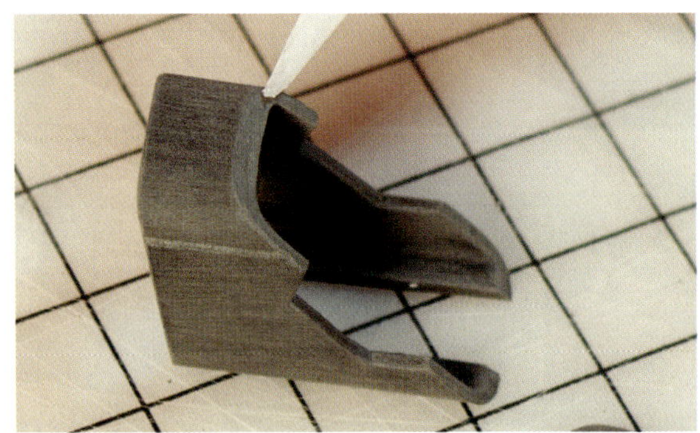

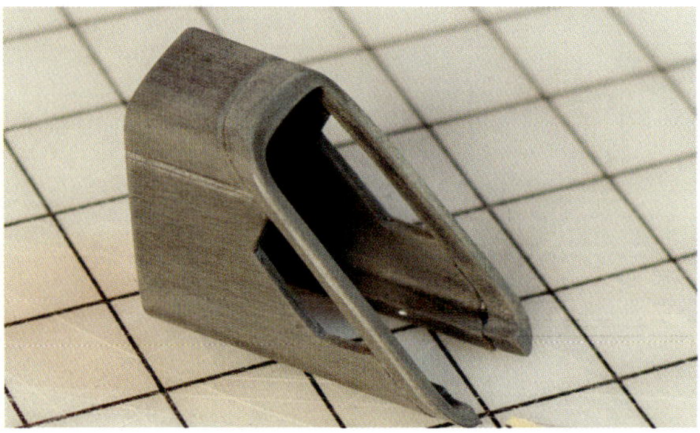

Super glue is an excellent bond for PVC foam.

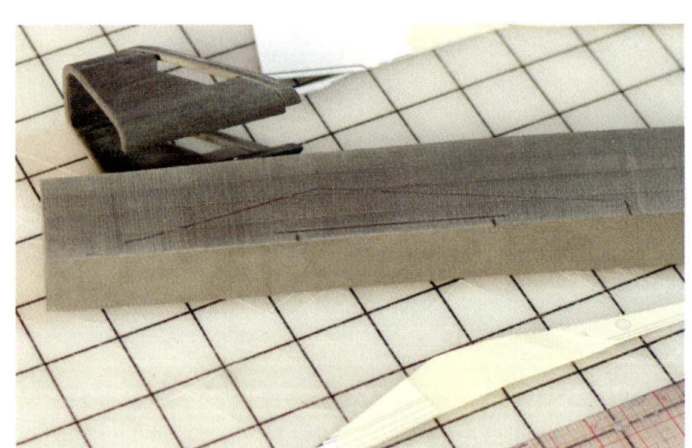

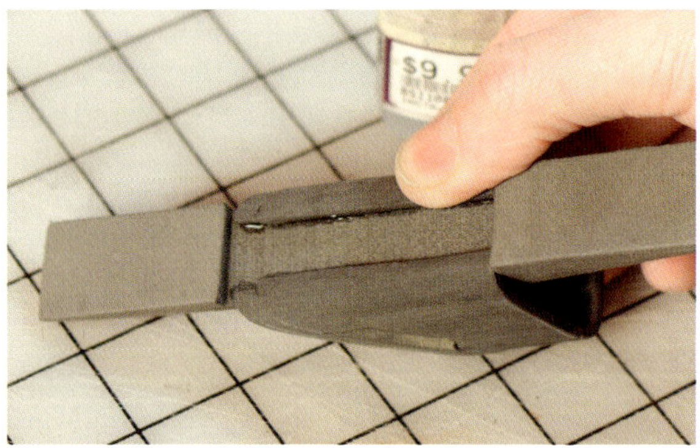

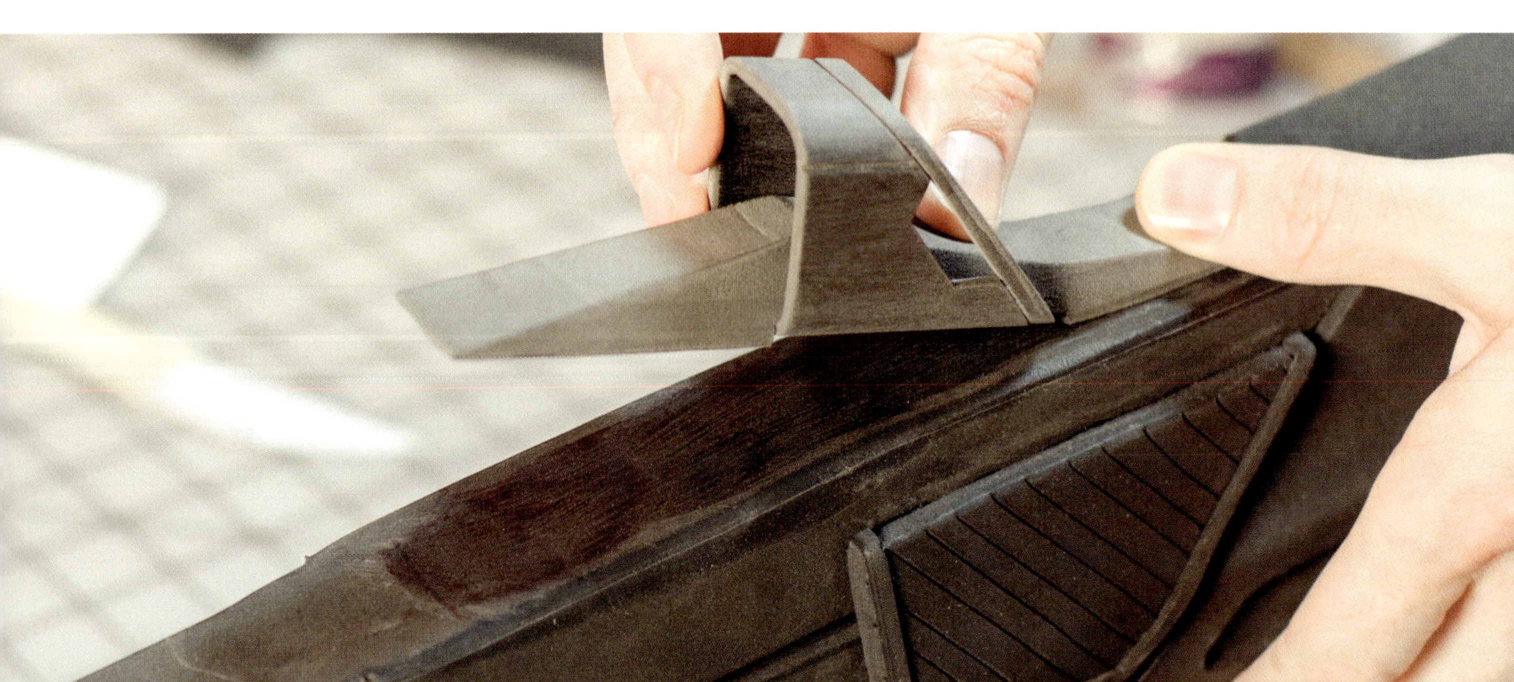

Front Rail

I cut a long, thin strip of foam for the front rail. The forward rail had a couple of half round slots cut into it. The quickest way to make these was to use a small sanding drum on my rotary tool to cut in the slots by hand. This was a little bit tricky, so I made sure to do some tests on scrap foam to perfect my technique. With the rail formed and cut to shape, it was glued down to the rest of the gun body.

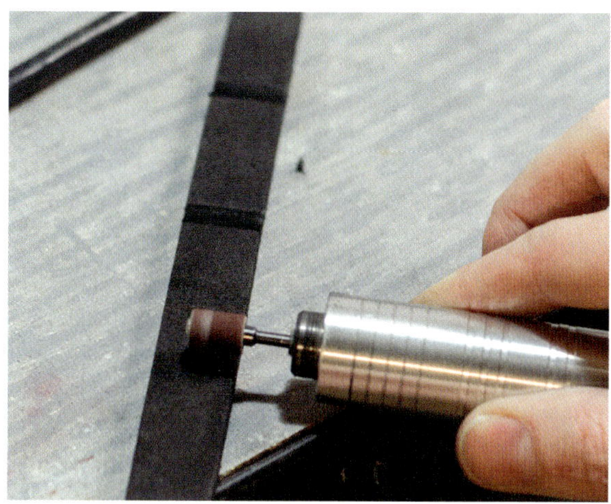

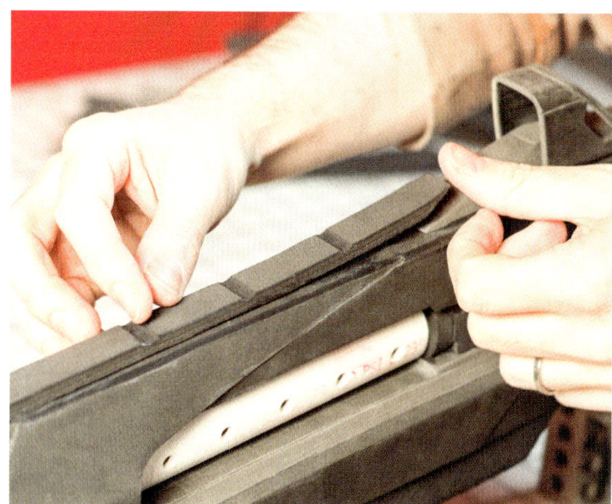

Sintra Trigger

The trigger was done in a similar fashion as the sight, using more PVC foam. The base of the trigger is extra long, so it will snug into the foam base and support any rough handling. A slot was cut into the bottom of the trigger area and the rigid plastic trigger was glued into place.

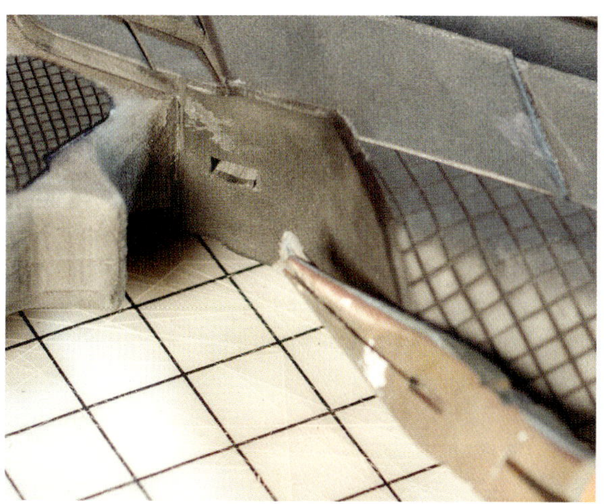

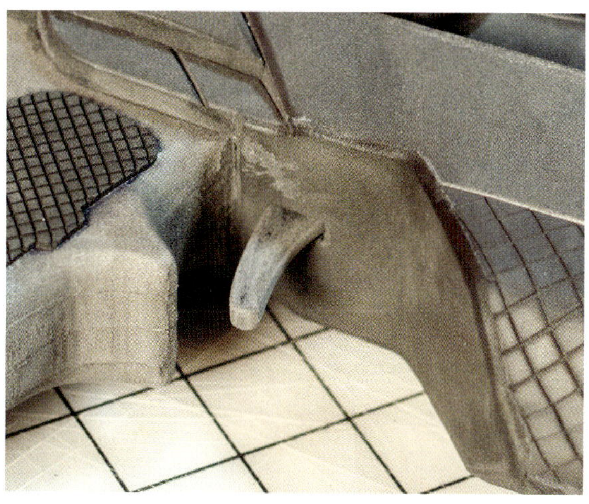

Screws

Future Space Screws

Since this is a gun from the future, it's covered in hex screws. I decided that the most efficient and accurate way to replicate them was to use actual screws. I picked up a bunch of set screws from the hardware store that were a perfect match!

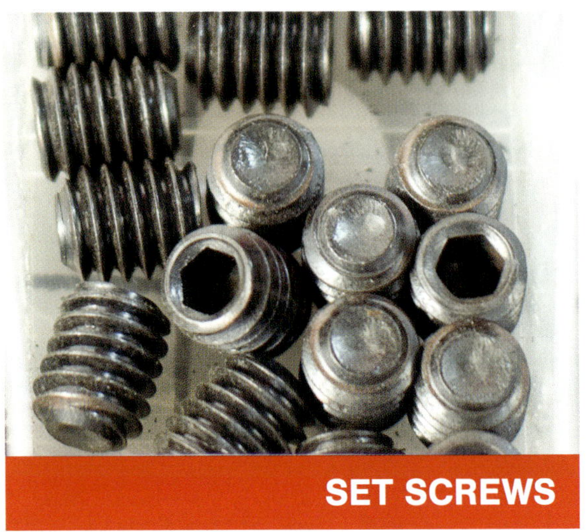

SET SCREWS

To punch holes for these screws I used my leather hole punch and then ripped out the offending material with needle nose pliers. This made room for me to screw in the hardware. A dab of super glue was applied to the hole and then I used an allen wrench to apply the screw.

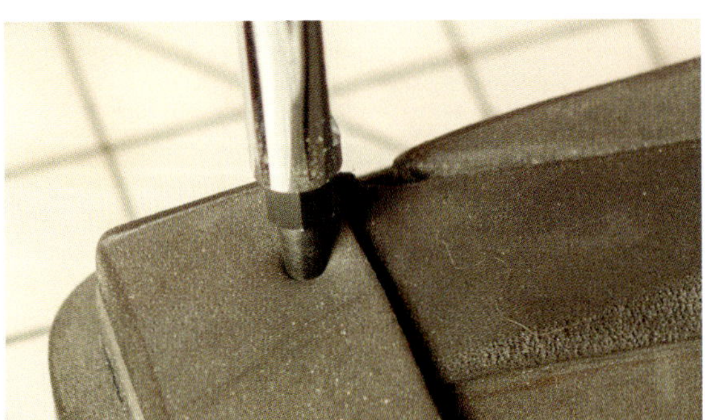

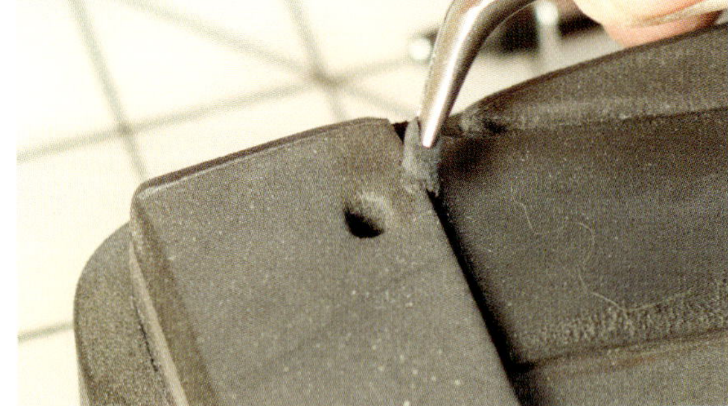

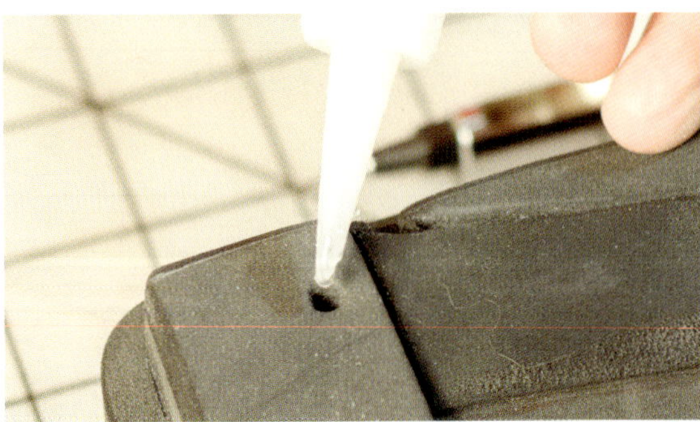

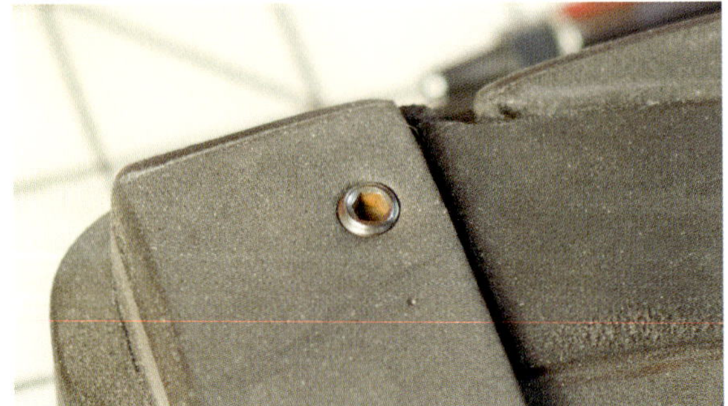

Sanding Drum Trick

Other circular greebles were added with the rotary tool. For the rivet head near the handle, I used the top of my smallest sanding drum. By pushing it straight down into the foam, I was able to cut a perfect little circle into the foam.

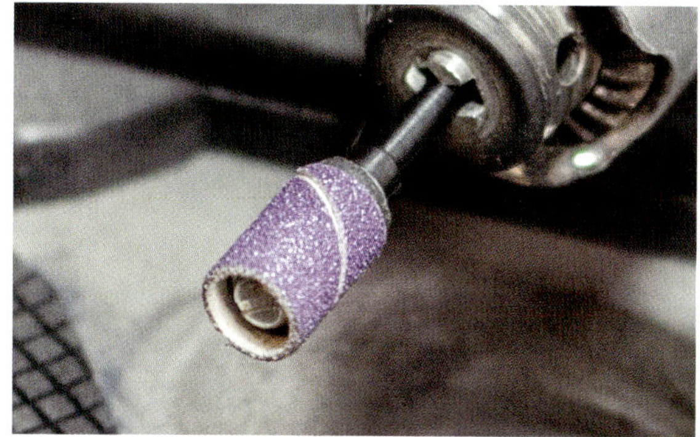

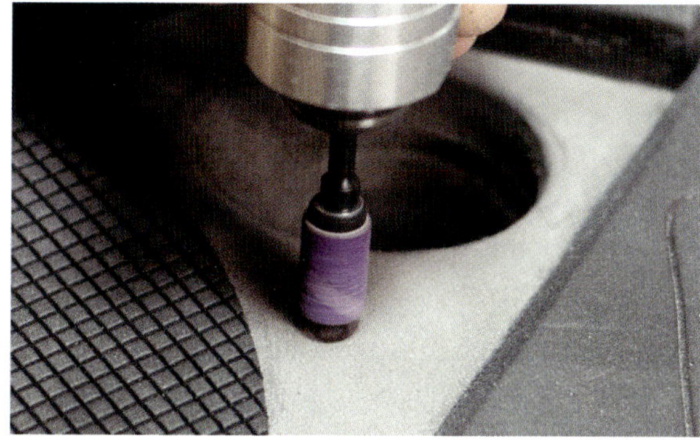

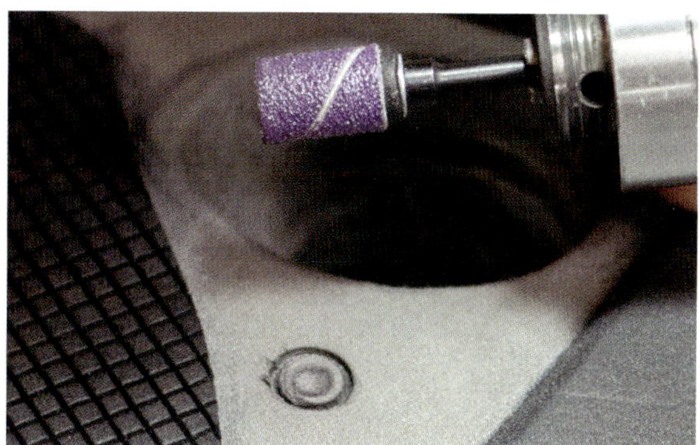

Clean Up

Those screw and rivet details were the last bit of fabrication on the gun and it was time to paint it! Before spraying the color, I gave everything a good once over with my grinding bit on the rotary tool to make sure all my edges were nice and smoothed out. Then I heat sealed everything with the heat gun.

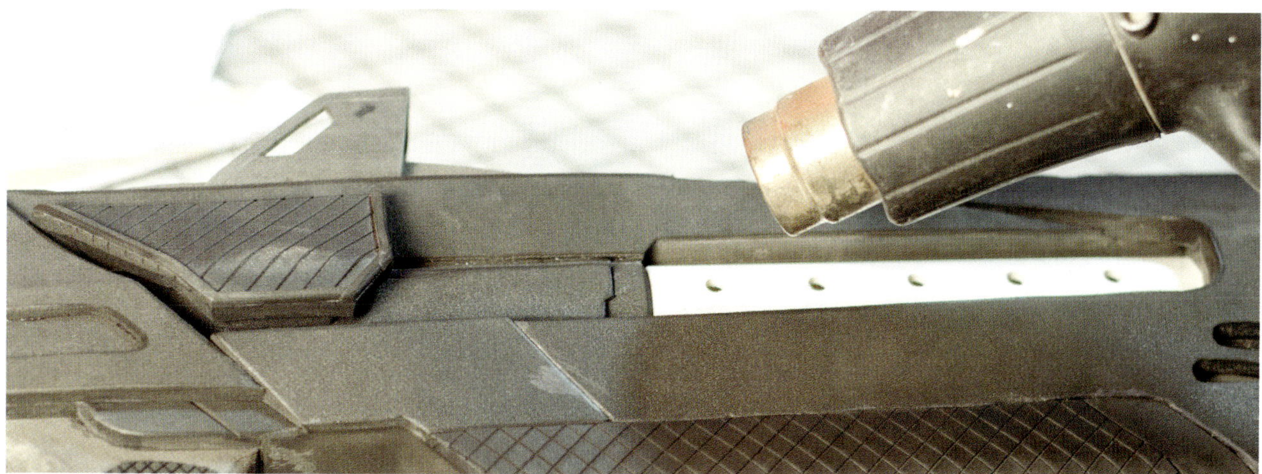

Sanding and Painting

Since I left the stock off the gun body, I could use that area to add a piece of wire for hanging my piece. This would allow me to hold the gun up without needing to touch it. This way I could paint all of the faces of the gun in one go instead of having to wait for one side to dry before flipping it over. Similar wires were added to the stock and the magazine.

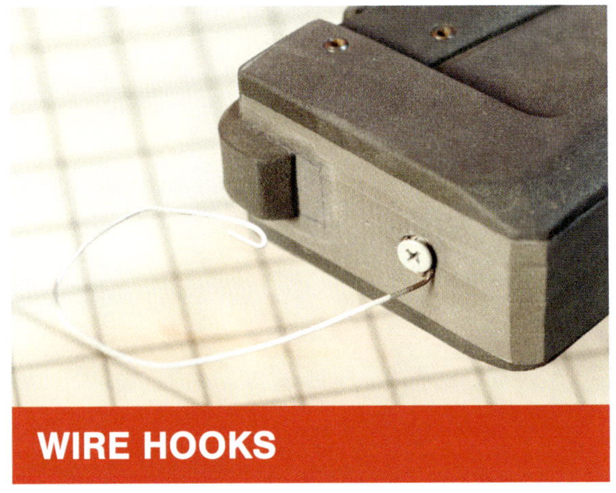

WIRE HOOKS

Seal with Paint

I didn't foresee this gun bending very much, so I opted to seal it with only spray paint. This is the quickest, most convenient way to get a base coat of color onto your foam props. My favorite paint for this is Krylon Fusion. It bonds really well to foam and acts like a primer. I started by applying a good four layers of the spray paint and then let it all dry thoroughly.

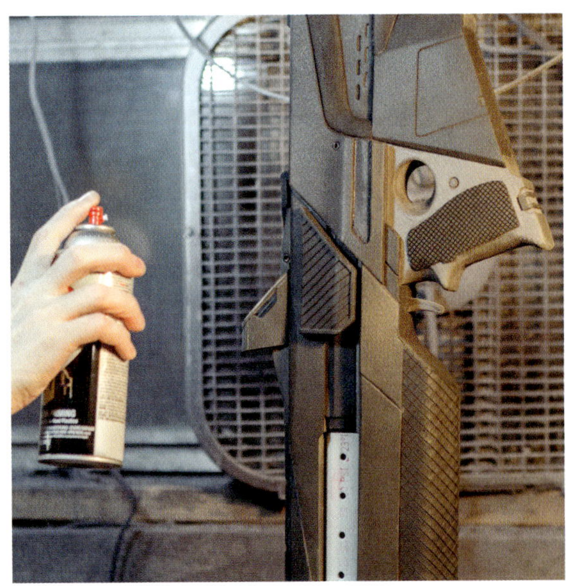

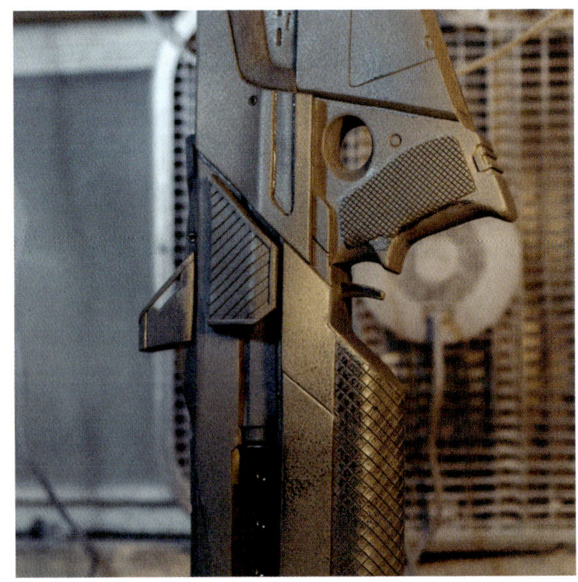

Read the can for drying times!

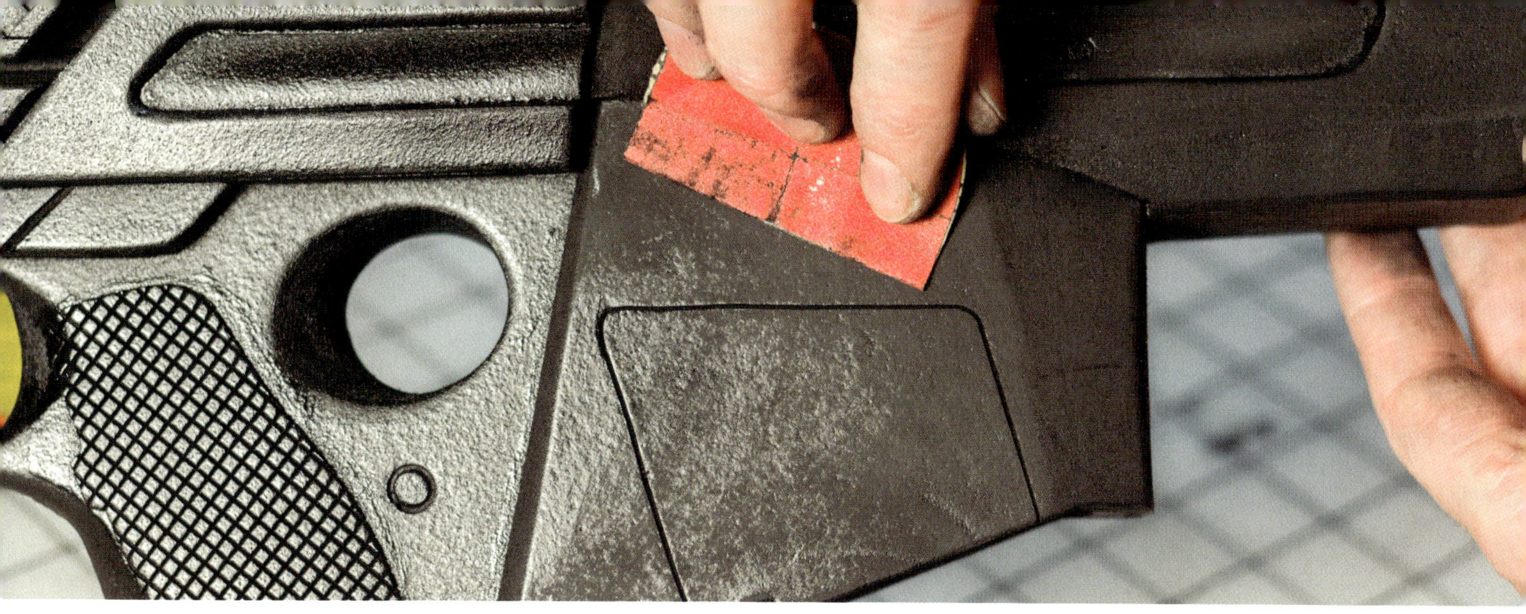

Sand All The Things!

Then everything got sanded! The goal with the sanding was to smooth down all of the flat surfaces. No matter what, you're going to end up with some texture from your foam and the sanding will help clear that up. I went with a 220 grit sandpaper for the majority of this work.

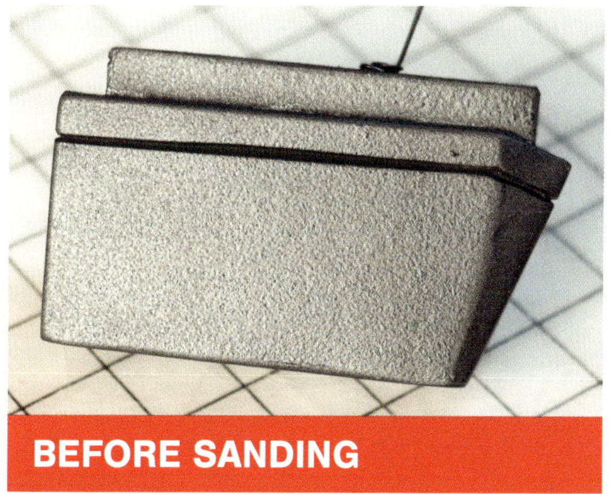

BEFORE SANDING

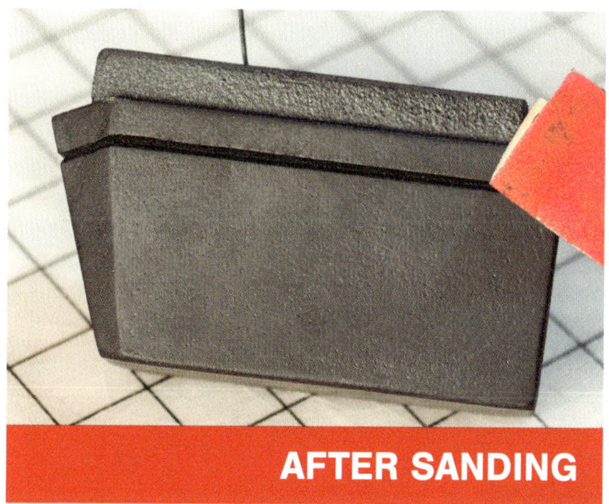

AFTER SANDING

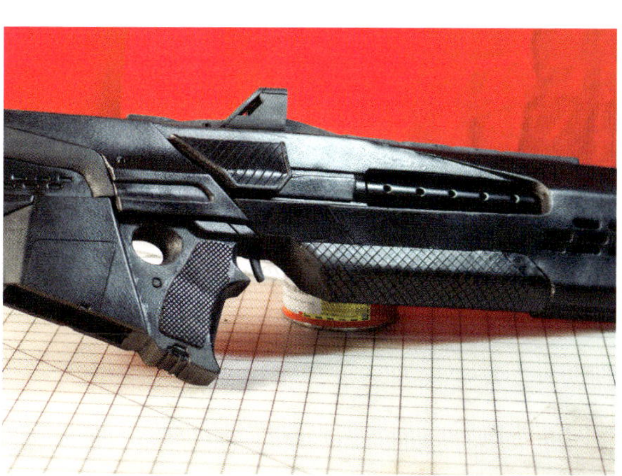

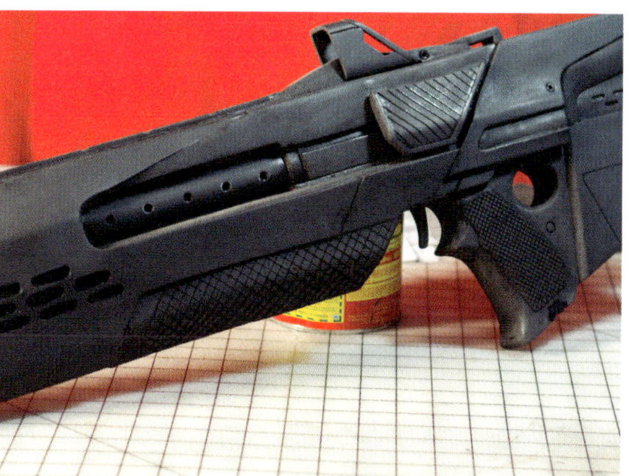

Filler Primer

At this point, I could have started laying down paint but I wanted to get just a little bit more refinement out of the surface. So, I sprayed on a couple of layers of filler primer. This is a thicker primer that does a great job of filling in any unwanted surface textures.

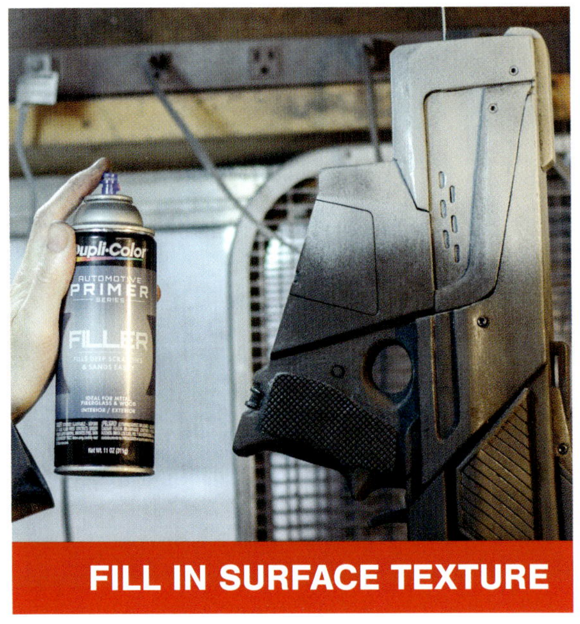

FILL IN SURFACE TEXTURE

Once the filler primer dried, you guessed it, even more sanding! The rough work was done with 220 grit paper and the final polish was done with a "fine" sanding sponge.

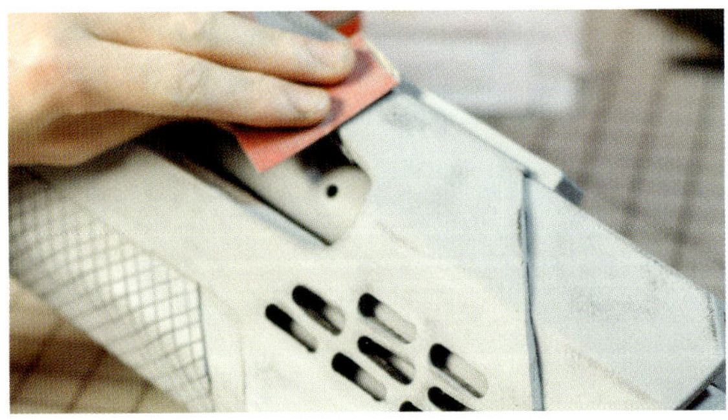

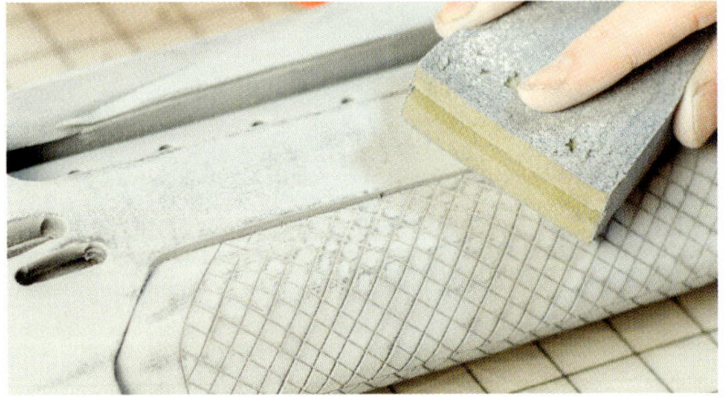

Warm Up Paint

Since I was spraying paint in the winter, I opted to warm up the spray paint cans in some warm water for a few minutes before applying them to my foam. This helped the paint exit the can in a much more favorable manner.

Warm spray paint has a finer mist.

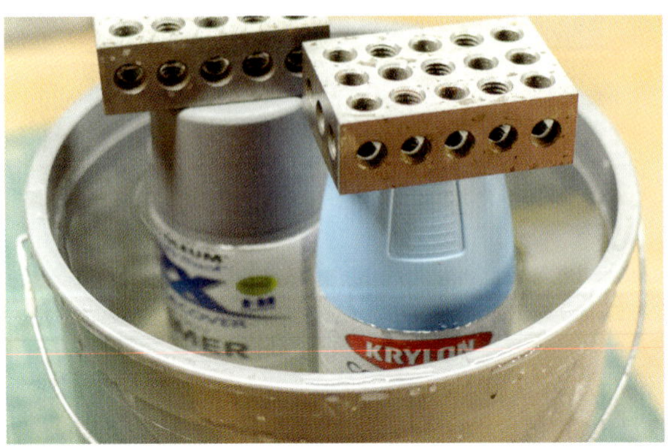

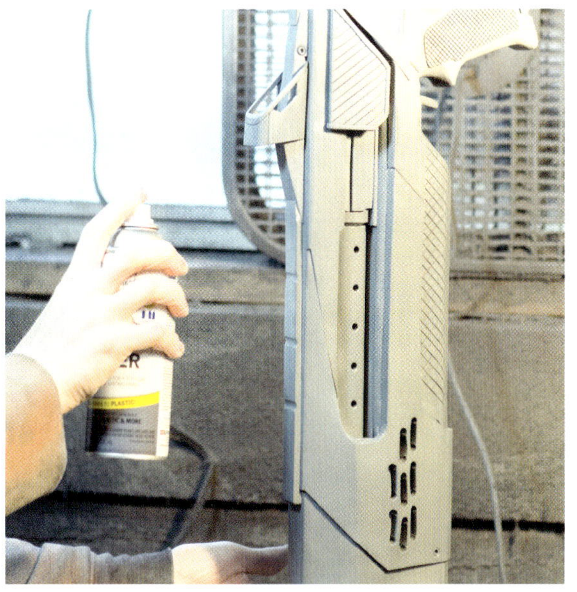

Primer

When I was finally happy with the surface texture, I could lay down some actual paint, starting with some normal spray paint primer. I applied a couple of thin coats and then let it dry completely before laying down my base colors.

Most of the Jade Rabbit is a dark gray. I couldn't find a rattle can with the exact color I wanted, so I mixed my own using acrylic paints. These paints were thinned with a little water and then applied to the foam gun with an airbrush.

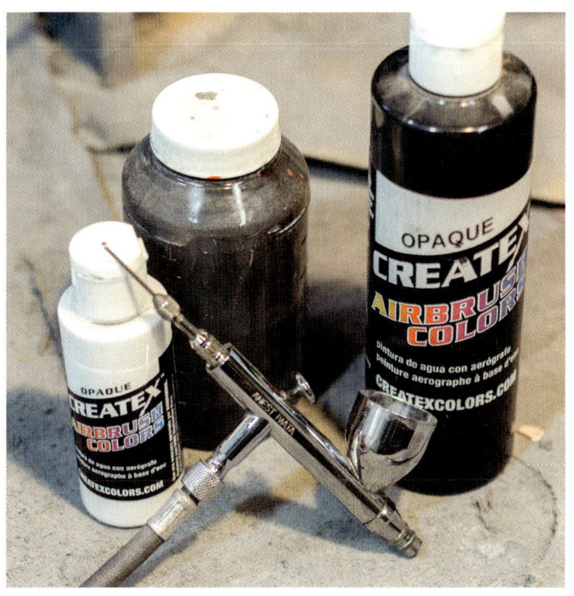

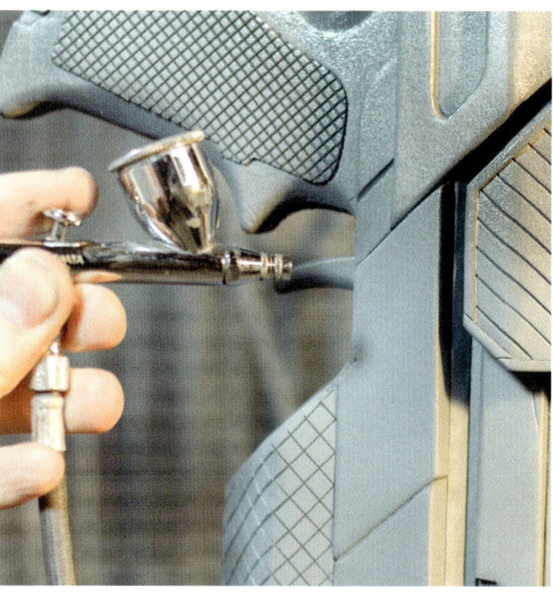

Masking

Again, I let this layer of paint dry completely before moving on. It doesn't hurt to leave a project like this overnight to be totally sure it's dry. When I was satisfied that the base coat was ready for it, I started masking off the areas that would be painted a light blue color. Using a "delicate surfaces" tape, I outlined all of the areas that needed to be covered. For small, intricate areas I laid down a big piece of masking tape and then trimmed it with a sharp hobby knife.

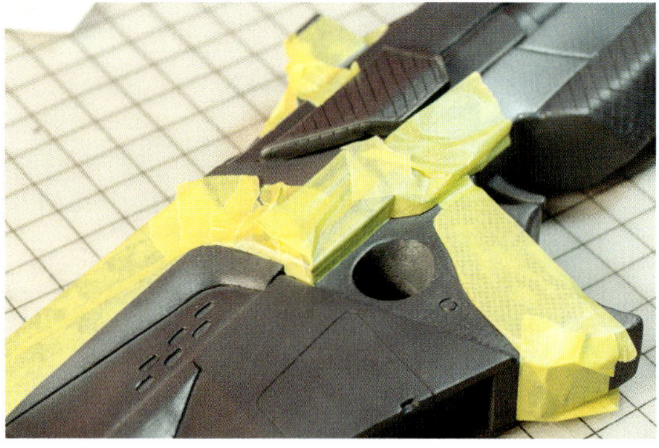

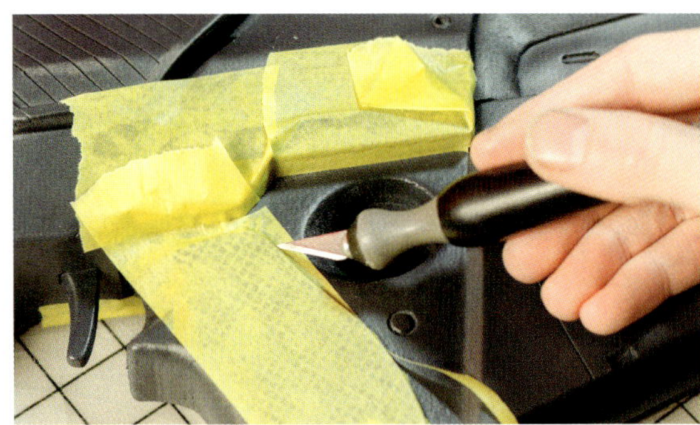

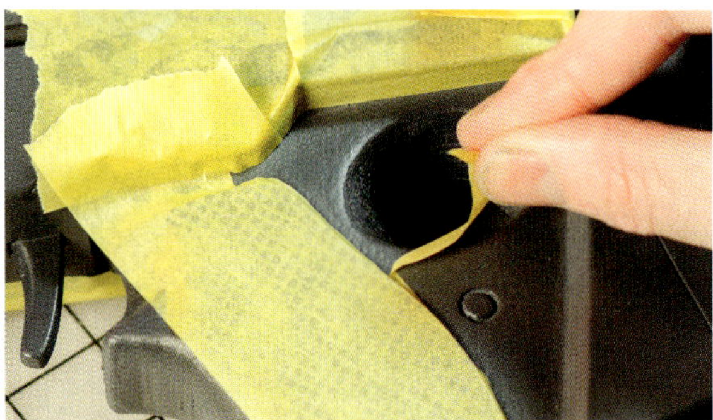

With all of the edges masked off, I used some masking paper and more tape to cover the rest of the gun. It was vital that every surface I wanted to stay gray be completely covered. It's really easy for the new sprayed layer to make its way through any gaps in your masking.

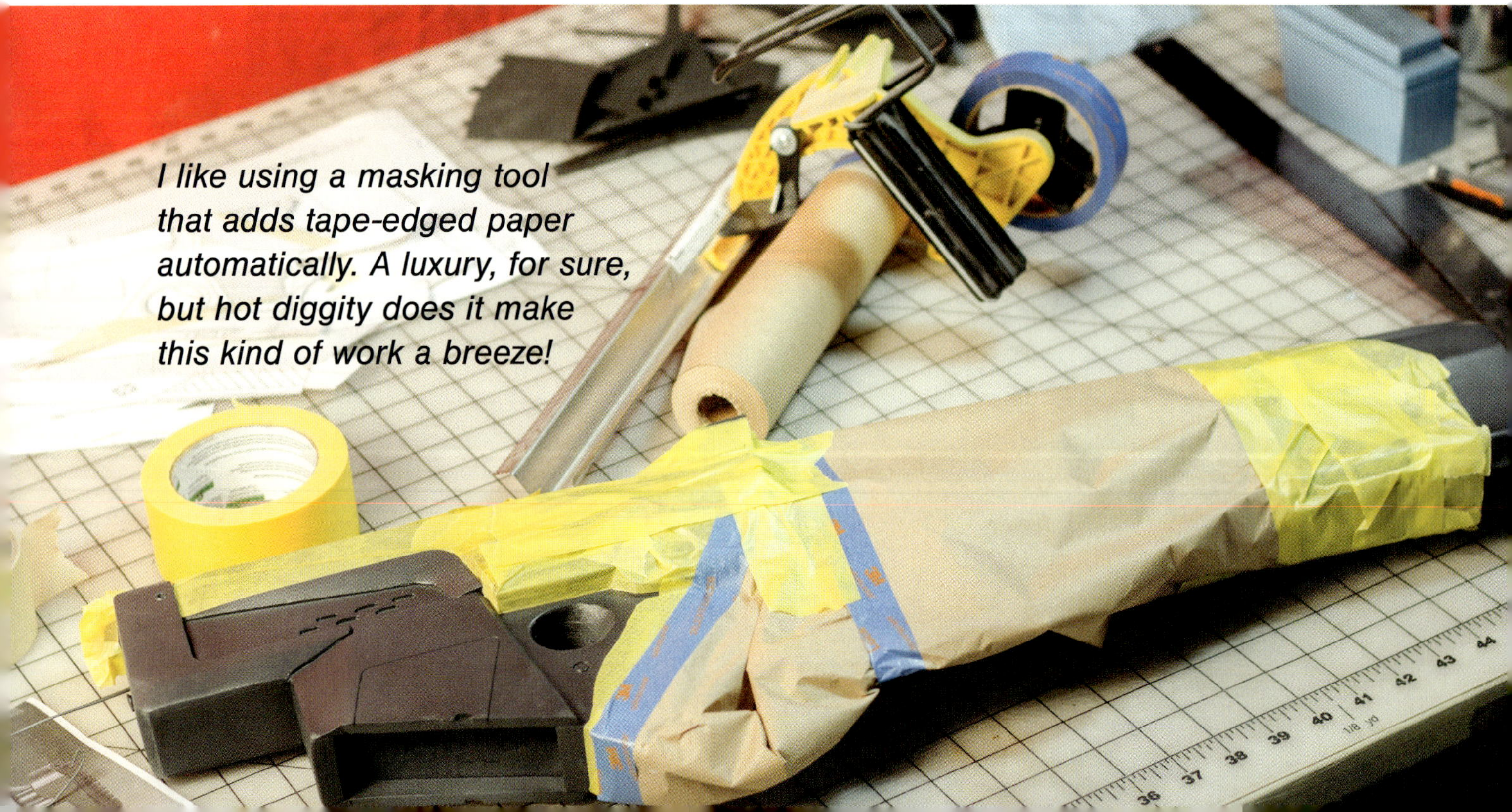

I like using a masking tool that adds tape-edged paper automatically. A luxury, for sure, but hot diggity does it make this kind of work a breeze!

When I was completely satisfied that the masking was solid, I got to spraying on the light blue layer of paint. I was able to find a rattle can that was the appropriate color for this layer, which made application a snap! Several layers of this paint were sprayed on and allowed to dry. The magazine was also painted this color with no masking required.

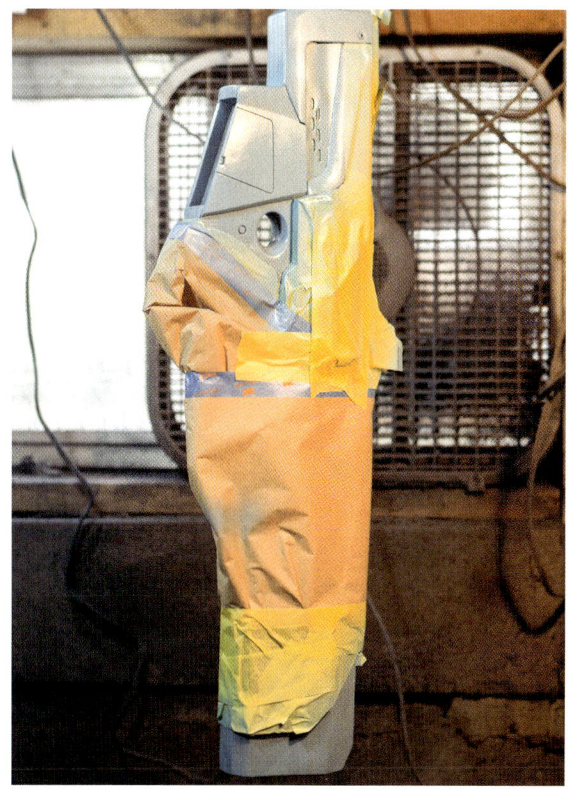

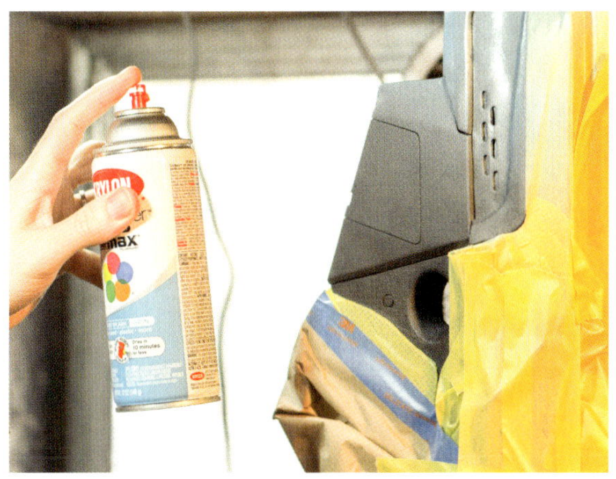

Once this blue paint was all dry, I could peel away the masking to reveal the nice, clean finish below! This is one of the most satisfying parts of any build.

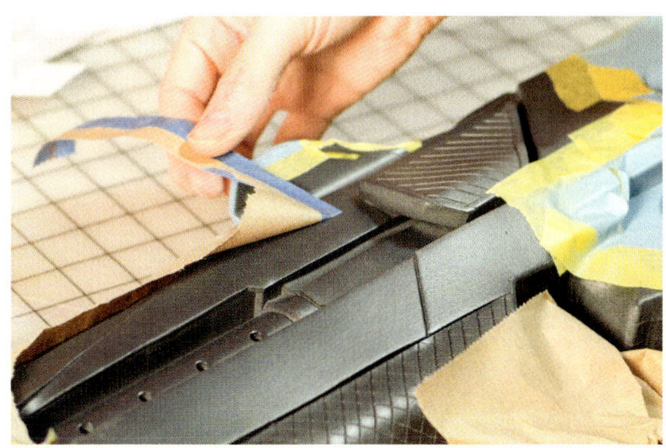

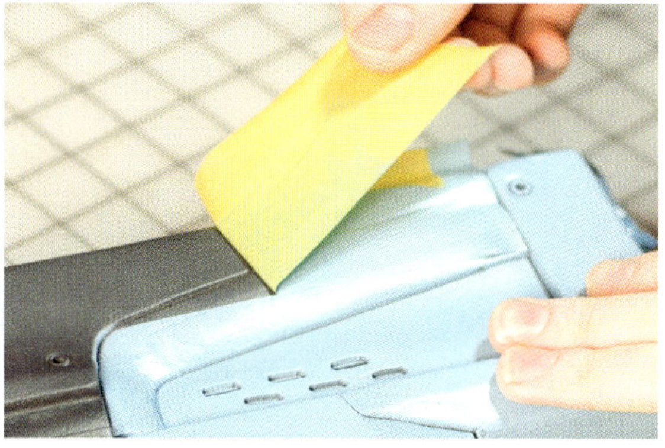

Invest in good quality "delicate surfaces" masking tape.

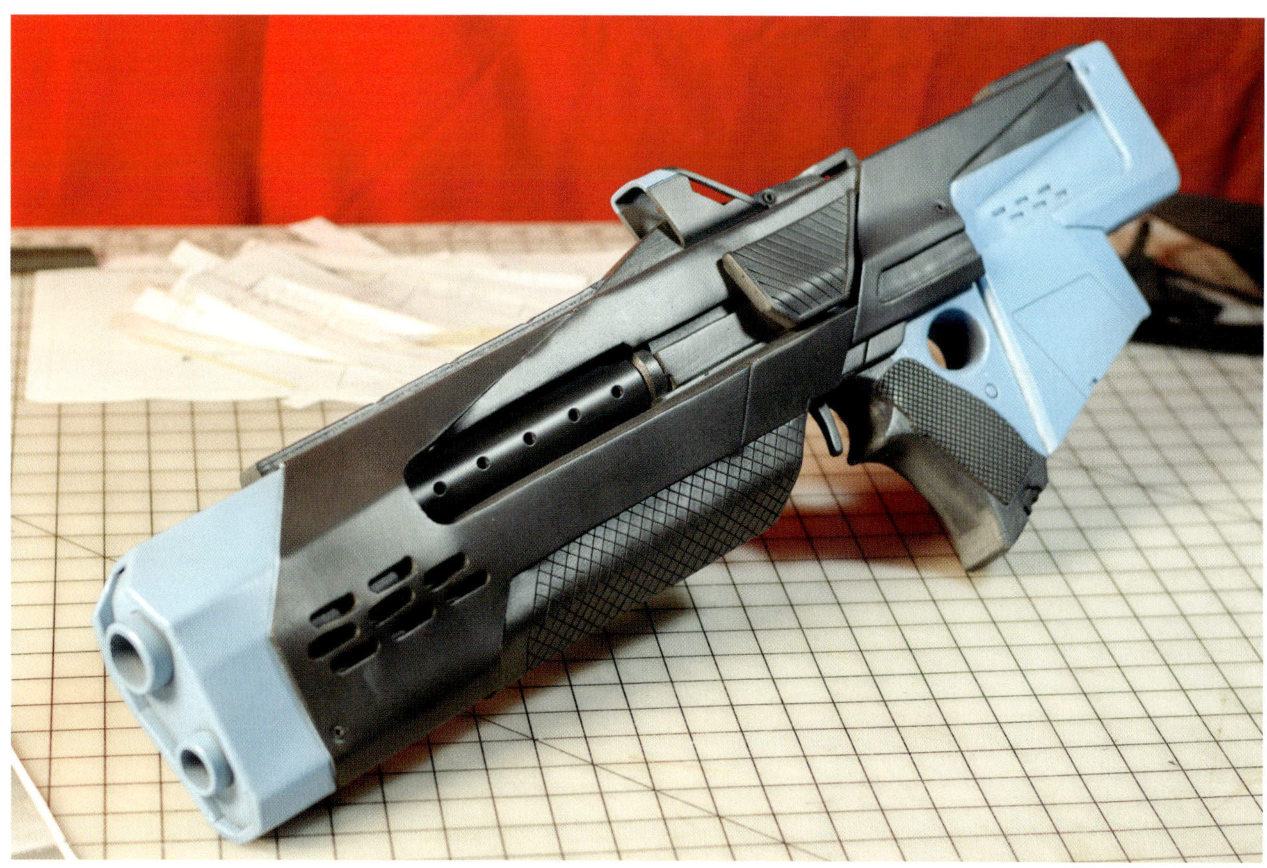

Brush on Layers

Some areas of the gun would have been difficult to mask, so I had to go back in with a brush and color them by hand. The front of the barrel was a perfect example. Since I already had the gray acrylic paint mixed up, I used it to brush on a couple of layers, covering up the blue below.

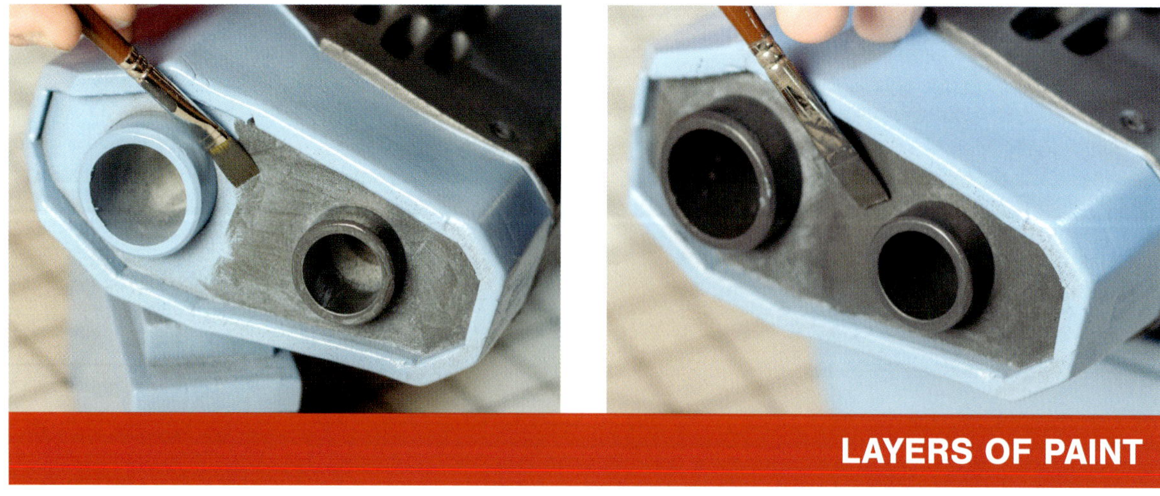

LAYERS OF PAINT

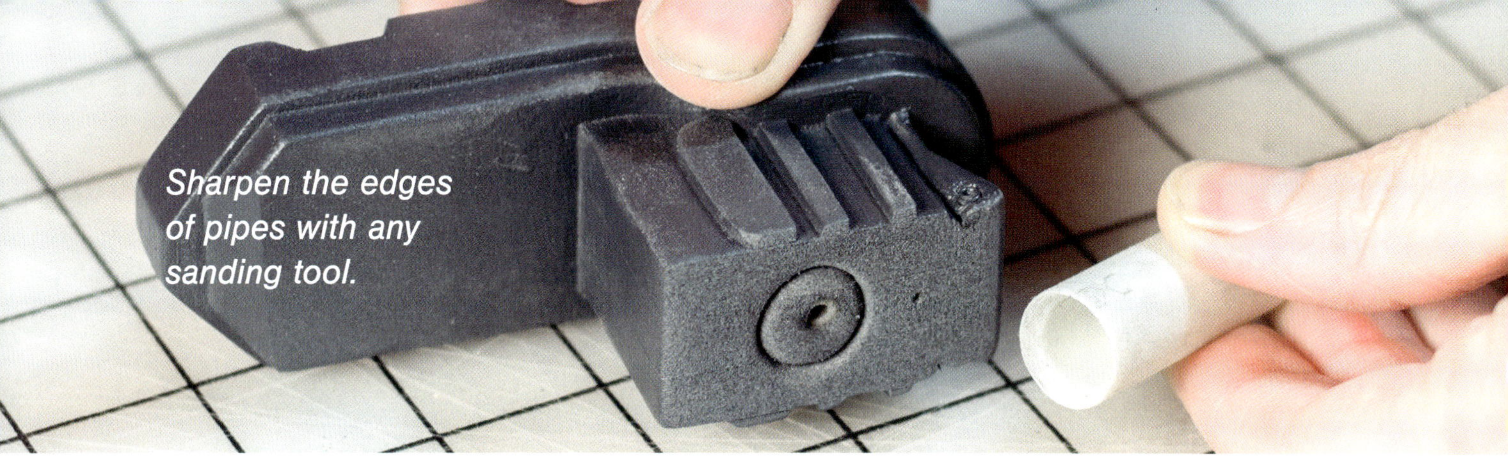

Stock Support

The stock didn't have any blue on it, so it didn't need any masking or brush up work. At this point, it could be permanently attached to the main gun body. To make sure the two parts would never come apart, I used a small PVC pipe to make an extremely strong connection. The PVC pipe was sharpened and used to cut a tube into the foam on the stock and in the rear of the gun body. Then this PVC pipe was glued into the stock, creating a sturdy protrusion.

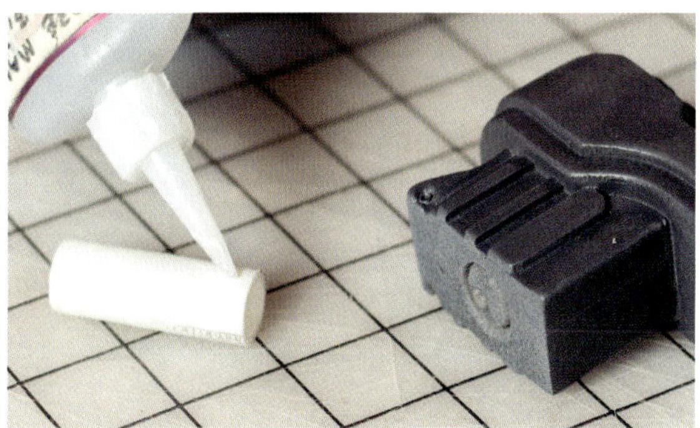

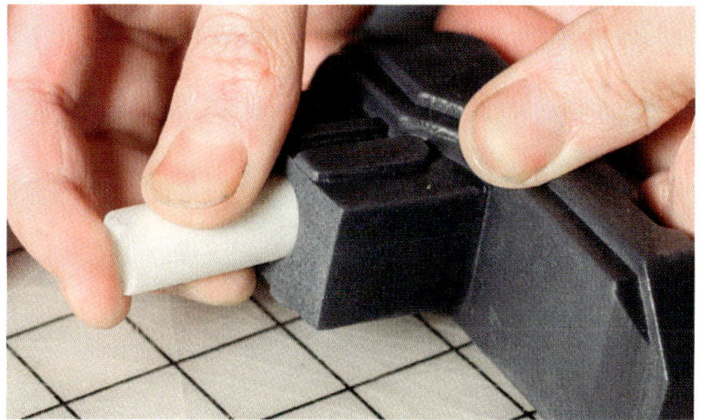

With a similar tube cut into the gun body, the stock could be glued to the body of the gun forever. Since the super glue dried really fast, it was vital that I get the position correct on the first try. I was repeating "do not glue it upside down" the entire time I was attaching the piece. I talk to myself a lot.

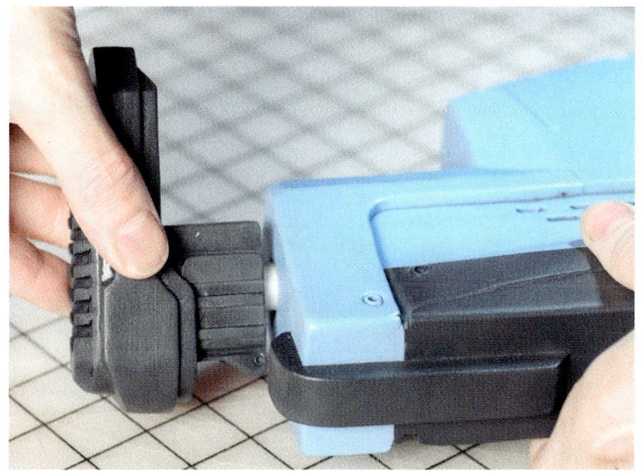

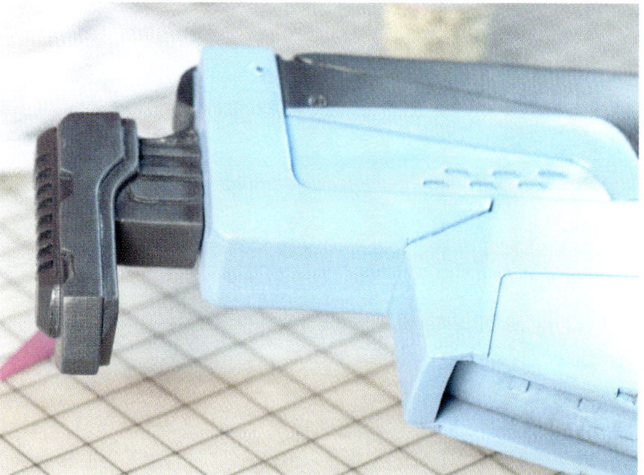

Foam Logo

One of the final bits of detail on this gun was the Jade Rabbit logo. This is another part that could totally have been cut out with a knife and a hole punch, but I went to my laser cutter. I also opted to use a self adhesive, white craft foam for this. No glue necessary! The cut out pieces were peeled away from their backing and laid down in place on the gun body.

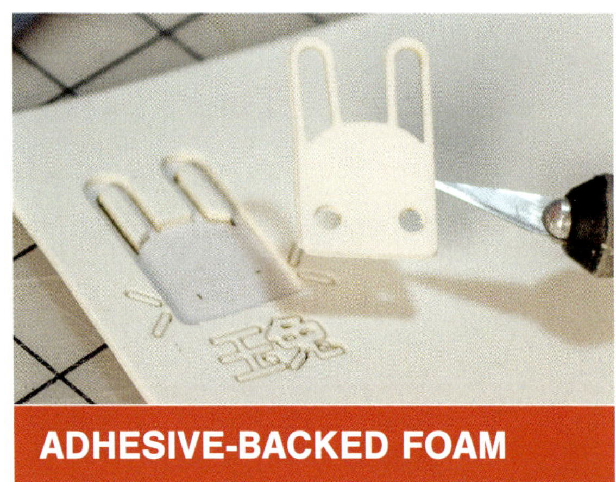

ADHESIVE-BACKED FOAM

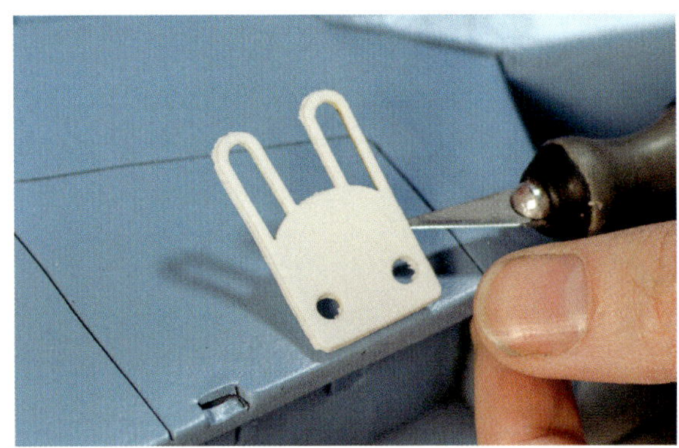

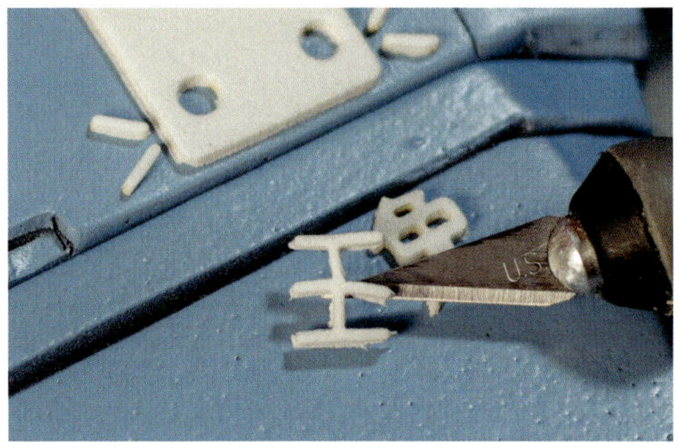

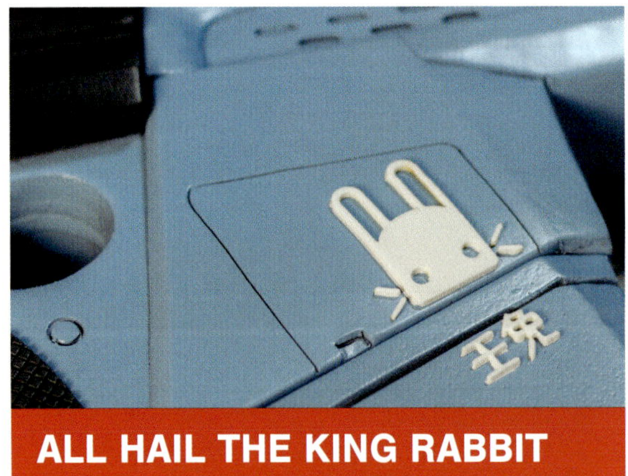

ALL HAIL THE KING RABBIT

The keen eyed observer will note that I lost part of the character for the word "jade", turning it, apparently, into the word "king". I'm OK with this.

The Jade Rabbit logo could have totally been done with a stencil and paint, but I really liked the 3D effect the 2mm adhesive backed foam achieved.

Stencil

For the other logo on the gun, I opted for a stencil. This could have been done in a number of ways. The cheapest would have been to hand cut the stencil from a piece of masking tape. I had mine cut out with a vinyl cutter from a transparent masking vinyl.

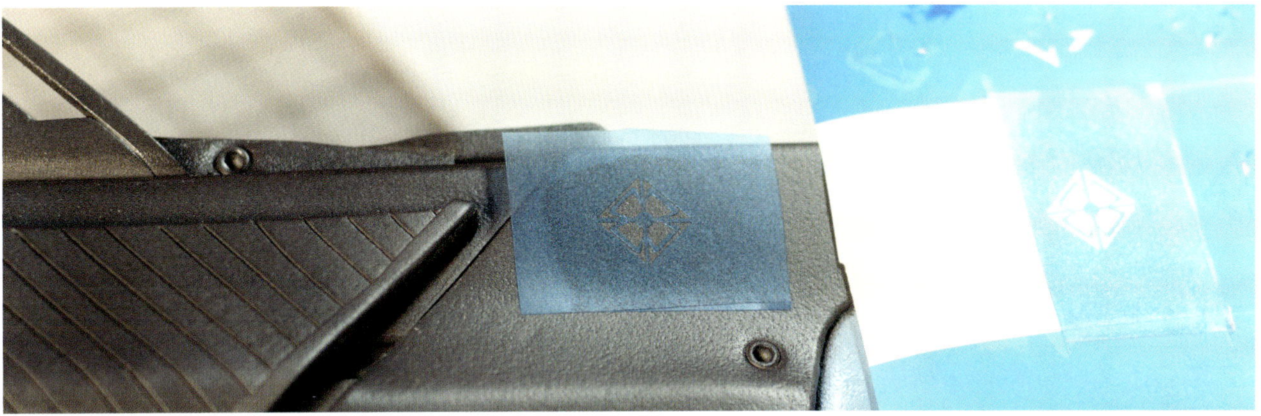

With the stencil in place on the gun, I dabbed on a couple of layers of white acrylic paint, allowing the paint to dry between layers. When it was completely dry I peeled away the stencil revealing the crisp logo below.

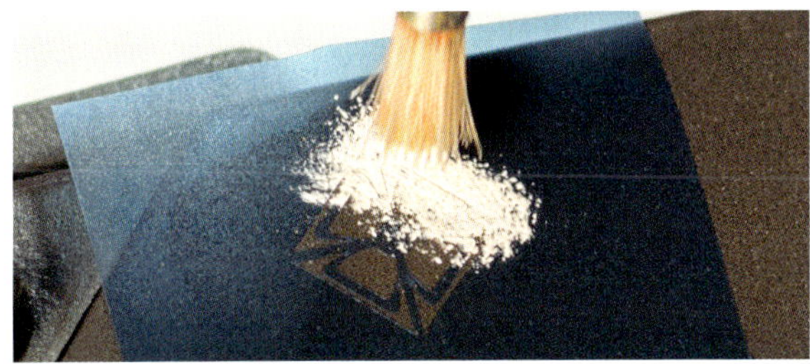

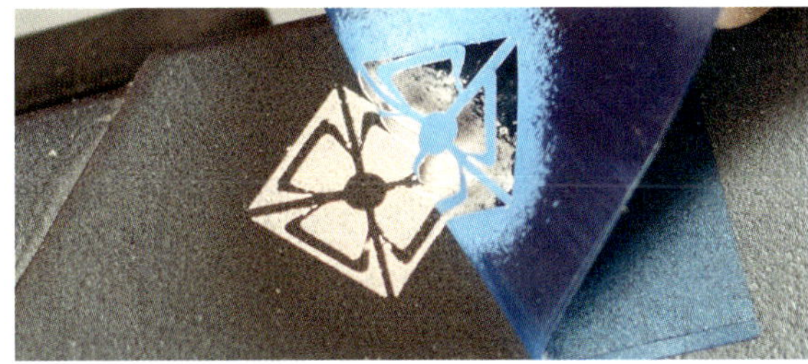

Clear Coat Before Weathering

Happy with the colors on the entire gun, I sprayed the whole thing with a clear Krylon paint. This would ensure that my weathering passes would not mess up this glorious paint job.

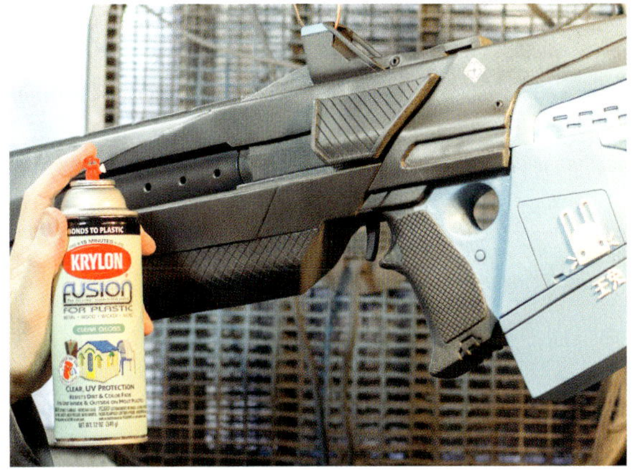

WEATHERING

In the video game, the Jade Rabbit isn't too dirty, but I prefer my space guns to be a little bit "world worn", so I opted to grime it up a bit. I also like the contrast that weathering adds to an otherwise plain paint job.

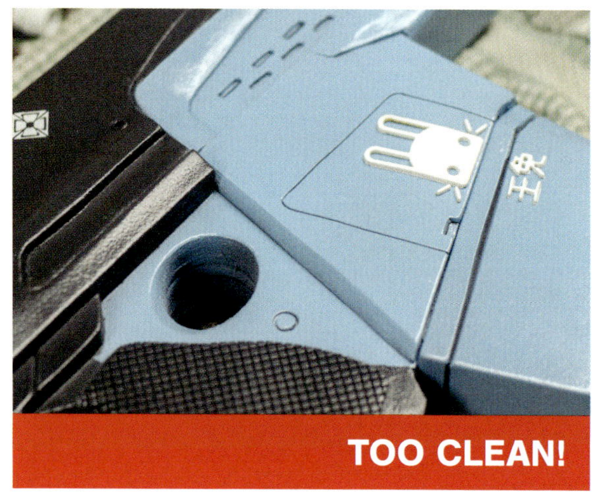

TOO CLEAN!

Some of this weathering paint was done on an internet live stream. It was super fun to paint along with my friends online!

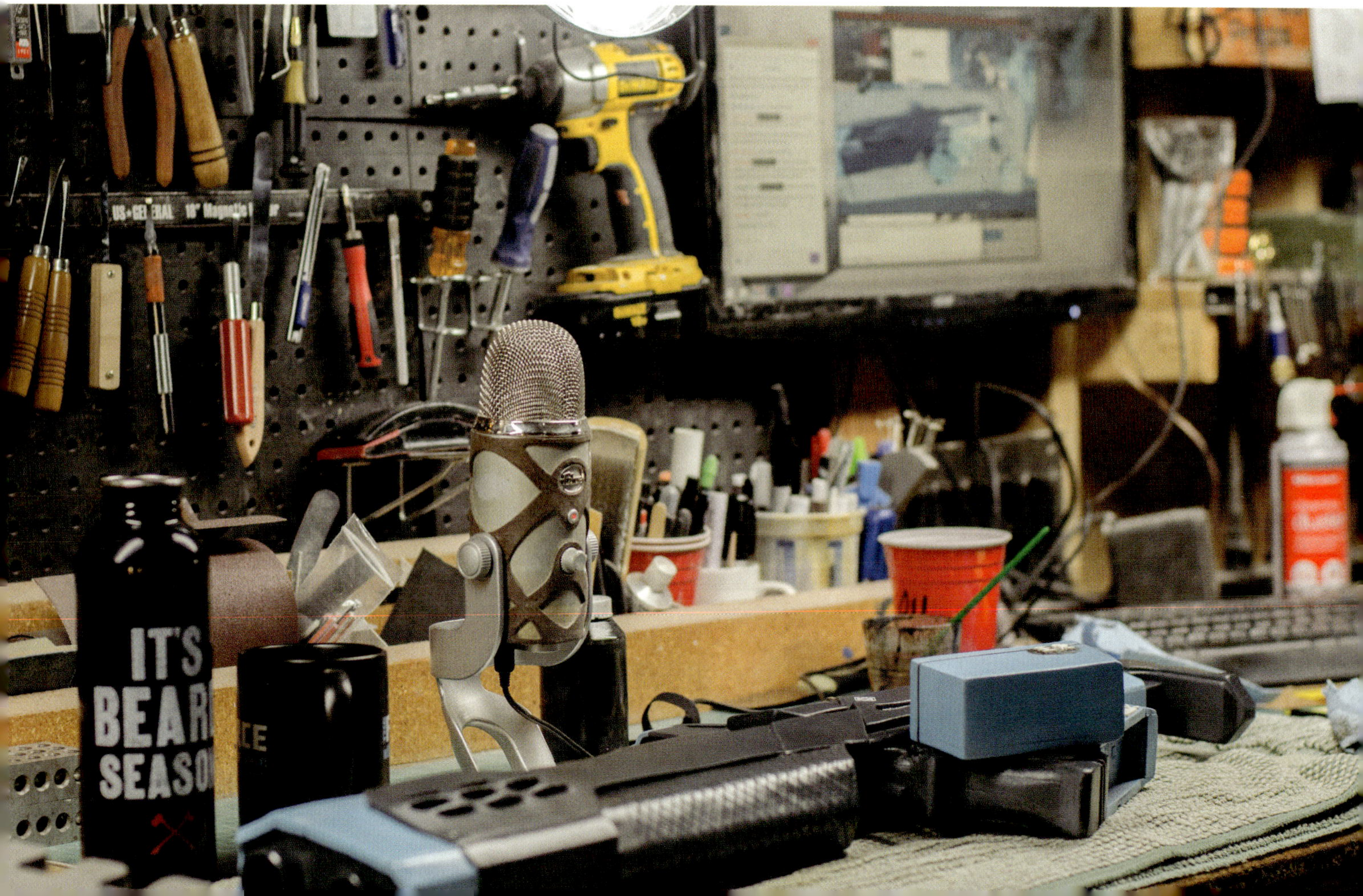

For this weathering scheme, I decided to go with “water mixable” oil paints. These paints gave me a lot of working time and achieved a “smeary” finish, much like real life oil and grease. These are my go-to paints for anything mechanical that would acquire some nice, greasy grime.

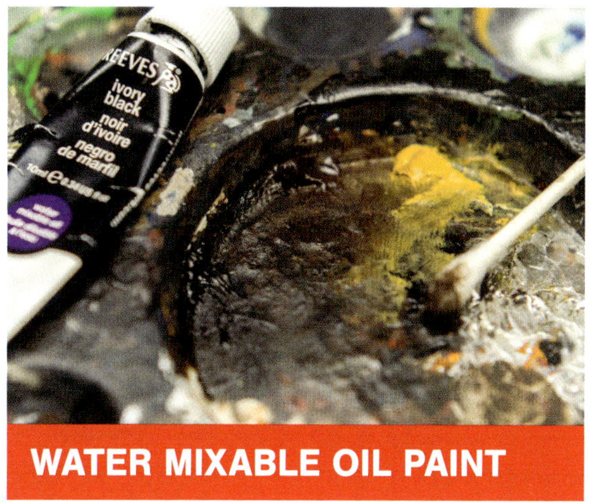

WATER MIXABLE OIL PAINT

Always test the layers of paints you'll be using on scraps first!

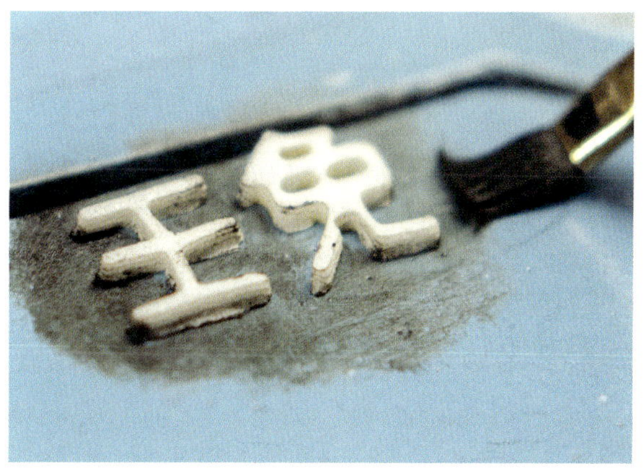

Using a variety of black, brown, and yellow ochre pigments, I applied the oil paints liberally to any of the low recesses of the gun. I tried to pick colors that would create some nice contrast, but I purposely did not mix them very much. The goal was to make the grime build up look natural.

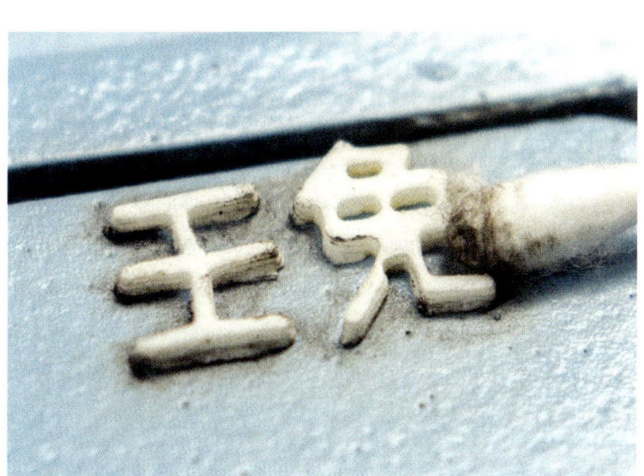

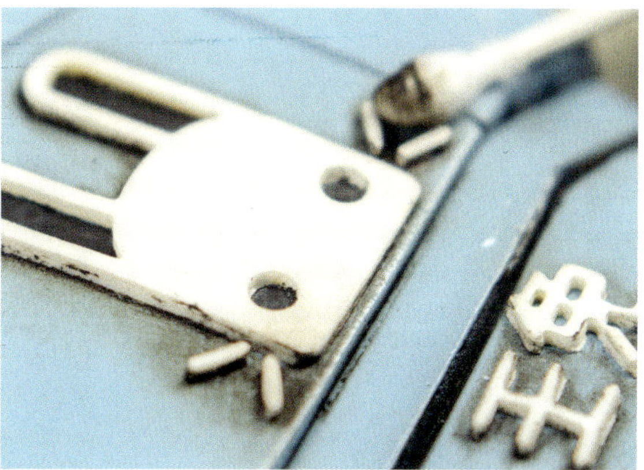

Apply and Wipe Away

Working in small sections, I would add the grime paint and then wipe away most of it with a paper towel. I was trying to make it look like the gun had gotten dirty and I tried to clean it hastily. Some of the smaller areas, like the Jade Rabbit logo, were cleaned up using a cotton swab.

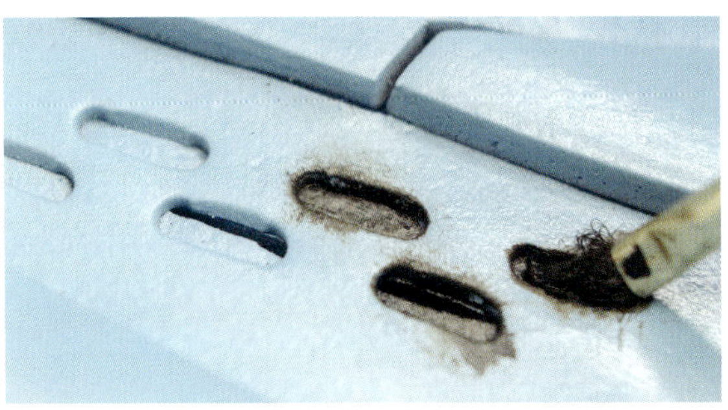

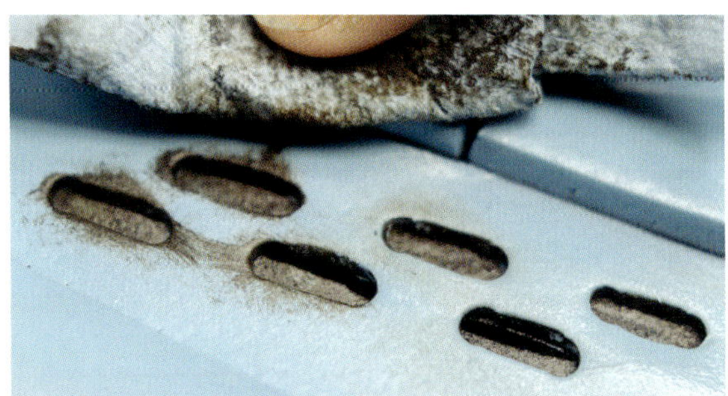

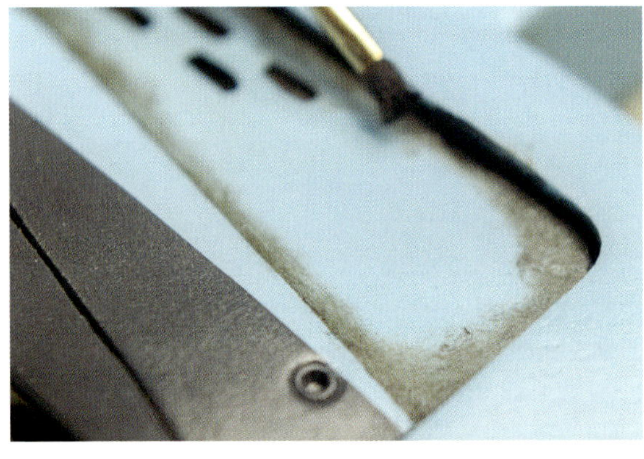

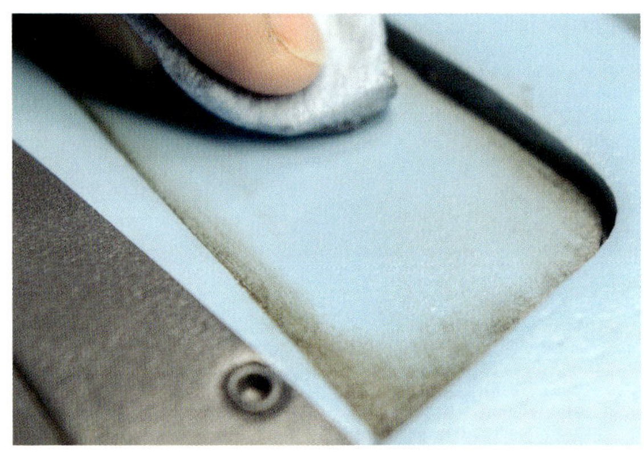

This weathering process was repeated over the entire gun. Paint was added to deep crevasses and then wiped away, leaving a nice, "world worn" finish on the gun.

Use lighter dirt colors on dark bases.

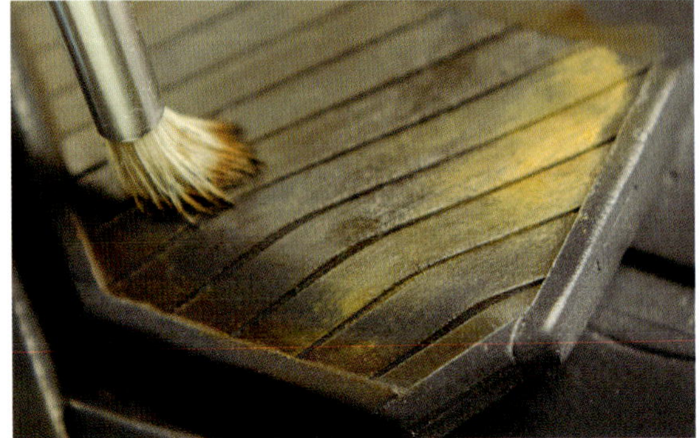

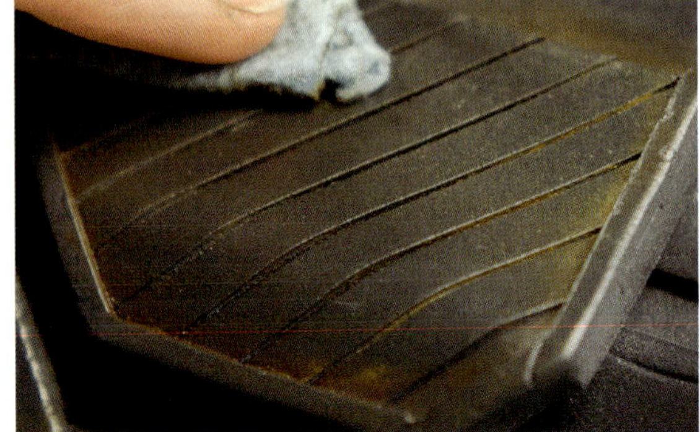

Metal Highlights

Some of the gun parts needed to be highlighted with a brighter metallic finish. The easiest method for this was using a silver permanent marker. All of the screw heads got this treatment. I also gave a quick silver finish to the "USB port" on the bottom of the handle.

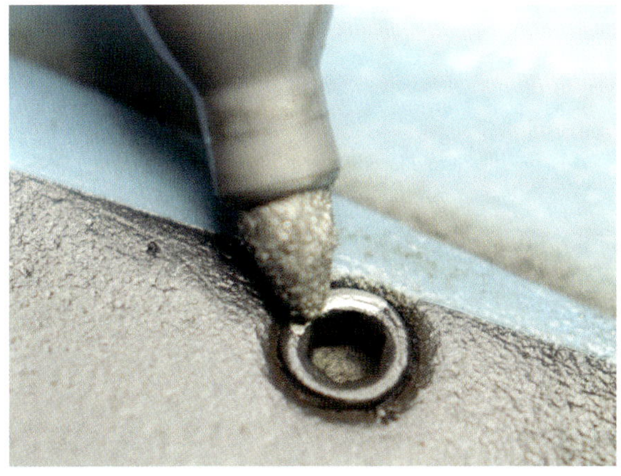

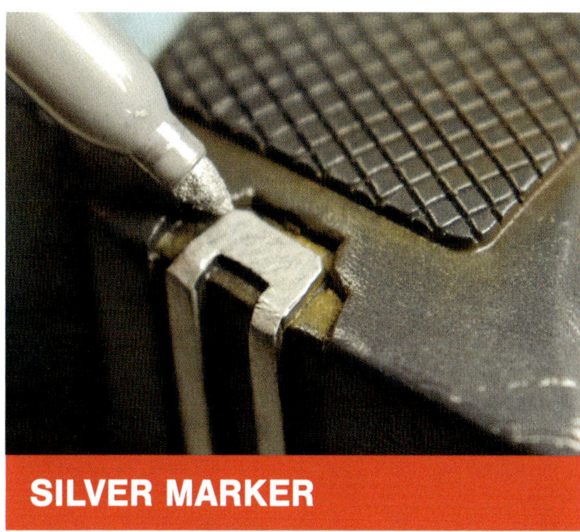

SILVER MARKER

I used the same silver marker to add some edge weathering to random areas on the gun. The goal here was to make it look like the paint had worn away, revealing the base metal finish underneath. I tried to be as conservative as possible with this edge highlighting. It's really easy to get all "Sharpie happy" and cover your gun in highlights. A little goes a long way.

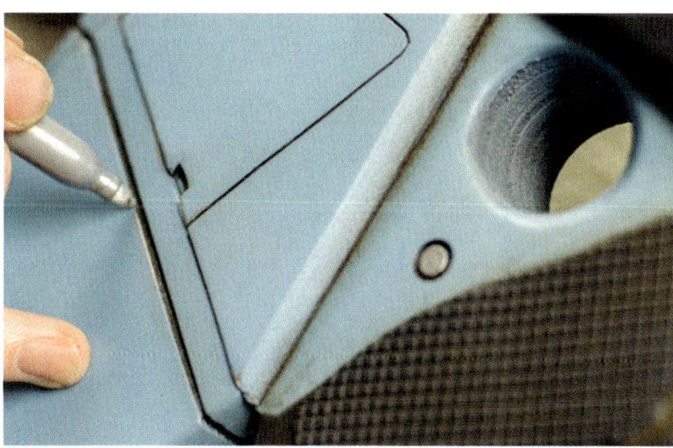

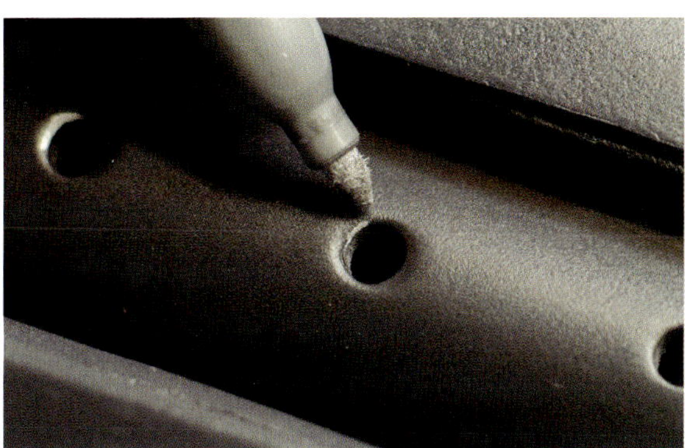

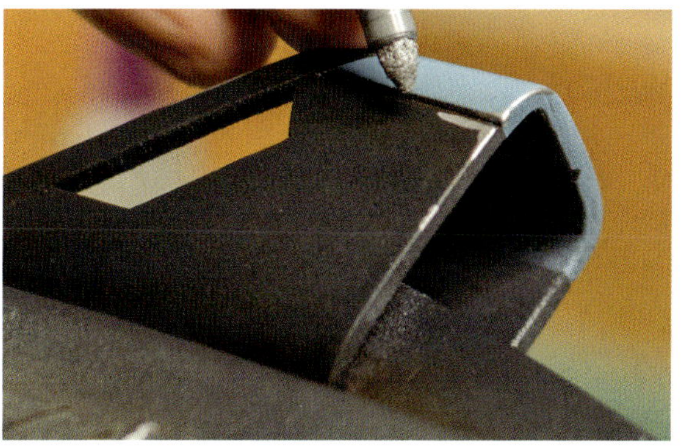

Weather in Layers

I did several passes on all of my weathering until I was completely happy with the finish. I prefer to add just a little at first and then layer on top of that to get the effect I want. Remember that it's easy to add more paint, but rather difficult to take it away.

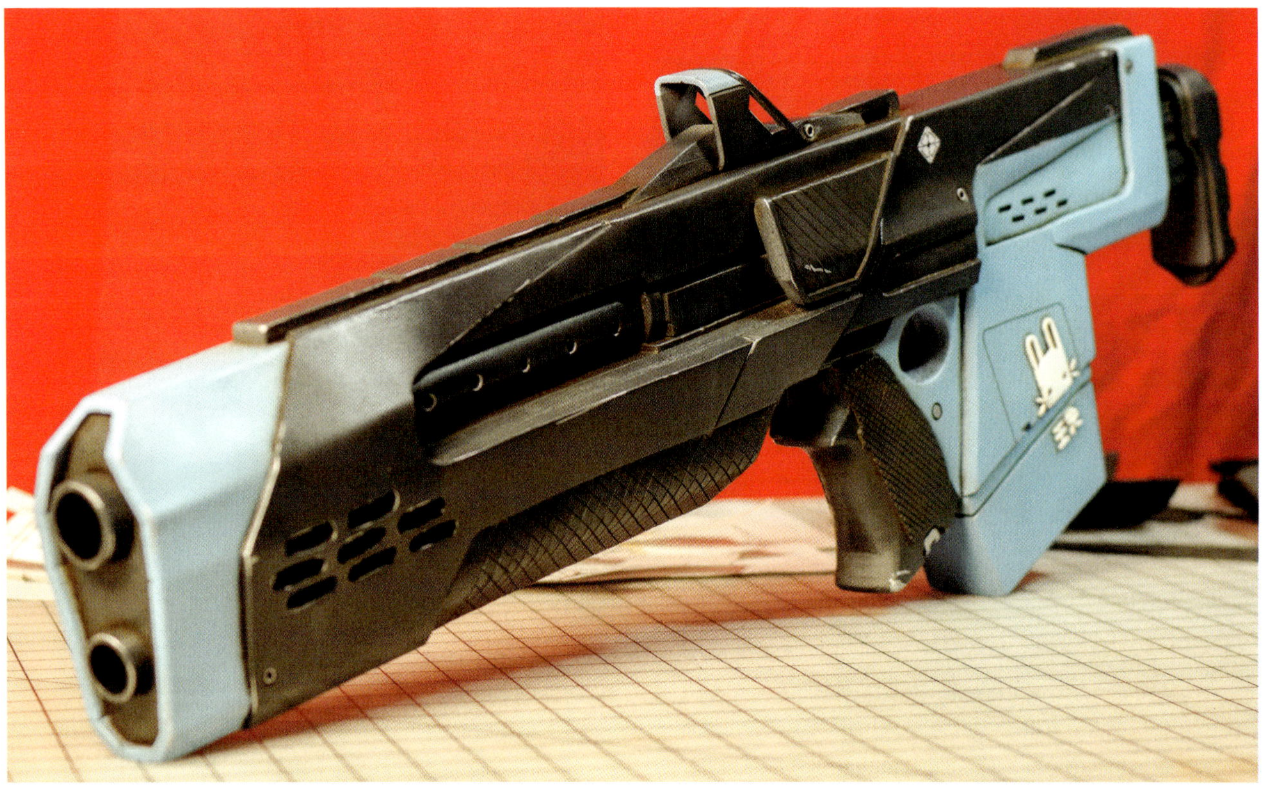

With all of the weathering done I declared the Jade Rabbit finished! Since the oil paints take a long time to dry, I didn't do a clear coat on top of them, at least not right away. It doesn't hurt to give oil weathering a good week or more before painting on top of them.

Tight deadline? Weather with acrylic paints, which dry quickly.

The Jade Rabbit was a really challenging, but extremely satisfying build. I think it goes really great with my Lord Shaxx costume, don't you? This particular project is a perfect representation of how I tackle this type of prop making problem solving! I hope you've enjoyed following my process from start to finish.

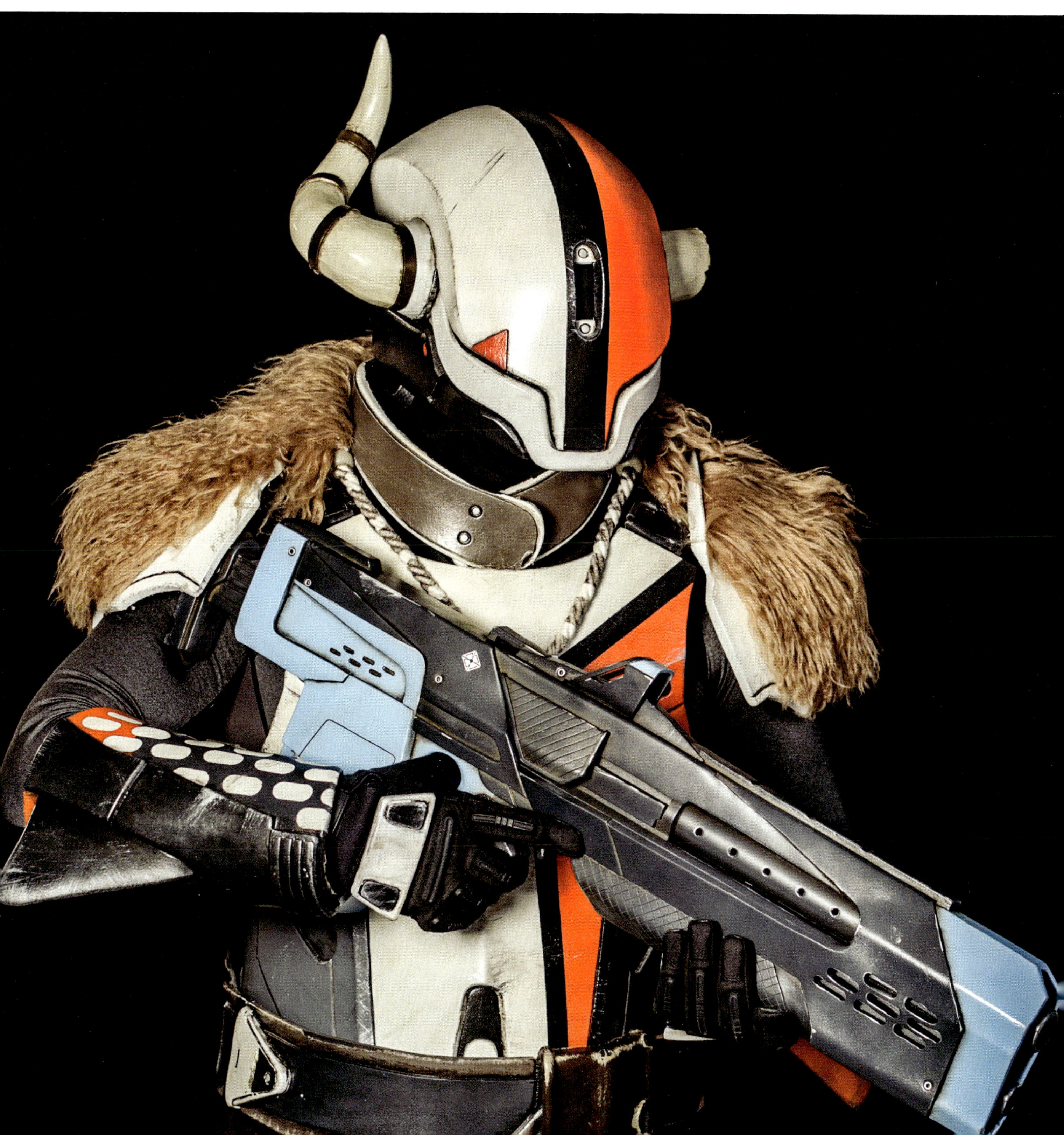

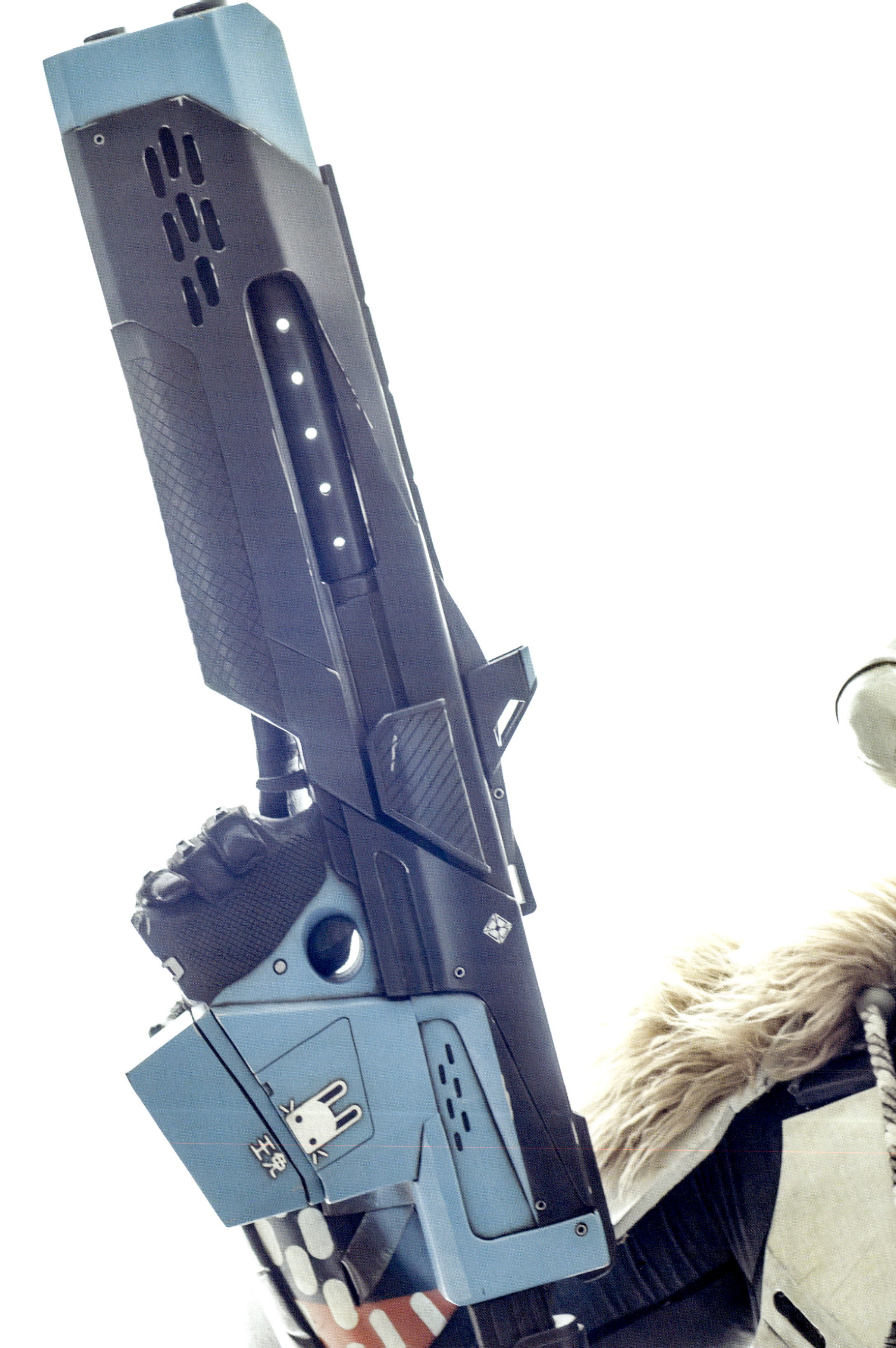

The Foamsmith Way

Hey gang, thanks for checking out this book. Your enthusiasm for crafting foam props and costumes fuels me and I couldn't be more stoked to see what you make with this knowledge. Like I said earlier, this book was designed to both teach you some new techniques and give you some major insight into my creative process. My hope is that you can take this information and create nearly any prop you can dream up using foam.

Also remember that my techniques aren't "the only way" to do it, so please explore with your own new techniques, tools, and materials. Consider the Foamsmith books as a foundation from which you can catapult your own creative endeavors. From my point of view, there's nothing more satisfying than teaching someone a technique and watching them more fully explore that technique and learn something new. That is the Foamsmith way.

Thanks again, you rule.

-Bill

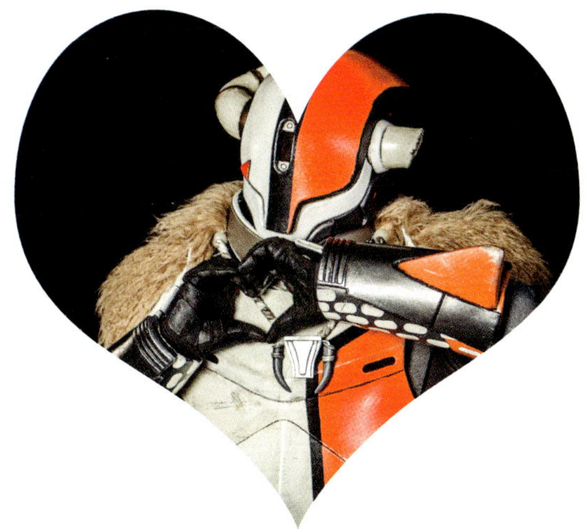

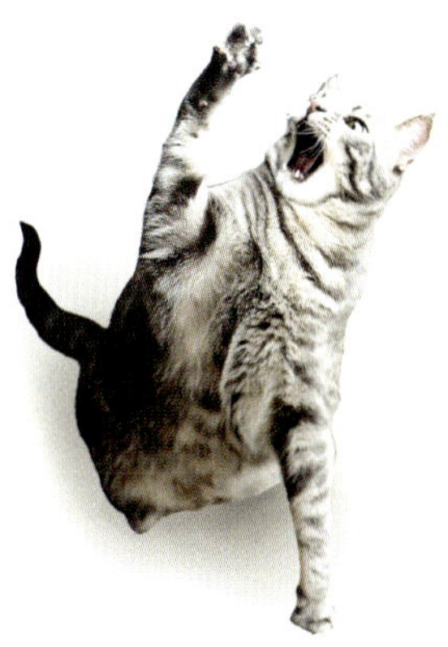

"At last! With these new Foamsmithing skills,
I can take over the world!"

- Buddhacat